Contents

ADVERTISING & PROMOTION

Don Milner

John Murray

Dedication

To my mother, Muriel

Success Studybooks

Advertising and Promotion	Geography: Human and Regional
Accounting and Costing: Problems and Projects	Information Processing
Book-keeping and Accounts	Insurance
British History since 1914	Investment
Business Calculations	Law
Chemistry	Management Accounting: An Introduction
Commerce	Management: Personnel
Commerce: West African Edition	Marketing
Communication	Office Practice
Economic Geography	Principles of Accounting
Economics	Principles of Accounting: Answer Book
Economics: West African Edition	Principles of Catering
Electronics	Statistics
Elements of Banking	Twentieth Century World Affairs
European History 1815–1941	World History since 1945

© Don Milner 1995

First published 1995
by John Murray (Publishers) Ltd
50 Albemarle Street, London W1X 4BD

Typeset by Colset Private Ltd., Singapore
Printed in Great Britain at the Bath Press, Avon

A CIP catalogue record for this book is
available from the British Library

ISBN 0-7195-5371-7

Foreword

This book is intended for anyone wishing to understand the theory and practice of advertising, promotion and publicity, whether for study or professional training purposes or for general interest. No previous knowledge on the part of the reader is assumed.

Those who wish to gain an overview of all aspects of the subject, from marketing research to a detailed breakdown of the stages of planning and carrying out a promotional campaign, will probably prefer to read the whole book in sequence. It need not, however, be read in this way. Different parts of it may be taken separately and in any order, according to the reader's own areas of interest.

Nevertheless, I do recommend that you begin by reading the first three chapters as these provide an essential framework for all that follows. The concept of the 'publicity surround' with its controllable and its uncontrollable elements provides both a background against which to understand the pro-active and reactive nature of promotional campaigns and the importance of research, analysis and planning. The distinctions between promotion and publicity and the wide variety of terms which can be used to describe publicity explained in the first two chapters are all helpful in understanding later parts of the book. The third chapter, on business policy, develops the point that advertising and other campaigns can never be viewed in isolation from the organisation's broader policies and objectives. Indeed, if promotional activities of all types are to be understood then some knowledge of business policy and strategy is essential.

The next five chapters on the use of agencies, the regulatory structure under which advertisers and others work, the nature of communications, the behaviour of the consumer and the contribution of marketing research all build on the first three in providing more details on matters which affect the decision making process when campaigns are being planned.

It is with the ninth chapter that we begin to look at specific types of campaigns beginning with a discussion of the media and all its ramifications. Although this chapter is of most interest and relevance to advertising it is also extremely useful in the general context of planning press (or media) relations campaigns and gives a background as to how, for example, direct response campaigns can be used. Chapter 10 discusses how a campaign is set up, beginning with the development of the brief and then looking at the selection and buying of media space and time, together with a consideration of the size of the campaign in such terms as cover, reach and frequency. It also introduces the creative brief as a precursor of the following chapters.

Chapter 11 focuses specifically on the space-based media of newspapers, magazines and posters and chapter 12 on the time-based media of television, radio and cinema. In each of these chapters there are detailed discussions of the creative problems to be resolved, together with some case studies.

For chapter 13, I am grateful for the partnership of Doreen Stone. It deals specifically with the issue of advertising and children and explores some of the ethical as well as the practical problems involved. Kids as customers (to borrow another author's phrase) are a fascinating area of study.

The next three chapters analyse the ways in which public and press relations can be used either separately from or in parallel with an advertising campaign. The last of these three deals with the sensitive problem of communications in a crisis situation.

The five chapters which follow deal with different sorts of campaigns. Direct marketing includes both direct mail and telemarketing. The coverage of sales promotions considers the whole question of pull and push factors from the motivation of the manufacturer's sales force to consumer promotions such as special offers. The use of sponsorship, not only to impress consumers but to impress suppliers, shareholders and trade customers as well, and the use of conferences and exhibitions are all fully discussed.

Chapter 21 looks in detail at business-to-business promotion and serves to reinforce earlier discussions on sales promotion, conference and exhibition management, telesales and sponsorship in demonstrating more fully the importance of other businesses as target audiences in a promotional campaign. Finally, chapter 22 deals with planning and shows the importance of being able to integrate all the different activities into one single co-ordinated campaign while paying attention to detail and keeping control over the various parts of the plan. It relates back to chapter 3 on business policy: the earlier chapter sets out the broad framework of policy and the later one the details of implementation. The two are deliberately separated because the intervening chapters provide the detailed information needed to move from policy to plan and from plan to promotion.

Throughout the book there are case studies and examples to serve as illustration and to bring the theoretical framework to life. There are also cross-references between chapters to enable a particular thought to be followed up.

No book of this size can possibly deal with all the many and varied issues involved in advertising and promotion but my hope is that you will find it comprehensive, interesting and encouraging and that you will feel motivated by it to develop further your own interests in this fascinating area.

Acknowledgements

I am grateful to my former colleagues at the London College of Printing and Distributive Trades and in particular to: Simon Cornes, Senior Lecturer in Radio Journalism, for his advice on the radio industry; Bill Offer, Deputy Dean of the School of Printing Technology, for his advice on printing processes; and Doreen Stone, the College's Marketing Manager, for many helpful comments.

I am additionally grateful to Doreen Stone for giving me access to her personal archives on advertising and children and to her 1993 MA thesis, 'The Extent and Effect of Child-Directed Advertising with Particular Reference to the under 12s in the UK Market in the 1990s'. Her co-authorship of chapter 13 is duly acknowledged with thanks.

Many of the short case studies could not have been written without the help and encouragement of a number of people. To Geoff Mayhew of Cornhill Insurance, Steven Newman of GAIA communications, Albert Kemp of Insurex Expo-Sure, Sarah Hill of the *International Herald Tribune* and Susie Helme of *Conference and Exhibition Fact Finder* my sincere thanks.

My thanks also to Miranda Kennet of the IPA, to Caroline Crawford of the ASA and to Ann Jonas of Maiden Outdoor for dealing with many queries.

The co-operation of agencies in projects of this sort is vital and I have been greatly helped by personnel at Saatchi & Saatchi, among whom I would particularly like to mention Angie Leese, the Press Officer, Karen Payne from Business Communications and Julian Diment, Account Executive. Ken Smith of Lowe Howard-Spink and Breda Power and Toni Townsend of Austin Knight are also to be thanked, as is Ron Wootton of Ronald J. Wootton Associates for providing the storyboard.

Nick Kyritsis and Keith Searle, Principal and Registrar respectively of the London City College, have lent a friendly ear on many an occasion and by being good listeners have often helped me to clarify my own thoughts.

Last but not least, thanks to Lauren Hotson for checking some of the details and helping in the compilation of the reference lists and index.

1 The nature and role of information

**1.1
Introduction**

Think of a place to which you have never been or a person to whom you have never been introduced. Think of some food or drink which you have never tasted or a film which you have not yet seen. You may be thinking of New York or Glasgow, the Prime Minister or the principal of the college you attend, malt whisky or bird's nest soup. Whatever you are thinking of, it must be something of which you, yourself, have absolutely no first-hand personal experience.

How is this possible? The answer, of course, is that you have been told about, or have read about, these things (and where there are gaps in your knowledge you use your imagination). You have been on the receiving end of the communication process, forming your view of the world partly on the basis of second-hand information. For no one relies exclusively on personal experience and our minds are full of ideas that do not depend for their existence on our own sensory experience.

**1.2 Sources of
information**

We receive information about things from a very wide range of sources. We may read of a place in a travel brochure or learn about it from looking at a friend's holiday snaps. We may form an impression of what sort of person a professional footballer is by reading an interview in a national newspaper. Our impression of malt whisky may depend entirely on the advertisements that we see for it in glossy magazines.

Of course, our own personal experience is also a vital source of information. But we can often manage surprisingly well without it.

If you were to summarise all the sources of information which contribute to this process of idea and image formation you would probably finish up with a list something like this:

- Things you know from your own personal experience.
- Things you have read in newspapers, magazines, leaflets and books.
- Things you have seen and heard on television and radio.
- Things told to you in a formal setting, such as a college lecture.
- Things told to you in an informal setting, such as a friendly chat.
- Things you overhear – in a bus queue, for example.
- Things you see – in a shop window, for example.

All the above represent different forms of **communication**. Amongst all that communication there will be many examples of publicity.

**1.3 Direct
publicity and
indirect
publicity**

A great deal of publicity emanates from an organisation in order to influence people's opinions and actions in favour of that organisation. Advertisements, direct-mail letters and speeches are examples. This is known as **direct publicity** and is sometimes also called **promotion**.

We can learn a lot about an organisation, a business for example, from the direct publicity it puts out. We can also learn a great deal from statements made about that organisation by other people. Documentaries on television, newspaper articles, competitors and consumers can all have something to say. This is publicity of an indirect sort – it does not come to us directly from the organisation.

Case Study

Bergerac and the Island of Jersey

Sometimes indirect publicity is an accidental by-product of a piece of work which was designed to serve quite a different purpose. The television detective series *Bergerac* was produced to provide thrilling entertainment but in doing so it gave a great deal of publicity to Jersey, the Channel Island in which the series was set. As a consequence of this publicity visitors to Jersey increased considerably, although the programme was not designed to boost local tourism. Paradoxically, some of the residents of Jersey objected to the attention which *Bergerac* brought to the island. They thought that it created the image of Jersey as a place with an unusually high, and violent, crime-rate.

How many people who have never visited Jersey have an image of it based almost entirely on watching the series *Bergerac*? And what sort of image would they have?

In common with most holiday destinations, Jersey does have a Tourist Office whose task it is to promote Jersey in the most positive way. There is nothing accidental about the television commercials which expound the natural and beautiful Jersey coastline. Neither is there anything accidental about the brochures describing holidays in Jersey which you can pick up in any good high-street travel agent. These are examples of planned and deliberate publicity using paid-for means of communication to enhance the image and performance of any organisation, product, etc. Jersey has its professional image-makers whose job it is to attract visitors (and business) to the island.

In fact, every product of every sort, a holiday, a car, an insurance policy, a tube of toothpaste or an ice-cream, has an image, and every product has its image-makers.

1.4 Image-making

Now imagine that you are one of those image-makers. You are probably either working for a business organisation or acting as one of its agents. Actually, you could be working for a political party, a charity, a religious organisation, the police force, local government or a branch of the armed services.

Your job is to use your communication skills to promote the interests of your employer in a positive way. Those interests may range from increasing sales to winning elections: from raising funds to attracting new recruits: from saving the church tower to fighting drug addiction. What-

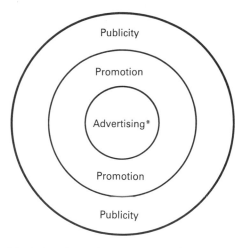

* Advertising is shown here as just one example of a promotional activity.

Fig. 1.1 The relationship between promotion, publicity and advertising

ever those interests are they will be undermined if your employer has a poor image and strengthened if your employer has a good image. It is your job to use a range of promotional techniques to enhance that image and support your employer's objectives and interests. It is also your job to be aware of all the indirect publicity that your employer may attract and, where it is unhelpful to your employer's purposes, to counter it.

It is almost certainly too big a task for just one person. A number of people with a wide range of promotional skills between them will have to work together to achieve the employer's objectives. Apart from promotional skills there is also a need for research, analysis and planning. That is what this book is about.

Figure 1.1 shows some of the above ideas in relationship to each other. In the large outer circle we have all the forms of publicity to which an organisation or its products might be exposed. Some of that publicity, as we have seen, arises indirectly and is outside the control of the organisation and some of it is direct and within the organisation's control. The Jersey Tourist Board had no control over the scripts for *Bergerac* but it certainly controls its own television advertisements.

In the middle circle we have those aspects of publicity which we can call promotion – all the communication which an organisation does on its own behalf to improve its image and to improve its chances of achieving its objectives. Promotion includes advertising, sponsorship, direct mail, personal selling, public relations, conferences, exhibitions, etc.

In the smallest circle we have just one example of a promotional activity – advertising. We could put public relations, direct mail or any of the other items into this circle. As we go through the book the two larger circles remain unchanged – there is always publicity in its widest sense and promotion as a particular kind of publicity in a narrower sense. It is the content of the inner circle that changes as we discuss different types of promotional activity.

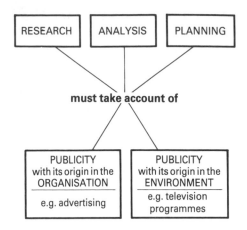

Fig. 1.2   The overall relationship between research, analysis and planning and internally and externally originated publicity

These promotional activities do not exist in isolation from each other. Organisations use them all and they must be seen as working together to provide the total image-formation effort. If all promotional activities communicate the same basic image, the total effect should be a seamless cloth. If they pull in different directions the result could be a patchwork quilt.

In fig. 1.2 we can see how such activities as research, analysis and planning fit in. You cannot operate effectively in the area of advertising or public relations unless you are prepared to undertake these activities. In fact, to be really effective you need to have a much wider knowledge of the whole field of business research, analysis and planning. It is difficult to set objectives for a public relations campaign, for example, if you do not first of all understand your employer's business objectives. Many of the business policy concepts discussed in this book will be found in any good book on business policy and strategy, but a simplified approach will be outlined in chapter 2.

Another aspect of fig. 1.2 is the clear distinction between direct publicity which is in the control of management and has its origins within the organisation and indirect publicity which arises outside the organisation and is not in management control. Whatever is said about a firm in the external environment also affects the firm's performance and needs to be monitored and analysed: newspaper articles, television and radio programmes, opinion surveys – in fact, anywhere where the name of the company or its products might be mentioned.

Figures 1.1 and 1.2 together provide a quick overview of the subject matter of the book.

1.5 Summary
- Your sources of information about anything at all are likely to be very varied and to include written and spoken as well as formal and informal statements.
- This is no less true of business and non-business organisations and the products and services they offer.

- Naturally, any organisation is concerned about what is said about it and puts a lot of effort into both issuing positive statements of all sorts and into countering any negative statements from other sources.

1.6 Assignment

Think of any organisation (your own college, for example) or a product which you have either recently bought or are thinking about buying and try to construct a list of the sources of information. Try to evaluate the value of each source to you personally. (For example, were you more influenced by college literature or by friends already attending?) In the case of a product you have already bought, have you subsequently been exposed to new information which either (*a*) confirmed the soundness of your decision or (*b*) made you wish that you had not bought it? In the case of a product you are proposing to buy, is there any other information you think you would like and how would you go about getting it?

2 What is publicity and promotion?

**2.1
Introduction**

Any business decision is developed within the context of the organisation's environment. This will be discussed more fully in chapter 3. Here we are concerned with a particular aspect of the environment which we will call the **publicity surround**. Any organisation is surrounded by publicity which pervades both its internal and its external environments. As we have noted, some of the publicity is direct in the sense that it originates from the organisation (we will later define this as **promotion**). Some, however, is indirect in that its origin lies elsewhere – this is obviously not promotion as such.

This chapter looks in more detail at the terms **publicity** and **promotion** and, finally, at some brief definitions of particular types of promotion such as advertising and public relations. Note, however, that words like advertising are not always used in the same way by everybody. Remember also that the word publicity is used here to include each and every statement made about an organisation.

**2.2 Different
perspectives
on publicity**

- **Publicity may be controlled or non-controlled** All managers have to accept that some things are outside their control and there are situations (such as when a company's products are under discussion in a consumer magazine such as *Which?*) where publicity comes into this category. Advertising, of course, is controlled publicity.

  Figure 2.1 shows an organisation's controlled publicity and fig. 2.2 shows its non-controlled publicity. Figure 2.3 shows all the aspects of publicity, both controlled and non-controlled, and indicates their relationship to each other and their effect on the company's image and performance. The word **publics** in these figures will be explained more fully later but, for now, it can be taken to mean any **audiences** which the company has.

- **Publicity may use any media** It may be printed – for example, in newspapers or on posters. It may be broadcast – for example, on radio and television. It may be spoken – for example, at a meeting between a salesman and a client.

- **Publicity may have different degrees of permanence** Advertisements in newspapers have a degree of permanence that broadcast announcements lack. A printed advertisement may survive for months, whereas a radio commercial lasts only for a few seconds – and a piece of 'sky-writing' will last only until the wind blows it away.

- **Publicity may be authorised or unauthorised** Any statement that an organisation makes on its own behalf, pays an agent to make for it, or permits a third party to make about it is **authorised**.

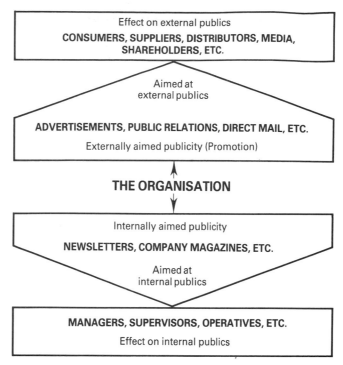

Fig. 2.1 Controlled publicity

However, any person is at liberty (within the law) to make unauthorised, and often unsolicited, statements about an organisation. The difference between unauthorised and unsolicited can give rise to misunderstanding, but generally a statement is **unauthorised** if it is made without the consent of the organisation under discussion.

- **Publicity can be solicited or unsolicited** Organisations may go out of their way to solicit publicity. Public relations offers an example of this when a firm sends out a press release announcing a new product in the hope that the product will be beneficially mentioned in the media. Another example would be when film critics are invited to preview a film prior to its release. In each case the objective is to solicit favourable comments. If, however, the comments are highly critical, as when a reviewer says that a film is not worth seeing, they can be said to be **unsolicited**. The film company did not encourage such things to be said.

  However, the negative film review could not be said to be unauthorised. If the film producers invite a panel of film critics to preview a film they are authorising the critics to express their honest opinions about it. The producers are deliberately exposing themselves to the possibility that the critics will not like their film. In such a case the negative reviews might be said to be authorised but not solicited and may be called an 'unsought consequence' (or unsolicited consequence) of authorising the critics to preview the film in the first place.

  Unauthorised or unsolicited statements are, of course, not always critical. A commentator can, and often does, make quite generous comments about an organisation without being solicited to do so.

Fig. 2.2   Uncontrolled publicity
*The organisation's external and internal publics or audiences are free (within legal limits) to comment on the organisation. The things said by members of one public may in turn affect the attitudes and opinions of members of other publics. The organisation may attempt to influence these comments but ultimately it has no real control.

- **Publicity may be friendly, neutral or hostile**   We would expect any publicity that an organisation puts out on its own behalf to be friendly. Unauthorised and unsolicited statements may, however, be hostile and any organisation (business, charitable, political, or whatever) must expect to attract some hostile comment. Comments can, of course, be simply neutral.

- **Publicity can be true or untrue**   Not all statements made about an organisation are true. We are not talking about differences of opinion here, as when one reviewer castigates a film which another praises but about what is, or is not, actually a matter of fact. Sometimes false statements are made in good faith by people who have simply got their facts wrong and intend no malice or deceit. There are times, however, when the publication of untrue statements may be made by people who know that what they are saying is untrue. In such cases the

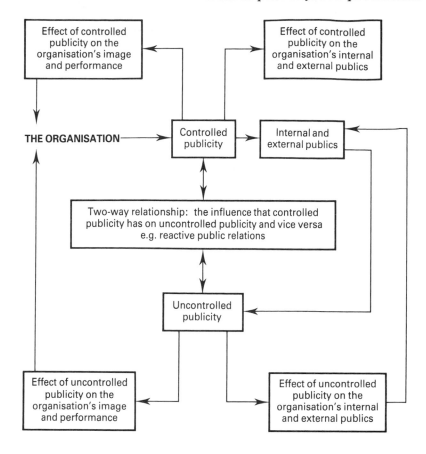

Fig. 2.3 The total publicity surround
NB The organisation is constantly surrounded by publicity. Not all of this is of
the organisation's own making. The effect of this publicity is felt by both the
organisation and its publics.

statements are made with the intention to deceive (and sometimes by
the companies themselves).

We must not make the mistake, however, of confusing 'hostile' with
'untrue'. Not all hostile comment is dishonest or untrue – the
reviewers are not lying when they say that in their opinion a film is
unworthy of the cinemagoer's attention.

**2.3 What do
we mean by
promotion?**
Promotion is that part of the publicity surround that can be identified
clearly as having been authorised, and paid for, by the organisation itself.
This definition clearly rules out unauthorised, unsolicited and hostile
publicity. Sadly, it does not rule out deliberate deception. There are
several ways of looking at promotion.

Pro-active promotional activities

Pro-active promotional activities are activities carried out with some forward-looking objective in mind. We might say that pro-active promotions are designed to bring about some state of affairs which the organisation thinks to be desirable.

Such promotional activities might be carried out in support of the organisation as a whole, or of a division or branch of the organisation. They might be carried out in support of a single product (as when a book publisher decides to promote one book from a list of 40 titles). They might be carried out in support of some marketing activity (such as launching a new product) or some financial activity or some corporate policy such as care for the environment.

Different industries have their own distinctive pro-active activities – the film industry invites reviewers to a private showing, the publishing industry organises author-signing sessions and a conference venue may run facility visits to woo potential conference organisers.

Reactive promotional activities

Reactive promotional activities are concerned with reacting, or responding, to situations which arise and which are not within the original plan. For instance, if a manufacturer were to suffer a factory fire, it would be necessary to reassure suppliers and customers that the company could cope with such a disaster and that it would be 'business as normal'.

Strategic promotional activities

Strategic promotional activities tend to be long term and are usually concerned with the overall direction that a company might take over a period of time. Entering a foreign market for the first time would be a strategic objective related to a market-development policy. Launching a new range of products would be a strategic objective related to a product-development policy. Holding on to market share would be a strategic objective related to a consolidation policy. All these policies would require a great deal of strategic promotional support.

Strategic promotional activities are pro-active.

Tactical promotional activities

Tactical promotional activities tend to be short term and concerned with some very specific objective such as shifting a surplus of slow-moving stock. Although such an objective might have only a limited impact on a company's overall situation, the combined effect of a series of tactical promotions will work together to take the company closer to its strategic objective – assuming, of course, that the company has an integrated plan in which tactical objectives are put in place to support strategic ones.

Tactical promotional activities may be either pro-active or reactive.

Promotional activities and internal and external publics

Promotional activities may be directed outwards at external publics or inwards at internal publics. It is often necessary to sell an externally directed strategy internally before it can be made to work and changes in company policy and procedure have to be internally promoted also.

2.4 Different types of promotional activity

Advertising

An **advertisement** is a message aimed at a specific audience paid for by an identifiable person or organisation (the advertiser) and appearing in any of the recognised media, such as magazines or newspapers. It is controlled by the advertiser. The fact that some newspapers give advertising space away does not undermine the general principle of advertising as a **paid-for message**. An economist would just say that the newspaper proprietors had set a **zero price** on their advertising space.

Press relations (media relations)

Press relations is an activity closely related to public relations with which it is often associated, as in the phrase 'public and press relations'. **Press (or media) relations** is a **method of promotion** designed to get messages into the editorial content of the media and it does so by developing professional relationships with journalists to get companies and their products mentioned favourably.

Some people dismiss this as 'free publicity' or 'free advertising', but that is to misunderstand the nature of both advertising and press relations.

Public relations

Public relations is wider than just press relations which it is often defined to include. Public relations is concerned with the systematic development and maintenance of mutual understanding between an organisation and its publics. Getting an organisation or its products mentioned on the radio, for example, is only part of this process.

Another way of looking at **public relations** is to say that it is concerned with **developing and sustaining a positive image** of the company and its products. Public relations is sometimes thought of as a supporting activity to marketing and advertising, but it is much more than this. Investors, suppliers, local councils, trade unions and government departments can all be target audiences for a public relations campaign.

Conferences and exhibitions

Conferences and exhibitions are discussed together because they have a great deal in common. Generically, they are referred to as **meetings** or **events**. A meeting is a formal situation where two (or more) groups of people, buyers and sellers for example, can come together to discuss matters of mutual interest and, sometimes, to carry out business transactions.

Sponsorship

Sponsorship is often called business sponsorship because most sponsorship deals today are funded by businesses. It is not a charity. **Sponsorship** involves a company **funding an activity** such as a football match or a pop concert in order to generate beneficial publicity for itself. The success, from the sponsor's point of view, of a sponsorship deal is the amount of good publicity it attracts. Sponsorship may be used to promote a corporate image or as part of a marketing campaign or a public relations campaign. Sponsorship support is usually, but not necessarily, in the form of money.

Direct marketing

Direct marketing is a generic term that covers a variety of ways of **promoting a product or service directly** to its final consumer or user without going through an intermediary. It involves the use of direct mail, telephone sales and calling on people at home. It is often associated with home shopping – shopping from home either by mail or telephone, for example.

Sales promotion

Sales promotion is another generic term that covers a very wide variety of practices which generally aim to motivate people in the closing stages of the purchase process and which are designed to bring about a successful sale. Sales promotions can operate at three levels: on the sales force, the wholesale and retail trade and, of course, the consumer.

Business-to-business promotions

All the promotional activities discussed above can be targeted at members of the consuming public. They may, however, also be targeted at other businesses so that we can talk of business-to-business advertising, business-to-business direct mail and so on.

2.5 Points to note

Under control

It should be observed that circumstances are rarely either totally controllable or totally uncontrollable. Something can go wrong with the best laid plans (a technicians' strike on television can ruin a carefully thought out advertising campaign). But situations apparently outside the company's control can still be influenced – by good public relations, for example.

Above and below the line

The terms **above the line** and **below the line** are often used and have their origins in the development of the advertising agencies. Originally, agencies made their living by buying media space on behalf of their clients. They made no profit on this from the client but instead earned a commission from the media. As the agencies expanded they took on more work on behalf of the client (sales promotion, for example) and on this they had to make a profit out of the client. The line in question was the one drawn across the page to distinguish the charges for media space (above the line) from the other charges (below the line) and the terms passed into common usage.

2.6 Summary

- Publicity, a term which can have the widest usage, also includes promotion which has a narrower meaning.
- Publicity includes all the statements made about a company or its products.
- Publicity may be controlled or non-controlled.
- Publicity uses any media.
- Publicity has different degrees of permanence.
- Publicity may be authorised or unauthorised; solicited or unsolicited; friendly, neutral or hostile; true or untrue.
- Promotional activities are those activities undertaken by (or authorised by) a company to get it positive publicity. It may be pro-active or reactive, strategic or tactical, inwardly or outwardly directed.
- Promotion itself further subdivides into a range of promotional activities often divided into above-the-line (media advertising) and below-the-line activities.

3 Business strategy and promotional campaigns

**3.1
Introduction**

Understanding strategy

Businesses, whether large or small, need to have clear strategic policies. In practice, there is unlikely to be a single strategy for the entire company but a family of strategies: financial strategies, product development strategies, market development strategies and, of course, advertising and public relations strategies. Overall, there has to be a corporate strategy for the whole business – to hold the lower-level strategies together and to give them a common purpose. It is impossible to develop good advertising strategies, for example, without being able to see how these relate to product and market development strategies and to corporate strategy as a whole. Advertising and public relations agencies will spend a lot of time studying a client's strategies before making their proposals and may even play a part in their development.

Understanding strategy is useful in two ways. First of all, it is useful in understanding one's own company and secondly, where business-to-business marketing is involved, it is useful in understanding the client company as well. This chapter is helpful background reading for business-to-business promotion (chapter 21).

Types of strategies

Strategies cannot be understood simply by reading a company's published policy statements. What actually goes on may bear very little resemblance to what the official documents say. Different types of strategies have to be recognised:

- **Official strategies** These have been agreed at different levels in the organisation and set out what should to be happening.

- **Emergent (or observed) strategies** These describe what is actually happening. They may differ from the official strategies.

Emergent (observed) strategies need not be a bad thing. They reflect the real-life experiences of the people at the sharp end who are often in a better position than those higher up to know what needs to be done. Official strategies may even be rewritten to accommodate emergent strategies. There is cause for concern, however, when the emergent strategies begin to diverge from each other to the point where they are no longer serving a common purpose.

A good overall corporate strategy will minimise the negative consequences of emergent strategies whilst remaining sufficiently flexible to take advantage of the positive contributions which they can make.

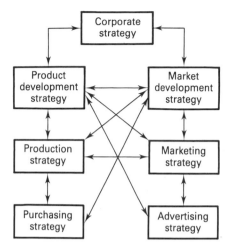

Fig. 3.1   The integration of corporate and lower level strategies
The product and market development strategies must relate to each other. The production strategy develops from the product development strategy and influences the purchasing strategy. All the strategies must be reconciled with each other and the corporate strategy. It is no use planning to market and advertise what you are not also planning to produce.

3.2 Top-down and bottom-up strategies

When a company is in a fairly stable and simple situation, it is often much easier to make most of the strategic decisions centrally at the top. In such situations local, lower-level managers may be quite happy to accept these top-down decisions and may even feel that they would, in any case, have made the same decision themselves. Where a company is in a dynamic and complex situation, however, it might be argued that local, lower-level managers are better placed to develop strategic and tactical responses and that central, higher-level management should be more concerned with developing and protecting the overall picture in the light of these bottom-up decisions. Where bottom-up policies occur, it is essential for departmental heads to meet together periodically with top-level managers to reconcile what is going on in each department.

The smaller a business is the more readily a centralised top-down policy will work. Large organisations, particularly those in dynamic and complex markets, are more likely to have greater local autonomy.

Figure 3.1 summarises some of the points made above.

3.3 Corporate mission statements

Many companies now have mission statements. These set out, sometimes in one sentence, what the organisation's fundamental purpose is. Often mission statements are along the lines of 'We aim to be the best at what we do'. Easy to remember, but it does not tell you very much about the company's activities. An advertising or public relations campaign should never lose sight of what the company's mission purports to be and the mission statement may itself be the inspiration for a promotional campaign.

Sometimes mission statements are couched in very specific terms and include such phrases as 'we aim to increase our market share by 10 per cent by the end of the decade' (which some people would say was really a strategic objective). Sometimes they are more general and may include such phrases as 'we aim to be a socially responsible organisation'.

Mission statements are at their best when they offer some sort of 'visionary' view of the organisation and send out positive statements to the company's internal and external publics. They may refer to social responsibility, environmental concern, equal opportunity policies, positive research programmes, growth strategies and ownership and control policies.

The fictitious example which follows is, itself, an act of publicity and promotion. Whoever reads it, employee, supplier, customer, consumer, journalist or whoever will have a clear picture of the vision set out for this company by its managers. Every decision taken and, therefore, every subsequent statement (advertisement, press release, etc.) can be judged against this mission (or vision) for the company's future.

We are a privately owned family business which has been trading in the cosmetics industry for the last half-century. We have grown as a result of internally financed development and the friendly and negotiated take-over of related businesses. We intend to remain in family ownership and our acquisitions policy will continue to emphasise friendly take-overs. Aggressive and predatory take-overs are not, and never will be, a part of our business policy. We have always taken, and will continue to take, a positive view of changes in the business environment and have incorporated into our business philosophy demonstrable concerns for social and environmental issues. None of our products currently in the market has been tested on live animals and we are proud to be one of the first cosmetics companies to adopt this policy. We will continue as an employer with a proven record in the area of equal opportunities. Against this background we have been a profitable and successful company providing both employment and quality products and we intend to take advantage of the Single European Market and other recent developments in world trade to continue in this way into the next century.

Mission statements which do not actually tell anybody anything about the company's purpose and direction are not worth making. Interested parties external to the organisation (such as animal rights groups) may well ask for copies of such a statement. In any case, a company which has gone to the trouble of producing a mission statement will wish it to be widely known and understood. It may feature as part of the chairperson's annual report or be sent out as part of a press release or press information pack. It may be distributed to suppliers and customers and made available to employees. People applying for jobs may be sent a copy.

When a company faces new circumstances, has been re-organised or has come under new management, an opportunity arises to rewrite the mission statement and to send out new messages.

Mission statements are not confined to the corporate level. Individual departments such as customer services departments may have their own mission statements but these should always reflect the corporate one. Divergent mission statements are as potentially mischievous as divergent strategies and may even reflect them.

3.4 The value chain

The value chain relates to many of the ideas involved in both the strategy as a whole and the mission statement. It can also inform the development of a promotional campaign. A manufacturer, for example, has certain corporate values (these may be as set out in the mission statement). To achieve its objectives it is desirable for the company to link up with others which share the same values. Specifically, the manufacturer will wish to favour suppliers who share the company's values and to sign up distributors who think in the same way. Even such decisions as appointing an advertising agency invoke the idea of a value chain. To what extent is the agency in sympathy with and supportive of the manufacturer's business values?

Case Study

Grundig Satellite

In July 1994 agency DFSD Bozell was appointed to create the ads for Grundig Satellite's £3 million advertising campaign. Marketing manager Anthony Sethill was quoted in the London *Evening Standard* as saying, 'We decided on DFSD Bozell because of its ability to understand and translate our business philosophy and communications strategy into innovative creative work.'

Figure 3.2 shows the concept of the company value chain.

3.5 Business strategy

Analysis, choice and implementation

Developing a business strategy is usually taken in three steps:

- Strategic analysis
- Strategic choice
- Strategic implementation.

In practice, they do not follow one after the other but have an interactive effect so that a later step may cause a company to rethink a decision taken at an earlier stage. Figure 3.3 depicts the relationships involved.

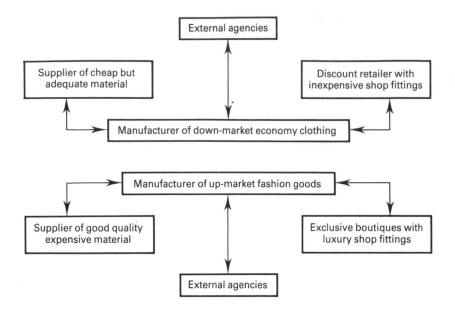

Fig. 3.2   Contrasting value chains
The selected suppliers, distributors and agencies have been chosen because they understand and can co-operate with the manufacturer's own value system.

Strategic analysis

Strategic analysis involves looking at the situation currently facing the company. It takes account of those factors outside the firm in the external environment and those inside the firm such as resources. It also takes account of the various power structures both inside and outside the firm which can be harnessed to assist the policy process or which can, if objections to the policy arise, provide stumbling blocks to impede its progress.

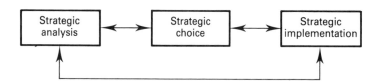

Fig. 3.3   The relationship between analysis, choice and implementation

Strategic choice

Strategic choice involves first of all generating a range of strategic options (what the company could do) and then deciding which of those options is actually best (what the company should do). There are three main criteria for making such a choice:

- **Suitability**   Does the proposal fit in with the company's mission statement, for example?

- **Feasibility**   Is the proposal such that it is within the power of the company to carry it out? (Does it have the resources?)
- **Acceptability**   Is the proposal such that it will meet the expectations and objectives of people both inside and outside the organisation?

If these criteria do not point to one strategic option that is clearly better than all the other options, there are a variety of techniques that can assist in the final choice. One such is a scoring device in which options are ranked against specific criteria such as those found in the mission statement. One such criterion could be 'the need to retain family ownership' and options which could foreseeably threaten to undermine family ownership would score low. Another criterion might be that of international expansion and options offering a better chance of overseas growth would score high.

Deciding between the two options would be assisted by weighting the criteria. If retaining family ownership was weighted twice as heavily as avoiding redundancies this would tilt the scales even more in favour of option 1 in fig. 3.4.

Criteria	Option 1	Option 2
Retain family ownership	√	X
Overseas opportunities	?	√
Avoid redundancies	?	√
Related diversification	√	?

√ = Yes (2 points)   X = No (0 points)   ? = Uncertain (1 point)
Option 1 scores 6 points; option 2 scores 4.

Fig. 3.4   A simple scoring device

In fig. 3.4 option 1 would allow the company to retain family ownership but could not guarantee that there would be no redundancies. Option 2 would avoid redundancies but only at the cost of surrendering family ownership. This example also illustrates the principle of **trade-offs** – neither option can guarantee both family ownership and no redundancies so one has to be traded off against the other.

Either option could meet with fierce resistance from different parties and this is where the power structures can come into play. Each option will have its supporters and the option which is eventually agreed may just be the one with the most power behind it – not necessarily the best one overall. For example, if resistance to redundancies proves insurmountable then, short of riding rough-shod over the objections, the company might in the end go for option 2 – the 'second-best' option – which raises the interesting observation that sometimes the second-best option might be the best thing to do.

It is in situations like this that public relations can sit in on the strategy-development process – pointing out where the resistance is likely to come from and proposing ways of responding to it. Some firms now insist that public relations sits in on all major policy decisions. Public relations can also identify the opportunities for getting some good publicity out of the proposals.

Strategic implementation

Strategic implementation involves putting the selected option into practice. At this stage detailed plans are needed. (Planning is considered in chapter 22.)

3.6 Strategic perspectives and constraints

In developing its strategy, a company should take account of three factors: the environment, its own resources and the expectations of the people who are going to be affected by it. The perspective the company adopts will show the priority given to one of these over the other two. The other two will then be seen as constraints.

The environment perspective

The **PEST** model is one way of looking at the environment. It stands for:

- **Political** In its widest sense, it can be taken to include legal and regulatory factors.

- **Economic** This includes such aspects as how unemployment affects the market as well as psychological factors such as consumer and business confidence and the propensities to spend, save, invest, etc.

- **Social** This includes factors such as concern for the environment, the emergence of a comparatively wealthy retired market, lifestyles and ethics.

- **Technological** Included here is the impact on marketing and advertising of such developments as interactive television, point-of-sale and telemarketing technology.

Case Study

Catalina: a technological breakthrough

In early 1994 ASDA, the supermarket chain, installed a new checkout device in over a hundred of its stores. This device (known as Catalina), a sort of 'electronic spy', identifies the brand names of the products purchased and issues on-the-spot discount coupons *for competing products* to be redeemed on the next shopping trip. The *Daily Mail*'s consumer affairs correspondent, Vikki Orvice, said, 'If, for example, a customer buys Pepsi, its rival Coca-Cola could, if it has bought access to the system, retaliate by offering a voucher offering discounts on Coke for their next visit.'

Catalina can also be used to promote ASDA's own-brand products, to reinforce purchasing habits by issuing same-brand coupons or to sell across the manufacturer's range by issuing coupons for another product made by the same producer.

Over twenty food manufacturers have already bought into the system and other manufacturers must be monitoring this technological breakthrough which will be seen as a threat by some and an opportunity by others.

What the PEST model does is remind us that there is not one single environment but a range of environments, including cultural, educational and religious ones, which can all be fitted somewhere into the PEST scheme.

Another useful approach focuses on what are called the **micro, meso** and **macro** environments:

- **The micro environment** is concerned with the firm itself and what is going on within it.
- **The meso environment** refers to the particular industry in which the firm operates. It could be taken to include all the aspects of value-chain analysis above as well as, of course, the competition and the market.
- **The macro environment** is the wider political, legal, cultural and social environment of the economy as a whole.

With respect to the meso environment, it is necessary to avoid the simple assumption that a firm operates in one industry only. Large multi-product firms with diversified product portfolios may well operate in several different industries at the same time. Such a company will develop separate strategies for each of the industries in which it operates or for each of the 'businesses' which make up the corporate whole.

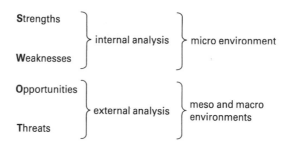

Fig. 3.5 SWOT model

SWOT

The SWOT model is also a useful frame of reference for developing and evaluating strategic ideas. SWOT stands for **Strengths** and **Weaknesses** (which relate to the internal environment of the company) and **Opportunities** and **Threats** (which relate to the external environment). Figure 3.5 portrays this model.

Important parts of the environment, from our point of view, are the 'publicity surround' (see chapter 2) and the regulatory framework (see chapter 5).

The resource perspective

The obvious concern here is whether or not the company has (or can acquire) the resources it needs to implement its preferred strategy. This can apply just as much to, say, a sales promotions strategy as to a production strategy. For instance, ITC (see chapter 5 for the Independent Television Commission) rule 35 requires that 'the advertiser is able to meet any reasonably foreseeable demand created by the advertising' and 'is able to fulfil orders within 28 days from receipt. . .' Setting up a strategy which could not be resourced to these standards would be folly.

Resources include anything to which the company has access, regardless of whether or not it actually owns them. A reliable supplier is a resource, as is a reliable distributor (we are back to the value chain). Looking after these valuable resources by developing good trade relations (a type of public relations – or relationship marketing) is crucial. A company's consumers may be seen to be the most important resource it has – why else will one firm take over another firm just to get its hands on the mailing list?

To develop a promotional campaign, a company needs access to media analysts, planners and buyers, **creatives** such as copywriters, designers and photographers, printers, mailing list managers and so on.

Some of these will be in-house and some will be out-house, but they will all be part of the resource base required by the company. Deciding whether to do these things in-house or put them out to an agency is itself a strategic decision tied in with such factors as loyalty and control. Agencies, and some of the strategic implications involved, are discussed in detail in chapter 4.

The expectations perspective

An understanding of the expectations and objectives of the people affected by the company's strategy is essential. A strategy will work either because people are committed to it and make it work or, if they do object, because they lack the power to do anything about it (or there may be a level of indifference involved). If, however, people judge that a proposed strategy is unacceptable to them (because, for example, they perceive that it will threaten their jobs) then they may try to resist it. Again, the extent to which they can resist it will depend on how much power they have; but if they have enough power, they can force a company into developing its second-best option.

Case Studies

1 Nestlé

Nestlé has, over the years, enjoyed a lot of beneficial media publicity from its Gold Blend advertising campaign. But in 1994 it also encountered two pieces of resistance to its policies from people who did not find those policies acceptable. The first arose when the company declined to interview a black boy for the role of the Milky Bar Kid (one of advertising's most famous characters) and the other was when demonstrators gathered outside the company's Croydon headquarters to protest about the sale of processed baby-food in the third world. The protest was in favour of breastfeeding and claimed that commercialised baby food was actually leading to avoidable infant deaths in countries where breastfeeding would be better. (This particular debate has been going on for many years – not only with Nestlé.) In both cases Nestlé made public statements defending its policies in the face of this hostile publicity.

2 McDonald's and Sainsbury's

McDonald's encountered enormous resistance from local residents when it proposed to open its first drive-in outlet in London and in one case Sainsbury's encountered similar resistance from local residents when it proposed moving its early morning delivery time back an hour (and it is facing similar problems now with the impact on local neighbourhoods of Sunday openings). Residents were afraid that their expectations of a quiet neighbourhood would be disturbed by late night traffic on the one hand and early morning traffic on the other. Resistance like this can be, and usually is, overcome – very often with the help of promotional techniques to win enough support for the proposals to go through. But companies cannot always ignore or neutralise such protest.

Companies are often prepared to spend a great deal of money on advertising and public relations to overcome such objections and to secure the level of acceptability needed. The tactics used may include any of the following:

- Advertisements in the media can be used to explain the benefits of the proposals.
- Direct mail can be used to give a more detailed and personalised explanation than a media advertisement can make.
- Press conferences can be used to gain media attention for the new strategy so that the company's point of view can be put across.
- Open days and exhibitions can be used to let local residents see what the company is about.
- Members of Parliament and local councillors can be lobbied.
- Discussion groups can be held with personnel who are worried about the proposals.

The main point is that a business's strategies affect the life of other people who may or may not have enough power and influence to make the company think again.

Constraints

Whichever of the three perspectives is adopted, the other two will then act as constraints. Suppose, for example, that a company adopts an environment-based perspective, seeking out and pursuing opportunities in the external environment. Its ability to do this will be limited by its resources on the one hand and by the expectations and power of people

Fig. 3.6 Perspectives and constraints: the relationship between the environment, resources and expectations

on the other. Similarly, a resource-based strategy will be limited by the business environment of the company and the expectations and objectives of others. Some companies elect for an expectations-based perspective, but if they do they will find that their ability to meet the expectations of others will, itself, be limited by the environment and resources.

Figure 3.6 illustrates these relationships.

3.7
Do-nothing
strategies

A 'do-nothing' strategy does not mean that the organisation does nothing at all, but that it carries on without changing anything. Simply leaving things as they are is often the best option of all. (As Americans say, 'If it ain't broke, don't fix it.') Some experts argue that a do-nothing strategy should always be evaluated, since it provides a basis of comparison with the other 'do-something' strategies and establishes a bench-mark against which they can be assessed. It works against the danger of 'change for change's sake' or of forming too favourable a view of the alternatives and it brings in some extra realism.

In fig. 3.7 suppose, for example, that the strategy of a new advertising campaign would increase market share from 9 per cent to 11 per cent

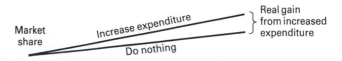

Fig. 3.7 Projected results of a do-nothing strategy compared with an increase in advertising expenditure

in twelve months at a total cost of £3 million. Suppose also that it is estimated that a do-nothing strategy (carrying on with the old campaign) would, in any case, increase market share to 10 per cent in the same time at a cost of £1 million. There is now a basis for evaluating the costs and benefits of making a change. Is it worthwhile spending an extra £2 million pounds to gain an extra 1 per cent share of the market?

3.8 Summary

- Organisations need policies and strategies and usually have a family of divisional and departmental strategies which, ideally, should be co-ordinated and integrated through an overall corporate strategy.
- In simple, static situations, policy decisions can easily be made centrally, but as situations become more dynamic and complex (and as the firm gets bigger) more decisions may be decentralised to lower, local levels.
- The concepts of mission statements and value chains are helpful in understanding and developing strategic positions.
- Advertising and other promotional strategies have to fit in with the general family of strategies.
- Understanding how policies and strategies are developed and agreed is helpful in creating promotional campaigns and, in business-to-business marketing, in understanding how the customer firm functions (what its purchasing policies are, for example).
- Agreeing on a strategy involves strategic analysis, strategic choice and strategic implementation. It also involves having a particular perspective, taking the environment or the resource requirement or the expectations and objectives of others as a starting point.
- The expectations of others are important because it reminds us that if enough people have enough power they can force a company into abandoning its preferred policy and adopting a 'second-best' policy instead. The environment, a company's resources and the expectations of others can also act as constraints.
- An organisation always has the option of 'doing nothing' – of leaving things as they are. Sometimes this can actually be the best thing to do.

3.9 Further reading

There are many good books on business policy and strategy. The ideas expressed in this chapter are more fully discussed in *Exploring Corporate Strategy* by Gerry Johnson and Kevan Scholes (Prentice Hall), which is strongly recommended.

3.10 Assignments

1. Write a mission statement for any organisation with which you are familiar. List the people to whom it might be sent and outline the impression you want to create.

2. Try to discover some situations in which an organisation (it need not be a business) is experiencing resistance to its policies (either at the local or the national level). Try to evaluate the strength and power of the opposition and to identify what it is that they want the organisation to do instead.

3. Discuss the situations in which you think that a do-nothing strategy might be the best one to adopt. In any case, explain why it is sometimes argued that a do-nothing strategy should always be evaluated.

4 The use of agencies

4.1 The choice between in-house and agency operations

As we observed in chapter 3, developing a strategy involves a consideration of the resources available to a company. Some of these resources may lie outside the company and some may belong to it. A manufacturer may decide to undertake its own deliveries or to pay an external carrier, or to manufacture its own component parts or to buy them in from outside. These 'make or buy' situations are widespread and no less common in the worlds of advertising and promotion than anywhere else.

When an organisation decides to do its own advertising we say that it is doing it **in-house** – in its own advertising department. When the organisation appoints an agency, we say that it is going **out-of-house** or just **out-house**. In this latter case, the organisation becomes the client of the agency and we talk of client–agency relationships.

However, even when the work is done in-house a form of client–agency relationship exists and this must be understood. An in-house public relations department, for example, does not work in isolation from the rest of the company pleasing itself as to what sort of public relations it will do and when. It works for another department of the company, or even the board of directors itself. In such cases, we say that there is an **internal client**. For example, the marketing department could be the **client department** of the PR department (which, in turn, is acting as a sort of **internal agent**). An in-house department needs to have as much care for its internal clients as an independent agency has for its external clients.

The decision whether to use in-house or out-house facilities is a complex one. When a company uses external suppliers (an advertising agency is a form of external supplier), it is operating in the external market with all the problems and benefits that external market operations involve. When it chooses to do the work itself, it abandons the external market in favour of its own **internal market** in which one part of the company is 'selling' its services to another part of the same company.

The question of whether to use an agency can be restated as the general policy question of whether a company is better off operating externally in the open market or operating internally in its own market. That is the question which we consider when we look at all the factors which will influence the decision as to whether or not to use an agency.

4.2 The range of in-house/out-house options

It is not a straightforward question of either doing all the work in-house or putting it all out to a single external agency. In practice, we may find any of the following options being pursued:

- The company does all the work in-house.
- The company gives all the work out to one agency.

- The company splits the work between itself and one agency.
- The company gives out all the work, but splits it between two or more agencies.
- The company keeps some of the work in-house and divides the remainder between two or more agencies.

Many firms change their approach to these options and it is doubtful if there are any managers who would say that only one of the above options could ever be right.

When IBM awarded its £300 million worldwide account to British agency Ogilvy and Mather in 1994, it 'sacked' 40 other agencies across the globe (some in this country). O&M, to avoid conflict of interest, 'resigned' from accounts with IBM rivals Microsoft and Compaq.

Furthermore, even when the company puts work out to agencies, it must still employ sufficient people in-house to liaise with them and to co-ordinate their efforts.

4.3 Criteria for deciding between in-house and out-house

There are many factors which could affect the decision. Some are given a higher weighting by some companies than others and the weighting given may, itself, be influenced by the kind of work under consideration. The following list of different types of agencies should be borne in mind. (The list is not exhaustive.) Note that in the rest of this chapter the word agency is used to mean any of the following and not just advertising agencies:

- Advertising agencies.
- Conference organisers.
- Copywriting agencies.
- Design studios.
- Direct marketing houses.
- Exhibition organisers.
- Full service agencies.
- Media independents.
- Press cutting services.
- Photographic studios.
- Production companies.
- Public relations consultancies.
- Sponsorship agencies.
- Venue finders.

Costs

In some situations, where outputs can be standardised, cost comparisons are relatively easy to make. However, the planning and creative work involved in promotional campaigns is seldom standardisable and it might sometimes simply prove impossible ever to know for sure whether or not an agency would be cheaper.

A complication is the method by which the company handles its **internal transfer pricing**, when one department does work for another. Internal transfer pricing methods vary from organisation to organisation with the possible consequence that in-house work may appear cheaper or dearer to the client than it actually is. The following internal pricing methods might be used:

- The internal supplier could be treated as a cost centre, there to provide a service, with its work written off and not charged to the client department.
- The work could be charged through on a full-cost basis, but with no mark-up for profit.
- The work could be charged on exactly the same basis as an external agency would charge for the same work.

There are no golden rules for deciding how internally generated costs should be distributed; but you should be aware that **zero price** and **full-cost** systems distort the comparison and **market-price** systems may be resented by a client department which is denied access to the market any-way. All of this supposes that the data exists to enable a comparison to be made.

Results

The problem with this criteria lies in the difficulty of ever knowing until after the event what results have been achieved as opposed to those which were hoped for. Results may be measured in such terms as having made X per cent of the public aware of the company's existence or of giving so many people an **OTS (Opportunity To See)** an advertisement. It is impossible to set up in advance an analytical model which will predict with total certainty whether an in-house campaign will produce better results than an out-house campaign, since there are too many non-controllable factors. Although a client might, subsequently, be disappointed with an agency's performance and suspect that it could have done better itself, it will simply never know.

Speed of delivery

Generally speaking, pro-active campaigns should be planned sufficiently well in advance that the pressure of time alone should not be a deter-mining factor in deciding whether or not to use an agency. There are reactive situations, however, such as the need to respond quickly to a crisis situation, where an agency might have the resources to make a quicker response than an in-house department. It could, of course, go the other way, with the in-house department able to provide the necessary service faster. A company may, for example, have its own in-house print shop or reprographics unit to run off press releases or direct mail letters. In an emergency, however, it might find that an external printer can handle a particular job faster.

Confidentiality

A manufacturer working on a new product may wish to limit the number of people who know about it. Appointing an external advertising agency would inevitably involve letting the personnel of that agency 'in on the act' and that might just not be acceptable. This is an instance where acceptability becomes the main criterion – it is not acceptable to the company to divulge information about its new product plans to outsiders.

Objectivity

A company might feel that it will get more objectivity, a more critical approach, from an agency than it will from its own personnel who might be suspected of being unwilling to risk upsetting an internal client by being too critical or, just as likely, be unwilling to take a hard look at its own efforts.

Commitment

An agency is unlikely to have only one client and there will, therefore, often be demands made on its resources from its other clients. A company may begin to worry about whether it is getting its share of agency attention or whether, under pressure, the agency will not favour some other client. Additionally, as the client has no direct control over agency personnel, it might fear that agency people working on its account might leave and be replaced by others less experienced and less competent.

Accessibility

One advantage of having in-house facilities could be that they are easier to get at. However, with multi-site companies, a public relations department based at head office may be just as inaccessible to a particular centre of operations as an external agency.

Accessibility (proximity) is an important factor in the choice of agency. A company based in Manchester might well prefer to sign up a Manchester-based agency because it is seen as more accessible than a London agency, whereas another company might go in-house simply because there is no suitable agency within easy visiting distance.

With both commitment and accessibility there may be a misconception associated with in-house operations. An in-house facility may be working for several client departments at the same time and the problems of divided loyalties and inaccessibility might just as easily arise. Ask anybody who is in charge of an in-house print shop or reprographics unit.

Expertise

An agency may offer a particular skill which is not available in-house. for example, the ability to run a direct-mail operation. In this case it may pay the company to go out-house, particularly if direct-mail exercises are not to become a major part of the company's overall promotional activity. However, if it is envisaged that direct-mail shots are to become a regular feature, then the company might just as well appoint its own direct-mail manager.

Experience

It is sometimes suggested that agency personnel have wider experience than in-house personnel. However, given the ease with which a practitioner in, say, advertising or public relations can move between in-house and out-house appointments such claims must be looked at cautiously.

Creativity

There is obviously a need for creative thinking and imagination in designing promotional activities and an organisation may well feel that it will get access to more original ideas by going out of house.

Dismissibility

It has been argued that one advantage of appointing an agency is that it is much easier for a client to 'sack' an agency than it is to sack an entire in-house department. This is a rather negative view and is open to question. If a firm got a reputation for being difficult to work with and of too frequently sacking its agencies, it might find that other agencies would not wish to take it on. In any case, many firms have had no difficulty in the past in getting rid of an entire department. Indeed, closing down an existing department might be just one factor in developing a new strategy.

4.4 Making the decision

At the end of the day, there is no hard and fast formula for making the decision.

One approach which attempts to bring all the above considerations under one umbrella is called **cost-benefit analysis (CBA)**. Here the management would list under two separate headings the costs and the benefits associated with each option. A comparison could then be made to see which option might offer the better balance of benefits over costs. Costs and benefits are not to be defined only in terms of money; such non-quantifiable elements as loyalty and creativity must be included. This method is subject to a considerable degree of subjective judgement, but, like the scoring method discussed in chapter 3, it does at least provide the opportunity to consider all the angles. CBA can be used to evaluate other strategic decisions as well and scoring systems can be used in deciding whether to go out-of-house or not.

Perhaps, for many organisations, it is a question of liaison, co-ordination and control. The more facilities are internalised, the more control an organisation might think it has; the more they are externalised, the less control the organisation might have. Many organisations have ten or more agencies on their books at the same time. How does this affect overall monitoring and control?

4.5 Dividing the work between in-house and out-house

It is not merely a matter of doing all the work in-house or putting it all out-of-house. An organisation might decide to do some of the work itself and put the rest out. In such a case the question would be where to draw the line. A company which will not put the advertising campaign for its new products into an agency's hands may be perfectly happy to allow an agency to handle its mature products where there is no longer the need for confidentiality and secrecy. Some of the reasons for splitting the work might include:

- The company has the occasional need for some service such as planning a sales promotion but does not run sales promotions sufficiently often to justify maintaining an in-house facility.
- There may be peaks of activity once or twice a year such as a new product launch. Maintaining a department big enough to handle this peak work would mean that personnel would be underutilised during the rest of the year.
- There might be an unusual event, such as celebrating the firm's hundreth year in business, and this might require extra advertising or public relations to be brought in.
- It might even be that the company maintains some external agency on its books just to keep the in-house personnel on their toes. In this case, the external agency would be seen by the in-house group as a competitor rather than a co-operator, and this might not be a good recipe for success.

4.6 Dividing the work between two or more agencies

The attractions of using one big **all-through** or **full-service** agency are fairly obvious. There is only one external body to deal with and client–agency relationships are much simplified. There is not the problem of co-ordinating the work between agencies as might otherwise arise. There may, additionally, be economies in employing an advertising agency which has its own design department compared with using a smaller agency which, in turn, contracts design work out.

On the other hand, a full-service agency may be like the curate's egg – very good in parts but otherwise not so good. Going for smaller specialist agencies extends the range from which a company can choose and, furthermore, limits the dependency which a client may feel when it has only the one agency. It is never a clear-cut situation.

During a business boom, when money is flowing in, there may be a tendency to go for the one full-service agency and put all the work out. As recession sets in, firms may cut back on their promotional budgets and feel more able to do the work themselves. However, there may be parts of the work which they might still want to put out. It does, at least, suggest that such decisions may have as much to do with the state of the economy as they do with anything intrinsic to the nature of advertising and promotion. Indeed some commentators suggest that it is little more than a matter of fashion. One year big full-service agencies are in; the next year the vogue is to go for the smaller specialist houses.

4.7 Agencies also go out of house

A big agency might have its own design and photographic studios. A smaller agency, needing the work of a photographer, may put the work out to an independent studio. The extent to which an agency may further subcontract work, the way in which it goes about it, and the basis upon which it eventually charges its own clients for the work involved is a matter of some concern and may be an additional factor affecting the choice of agency.

A client company would certainly be well advised to ask about such matters before signing a contract. The more an agency subcontracts the less control the client may have (will it have any influence, for example, on the agency's choice of a designer?). The more the agency **marks up** the money paid out by it before passing the charge on to its client, the less value for money the client will receive. Agency practices vary enormously from making no mark-up to modest administrative costs to a profiteering 25 per cent.

4.8 Appointing and working with an agency

If the decision is made to appoint an agency, the following points should be considered:

- Preparing the **brief**.
- Selecting and appointing the agency.
- Client–agency relations.
- Contractual and financial arrangements.

Preparing the brief

The following comments are fairly general ideas that would be useful in considering a brief for any kind of agency from direct mail to design or advertising to public relations. Advertising briefs are discussed more fully in chapter 10.

The brief is a written statement setting out what the client wants the agency to do. No agency likes to work for a client who does not know what it wants and the ability to write a good brief is crucial – a good agency will help to sort out the brief if necessary. At the end of the day the brief should be something to which both client and agency can commit themselves and it should be a result of discussion and negotiation. It is important for the client to be as open as necessary with the agency. Holding back vital information which the agency might need is unfair to both sides. The agency is handicapped and the client cannot get the best service.

The brief will cover the client's objectives, the time-scale involved and the size of the budget. It would be usual for the client to say how much it is prepared to spend, but the agency may produce good reasons for increasing the budget. It would not be unknown for an agency to decline an account if, in its opinion, the proposed budget was too small to get the sort of results the client was looking for. Finally, the brief might include a statement of the methods or tools to be used: for example, is it to be primarily a television campaign, or will direct mail play the major role? If more than one agency is to handle different parts of a project, then it is a good idea to let each agency see all the briefs and not just its own.

The client should be prepared with the clearest possible ideas as to what it wants. An insufficiently prepared client might find that the better agencies will not want to talk to it; or, what would be worse, the client might be talked into accepting unsuitable proposals by an agency that does not truly understand its needs. The client has a right to approve the brief and must not be afraid to say no. If the client does not like a proposal, the agency must justify it.

Selecting and appointing an agency

First of all, the client should look around to see what is available. The client might approach one of the professional bodies for a list of agencies or look for information in a trade journal such as *Campaign* or *PR Week*. A company might find that agencies approach it directly by putting it on their mailing lists or sending a promotional video or a representative.

At this stage, the company should try to match the profiles of the agencies against its own requirements, eliminating unsuitable ones and drawing up a list of the possibles. For example, a major retailer would want to look at agencies with retail campaign experience – some agencies have teams of retail specialists just as others have teams with business-to-business expertise. What sort of experience do they have, what about the people who work for them, what accounts do they currently handle, what accounts have they handled in the past, how long have they been in business, what is the size of their annual turnover or billings – these are all questions that should be asked.

Agencies may at this stage be invited to make what is called a **credentials pitch** – an opportunity to make a presentation proving their worthiness to be on the shortlist. They may not actually say very much about what, specifically, they would do for the client (it might be too early for this and, in any case, the preliminary brief would not give too much vital information away) but they would talk about their own track record and prove that they were worth considering. Credentials pitches do not always happen, for a client may be quite clear as to which agencies are to be shortlisted without such a formality.

Shortlisted agencies would then be invited to pitch for the account – to make a detailed **proposals pitch**. Advertising and public relations agencies put a lot of time, effort and money into pitching, sometimes going so far as to build special sets and put the presentation team into costume. Pre-pitch activities are not unknown either – an agency might pay for a hot-air balloon to be flown in full view of the client's windows.

The decision as to which agency to appoint would depend almost entirely on the quality of the proposals, the creativity and originality of the ideas and the extent to which the agency seemed to understand the client's needs and requirements. A client must be careful, however, not to be taken in by a polished presentation which cannot fully be carried out because the agency staff who will work on the account lack the necessary experience.

Sometimes the people making the pitch are not the people who will work on the account. It is usually wise to clarify this; if the people who will work on the account are not present at the pitch, the client should insist on meeting them, before signing anything. The ability to make a good pitch is not, in itself, evidence of ability to run a good campaign.

An agency may decline to pitch and may decline to make a proposals pitch even after it has made a successful credentials pitch. Reasons for declining might include:

- The agency is too busy to take on a new account. An agency may be interested in two different accounts at the same time, knowing that it cannot handle them both. If it wins one account, it may actually pull out of the other even after accepting the invitation to pitch.

- The agency does not like the competition: a less well-known agency may not wish to pitch against an agency with an established reputation in a particular field. Agencies do not, however, always know who the competition is nor, even, how many other agencies have been invited. For reasons of security a client may wish to keep this secret.
- The agency does not like the nature of the account: some agencies will not work for tobacco companies, for example. The agency might feel that it cannot work happily with the client or that the client is not prepared to spend enough money.
- The agency cannot afford at that time the cost of preparing a pitch which can run to many thousands of pounds. (An agency in this position might be unwilling to admit to it and, if pressed, might offer a different reason.)

Client–agency relations

The agency should be seen as an extension of the client's organisation, not as an outsider. There may be a need to reveal sensitive information and this requires (*a*) that the client is willing to divulge it and (*b*) the agency personnel keep it confidential. In some agencies personnel are discouraged (even forbidden) from talking about the account they are working on with other members of the same agency. To some extent they become a quasi-department of the client and some of them will spend a considerable amount of time on client premises talking to and working with client personnel. It is in the interests of the client, when agency personnel are on its premises, to afford them every consideration in terms of a place where they can work, access to company records and access to company personnel. Similarly, on those occasions when the client visits the agency, the client should feel he or she is visiting colleagues not strangers. There will, of course, be conflicts and disagreements, but such things are just part of organisational life anyway and it would be a mistake for the client to think when coming away from a particularly difficult meeting that 'all the unpleasantness could have been avoided if we had just stayed in-house'. Figure 4.1 illustrates the difference between the agency seen as an outsider and the agency seen as an insider.

However, clients should always remember that agencies do not work for them full-time: agencies have their own business concerns as well. There are too many cases of clients who call unnecessary meetings and make other unreasonable demands on agency time only to discover that, at the end of the day, the time has found its way on to the agency's bill. Insisting that agency staff come to the client for discussions rather than the client going to them might show who is the boss, but the client shouldn't be surprised to be charged for the agency's time and expense involved.

Written reports are often as useful as meetings and less demanding on everybody's time – meetings should only be held when necessary. The client should ask for, and expect, routine progress reports and special reports, such as how the agency dealt with some unexpected contingency (see pages 288–90). Similarly, if the client has in-house meetings at which the agency is not represented, a report should be sent to the agency.

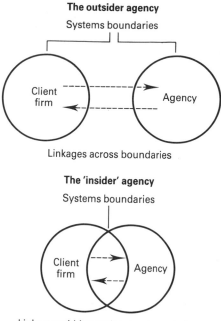

The outsider agency

Systems boundaries

Client firm

Agency

Linkages across boundaries

The 'insider' agency

Systems boundaries

Client firm

Agency

Linkages within overlapping boundaries

Fig. 4.1 The agency seen as outsider or as insider

The agency should know who is the contact person in the client's organisation and how contact can be made. The agency should also have a clearly identified person to liaise with (such as the account handler in an advertising agency). This is particularly important when trying to co-ordinate the work of several agencies or to co-ordinate in-house work with agency work.

The contractual and financial arrangements

It is sensible, before making a final decision, for the client to be clear about the legal and financial arrangements. Signing an agency up for three years may prove a costly mistake if after six months the client feels that things are not working out. The legal conditions for terminating an agreement must be clearly understood and set out in the contract. Break clauses may be used which say, for example, that the contract is for three years subject to an annual review. This lets the client get out of an unsatisfactory contract and also gives a dissatisfied agency the ability to quit. Generally speaking, the duties and obligations of both parties must be clearly defined, together with the procedures to be followed at all stages. There are no standard industry-wide contracts and it is in the interests of both parties, as the Society of British Advertisers puts it, 'to avoid misunderstandings that might damage the relationship. . . . Legal advice should be sought where special provisions need to be included.'

A constant source of unhappiness between client and agency is the financial relationship and this particularly should be very carefully

Table 4.1   A £15 million media campaign

Agency invoiced by media at rate-card price less 15 per cent	£12.75 m
Agency invoice client at full rate-card price	£15.00 m
Agency mark-up	£ 2.25 m

NB £2.25 million is actually 17.65 per cent of £12.75 million. A mark-up of 17.65 per cent to the client is the equivalent of a 15% commission from the media.

covered in the contract. There are several ways of paying an agency or, to put it differently, there are several ways in which an agency can charge for its services.

Commission

Commission is the traditional method for advertising agencies. It was used exclusively in the early days of agencies and insisted upon by media owners. The agencies buy advertising space at a published rate (as on 'the rate card') from the media and sell it to the advertisers at the full rate-card price. The media, however, charge the agencies the rate-card price minus 15 per cent commission. In effect, this means that the agencies were making their profit out of the media and providing their services to the advertisers 'free of charge'. But it was not always perceived this way by the advertisers who saw themselves being charged a mark-up of 17.65 per cent and soon began to question the fairness of the system. Some thought that they should buy from the media direct and pocket the commission themselves; others thought that the agencies should share the commission with them (now called 'commission rebating') and many complained that the system simply encouraged the agencies to spend money recklessly on the client's behalf to boost their commission earnings. Table 4.1 shows how such a system works, using a £15 million media campaign as an example. If, as often happens now, there is a rebate in operation, the agency might pass on, say, 5 per cent of the commission to the client and take only £1.5 million itself. The rigid commission system is no longer enforceable and specialist media buying companies can work on a profit as low as 2 or 3 per cent, rebating as much as 12 per cent to the client. A less happy development is the suspicion that the media buyers give a larger than proportionate rebate to their biggest clients and a smaller rebate (sometimes no rebate at all) to their small clients in spite of the fact that all the space is equally rebatable.

Fixed fees

An agency may work on a fixed period fee, usually annually or quarterly. For an agreed fixed sum, it performs the client's needs for the contract period. Difficulties arise when the agency is unusually busy on the client's behalf and feels, towards the end of the period, that the money has all gone and that the client has had all the advertising or public relations to which it is entitled. The client may not see it this way and may insist that the agency carry on as per contract. Sometimes the client can be persuaded to top up the fee and sometimes an agency will carry on even though it is no longer making a profit on the account. On the other hand, the agency may have a quiet time and the client may wonder just what it is getting for its money.

Ad hoc fees

Another kind of fee is where the agency contracts to carry out one specific task, for example, a direct-mail shot or a sponsorship deal. It is unwise for either party to sign an *ad hoc* contract before the project in question is fully costed out, otherwise the same problems can arise as with fixed fees: one side feels cheated and the other is more than satisfied with the outcome.

Hourly rates

Hourly rates are used by some public relations agencies, particularly on small accounts where there might not be much in the way of creative or production costs and the major input into the account is time itself. Hourly rates may be as much as £250 an hour for a senior executive or as low as £25 an hour for clerical assistance.

Payment by results

It is suprising that any agency will contemplate a payment by results system when the results of its efforts are so often outside its direct control and in some cases may be extremely difficult to measure. It may be thought that only new agencies anxious to make a reputation for themselves or agencies struggling to attract new business against a shrinking client list would expose themselves to the risks involved. The conventional view is that a client pays the agency for its efforts on its behalf and that it is the work done by the agency that the client pays for. Results are, of course, important and may affect the decision to carry on with the agency, but paying the agency on a basis directly related to those results may be to pay an agency for 'results' arising out of some other circumstance (such as a competitor attracting some very bad publicity) or to penalise an agency for circumstances outside its control, such as results being adversely affected by poor distribution.

There are some situations where payment by results might work. A direct-response advertising campaign where the number of responses can be directly measured, for example, or a public relations campaign to raise name awareness. But even with these, payment by results is not an entirely satisfactory method. A reversal of this thinking is the practice of rebating part of an agreed fee if performance does not meet an agreed standard. A direct-mail list-broker may rebate if too many letters are returned unopened. This is not so much payment by results as penalties for non-results.

Retainers

A company may pay an agency a small annual fee as a retainer in case that agency should be required. Even if the agency is not required, it keeps the retainer.

Mark-ups

Mark-ups are not in themselves a method of payment and may be used in connection with any of the above systems. The basis on which an agency marks up the work which it itself contracts out to another house is, nevertheless, part of the financial package and should be considered in this connection.

Some agencies prefer to stick to one method of charging, but others will use more than one method. It has been argued that if, after seeing the pitches, it is difficult to choose between two agencies on the basis of the proposals, then the client might as well choose on the basis of the financial packages the agencies are prepared to negotiate.

4.9 Terminating the relationship

A relationship may be terminated by mutual consent without acrimony, but if for any reason the client is dissatisfied with the agency the client may terminate the relationship. It is usually easier to do this when the contract comes up for renewal, but in extreme cases it may be thought necessary to 'sack' the agency in mid-contract. This, of course, is easier if the contract is worded in such a way that the law is on the client's side. It is usually wiser to look for a new agency before sacking the old, otherwise the client may be unrepresented at a crucial time.

It is possible to terminate a relationship simply because the client believes that a new set of ideas and fresh minds are called for or because the work is being taken in-house or because the client can no longer afford it. Whatever the reason, the decision to seek a new advertising or public relations agency will almost certainly involve the decision to begin a new campaign. The existing campaign will have come about as a result of the creative talents of the current agency and cannot just be taken over by the new agency. The new agency will want to develop its own ideas anyway.

However, it may be the agency which does not wish to carry on and which, in effect, 'resigns' the account. Again, the usual time to do this would be when the contract comes up for renewal, but if the agency felt in mid-term that it could not carry on working with an apparently unreasonable client it might seek to resign the account earlier. When the tide began to turn against the commission system, some agencies resigned accounts rather than give in to demands for commission rebates.

In the relatively small worlds of advertising and public relations, it may prove hard to keep secret the intention to terminate. Whatever the reason for terminating (and whoever's decision it is), the other side should not hear of it from a third party. It is very unsatisfactory for an agency to discover that one of its clients is looking for a replacement other than from the client itself; this only adds further rancour to a possibly unhappy situation. In any case, it is possible that both sides can get together to discuss why either or both of them wishes to part company and any difficulties might be resolved.

Case Studies

1 Saatchi & Saatchi

Large, internationally known firms do sometimes deliberately break up into smaller companies for good strategic reasons. ICI and Zeneca provide an example. However, when the world-leading advertising agency Saatchi and Saatchi broke up, the break was far from amicable and the story gained headline media attention across print, television and radio. Leading light and co-founder Maurice Saatchi was forced out of position after a bitter boardroom struggle and promptly put in place steps to set up a new advertising agency to compete against his former brain-child.

The threat of a new Saatchi-led agency compounded the difficulties faced by the original firm which took on all the characteristics of a crisis situation (see chapter 16). The reputation of the firm suffered as the boardroom disputes were widely reported and rumours of managerial incompetence at the highest levels added fuel to the fire. The share price collapsed, savaging (by about 30 per cent) the value of the original firm and triggering off elements of a financial crisis as major lenders nervously looked on. The resignation of top account and creative directors in support of Maurice Saatchi and the steps taken by major clients to move their accounts elsewhere – notably into the proposed new Maurice Saatchi agency – added to the firm's operational difficulties.

Major clients British Airways and Mirror Group Newspapers quickly removed their multi-million pound accounts and, at the time of writing, question marks hung over the Dixons and Tory Party accounts. Saatchi directors embarked on a crash programme of personal visits as they fought to hold on to threatened accounts and lawyers scrutinised every word of the contracts.

The *Evening Standard* of 12 January 1995 made much of a story that a secret £1m loan from Saatchi & Saatchi to the Conservative Party effectively tied the party to the agency whilst elsewhere it was claimed that only Maurice Saatchi had the stature to run the Tory account anyway. Threats of legal action to prevent Maurice Saatchi from poaching accounts were in the air.

Client contracts were not the only ones to be scrutinised and the contracts of employment of Saatchi & Saatchi executives were also put under the spotlight, particularly with respect to their freedom to accept positions with the new agency. Typically, resigning executives are contractually prevented from setting up new agencies or taking senior positions with competitive agencies within a stated period of time but in practice such requirements are often overlooked.

In setting up a new agency, as Maurice Saatchi decided to do, an entrepreneur has three strategic options (see chapter 3). He can wait for the share value of the original firm to fall so low that he can simply buy it back and change its name. He can seek to buy an established agency with global connections and change its name or he can start from scratch, building on the loyal team which followed him out.

Such a new company would be initially small and would probably consider networking worldwide with local agencies (building a sort of international value chain) and sub-contracting out specialist functions like media-buying.

2 Kenning Tyre Services

What must count as one of the shortest relationships on record was the ill-fated signing by Kenning Tyre Services in 1988 of agency Klein Grey. After a four-way pitch, Klein (the business-to-business arm of Klein Grey) won the £2m account only to lose it a fortnight later. Apparently irreconcilable differences emerged almost immediately after the signing (and this in spite of Klein Grey's obviously winning pitch). Kenning Tyre Services notified Klein of its decision, effectively sacking the agency, and almost straight away went back to considering other agencies, some of whom had been amongst those involved in the original contest.

4.10 Summary

- A very wide range of promotional activities can be carried out either in-house or out-of-house and there is an equally wide range of agencies to do them.
- A company has to decide between in-house or out-house activities and there are several criteria which can help such a judgement.
- If the decision is made to go out-house, the question becomes whether to seek one full-service agency or to split the work between two or more agencies.
- Selecting an agency should be done with care and involves short-listing, credentials and proposals pitches.
- Client–agency relationships are very important. The agency should, ideally, be treated as an extension of the client and not as an outsider.
- If the relationship becomes strained, the client can 'sack' the agency or the agency can 'resign' the account; but, in any case, the two might part company quite amicably when the contract has run its course.
- One of the most common causes of poor client–agency relationships is the financial arrangements. It should be established as clearly as possible what the terms of business are and agencies should account for any money spent. There should, in any case, be a clearly drawn up contract.
- The circumstances in which an agency might be used vary from relatively simple exercises, such as renting a mailing list, to very complex international advertising campaigns and this should be borne in mind in giving weight to any of the comments made in this chapter.

4.11 Assignments

1. With reference to a specific problem, such as opening up a new market or launching a new product, discuss the arguments for and against using an external agency.

2. Choose an established product, preferably one for which you can get recent data, and take note of current and recent campaigns for it.

From the point of view of the client, explain how you would go about selecting either an advertising agency or a public relations agency for this product.

3. Discuss the importance of good client–agency relationships and the steps which can be taken by either client or agency to maintain good relationships.

4. What would be the advantages and disadvantages of using a full-service agency?

5 The regulatory structure

5.1
Introduction

In chapter 4 we saw that the decision to use one or more agencies or to do the work in-house was itself part of the policy and strategy of a company. The regulatory system is also part of the framework of policy and strategy and here we look at some aspects of regulation as they apply to advertising and promotion.

No chapter of this length can make the reader an expert in the law or any other regulations. What it can do is to signal the sorts of problems that might be encountered in setting up a promotional campaign and to point the reader in the right direction. In practice, some of the issues are fairly straight forward and unambiguous – for example, no tobacco products may be advertised on UK television. In other cases there is room for differences of opinion and a judgement may be required. When is an advertisement 'offensive' or 'frightening', for example? Where such judgements have to be made, advertisers are advised to clear the copy with the relevant body first before production and other costs have been incurred. The suspicion is that some advertisers deliberately cross the line for the sake of the publicity that the subsequent complaints can generate and, to quote Sir Timothy Raison, Chairman of the Advertising Standards Authority, in his 1993 report: 'Overall, our main concern now is that there are still some media who have been willing to publish advertisements that ought not to be published.' 1994 saw a considerable improvement.

It is not just above-the-line advertising that is subject to laws and regulations. Any promotional activity from word of mouth to press releases, from free samples to direct mail and from sponsorship to sales promotion is subject to control of one sort or another: not only, incidentally, controls specifically set up to regulate promotional activities as such, but also controls which were set up with a wider purpose in mind. If a company is planning some aerial advertising, it would be well advised to consult the laws relating to aviation if it does not wish to be prosecuted for flying in a commercial plane's flight path (the same laws apply to kites and model planes) and poster contractors must get permission from local authority planning departments before erecting new sites. Local authorities and police forces frequently need to be consulted before signage is erected outside an exhibition hall or sports ground and stories abound of such signage being unceremoniously pulled down because the right permissions had not, first of all, been obtained.

Regulations and controls can be a minefield for the unwary and just when a company thinks that it understands what is required it finds that things are different in another country. Slimming aids and face creams which can be sold **over the counter (OTC)** in the UK will come under the Food and Drugs Administration (FDA) in the USA and may be reclassified as medical products to be sold on prescription only. There is currently a storm brewing in the USA as the FDA moves towards attempting to reclassify tobacco as a drug. The UK, as a member of the European Union (EU), is part of the Single European Market, but we are a long way from having single European laws and controls change from country to country within Europe. There are proposed European directives on such things as advertising to children and advertising tobacco products but no European laws as such – for the time being at least, Brussels appears to recognise the self-regulation of member states. However, as between Europe as a whole and the USA there are some polarisations which merit attention. For example, the USA is more open about the compilation of direct mailing lists and companies are rarely restricted as to the sources or methods used to put a list together. In contrast to the freedom of access to information which characterises the USA, European thinking on list-building tends more towards confidentiality and the rights of privacy.

5.2 Government legislation

The ITC (Independent Television Commission) Code of Advertising Practice contains a list of no less than 57 statutes which affect broadcast advertising and the ASA (Advertising Standards Authority) *Background Briefing* (June 1993) states that there are 'at least 80 statutes' affecting advertising as a whole in the UK. Local government regulations are not included in this list. Nevertheless, within the local government area in which such regulations may be made they have the same force of law.

Laws relating to children and education, to racial and sexual equality, to gambling and lotteries and to finance and insurance are all included. Some of the statutes (the Trade Descriptions Act 1968; the Fair Trading Act 1973) affect all industries and others (the Medicines Act 1968; the Food Safety Act 1990) are industry specific. Some relate to non-business advertising (the Charities Act 1992).

Three important statutes protect the rights of businesses in the design and identity of their own products and services: the Trade Marks Act 1938 (updated in 1994), the Registered Designs Act 1949 and the Copyright Designs and Patents Act 1988. Issues involving trade marks, designs and patents were at the forefront of much of the debate and antagonism in 1994 between the supermarkets with their supposed 'look-alike' own brands and the manufacturers of branded goods.

Case Study

The British Retail Consortium versus the British Producers and Brand Owners Group

The passage of the Trade Marks Bill (1994) illustrates the extent to which one piece of legislation may be viewed differently by two groups. Originally no more than an updating of the old 1938 Act and an opportunity to incorporate some elements of EC law, the bill became a focal point for the newly formed British Producers and Brand Owners Group who hoped that it would give them more protection against the rising tide of 'copycat' supermarket own-brands. The British Retail Consortium in the opposite corner enlisted the aid of consumer groups to lobby Parliament against what it saw as an anti-consumer, anti-competition argument.

Department of Trade and Industry spokesman Patrick McLaughlin said the brand owners had left their action too late to affect the wording of the bill and that, in any case, it would not be the right place to tackle the problem of copycat products which was not, in itself, a trade mark issue. The bill does, however, offer a little consolation in that it contains provision for brand owners, like Toblerone, to register the distinctive shapes of their packaging.

As Tom O'Sullivan says, writing in *Marketing Week* (20 May 1994), 'Currently the only option open to the owners is to use common law and prosecute a rival for "passing off" a product. But it is a notoriously difficult method and the next move for the owners will be to lobby for changes in competition law.'

Coca-Cola's success in forcing Sainsbury's to back down over its Classic Cola product may work against the owners in reinforcing the widely held view that the brand owners and retailers do already have a forum for sorting things out.

The dispute shows, if nothing else, that legislation need not be perceived by businesses as something handed down to them but as something which, if they act decisively, they can seek to modify to reflect their own interests.

One of the most important statutes is the Control of Misleading Advertisements Regulations 1988 which incorporates into British law some of the requirements of the EC Directive on Misleading Advertising. It provides an additional sanction which the Advertising Standards Authority (ASA) can invoke through the Office of Fair Trading (OFT) and the Independent Television Commission (ITC) and the Radio Authority can apply directly using their powers under the Broadcasting Act.

5.3 Regulatory bodies

To assist (and control) advertisers in developing legally and morally acceptable campaigns, regulatory bodies have been set up to develop and administer codes of practice within the law. The three main bodies are the Advertising Standards Authority (ASA), the Independent Television Commission (ITC) and the Radio Authority, all of which produce codes covering between them advertising, sales promotion and programme sponsorship. Not surprisingly, there are vast similarities in the scope and content of their codes and all of them contain the familiar injunction that advertisements (and sales promotions) should be 'legal, decent, honest and truthful'. For prepublication clearance of advertising copy and advice generally to advertisers, agencies and publishers, there are also the Committee of Advertising Practice (CAP) for non-broadcast advertisements and the Broadcast Advertising Clearance Centre (BACC).

The Committee of Advertising Practice (CAP)

The Committee of Advertising Practice was set up in the early 1960s as a self-regulatory body. Organisations from both advertising and the media are members, including the Newspaper Society, the Periodical Publishers Association, the Institute of Practitioners in Advertising, the Advertising Association and the Broadcast Advertising Clearance Centre. Direct mail, outdoor advertising and cinema advertising associations are also members. Its work has included the drafting and revision of two codes of practice:

- The British Code of Advertising Practice (BCAP)
- The British Code of Sales Promotion Practice (BCSPP)

which in January 1995 were republished jointly as a single document:

- The British Codes of Advertising and Sales Promotion.

With respect to advertising, two of CAP's recent activities have been investigations into health-related products and the growth of **advertorials** – advertisements designed to imitate the editorial style of the magazine or newspaper in which they appear and which might violate the requirement that all advertisements should be clearly recognised as such. With respect to sales promotion, it set up in 1992 a working group to both increase awareness of the BCSPP and improve its efficacy.

CAP codes cover all print advertisements, posters, leaflets, direct mail, teletext, video cassette commercials, cinema advertising – collectively referred to as **press and print** and comprising all non-broadcast advertisements – and non-broadcast interactive media such as computer games. CAP is generally concerned with promoting and implementing a voluntary pattern of good behaviour among both advertisers and the non-broadcast media. To this end, it offers a free prepublication rapid-response copy advice service which is compulsory for cigarette advertisements but extensively used by agencies, advertisers and publishers across all advertisements. As a self-regulatory voluntary body, CAP has no powers of enforcement either in its own name or through its supervisory arm, the Advertising Standards Authority. Nevertheless its use of peer group pressure to implement sanctions is very effective and it is through membership of CAP that publishers can deny advertising space to uncooperative advertisers. The ASA has been recognised by the courts as exercising an 'important public law function'.

The Advertising Standards Authority (ASA)

The ASA was set up to be independent of both government and the advertising business with the remit to implement the CAP codes in the public interest. The chairman and most of its Council members have to be free of any advertising interest. Having no legal powers, it relies on persuasion reinforced by adverse publicity in the ASA Monthly Report. Additionally, media owners can be asked to refuse to provide more space to persistent offenders and both media and advertisers alike stand to forfeit any benefits they may get as members of trade associations and professional bodies if they do not comply. The combined weight of all these pressures, together with a desire on the part of most advertisers, agencies and media owners to do the right thing, operates to keep the majority of non-broadcast advertisements and sales promotions within the codes.

The ASA is the regulatory arm of CAP and deals directly with the public in handling complaints. It is funded by a levy on all display advertising which, to preserve its impartiality, is independently collected by a separate body, the Advertising Standards Board of Finance.

Advertorials: the ethical problem

A growing practice, particularly it seems with food and house-keeping magazines, is the advertorial. It is really an advertisement but it is deliberately designed to look like an editorial feature. The ethical problem centres around how the reader perceives it. If it is seen as being an advertisement then, its critics would say, no harm is done. But if it is seen as being a real editorial then readers may be misled into believing that it is a genuine independent third-party endorsement of the product. The problem has been sufficiently recognised for a set of guidelines to be produced jointly by the Periodical Publishing Association and the British Society of Magazine Editors to advise editors as to how advertorials should be presented. The guidelines say: 'The words "advertisement", "advertising", "advertisement feature" or "advertisement promotion" should be used.... The term "promotion" should NOT be used in isolation but may be used in conjunction with the name of the magazine or advertisement concerned.'

Some magazines have, nevertheless, simply used the one word *PROMOTION* or have printed words like *advertisement* or *advertising feature* in such a small or delicate typeface as to make them almost unnoticeable. Printing white letters against a multi-coloured background enhances this effect.

Advertorials can be an important source of income for a publication and some publications have a specialist sales team within the advertisement department to promote them. The Advertising Standards Authority has no special rules for dealing with advertorials. As far as the ASA is concerned they are just advertisements and must, like any other advertisement, be legal, decent, truthful and honest. However, it is not their honesty, *per se*, that worries the critics. What the advertorial contains may be honest enough. It is the way the advertorial is presented which is the concern. The ASA Annual Report 1993 said that over a three-month monitoring period it found the results encouraging in that 'only 6 per cent were difficult to identify'.

Nevertheless, advertorials (which grew in number by 50 per cent in 1993) seem to be here to stay. Whether self-regulation will meet the critics' objections or whether a change in the law will come about remains to be seen.

The Broadcast Advertisement Clearance Centre (BACC)

The BACC exists to give advice to advertisers and agencies on the suitability of a proposed broadcast commercial and, in the case of radio, to give clearance certificates to all advertisements intended for a national campaign or which, in any case, fall within prescribed categories such as finance, health, charities and religion. Otherwise, radio commercials intended for a local campaign (one station only) may be cleared by recognised station staff and regional advertisements by nominated senior sales people within the region. Television advertisers may additionally seek guidance from the particular stations they intend to use or from the ITC itself. The ITC, however, will not make prebroadcast rulings on the acceptability of a commercial. Proposals are rarely put forward other than at the script stage and there may be impressions and effects in the finished article which could not be anticipated from the script alone. For example, ITC rule 22 says '. . . no advertisement may contain anything that might reasonably be thought to encourage or condone cruelty or irresponsible behaviour to animals' and it might not be obvious from the script alone that this rule might be breached.

The Independent Television Commission (ITC)

The ITC came into existence on the first of January 1991 when it replaced the old Independent Broadcasting Authority (IBA) and the Cable Authority. It derives its powers from the Broadcasting Act 1990. Its powers extend not only to the control of television advertising and programme sponsorship but also to the actual licensing of the television companies which transmit the programmes (and produce some of them).

The ITC has two codes. They are:

- The ITC Code of Advertising Standards and Practice
- The ITC Code of Programme Sponsorship.

Unlike the CAP/ASA code, the ITC codes are not set up on a voluntary self-regulation basis but under a statutory duty derived from the Broadcasting Act 1990. The ITC actually has the power to require advertising which violates the code to be withdrawn and also has the power to exclude whole classes of advertisements, such as 'clinics for the treatment of hair loss' and 'breath-testing devices and products which purport to mask the effects of alcohol'. The ITC may even go so far as to fine a licensee and even to revoke or shorten its licence for persistent failure to comply with the Broadcasting Act 1990 and the ITC codes.

The Radio Authority

The Radio Authority came into existence at the same time as the ITC and also derives its powers from the Broadcasting Act 1990. It also regulates the whole independent radio service and not just the advertising and programme sponsorship aspects of it. In a broad sense the Radio Authority does for independent radio what the ITC does for independent television.

It publishes one code:

- The Radio Authority Code of Advertising Standards and Practice and Programme Sponsorship.

5.4 Broadcast advertising

The advertising code requirements do not differ greatly between the ITC and the Radio Authority. Clear breaks must be made between programmes and advertisements so that it is always clear which is which; testimonials must be genuine; unreasonable appeals to fear may not be used; rival products may be mentioned for the purpose of a valid comparison but not for the purpose of denigrating those products; price claims must conform to the requirements of the Consumer Protection Act 1987 and so on. Both codes have detailed appendices relating to advertising and children, financial advertising, health and medicines, charity advertising and religious advertising. An interesting feature is the responsibility laid on the broadcast media to exercise judgement on the distribution of advertisements within or adjacent to particular programmes. The ITC acted to censure Meridian Television for transmitting an advertisement featuring Helen Lederer during a break in a programme in which she also appeared (contrary to ITC rule 6c) and in one of its helpful 'practice notes' the Radio Authority suggests that a planned airline commercial should be withdrawn if it followed a news bulletin featuring a plane crash.

Radio being a voice-only medium lends itself to 'presenter-read' advertisements. A radio presenter may voice an advertisement providing that he or she does not (even by tone of voice) suggest an actual endorsement of the product.

5.5 Product placement

Product placement where the licensee receives money from the manufacturer to include a reference to the product within the programme is not allowed, although a legitimate, in context, reference to a product, brand or manufacturer may be permitted (in a documentary, for example). In a television drama a packet of, say, Kellogg's Corn Flakes may be seen on a breakfast table as part of the scenery without any explicit reference to it and this would be acceptable (providing that no money had changed hands). On radio a character might say 'Pass me the corn flakes', but not 'Pass me the Kellogg's Corn Flakes.' That would constitute **indirect advertising** and is not permitted.

The ITC's *Television Advertising Complaints Report* (March 1994) is fascinating in this respect:

> Anyone who believes that rules such as this are unnecessary should take a trip to Spain. The second largest commercial channel there readily admits that many of its programmes are specifically devised to serve as vehicles for product placement. There is a rate card for background placements and if you pay triple you can have your product manipulated and mentioned by a character in a soap.

5.6 Programme sponsorship

The sponsorship of printed media products, such as single sections of multi-section newspapers, is relatively new and, as yet, no sponsorship code exists. Both the television and the radio codes cover sponsored programmes largely along the lines of the requirements in the EC Directive on Television Broadcasting.

Sponsorship is defined as the broadcasting of a programme in return for a payment in cash or in kind (to the licensee). Such payment could actually be the programme itself. The codes are concerned with the sponsorship of programmes as such, rather than with the programme (editorial) coverage of sponsored events. The latter are, nevertheless, referred to in the television code where a sponsored event may be featured during a programme with a different (programme) sponsor. This must not be done in such a way as to imply that the programme sponsor is also the event sponsor.

Any programme, with the exception of news programmes, can be sponsored. Sponsors may choose programmes or features which have a recognisable connection with their products but they may not sponsor programmes which, without their sponsorship, might have had editorial content at issue with their own interests. Peugeot sponsor the Weather Update and Fiat the Traffic and Travel announcements on commercial radio – neither of them should sponsor a consumer advice programme dealing with car safety. Where the ban on product placement is concerned with keeping out what ought not to be in this insistence on not compromising editorial freedom is designed to keep in what might otherwise be forced out.

Licensees should always retain ultimate editorial control of (and responsibility for) the editorial content and this control should not be seen to be compromised by sponsorship involvement. In fact, nothing that can be perceived as 'promotional' of the sponsor's interests may appear (aurally or visually) in the programme. Manufacturers of products (such as cigarettes) that cannot themselves be advertised cannot sponsor programmes at all.

Sponsors may buy advertising time before or after the programme and in the commercial breaks. Sponsor credits, themselves, should be 'brief, precise and capable of substantiation' (Radio Authority Code: Section C rule 6) and may appear at the beginning and end of the programme or as 'buffers' leading into and/or out of a commercial break. Sponsor credits, which are strictly limited in length and style, should be non-promotional and be clearly distinguishable from both advertisements and programme content.

5.7 How the codes work

The ASA is a self-regulatory body with no legal powers which, if all else fails, can refer offenders to the appropriate statutory body or, as a last resort, to the Office of Fair Trading for action under the Misleading Advertisements Regulations 1988. The ITC and Radio Authority both have legal powers derived from the Broadcasting Act 1990 which include the power to apply the Misleading Advertisements Regulations directly.

The ITC and Radio Authority enforce compliance through a variety of sanctions, whilst the ASA depends much more on persuasion and peer-group pressure. They all act in consultation with advertisers, agencies and the media as well as representatives of consumer and other interests in framing and revising their codes and all offer advice through either CAP or the BACC. All of them have requirements which go further than the law, and industry members are expected to observe the spirit of the codes and not to use legal and semantic arguments in an attempt to justify actions which the codes clearly do not intend. Industry-based organisations such as the Periodical Publishing Association and the British Society of Magazine Editors play their part in drawing up guidelines and publishing codes of conduct for their members.

To assist them in implementing the codes, all the bodies depend to a large extent on the vigilance of the reading, listening and viewing audiences in spotting breaches that might otherwise go unremedied. The ASA, for example, runs a press and poster campaign which tells people of their right to complain using the current strapline 'keeping tabs on ads' and it publishes a monthly review of the complaints it has handled. However, the ASA need not wait for a complaint to arise as it constantly monitors the advertising scene and can take immediate action when it sees something which violates the code.

It is not necessary to be a consumer of the product in order to complain about an advertisement. Many complaints do arise, of course, from people who have responded to the advertisements and feel that they have been misled, but others arise from members of the public who simply feel that the advertisement (or the timing of it) is inaccurate, in poor taste or otherwise offensive. A company could complain if, for example, a rival's commercial showed it or its products in a denigrating way. Religious or political parties may complain if they think that an advertisement in some way misrepresents them. An individual may complain that his or her identity has been used in a commercial without permission in some circumstances. These 'reluctant celebrities' usually only have a case if they can show that they have been represented in such a way as to hold them up to ridicule or otherwise harm them. The ITC is somewhat stricter than the ASA, but the principle is broadly the same.

Reluctant celebrities

A practice about which there is very mixed opinion is that of using celebrities without their consent. It is not actually illegal to do so, and the Advertising Standards Authority code 'allows for the robust treatment of public figures', according to spokeswoman Caroline Crawford (quoted in the *Guardian* 25 October 1993). Celebrities may be used without their consent providing that it is not inconsistent with their public images and does not damage their ability to make a living. England football manager (now ex-manager) Graham Taylor objected to the unauthorised use of his name in a TWA advertisement which said 'Dear Graham, here's how to get England to the next World Cup' because, he said, it implied that he endorsed TWA. Creatives are divided in their opinions, but a frequently expressed view is that such tactics are often a substitute for a good idea. Because such advertisements tend to make use of archive photographs they may be more frequently found in press and poster campaigns, but still pictures, archival film or video footage can be incorporated into a television commercial.

A reluctant celebrity who never actually appeared in an advertisement but nevertheless successfully complained to the ITC is Norman Lamont MP. He complained that a Visa Delta card advertisement featuring another ex-Chancellor of the Exchequer, Denis (now Lord) Healey, made an implied reference to a press story about him which was subsequently shown to be untrue. The complaint was upheld. It should be noted that Mr Lamont was the only person to complain but that does not matter – the authorities do not insist on any minimum number of complaints before they will investigate.

5.8 Legislation versus voluntary codes of conduct

There are those who argue in favour of regulation through legislation as being the best way to prevent abuses within any system and, as we have seen, there is no shortage of statutory measures affecting the communications and promotions industry. The pro-legislation argument stresses:

- **Clarity** The law is clearly spelled out.
- **Certainty** Offenders will be dealt with.
- **Equity** The large and the small, the weak and the strong are equally governed.

The arguments against legislation are that:

- However carefully the law is worded, there will always be people who look for a loophole (and often find it).
- The legislative process is slow (the Trade Mark Bill has been three years in the making).
- The judicial process is often slower.

The case for self-regulation includes:

- **Accessibility** Complainants need only write a letter.
- **Speed** A misleading advertisement, for example, can be withdrawn within days, even hours.
- **Flexibility** A code can be updated to meet new circumstances far quicker than the law can be revised.
- **Economy** No vast legal fees are involved.

Furthermore, it is said, codes encourage a moral rather than a legal attitude. Parties are usually expected to follow them in spirit and not to wrangle over legal technicalities. Where complaints have to be investigated, codes often reverse the normal process of law where the burden of proof is on the prosecution and place the burden of proof on the defendant. All advertisers have to be prepared to justify and defend their decisions under the code.

There are those, however, including some (but not all) environmental groups, animal rights groups, consumer groups, parent–teacher associations and so on, who think that some voluntary codes of conduct lack

Case study: not on my patch

ASA has become all too familiar with the sharp end of mail order advertising over the years. No case in 1993 more typified the reasons why than that of unauthorised transdermal nicotine and slimming patches.

"Giving up is easy – I've done it lots of times", runs the hardened career smoker's favourite gag. At the end of 1992, though, would-be kickers of the habit had cause to believe there was new hope – with the help of the nicotine patch.

Previously only available on prescription, their status had been recently reconsidered by the medical authorities. A number of potent licensed patches had become freely obtainable over the local chemist's counter. Manufactured by major pharmaceutical companies, these patches were licensed in November 1992 after thorough testing for safety and to make sure they dispensed nicotine through the skin into the bloodstream as they claimed. All advertisements for the patches were sent for checking by the ASA before they were published.

But in early 1993, the opportunists struck. The Authority began receiving enquiries from national newspapers about off-the-page advertisements for new patches which were untested and unlicensed. Similar in appearance to a sticky plaster, they were easy to produce and quick to sell. Advertisements placed by a number of mail order companies made unacceptable claims that their product was all that was needed to give up ("or your money back"). Untested, these 'alternative' patches never were shown to work.

Our advice to media was unequivocal: the advertisements should not be run until the legality and safety of the patches had been established by the Department of Health. After a short time, the advertisements stopped appearing.

Within weeks, however, the first derivative of the patch fad surfaced: the slimming patch. This product contained seaweed extracts which, when taken by mouth, were licensed as an "aid to weight loss". But there was nothing to show that the patch could deliver these extracts through the skin. Again, we issued strong advice against these advertisements, and media responded quickly and positively.

An evening primrose oil patch made a brief appearance, as did a vitamin C patch. In both these cases, the advertisers were happy to take advice to ensure that untoward claims were avoided.

Fig. 5.1 From Advertising Standards Authority Annual Report 1993

weight, are insubstantial and, as in the case of the tobacco industry, ultimately self-serving. There are even practitioners in a particular field who will argue for legislation rather than self-regulation on the grounds that the law provides a level playing-field whereas codes can be too easily ignored by unscrupulous competitors.

The ASA may be one of the best models of self-regulation. It has the support of law on those rare occasions where problems cannot be resolved within the code and, in 1979, an OFT investigation concluded that no benefits could arise from making the ASA a statutory body. To quote Sir Timothy Raison again: 'In many ways the Control of Misleading Advertisements Regulations provide a valuable model for self-regulation as the basic mechanism but with the law as an ultimate back-up.'

5.9 Summary

- There is a vast body of statute law as well as industry codes which affect advertisements and sales promotions. Product placements and programme sponsorship, as well as event sponsorship itself can all be affected.
- The responsibility for not offending either against statute law or the appropriate codes lies first of all with the advertiser who may, nevertheless, depend on the agency for advice and secondly with the media which should exercise good judgement as to the advertisements accepted and the timing or positioning of them.
- Advice can be obtained from CAP and the BACC among others, but unless some form of clearance certificate is issued the receiving of such advice is not, in itself, a guarantee of immunity against future complaints and consequent action.
- The cost of changing an advertisement after it has been produced can be considerable and generally the best advice is to check before starting production. Mistakes may still occur, even then, but the risk of going ahead without any clearance checks at all are too great to be justified.

5.10 Assignments

1. Argue the case for and against voluntary self-regulation as opposed to control through legislation.

2. Carry out a survey of recent press and broadcast advertisements that might be thought offensive, frightening or in bad taste. Discuss whether or not you think it worth making a complaint and, if you do, draft a letter to either the ASA, ITC or Radio Authority setting out your reasons. Remember to do this as a member of the public and not as a student of advertising.

3. Do you think that the law should expressly forbid either the mentioning of rival products without their manufacturers' consent or the use of people in advertisements without their consent? How far do you think an advertiser should be allowed to go in either case?

6 Models of communication

Communications are a part of the framework of policy and strategy. Some companies undertake a communications audit as part of their strategic analysis to see where their strengths and weaknesses lie in this area. A foreign language audit is a specialised form of communications audit which can be carried out by, say, a British firm thinking of entering the European market for the first time.

This book is about communication in a wide variety of forms and about the circumstances which influence the effectiveness of communication. We have already seen that communication about an organisation can originate from within the organisation or from some external source. Communications can be authorised by the organisation (this includes some externally originated messages) or unauthorised (even some internally originated messages can be unauthorised). Models of communication generally assume internally originated and authorised messages and that is what is assumed in this chapter. Unauthorised and externally originated messages will be built in to show the sort of effect that they can have.

In this chapter the word **communication** is virtually interchangeable with the word **publicity** but not entirely. All forms of publicity can be called communications, but not all forms of communication can be called publicity – instructions, requests for information, answers to such requests and formal reports are all communications which we would not want to call publicity. Models of communication, therefore, have a wider application than that which is under consideration here.

Every communication must have a purpose in mind. Advertising objectives are often classified under the two headings of to inform and to persuade. These two headings cover all sorts of communication and it is difficult to think of any promotional activity that does not contain elements of each.

Inform

Target publics need to be informed of all manner of things: product specification, product availability, prices, after-sales service and many other items as well. When something new is being introduced to the market – a new product, a new service, a new branch of a retail chain – then the need to inform is very high. It is not only consumers who need to be informed and techniques such as public relations, direct mail and conferences can be used to inform employees, shareholders, local communities and government departments as well.

Persuade

Persuading is harder than informing. It may require the receiver of the message not only to understand what is being said but also to act on it in some way. Persuading may be at the level of simply changing somebody's perception of something (as in convincing worried employees that there are no redundancy plans in preparation) but usually we want people to do more than just change their minds. We want them to do something: buy a new product, carry on buying an old product, recommend the product to a friend and so on.

The relationship between informing and persuading is frequently summed up in what is sometimes called a **hierarchical** model. It is called hierarchical because it is believed that people begin at a lower-order level and move through progressively higher levels until they reach the highest-order level. In simple terms these would be:

- **Cognitive** The lower-order level of simply knowing something.

- **Affective** A higher-order level of letting what one knows influence what one actually thinks and believes.

- **Behaviour** The highest-order level of translating what one thinks and believes into action.

In practice, it may not actually work out in such a neat hierarchical way. Some people do not progress beyond the cognitive stage. Others jump straight from the cognitive stage to the behaviour stage (the impulse factor). People at the behaviour stage may loop back to the affective stage to allow the experience of trying the product to modify what is understood and believed. They may even loop back to the cognitive stage because now they have tried the product they have new information or knowledge about it which they did not have before. Nevertheless, the hierarchical model for all its imperfections produces a **message model** of communications objectives based on the ideas of:

- Messages which merely inform.
- Messages which aim to change opinions and attitudes.
- Messages which encourage action.

Share of mind, front of mind and share of market

These different types of messages are sometimes associated with the concepts of **share of mind** and **front of mind**. We do seem to be limited as to what we can take in. Some things get into our minds and others don't. Whatever gets in has a 'share' of our minds and the more we think about things the greater the share they have. We are said to push things to the back of our minds when we do not wish to think about them, but this is the opposite of what the advertiser wants. The advertiser wants things at the front of our minds so 'share of mind' is often associated with the allied concept of 'front of mind'. The first two 'message models' listed above – messages that inform and messages that change opinions – are designed to get this share of mind/front of mind awareness. Because the third model is to do with action (actually buying something, for example),

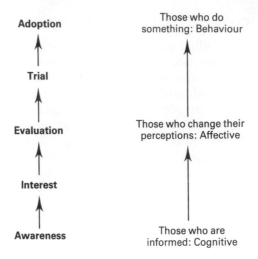

Fig. 6.1   The Rogers adoption model

it is common to associate it with **share of market** – the more products are sold as a result of such messages the greater the share of market will be.

6.3 Some related models

We can use the word hierarchy in a different sense to suggest something that is wider at the base than it is at the top, like an organisational hierarchy. Such a view recognises that it is easier simply to inform people, a bit harder to get them to change their minds and harder still to get them to do something, so at each level there will be fewer and fewer people. This is illustrated in fig. 6.1.

Rogers adoption model

The well-known Rogers **adoption model** (1962) explains the process by which a potential user adopts a product and thus becomes an actual user. (The difference between trial and adoption lies in the fact that trial may be just a one-off usage of the product, whereas adoption implies repeat regular usage.)

The AIDA model

The **AIDA** model is a simpler **hierarchical** model and stands for **Attention – Interest – Desire – Action**. Again, the number of people whose attention is obtained will be greater than those who eventually take action.

6.4 A simple model of communi- cation

At its simplest, a communications model has four elements: **sender, message, medium** and **audience**. Figure 6.2 may suggest that the message is always decided upon before the media is chosen. This is not so – the decision to use a television campaign may, in some circumstances, precede the formulation of the message, whereas in other cases the formulation of the message may precede, and even dictate, the choice of media. The choice of media may, in any case, be determined by other factors, such

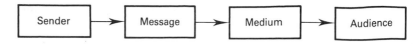

Fig. 6.2 Simple communications model

as the urgency of the message (as opposed to its content) which may indicate that the telephone should be used in preference to a letter. What is clear is that the message and the medium come between the sender and the audience regardless of which is selected before the other. Figure 6.3 may indicate this more effectively.

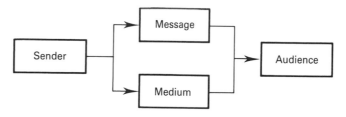

Fig. 6.3 Communications model

The sender

By sender we mean the originator of the message. Where, for example, an advertising agency is used, it is the client and not the agency that we should identify as the sender (or originator) of the message. The average consumer is not the least bit interested in the identity of the agency but does want to know who the message is coming from, as this information can influence the way in which the message is understood. An advertisement praising a product will be perceived differently from an editorial piece praising the product because the source (another word for origin) is different.

Any sender, whether an individual or an organisation, needs to develop a certain sense of self-awareness as the sender of a message. For example, an organisation can use the following tests:

- What are our objectives in sending this message? Where do we hope to be as a result?
- What aspects of our current situation are relevant? What do we say about ourselves which will improve our chances of success?

The message

The concept of the message recurs frequently throughout the remaining chapters of this book. The general principle, however, should be:

- Is this message likely to be effective in achieving our objectives?

This principle relates back to the sender's objective but also forward to the audience:

- Will this message be understood by our audience in the way that we wish it to be understood? Is it likely to get our audience to respond as we wish them to respond?

In this latter context, we often need to take account of the fact that the audience may not have as big a vocabulary as the sender, or may have a different vocabulary or may just use the same words to convey different meanings. Use language as the audience would use it and not as you yourself might use it – research the audience's vocabulary and use of language.

The medium

There is no doubt that the choice of medium can seriously affect the effectiveness of the message. People may be more or less responsive to a printed message than to a broadcast message and this can be the subject of a great deal of research. The voice as a medium (the spoken word) can have a powerful effect. People's attitudes to the media vary from, in the words of the old song,

> It must be true, it must be true
> I read it in the papers so it must be true

to 'You can't believe anything you read in the papers.'

The Canadian writer Marshall McLuhan popularised the notion that 'the Medium is the Message', suggesting that people are more influenced by the former than by the latter. However, whilst recognising the power of the medium itself to shape the audience's perception of the message, it is generally simpler to stick to the ideas that 'the message is the message' and 'the medium is the medium'.

The choice of a medium must be influenced by asking the following question:

- Is this newspaper (or this TV programme) the type most likely to be read (or watched) by the audience we want to reach?

One of the most powerful media, by the way, is good old-fashioned word of mouth.

Case Study

Word of mouth (WOM)

Estée Lauder, head of one of the world's biggest cosmetics companies, is fond of saying, 'There are three ways of spreading a message – telephone, television and tell a woman.' She isn't being sexist: what she is saying is that one of the biggest assets a company can have is the goodwill of its customers – people who will then pass the message along by talking about their good experiences with the product. In a television programme, The Beauty Queen, she told how, at the beginning of her career, taking time and patience with a woman who did not speak English led to Estée Lauder products being popularised in Mexico. The woman responded to the attention she was getting by buying up large quantities to take back to Mexico for her friends.

Companies try to build *word of mouth* (*WOM*) publicity in various ways. Special promotions that give gifts to existing customers for bringing in new ones have been used by insurance companies, credit-card companies, mail-order companies and many others.

Of course, WOM can work against the company if people complain about it to others. A much used slogan is:

'If you like what we are doing – tell others.
If you don't – tell us.'

It is far better to get dissatisfied customers to talk to you than to have them talk to somebody else. Dealing competently with consumer complaints itself generates good WOM – dealing with complaints in an off-hand way only makes things worse.

WOM really begins with the organisation's members. How they talk to people (not just consumers but suppliers and dealers as well) is important. Sullen sales staff or waiters create a bad impression, whereas a cheerful, polite waiter can put the finishing touches to what is otherwise a fairly ordinary meal.

The audience

In promotional terms, we can just as easily use the words *public* or *market*. It has been said that it is impossible to know too much about your audience. However much you know now you can always learn more. The amount of money spent on audience research and market research certainly underlines the thirst for such knowledge. Particularly as audiences themselves change. Just as you think that you understand what they like and what interests them they pick up on a different interest and you have to start all over again.

From a marketing point of view, we should always remember that the products and services we offer are *solutions to the consumer's problems*. In a very real sense audiences want to be told about themselves and their problems not about you as the sender and your problems. So you do really have to understand the problems, hopes and aspirations of your audience.

Audiences do not want to be either patronised or confused and the easiest way to avoid these problems is to put yourself in the position of the people receiving the message. Really try to identify with them, don't talk down to them and don't use words and concepts that they are not likely to understand. Try to think like a consumer rather than like a producer.

'We had trouble getting our deliveries out on time until we introduced our new computer system' is a producer-orientated message (the consumer does not want to hear about your problems). 'You like to get your milk early in the morning and and our new computer system is designed to make sure that you get it' is a consumer-orientated message (it deals with the consumer's problems). The key question must be: 'Do we fully understand our audience?' To which the answer might be: 'Probably not, but we never stop trying.'

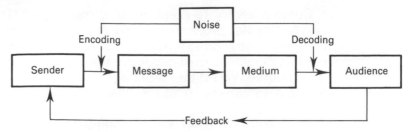

Fig. 6.4   A more realistic communications model

6.5 A more complex model of communication

To make the communications model a little more realistic, we need to introduce four additional concepts: **encoding**, **decoding**, **noise** and **feedback**. Figure 6.4 illustrates their place in the model.

Encoding

The message begins its life as an idea in somebody's head, but in order to achieve its purpose it has to finish up in somebody else's head. To achieve this transference, the message first needs to be *encoded* – it needs to be rendered in some oral and/or visual form. The idea may be encoded in words (written down or spoken aloud) or in diagrammatic form. For example, the creator of a TV commercial may write down his or her idea in the form of a **scenario** (a written description of what the commercial will look like) or in the form of a **storyboard** (a visual depiction of what the commercial will look like). In trying to convey the idea to the client the scenario or storyboard can be put over verbally – talking the client through the idea scene by scene.

Although we all use encoding whenever we speak or write, doing it for professional purposes, for example, writing a press release, requires special skills and training which we do not all possess. The person who has the original idea may hand it over to such a skilled person to develop it. The art director in an advertising agency may, in fact, be a lousy artist. Nevertheless, he or she has the ability to 'visualise' the idea and to explain to a competent artist what is required. Good professional encoding depends on a good understanding of the decoding process as well.

Decoding

Decoding is performed by the recipient of the message. The coded message (a printed advertisement or a radio commercial) has to be interpreted and understood if it is to be effective. Decoding is also an acquired skill – learning to read is, in fact, learning to decode (so is learning to listen, so why is more emphasis put on learning to speak?). Understanding the decoding process is very important for the advertiser who must always ask the question, 'Will the consumer who sees this advertisement understand it in the way in which I wish it to be understood?' or to put it another way: 'Will the idea presently in my head be the same idea when it reaches the consumer's head?' Guinness cancelled a series of television commercials after research showed that people did not understand them.

The process of both encoding and decoding is made more complex, but more interesting, by the use of such literary devices as similes, metaphors and puns. The **rebus**, a visual pun much used in heraldry, is often used in advertising and engages the attention of the reader as he or she tries to solve the puzzle.

Slogans and jingles are powerful coding devices – a cleverly worded slogan can encapsulate a whole set of product values and tell a story in a few words. The following are famous examples:

- A Mars a day helps you work, rest and play.
- Go to work on an egg.
- Beanz Meanz Heinz.

The Heinz slogan was disparaged by some literary purists for encouraging bad spelling, but they missed the point. The advertiser was having a bit of fun with the consumer and the consumer shared in, and appreciated, the joke.

Today, some people believe that the modern consumer is getting much better at decoding advertisements. If this is true, it enables advertisers to be more sophisticated in their thinking and more adventurous in their campaign planning; but it also puts them on their guard against trying to fool the consumer.

Noise

Noise, in this context, may paradoxically be quite soundless. Interference may be a better word. Anything that prevents the message from getting through to its intended audience intact can be called noise. The obvious examples are distractions such as the telephone ringing half-way through a commercial break on TV or the noise of traffic drowning out a lecturer's voice in a city centre college. Less obvious, but just as damaging, are things like poor design in an advertisement, press release or direct mail letter. This may involve poor use of colour, poor choice of typeface or even poor quality printing. Noise is anything, in fact, that distracts the attention of the reader away from the message itself. The editorial position of a newspaper may, in some situations, constitute noise and media planners are very careful to place their advertisements in a supportive, noise-free environment. Some advertisers withdrew their support from the *Daily Mirror* when its coverage of the Princess of Wales was thought to be creating too much noise.

Other advertisements (not necessarily for rival brands) can also constitute noise as they clamour for the audience's attention. Unauthorised and hostile comments made about the company and its products from any source are a type of noise. All this noise in the organisation's publicity surround has to be taken into consideration and, where possible, neutralised.

Noise does not, however, affect only the decoding process. The process of encoding can also be interfered with in a similar way.

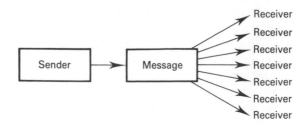

Fig. 6.5   One-step model (no intermediary)

Feedback

Feedback is the message received by the original sender from the audience telling him or her that the message has been received and understood – or not.

There are two kinds of feedback: positive feedback and negative feedback.

- **Positive feedback**   The audience responds in the desired way, thus indicating that they have received, understood and agreed with the message. Feedback does not always come directly from the audience to the sender but may have to be researched. The feedback from a public relations campaign designed to raise name-awareness can only be assessed if the sender takes the trouble to carry out the research. The feedback from a direct-response advertising campaign is more easily measured by simply counting the number of responses.

- **Negative feedback**   The audience either misunderstands a message or, having first understood it, disagrees with it.

In a mass-audience communications model such as advertising, the response is likely to be a mixture of positive and negative feedback. Some people will love an advertisement and others will complain about it to the appropriate body. Some will buy the product and become regular users and other will never try it.

Both positive and negative feedback are essential if a company is to get a realistic assessment of the success of its communications activity. Positive feedback is always welcome, but it is often said that negative feedback, although the least welcome, can be the most useful. It is the indicator that things are not working, provides a rich field of study and is an essential part of the learning process.

6.6 One-step and two-step communications models

One-step and **two-step communications models** are illustrated in figs 6.5 and 6.6. For convenience, the medium has been left out and the word **receiver** is used to indicate one single member of the audience.

In a one-step model, the message goes directly to the intended audience without any intermediary intervention. In principle, advertising is a one-step process, with the advertisement being seen and/or heard directly by the audience. In contrast, press and public relations is a two-step process, the message being first sent by the company to the media and then communicated onwards to the intended final audience. The problem for the originator of the message in a two-step process is what the

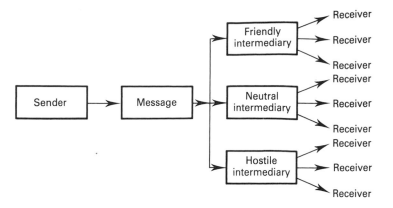

Fig. 6.6 Two-step model (with intermediaries)

intermediary audience (newspapers, radio, television) will do with it. They may enhance it, pass it on unchanged or diminish it. Or they may just ignore it and not pass it on at all. The role of the media as an intermediary audience is discussed in chapter 15.

6.7 Multi-step models and opinion leaders

Although advertising can be seen as a one-step model, it may combine some of the elements of a two-step model with some of the receivers acting as opinion leaders on the remainder. (In fact, the media in the above press and public relations example can also be termed opinion leaders.) Figure 6.7 illustrates this possibility. Opinion leaders may exist in any social group. A neighbour, a member of a young mothers' group, a member of a workplace friendship group can all be opinion leaders. Like the media

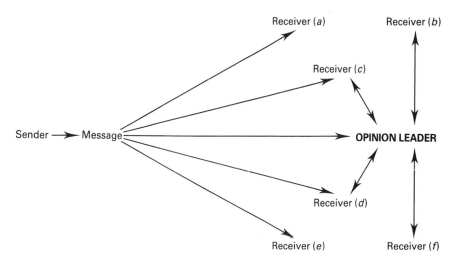

Fig. 6.7 Multi-step model
Receivers (*a*) and (*e*) see the advertisement but have no contact with the opinion leader. Receivers (*b*) and (*f*) do not see the advertisement but do have contact with the opinion leader who may tell them about it. Receivers (*c*) and (*d*) both see the advertisement and have contact with the opinion leader who may influence their perception of it or the product.

opinion leaders may enhance or diminish the original message or just pass it on unchanged. Opinion leaders tend to be the more outspoken and extrovert members of a group; they are more likely to try new products first and their influence as opinion leaders is given more credibility by this experience. Their importance to advertisers is that if it is possible to identify and get access to them, then it may also be possible to exploit their position and to use them in promoting the product.

If it is true that opinion leaders are more likely to try new products first, then introductory special offers at 'give away' prices may pay off if those who try the product pass on their opinions of it to others. Such arrangements can backfire, of course, if those who first try the product do not like it. It has often been remarked that bad news travels faster than good.

6.8 One-way and two-way communications

In figs. 6.7 and 6.8 some arrows are double-headed to indicate the two-way nature of some communication. Mass media advertising tends to be one-way with the message travelling from sender to receiver without any discussion or interaction (feedback may follow later, of course). But recent changes in interactive TV technology providing for immediate responses may change the nature of TV advertising from a one-way to a two-way system, particularly as the opportunity for the viewer to interrogate the TV arises and more so if, as seems very likely, telephone and television technology are combined into a single system. For the present, personal and telephone selling are the most important examples of two-way communications.

6.9 Total communications model

The **total communications model** (fig. 6.8) shows that communication is a multi-step, two-way process. Publicists, whether in advertising or public relations or some other branch of publicity, need to be aware of the complexity of the process.

6.10 Summary

- Communication is about both sending and receiving messages. At its simplest, communication involves a sender, a message, a medium and a receiver (or audience). This communications model becomes more complex when other dimensions are added in.
- Encoding is the process of translating the ideas in the sender's mind into recognisable symbols such as words and pictures.
- Decoding reverses that process so that the symbols become in turn ideas in somebody else's mind.
- Noise may interfere to distort the message.
- Feedback can help us know how successful our communications have been.
- One-step models show the message going directly from the sender to the receiver.
- Two-step models take account of the presence of an intermediary passing the message along. The intermediary may sometimes distort or enhance the message in some way. Opinion leaders play a significant part in this process.

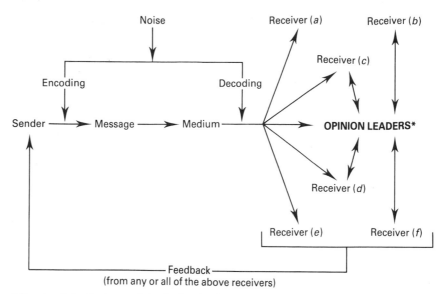

Fig. 6.8 Total communications model

- Some systems (for example, media advertising) are one-way and others (for example, telephone selling) are two-way. The most complex model is both.
- Whatever system is used, there are always communications objectives to be achieved. These can be described as ascending from the simple transmission of knowledge, through changing the way somebody actually thinks, to affecting somebody's behaviour.

6.11 Assignments

1. Get a friend to talk to you for two or three minutes about something important to him or her (like a hobby). Then try to relate back in detail what you understand your friend to be saying. Don't just repeat – show that you understand. Discuss together afterwards to see whether true understanding did take place and if not what could have been done about it. Change places.

2. Discuss the circumstances in which you think that a spoken message would be more effective than a written message and vice versa. Look at some of the wordier print advertisements and see how easy (or hard) it is to make the same points in speech – for example, over the radio.

3. Explain the difference between positive and negative feedback and justify the proposition that 'negative feedback is the least welcome but the most useful of the two'.

7 Buyer Behaviour

7.1 Introduction

This chapter looks at some of the factors that influence the buying and consuming process. Where people shop, what their attitudes to shopping and buying are and the psychological and sociological explanations of such behaviour are of interest because of the effect they have on campaign planning for both manufacturers and retailers. Our main concern here is with the consumer and the buying process in consumer markets (professional buying is dealt with in chapter 21). The person who buys is not necessarily the person who consumes the product. The majority of chocolate Easter eggs are bought by one person for another and a great many married men are quite happy to leave the buying of their shirts to their wives. This difference between buying and consuming can affect where advertisements are placed and how they are worded. James McNeal, an American expert on the consumer behaviour of children, distinguished three types of buyers:

- **Primary buyers** The consumers who actually make the purchase whether or not they are buying for themselves or for another.

- **Secondary buyers** The people for whom the primary buyers may be making a purchase. They strongly influence the purchase decision to the extent that the primary buyer will seek to anticipate what the secondary buyer will like. Secondary buyers may influence the decision directly by a whole range of behaviours from dropping subtle hints to actually saying, 'What I want is . . .'

- **Tertiary buyers** These might be called future buyers. A company specialising in providing holidays for the over-fifties may well take an interest in people in their late forties who are the market of the future. A restaurant that encourages family parties is sowing the seeds for a future market as children carry the 'eating out' habit into adult life.

7.2 Shopping behaviour

In this chapter we are mainly concerned with the primary buyer and one aspect of this is what is sometimes called **shopping behaviour**.

Shopping goods and convenience goods

For **shopping goods** the buyer is usually prepared to 'shop around', going from shop to shop to compare products and prices. When the product is an expensive one, such as a video, the buyer might visit several shops and travel some distance to do so before making a purchase. Buying shopping goods may entail several shopping trips, gathering up a great many promotional leaflets and considerable thought.

Most people regard the weekly visit to the supermarket for **convenience goods** as a chore, even though many supermarkets go out of their way to make the trip as agreeable as possible with their own form of 'retail theatre' (bright lights, colourful displays, background music, etc.). Generally, we see convenience goods as involving convenience shopping, and most shoppers are not prepared to shop around for bread, potatoes, newspapers, petrol, etc.

Against this background of convenience and shopping goods, it is possible to distinguish different attitudes to shopping in general:

- **Social shoppers** These people enjoy the possibility of social contact and patronise the local shop where they might be known by name rather than the supermarket. A visit to the shop is an opportunity for a chat and is often indulged in by the retired and the unemployed for whom 'getting out to the shop' might be a break in an otherwise dreary day. Social shoppers may shop for small amounts every day rather than for large amounts every week because this maximises their opportunity for social contact.

- **Economic shoppers** These people are not just interested in economy in terms of money but in terms of time also. They do not wish to shop around or engage in conversations with retail staff. They just want convenient local one-stop shopping and to get it over with as quickly as possible. Economic shoppers tend to favour self-service supermarkets.

- **Recreational shoppers** This might seem like an odd concept – shopping as a hobby – but it is not so odd. Some people really do like to go 'shopping' without any real intention of buying anything. In the USA spending the day at the 'mall' is an accepted thing to do – an extension of the time-honoured tradition of 'window-shopping'. People just go around the shops to see what's new, what's on offer, to try things out and generally to enjoy the retail theatre.

We can now turn to some of the psychological theories that can help us to understand consumer behaviour. There are many different schools of psychology, some of which totally contradict each other. All of them, however, offer explanations of human behaviour and it is not our job to decide which is right and which is wrong. They can all give us insights into the way in which people conduct themselves. One group concentrates on behavioural outputs such as 'buying' in response to stimulus inputs such as 'price'. Another group is more concerned with the mental processes which intervene between the inputs and the outputs. Some of this second group stress the rational, problem-solving nature of man; others stress the non-rational, subconscious nature. All have been brought into service in creating promotional campaigns.

**7.3
Behaviourist approaches and the black box**

Behaviourist approaches to human psychology are built around the idea that what goes on in the human mind is sealed inside a **black box** and cannot be understood. The most extreme behaviourists claim that there is no such thing as thinking and free will and that what we call thinking is merely a set of predetermined chemical or electrical activities. What

Fig. 7.1 Black box model

goes on in the brain is beyond our observation and comprehension and the only real guide we have to the human condition is what can be observed, namely the connection between the stimulus to which we are exposed and our subsequent behaviour. For this reason, behaviourist theory is sometimes called stimulus-response theory or connectivist theory. Figure 7.1 illustrates the black box approach, while fig. 7.2 gives a list of advertising and promotional stimuli and the possible appropriate responses.

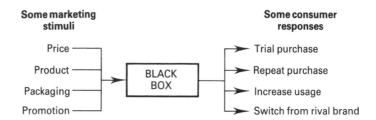

Fig. 7.2 Consumer responses to marketing stimuli

Behavioural theory and learning

According to behaviourists, we learn by the **pleasure–pain** (or **reward–punishment**) principle that is sometimes called **conditioning**. Conditioning is a process by which our behaviour is shaped so that we learn to avoid things which are unpleasant (punishing) and to repeat things which are pleasant (rewarding). This can be affected by our bodily condition. If we have already eaten to the full, the prospect of eating a cream cake may be unpleasant because our past experience has conditioned us to the discomfort that can follow from overeating. On the other hand, if we have not eaten for some hours the prospect of eating that cream cake will look entirely different.

This principle is so well known that women's magazines have advised their readers not to go shopping on an empty stomach. Food always looks more appetising when you are hungry and you will finish up buying more 'goodies' than you intended because you will be particularly vulnerable to the supermarket stimuli. The corollary to this is that if you have to take your children to the supermarket make sure that they have eaten – a hungry child is far more demanding.

Since advertisers do not want to punish anyone, the emphasis is on rewards. Word of mouth comes into this again – if we are always met with a friendly greeting when we visit the local shop we are 'rewarded' and will want to repeat the experience. The reward, of course, can be built into the product as well as into the service – a nice clean fresh mouth is a reward for using a particular type of toothpaste and conditions us to use that toothpaste again.

Reconditioning, deconditioning and new behaviours

The association must be kept alive by a constant repetition of the reward process. That friendly greeting should always be given, that toothpaste should always leave a nice clean mouth and so on. If the repetition-association process breaks down, the behaviour becomes deconditioned and consumers turn away from the product. Businesses can try to win them back by reconditioning the behaviour. This might be done by repeating the old rewards or by offering some new ones – sales promotions can be used here.

However, deconditioning an old behaviour is not always a bad thing and is often a necessary process in clearing the ground for the conditioning of a new one. We cannot remain children forever – old patterns of consumption are discarded and new patterns of consumption are acquired. In this context it is important to stress that advertising is not the only (nor even the strongest) source of 'rewards and punishments'. Family and friends, colleagues and social institutions all play a part. Young people come under peer-group pressure to do as their friends do – to feel rewarded by being included in the group and punished by being excluded.

The problem of too many stimuli

In the course of a day we are subjected to so many stimuli (not just advertisements) that we are unable to take them all in. One explanation has to do with the brain itself and might be called the **highway** theory. This suggests that there is only so much traffic that the brain can cope with and that after a while it is a bit like a congested motorway during the rush hour. New traffic can only get on to the motorway if some of the traffic already on it gets off. Another explanation suggests that it is in the nature of the stimuli themselves: those that stand out the most grab our attention. On this basis, it is a question of the clarity, size, shape, colour and sound of the stimuli that determines which ones get through and which ones do not. Stimuli characteristics such as shape, size and colour are clearly important in designing both advertisements and packaging and much research goes into such questions.

7.4 Mentalist or cognitive theories

A diametrically opposed view of human behaviour is to be found in the **mentalist** (or **cognitive**) camp. All the issues discussed above (such as learning new behaviours and the problem of too many stimuli) are still valid but can be looked at in a different way. **Cognitivism** (or **mentalism**) opposes the black box theory that the brain is just a machine and insists that thought processes are real phenomena that can be examined and understood. Consumers are intelligent: they think, they solve problems, they make decisions and they can be reasoned with. All these factors greatly increase the scope for creativity and imagination in the promotional arena.

Fig. 7.3   Intervening variables model

Cognitivists have opened the black box and claim to have discovered what goes on in there. Stimuli and responses are still important, but this model claims to understand something about the intervening factors as well. Here **intervening variables** have replaced the black box (see fig. 7.3). The term intervening variables describes the processes at work within the mind by which stimuli are interpreted, understanding arrived at, and decisions made. These variables have been described as perception, attitudes, expectation, learning and motivation.

Perception

Perception is the way in which we interpret the things around us. Two people may perceive the same phenomena in entirely different ways. A pessimistic theatre manager may complain that half the seats in the theatre are empty whereas an optimistic theatre manager may be very pleased that half the seats are full. A traveller on a train might be quite annoyed to find another passenger entering the compartment which he had hoped to have to himself. Another passenger might be glad of the company.

It is not just about differences between people. The same person may perceive the same phenomena differently on two different occasions. Selective perception is another factor, for we tend to see the messages that interest us the most. A smoker, for example, will screen out the health warning on the side of the cigarette packet because he does not wish to be reminded of his own mortality. Perception is influenced by attitudes and expectations.

Attitudes

The knowledge that a product originated in a country of whose political system the purchaser disapproves can affect the perception of that product. Before South Africa began its process of dismantling apartheid many shoppers would not buy South African sherry. Attitudes towards any country of origin, manufacturer, product, service or retail outlet may even be formed without any prior experience.

Expectations

Elementary economic theory tells us that when price rises then demand will fall. This is a simple behaviourist stimulus-response model. However, if people expect that one price rise is an indicator of further price rises to come, then you will see the paradoxical behaviour of a price rise being followed by an increase in demand as buyers try to keep ahead of the market. If a fall in price is seen as the first of a series of price cuts, then buyers may hold back and wait for prices to drop even further. The Stock Exchange and the housing market have both experienced this type of expectancy-based behaviour.

Learning

Cognitive theory does not rule out the stimulus-response pleasure–pain aspects of learning but it goes further. We may learn about something by using the processes of thought, by constructing possible situations 'inside our heads' and by asking 'what if?' questions. Classical probability theory exemplifies this process of *a priori* (before the event) learning when we learn the odds of picking an ace without ever holding a pack of cards.

Motivation

Motivation is defined as the basic drive which leads us into doing that which satisfies our needs. What those drives are and where they come from is answered differently depending on our point of view. Cognitivists tend to stress the view that people are rational and intelligent and driven by conscious motives. Psychoanalysts, on the other hand, stress the subconscious and non-rational nature of man.

7.5 Non-rational and rational motivations

The basic premise of psychoanalytical theories (commonly referred to as Freudian after Sigmund Freud) is that the motives which we claim to have are seldom our real motives. A Freudian might say that our **rationality** (the way in which we explain ourselves) is merely a veneer which we draw over our real selves because we do not like the truth. The difficulty which some people have with this is the apparent obsession with sex and with emotions such as fear, guilt and shame. The following are some typical ideas:

- Mothers buy washing powder because they fear the stigma of being labelled bad mothers if they do not.

- Middle-aged men buy sports cars to bolster their self-confidence in the face of declining sexual virility.

- Healthy people donate money to medical research because they feel guilty about being healthy.

For such people, these motives of fear, sex and guilt are beneath the surface of their consciousness (in the subconscious as Freudians might say) and would not be the explanations that they would offer if asked to do so.

Psychoanalysts also suggest that the root of these subconscious motivations is often to be found in some, usually disturbing, childhood experience long since forgotten. A man may be afraid of flying because of a childhood incident in which he saw some flying ducks being shot down by hunters. The man may subconsciously believe that if he flies he also will be shot down.

The critics of the application of psychoanalytical thinking to marketing say that it is one thing to use such techniques to help a person to overcome an irrational fear of flying and quite another to use them to play on a woman's fear of being thought a bad mother to sell washing powder. They see nothing wrong in treating people as rational and logical and in accepting at face value the explanations that people offer. On this view, all we need to know about the man who is afraid of flying is that he fears a mid-flight accident. It is perfectly rational and reasonable to fear a mid-flight accident because mid-flight accidents do occur. Therefore, it is perfectly reasonable for us to accept his explanation at face value without probing into his mind and coming up with stories about dead ducks.

Why not, the rationalists would say, simply accept a mother's explanation that she buys soap powder to get dirt out of her family's clothes? Rational appeals to removing the dirt, removing bad smells, preserving the colour and softening the material do not need to be supported by playing on feelings of guilt.

7.6 Gestalt theory

The word *Gestalt* signifies 'totality' or 'completeness'. The **Gestalt theory** is a particular view of rationality and problem solving based on the idea that 'nature abhors a vacuum' and should a vacuum occur the forces of nature will act to fill it. A gap in our knowledge is rather like a vacuum or, at a simpler level, like the missing pieces of an otherwise complete jigsaw puzzle. We do not like gaps, incomplete stories and half-finished messages and our active imagination will work to complete them. The human mind is capable of doing this at such a speed that we are often not aware that we have done it. At other times the process of **closure**, as it is called, can take time as we consciously wrestle with the problem in order to effect completeness.

This tendency to closure can, of course, lead to the picture being completed inaccurately and this danger is more likely when there are many pieces missing or when one of the missing pieces is vital. Consider the following:

2 + 2 = ? is straightforward: we supply the missing 4 easily.

? + ? = 4 is infuriating. Even if we assume that the missing numbers are whole and not fractions and that they are positive and not negative, there are three possible answers: 1 + 3, 2 + 2 and 3 + 1.

Without more information, accurate closure is impossible and yet, such is the tendency to closure, many of us will fill in the gaps one way or the other.

In fact, if the assumptions about fractions and negative signs are wrong, then there is a quite unlimited range of possible answers. Nothing would make sense and if the world were perceived to be like this all of the time it would be a frightening place to be. Closure is a way of making sense and failure to achieve closure (completeness) is frustrating and, possibly, frightening.

The use of Gestalt theory in advertising

Advertisers make use of the Gestalt theory when they play games with the consumer. Advertisements that require the message to be completed reward the receiver with a flattering sense of achievement, may even generate discussion about the advertisement and generally enhance the image of the product. However, if insufficient clues are given so that completeness cannot be achieved or inaccurate closure takes place, the campaign will backfire.

The brewers of Double Diamond used the slogan:

R U E 4 A DD

which was printed in black but with a red E to give the message 'Are You Ready [red E] for a Double Diamond [DD being a recognised abbreviation for Double Diamond]'. The power of the mind is such that we are able to make sense of such apparently meaningless messages.

More recently Oranjeboom, in the style of *'Allo, 'Allo* anglicisation of European languages, produced the tube-card (a mini-poster inside a London Underground train):

Tuk Bak Uur Ton Cels
Heer Kommen de Oranjeboom

with the strapline:

Not everyone will get it.

All such usages need to be carefully researched to make sure that they will work.

7.7 Using psychological models in advertising

Some promotional campaigns seem to lean more heavily on behaviourist models with an emphasis on incentives and rewards for repeated behaviour, while other campaigns use a cognitive, intellectual approach that engages the prospective purchaser in a reasoning process. Yet again, some campaigns may try to exploit those deeper subconscious motivations associated with Freud.

Perhaps behaviourist approaches work best with relatively cheap fast-moving goods which depend on repeat purchases and cognitive approaches work best for the items which are bought at long intervals and into which a great deal of thought must go. Again, cognitive approaches may be best for general advertising campaigns aimed at getting share of mind and behaviourist approaches for sales incentives aimed at getting share of market. But it is sensible to keep one's options open and be prepared to consider any solution to a problem without pretending to be an expert in an area which requires years of devoted study.

7.8 Some sociological approaches

Sociology is concerned with the way in which people live together in societies and groups. It suggests that human behaviour can be explained by the way in which a particular society is organised: for example, the extent to which it is clearly diversified into different groups and the extent to which it is stable over time. The traditional British socio-economic groups defined as A, B, C1, C2, D and E suggest a stable clearly defined structure but may no longer be as useful as once thought. The concept of the family, a mainstay of many an advertising campaign, is no longer valued as it was and advertisers are still wrestling with how to respond effectively to such changing structures. The diversity of ethnic groups, divorce and remarriage, single-parent families, live-in partners, gym-slip mothers, latch-key and 'home-alone' kids are all social realities which cry out against over-simplification.

The rules and norms of each society influence the patterns of purchase and consumption. Rules may be thought of as those things which are prescribed by law (the minimum age at which it is legal to drive a car, for example) and norms may be thought of as those unwritten practices which count as standard behaviour (for example, a man opening a door for a woman and letting her go through first). Western manufacturers of sewing machines entering the Middle-East market experienced an interesting norm. They tried, unsuccessfully, to sell their products to women until they found out that it was traditional for the husband to decide on such things. They switched their marketing to the men with much improved results. But it is not only the rules and norms that are important: so too is the extent to which they are adhered to. It has been observed that Hong Kong and Singapore have similar rules but that Hong Kong is not so strict as Singapore in enforcing them.

Social theatre

We might say that people consume goods as a result of the social structures and social pressures under which they live, acting out a series of roles by which they both identify themselves and meet the social expectations of others. These roles involve the use of the right words (the script), the right clothes (the costume) and the right products (the props). Young executives learn to play golf because 'it is the thing to do'. The children of certain professional families go to dance classes or take riding lessons because these are seen to be expected. Teenagers want to wear the same designer labels as their friends because they 'feel out of it' if they do not. Products can, all too easily, become the props for acting out the role and the badges that tell other people who we are and which group we belong to. There is the story of the young executive who always had a set of golf-clubs in the boot of his car even when he went shopping to the supermarket with his wife. Whenever the boot was open his clubs were on display sending out a message.

Lifestyle groups

Lifestyle concepts demassify the mass market concepts of C1s and C2s etc. into smaller groups or clusters based on the idea that members of a particular cluster are likely to consume the same sort of things. Rosemary Stefanou in her book *Success in Marketing* (John Murray, 1993) summarises the characteristics of nine different groups based on the American **VAL (Values and Lifestyles)** classification and seven different groups based on the UK Taylor Nelson survey. **Societally conscious** (VAL)/**social resisters** (Taylor Nelson) are described as supporting causes and caring about the environment – they are likely to be members of the so-called green market which has strongly influenced both product and package design in many areas. Lifestyle concepts are a convenient way to identify smaller and more meaningful groups often cutting across the socio-economic groupings (an environmentally concerned consumer can come from any socio-economic group), but such concepts have to be used with care. Both the above surveys identify **survivors**, but the American definition (4 per cent of the US population) paints a bleaker picture of the 'old and the sick' than the more robust 'hard-working and stable' survivors defined as 16 per cent of the UK population.

As well as the green market, there are the grey market (those over 55) and the pink market (gays and lesbians). Nobody talks about the black market (that term has long meant something quite different) but ethnic markets are well known. Researchers tell us that 'we are are what we eat', 'we are what we read' (it has been said that you can learn anything you want to know about *Sun* readers by following the cartoon strip 'George and Lynn') and 'we are where we live'; these observations all reflect attempts to identify target markets.

Advertisers like to have these little pictures or snapshots to aim at, from the American 'pools and patios' representing the people who have made it to the top to the UK 'videos, crisps and lager' representing people who probably like it where they are. More recently, advertising agency Leo Burnett has produced another set of labels based on residents in the London ITV region with such tags as articulate metropolitans (socially active and style-conscious), suburban homemakers (keen on DIY and gardening) and disgruntled townies (disenchanted and feeling under threat). In common with many lifestyle classifications, these groups are identified by where they live and, in particular, by postcode – very useful for direct-mail shots.

Parochials and cosmopolitans

Parochials are people who basically only feel comfortable with what they are used to. They have, as the word implies, a fairly narrow view of the world. They may not travel much, but when they do they expect to be able to continue their lifestyle in whatever part of the world they happen to be. English parochials might say 'France is all right but you can't get a proper cup of tea' (a coded way of saying 'it's all right but it isn't England'). The consumption pattern of parochials is likely to remain unchanged year after year. **Cosmopolitans**, on the other hand, have a world view; they probably travel a lot and when they are in another country they will eat the local food. Cosmopolitans are very likely to be experimental and to change their consumption patterns.

Leaders and laggards

In every society or social group there are going to be people who are identified as **leaders**. E. M. Rogers, in his book *Diffusion of Innovations* (Free Press, 1962), used the term **innovators** to describe those leaders who were the first to adopt new things. He identified the acceptance of new products and ideas into society as a process involving different types of people. Rogers claimed that about 2.5 per cent of all purchasers of a new product were innovators followed by another 13.5 per cent he called **early adopters**. Innovators and adopters are very likely to be cosmopolitans as well. Another 34 per cent make up the **early majority** and will be the next group to try the product followed by the **late majority** (also about 34 per cent). Finally come the **laggards** (about 16 per cent) who are the last group to purchase the product and who may come into the market months, or even years, after the innovators. Laggards may also be parochials. Figure 7.4 illustrates this.

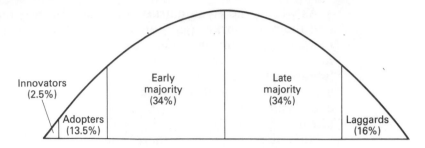

Fig. 7.4   Innovators and laggards

It should be clear that social change (including the adoption of new products) is most likely to come about as a result of the influence of cosmopolitans, leaders and innovators. These are the adventurous and experimental elements of society and are often associated with the lifestyles of **achievers** and **conspicuous consumers**. Parochials and laggards are not likely to act as **agents of change**. Obviously, marketers will be interested in identifying cosmopolitans and innovators when they are launching new products and entering new markets. Their role in a two-step model of communications cannot be ignored. Sky Television, the satellite broadcaster, sells advertising air-time on the back of lifestyle identifiers such as 'decision makers in satellite homes are more likely to be adventurous and to want to try new products than those in non-satellite homes'.

7.9 Some additional personal factors	**Post-purchase dissonance**

Post-purchase dissonance

Many people, having made a purchase, then begin to worry about whether the purchase was wise: they are suffering from post-purchase dissonance. What they need is **post-purchase reassurance**. Advertisers recognise this and some advertisements are designed to overcome such dissonance or anxiety. An advertisement for a pensions scheme may begin, 'If you are one of those thoughtful, far-sighted people who have already bought an ABC pension then this advertisement is not for you. Read no further. You have already made the right decision': actually, the advertisement might be for those who have already signed up – to keep them paying the premiums.

Thresholds

The most common threshold is probably price. A couple buying a house may tell the estate agent that they want something in the range of £100 000 to £120 000. Other thresholds may specify a minimum of four bedrooms and a garage. Thresholds define the product characteristics that are being sought and, to some extent, define the benefits the purchaser is looking for.

Trade-offs

These occur in situations where the products on offer do not have all the desired threshold values. The couple may be offered two properties in the specified price range: one with four bedrooms but no garage and the other a three-bedroomed house with a garage. They will have to trade-off the garage against the bedroom.

Scoring methods

The couple could list all the desired attributes of a house and weight them on a scale of one to ten. Attribute scores would be multiplied by attribute weights for each house and the results totalled. The house with the highest score would be bought. If the fourth bedroom and the garage were both given the same weight then neither house would do. The couple might look at the weight attributed to 'neighbourhood', see that it was only a six and consider a house-search in a cheaper area (another type of trade-off).

Decision-making units (DMUs)

The couple buying the house are a **decision-making unit**. If they had teenage children, these also might join in the evaluation process to make a bigger DMU. All sorts of purchases, from cars to holidays and from furniture to house-buying, can be resolved by such a group.

7.10 Towards a more complex model of buying behaviour

Taking all the above factors into consideration, together with what was discussed in chapter 6 on communications, we can summarise the buying process as a flow diagram. Figure 7.5 illustrates this.

7.11 The Howard–Sheth model

The Howard–Sheth model (1969) is still one of the most comprehensive models of buying behaviour. It breaks down into three distinct phases each with its own characteristics.

The extensive problem solving stage (EPS)

This covers the circumstances surrounding a prospective buyer for whom this is a first-time purchase and for whom the problem posed is an unfamiliar one. In this situation, the prospective buyer will spend a considerable amount of time searching out information and will take time to make a decision. Because the buyer is inexperienced a great deal of attention is likely to be paid to the opinions of others. Sales assistants, friends and colleagues will all be listened to and any relevant media articles and programmes attended to. The **EPS** stage may last through the first three trials.

The limited problem solving stage (LPS)

As the buyer gains experience in the use of the product there will be less search for more information. The buyer will come to depend increasingly on his or her own judgement and will be less influenced by friends and colleagues. Newspaper articles will be read less as part of a search for knowledge than in the pursuit of confirmation that the buyer is on the right track.

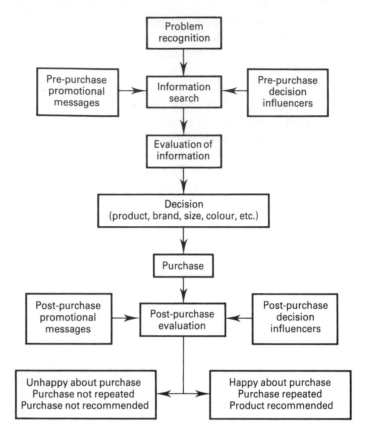

Fig. 7.5   Flow diagram of buying process

The automatic (or routinised) response behaviour (ARB or RRB)

At this stage the person is an experienced buyer. There is very little need felt now for new information and the opinions of others are virtually disregarded. The buyer feels more and more confident in his or her own judgement based on considerable experience of the product and does not put very much thought into making the next purchase.

The Howard–Sheth model fits in rather well with the **product life-cycle** and contributes to the concept that the advertiser's message should change as the product moves along the PLC curve. Figure 7.6 illustrates this.

7.12 Summary
- The distinction between shopping goods and convenience goods is a useful one when discussing the buying behaviour of consumers, as are the distinctions between social shoppers, economic shoppers and recreational shoppers. Taken together, they can reveal a wide variety of shopping behaviours.
- Consumer behaviour can be looked at from a variety of psychological and sociological perspectives. The two main psychological approaches are based on observable behaviour (and the observed relationship between inputs and outputs) on the one hand and on mental processes on the other.

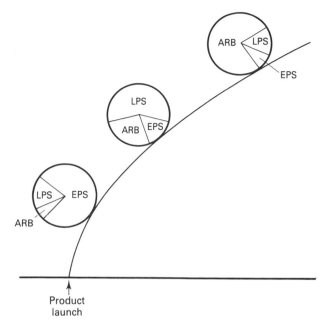

Fig. 7.6 Adapting the Howard–Sheth model to the product life-cycle
The ratio of people in the EPS, LPS and ARB stages should change over time
as the product approaches maturity.

- The first (the behaviourist approach) sees the human mind as a black box and says that we cannot actually know what goes on between the inputs (for example, price) and the outputs (for example, purchases).
- The second (the cognitive or mentalist approach) claims to have opened the black box and identified a range of intervening variables such as perspectives and attitudes.
- This psychological view that we can understand the human mind at work tends to divide into a concentration on the rational and problem-solving nature of man on the one hand and the irrational and emotional nature of man on the other.
- Whilst some advertising specialists follow a particular school and specialise in developing campaigns around it, most are eclectic and will consider all the different explanations of human behaviour in looking for solutions to a client's problems.
- Sociological approaches are also useful in looking at social classes and groupings as a clue to human behaviour. Concepts such as social theatre, cosmopolitans and parochials, leaders and laggards indicate the wide variety of social behaviour.
- Lifestyle classifications can be used to pinpoint specific groups or clusters which can be targeted for a particular campaign.
- All these ideas can be incorporated into a complex model of consumer behaviour such as the Howard-Sheth model.

**7.13
Assignments**

1. Think about a shopping good which you have recently bought and describe the decision-making process you went through. In particular, try to recall the span of time involved, all the sources of information you used and the number (and location) of the shopping trips you made in connection with this particular purchase. Explain briefly why you wouldn't go to that much trouble for a jar of coffee.

2. Divide a group into role-players and observers. Let the role-players form a DMU to make a purchase decision (say, a group holiday) and the observers take notes on how the discussion develops, who makes positive suggestions, who is more cautious and so on. Set a time limit and discuss it afterwards.

3. Make a collection of print advertisements and try to classify them according to what you think the basic psychological or sociological platform of each advertisement is (try to relate this to the newspaper or magazine where you found the ad). You could even edit a reel of TV ads and do the same. Remember that it is your perception of the ads that matters – don't try to guess at what was going on in the copywriter's mind.

8 Marketing research and market research

**8.1
Introduction**

Marketing research embraces any and every aspect of marketing from packaging to pricing and from the product to promotion. Market research is a much narrower term and is used to describe research into the market itself. Both consumer and user market research are included. This chapter is not about the specific techniques of marketing or market research as such, although they will be referred to. It is, instead, an attempt to show where research plays its part in the setting up and monitoring of a promotional campaign. But first, why do research at all and what is it?

**8.2 Why do
marketing
research?**

Management is about making decisions and, in an uncertain environment, the possibility of making the wrong decision is considerable. Research removes some of the uncertainty by giving us a better and clearer picture of what is going on. Reducing uncertainty also reduces risk – specifically, the risk associated with making the wrong decision. This, in turn, should lead to better decisions being made. The reasons for doing research, then, are:

- To reduce uncertainty.
- To reduce risk.
- To improve decision-making.

Note that we are not talking about *removing* risk and uncertainty only *reducing* them. We are not talking about always making the right decision but about not making too many wrong ones.

Many decisions made without the benefit of research (sometimes in defiance of the research) prove to be successful and many research-based decisions prove to be wrong. Research can lead to the wrong conclusions being drawn and should not be the only criterion for decision-making. Management flair, intuition, experience and judgement also play an important part. Research is not, in any case, a *decision-making* process: it should be thought of as a *decision-assisting* process.

What is research?

- **Research** can be defined as the systematic and objective gathering of relevant **data** (facts) about a clearly defined problem and the analysing and processing of that data to yield essential **information** to assist in the decision-making process.

Our definition uses both the words *data* and *information* – words often used to mean the same thing. In this context, however, something different is intended. *Data* is used to refer to the unprocessed raw facts which have been gathered in the initial data-collection stage and *information*

Table 8.1 The difference between data and information

Data	Information
Annual sales figures	
1989 100.00	Over the last four
1990 109.50	years, annual sales
1991 122.00	have grown by
1992 132.50	approximately* 10%
1993 144.75	per annum.

* Note the use of the word *approximately*. In extracting information from data, it makes sense to learn to approximate. The decisions you are going to make are unlikely to be affected by knowing that the rate was actually 9.7 per cent or 10.4 per cent. In almost all cases, using a phrase like 'approximately 10 per cent' is a perfectly adequate way of presenting the information.

means what the facts tell us after they have been processed and analysed. A simple example might help: see Table 8.1.

Another important element in our definition is the reference to a 'clearly defined problem'. Unless you are in a position to define the problem clearly, you are not going to be able to decide what, or how much, research to do. If you do not know what you want to research, or why you want to research it, you might as well not bother. Whether the research is done in-house or out-of-house, you will need to be able to negotiate a proper research brief and defining the problem is the only place to begin.

8.3 Primary and secondary research

In general, market research is split into two broad categories. There is **secondary research** which involves the use of secondary data and **primary research** which involves the use of primary data.

- **Secondary research** This involves the use of research which has already been carried out, possibly in connection with the current problem, but at an earlier date. It may involve the use of data which was not collected with the present problem in mind but which may, nevertheless, prove to be relevant and helpful. Sources of secondary data may exist internally in the company's own records (sales figures etc.) or they may lie outside the company in the form of commercial research reports, government reports, trade association reports and the like. Even newspaper articles can be a valuable source of secondary data. Because secondary research is very much a matter of reading books, reports, articles, etc., it is sometimes called **desk research** or **library research**.

- **Primary research** This involves starting from scratch, setting up a research project and paying professional researchers to get some new information which is not covered in the secondary data. It is sometimes called **field research** and the people who carry it out may be called **field-workers**.

The use of secondary and primary research needs to be understood. Because of its pre-existent nature, secondary data is always quicker and cheaper to obtain than primary data. Where it is internal it has the merit of relating specifically to the company itself, but it cannot tell you much about the industry or the market as a whole. External secondary data may not tell you anything at all about the company, but it should tell you about the market or industry. Internal secondary data can be quite new and up to date, but external data is often relatively old and out of date. External data may suffer from other difficulties. Different base years may have been used, or different research techniques or even different definitions (for example, what is a 'teenager', a 'housewife', a 'regular reader' or a 'heavy smoker').

Nevertheless, in spite of these difficulties, it is always recommended that secondary research is carried out before primary research is begun. There are some good reasons for this:

- Secondary research is both quicker and cheaper.
- Secondary research sometimes throws up answers to the current problem without the cost of doing primary research.
- It may show that the problem has already been researched and that it is unlikely that you will learn any more.
- It may pinpoint areas which have not yet been researched so that you can focus your efforts on breaking new ground.
- It may help you to identify the best methods to be used in doing primary research into a specific area.
- It may put you on your guard against thoughtlessly repeating mistakes made by earlier researchers.

For all these reasons, it is always advisable to do secondary research first. Why spend three months and £25 000 to find out something you could learn today by buying a £2 000 report?

8.4 *Ad hoc* and continuous research

Ad hoc **research** (done for a particular purpose) is sometimes referred to as *one-off* research. It is set up for a specific reason, such as pretesting consumer reaction to a new advertising concept before embarking on the expense of producing a new TV campaign. Some preliminary *ad hoc* research, such as an investigation of an overseas market to determine its potential, can be based on secondary data, but much *ad hoc* work involves primary research. **Continuous research** can measure what is going on over a period of time in a particular situation. Commercial market tracking studies such as those carried out by the British Market Research Bureau (BMRB) and Broadcasters Audience Research Board (BARB), which are discussed below, come into this category.

Changes in EPOS (Electronic Point Of Sale) technology increasingly improve the process of continuous research. It is now technically possible using a particular type of preprogrammed credit card or charge card to monitor not only what products are going through the cashpoint but who is actually buying them. This should only be done with the shopper's consent and shoppers in the USA are being rewarded for agreeing to use such cards and taking part in trial runs. The results will be invaluable to direct mailers.

Omnibus research, where many different companies can share the cost by paying a 'per question' fee to have questions included in a survey, can be used on a regular basis.

8.5 Secondary research and promotional campaigns

The promotional campaign planner, whether the campaign is advertising, public and press relations, direct mail or whatever, is well served by secondary data. There are three main reasons for this:

- The provision of secondary data has become an industry in its own right and many professional companies exist solely to provide commercial research reports to campaign planners.
- A large number of media owners depend on advertising revenue to stay in business and have developed their own databases as a selling point when dealing with media buyers.
- Professional bodies representing different branches of the media also produce reports. RAJAR (Radio Joint Audience Research), VFD (Verified Free Distribution – for free newspapers), ABC (Audit Bureau of Circulation – for paid-for papers), OSCAR (Outside Site Classification and Audience Research – for posters) and CAVIAR (Cinema and Video Industry Audience Research) are some examples.

Additionally, there is a substantial body of government-financed research, both nationally and internationally, and a great deal of interesting research is constantly being carried out in universities, some of which have gained a reputation for their expertise with particular industries, such as travel and tourism.

8.6 Commercial research reports

Reports of this sort are based on research done by professional companies who then sell the results to advertisers, agencies or media owners. There are two main kinds of reports in the consumer markets: those which report on consumer buying behaviour and those which concentrate on retail sales or **retail audits**. TGI and AGB (see below) are among the best known consumer reports.

Target Group Index (TGI)

TGI (published by the British Market Research Bureau (BMRB)) is available both in the UK and the USA and analyses a large number of categories and subcategories of major advertised brands. Some 4,500 brands across 500 product categories are reported on. The report, which is based on 24 000 self-completed questionnaires, includes data on such items as alcohol, cars, proprietary medicines and tins of baked beans.

The users of each product are categorised under such headings as age, sex, socio-economic and geographic status which are further broken down into the categories of 'heavy users', 'medium users' and 'light users'; even 'non-users' are included. Users may be further classified as loyal to one brand (**solus users**), having a preference for one brand but likely to use others as well (**most often users**) or having no fixed preference (**minor users**).

A particularly useful feature of TGI is the internal cross-referencing of users of all types against their own reported newspaper reading and television viewing habits. This feature is invaluable to the media planner.

Indeed, internal cross-referencing can be done against any two or more categories in the survey. For example, it can be done against what are termed 'lifestyle' questions in which panel members answer questions on anything from the sort of holidays they like to what they think of health and fitness fanatics. Lifestyle questions can introduce an *ad hoc* element into what is otherwise continuous research.

Audits of Great Britain (AGB)

AGB (published by Broadcasters Audience Research Board (BARB)) is the other major provider of consumer panel data in the UK and it compiles the BARB reports which are regarded as essential for both TV programme planners and advertisers. The process begins with a random selection of around 43 000 representative households from which one in ten is invited to join the panel. About 25 per cent drop out and are replaced each year. Their identity is a carefully guarded secret to discourage attempts to pressurise them into changing their viewing preferences.

The secret of the BARB system is the **people meter**, an engineer-installed master control which links up all the televisions in the home. The meter records which programmes are being watched, including cable and satellite where these are installed. It even flashes a reminder if people forget to 'log-in'. Even brief absences from the room are noted and there is a special code which records long absences like holidays.

The master control pushes the previous evening's viewing figures down the phone to a central computer. The analysed results are available to both programme planners and advertisers by ten o'clock in the morning and are seen in summary form by the rest of us in the weekly TV ratings.

The problems with any voluntary consumer panels, such as TGI and BARB, are that (*i*) they may not be truly representative of the whole population (people who refuse to take part may have different habits) and (*ii*) panel members may consciously or unconsciously change their natural patterns of behaviour to take account of the research process. Nevertheless, they are widely used and much relied on.

Target Group Ratings (TGR) and data fusion

Another problem about which there are different opinions is the relatively limited amount of information which can be got from any one respondent. One view is that too much should not be asked and that the present 'work-load' imposed by, for example, TGI and BARB is about right. The opposite view is that once a volunteer has been recruited as much information as possible should be obtained. BARB, for instance, is interested in finding out not only what people watch but how they rate the programmes they see, although this will impose additional burdens on the panel members.

One solution to the problem is to fuse the data from two or more different surveys. This involves matching a sample of respondents from one survey exactly with another sample from a different survey (age, income, marital status, etc.) and to treat them as though they are, in fact, the same people. TGR (operated jointly by BMRB and BARB) matches consumers from BARB households with an equal number from the TGI panel to enable advertisers to achieve a tighter focus for their campaigns.

National Readership Survey (NRS)

The NRS reports provide readership patterns of magazines and newspapers analysed by demographic classifications. Twenty-eight thousand consumers are surveyed and approximately 250 publications are reported on. Reports come out annually and bi-annually, but the process, whilst of some use to media planners, is not without its critics. The demographic classification is thought to be out of date and the concentration on the 'male head of household' as the source of information is questionable. The definition of reader allows the inclusion of people who only read one part of a paper (say, the sports section) and people who really only see the paper once in a while – in other words, you do not have to read all the paper every day to be counted as a reader.

The National Shoppers Survey (NSS)

The National Shoppers Survey (NSS) holds a database of three million households classified by lifestyle groupings.

Retail audits

The principle behind retail audits is similar to that of consumer panel research. A panel of retail outlets is recruited to represent the retail market as a whole. Participation is voluntary and the representativeness of the panel is distorted by the fact that several large retailers such as Marks & Spencer, Sainsbury's and Boots will not take part. To compensate for this the results are weighted and adjusted – essential since Sainsbury's alone has around 11 per cent of the retail grocery trade.

Manufacturers in the fast-moving consumer goods (FMCG) sector will find this research most valuable. It provides information on the average prices being charged, how much of the manufacturer's goods are being held in stock and, of course, information on competitors' products. Participating retailers are not expected themselves to undertake the massive task involved and teams of trained auditors go from shop to shop doing the work.

A. C. Nielsen are the main UK providers in this field. It employs over 250 auditors to visit 1 400 shops every two months checking purchasing patterns, stockholdings, invoices and delivery notes to determine total sales, market shares, unsold stock, effectiveness of different types of outlets and seasonal variations, etc. Nielsen constantly updates its own product range to provide more frequent reports, on-line telephone services and so on.

MAID to measure: Market Analysis and Information Database

Established in 1985, MAID today provides its Newsline, Researchline, Brokerline and Companyline services to over 500 top clients around the world. A subscription-only service, MAID employs over 60 analysts working around the clock to extract information from thousands of commercial research reports, broker reports and newspapers and to summarise it into an easily understood format and pass it down the phone instantaneously to waiting monitors.

8.7 Quantitative research and qualitative research

The foregoing deals with **quantitative** research which involves the collection of a large amount of facts or figures and is often characterised as asking a large number of people to answer a lot of fairly easy questions such as what income group are they in and what newspapers have they read in the last month. These are questions which really require only a feat of memory on the part of the respondent. Questions which call for an opinion may be more taxing but can be fairly easily included.

Qualitative research (often associated with motivational models of buyer behaviour) attempts to go deeper and to try to find out just why people buy the things they do. It is often characterised as asking a small group of people some fairly complex questions. Each interview takes longer (two or three hours (or more) as opposed to, perhaps, 10 or 15 minutes) and usually involves greater interviewing skills on the part of the researcher. 'Accompanied shopping' where the researcher might spend a whole morning going around the supermarket with the respondent is an example. Each purchase decision is discussed as it takes place to discover why one brand was selected rather than another.

Below we are going to look at some examples of research applied to advertising and public relations campaigns.

8.8 Primary research and advertising campaigns

After an advertising campaign has begun to roll, it is possible to conduct post-launch research to try to measure the impact it is having. It is not necessary to wait until the campaign is over and, in fact, research carried out during a campaign can point to necessary changes – a change in copy or frequency, for example.

DAGMAR and AIDA

Of course, it is difficult to measure the results of a campaign if no clear objectives were set out to begin with. The DAGMAR model draws our attention to this problem by at least making us think of **D**efining **A**dvertising **G**oals for **M**easured **A**dvertising **R**esults. The objectives could, for example, follow the AIDA stages (**A**wareness – **I**nterest – **D**esire – **A**ction) and the goals of the campaign could relate to, say, increasing **A**wareness or increasing **A**ction (sales). However, to measure the effect of a campaign it is first necessary to take some pre-campaign measurements or there will be no baseline to measure the result against.

Models such as DAGMAR and AIDA remind us that we are dealing with a process that takes place in the mind of the consumer: it is not the advertising, *per se*, which we are researching but how it is perceived, understood and reacted to by the intended consumers. Before and after research enables us to monitor this process.

It is necessary to remember that, in any case, advertising is not the only thing which impacts on awareness and sales. Sunshine may have as much effect on the sale of ice-cream as advertising does and negative editorial comment in the health and fitness pages on 'non-dairy' products ('Is your

Fig. 8.1   Monitoring frequency

ice-cream made from pig's fat?') don't exactly help. Not only is it sometimes difficult to isolate the effect of advertising from other factors such as retailers' merchandising policies, but also it is difficult to judge correctly the time-scale and frequency for taking measurements. Cumulative effects and time-lags come into play here:

- Cumulative effects may mean that the advertisement will have to be seen several times by the same person before it begins to take effect. Taking measurements too early may panic an advertiser into believing that nothing is happening.
- Time-lags may indicate that a consumer needs time to think before acting. Assuming that an advertisement today will result in a sale tomorrow can produce the same sort of panic as ignoring the cumulative effects. A consumer may buy something today as a result of an advertising campaign seen several weeks (even months) ago.

Cumulative effects combined with time-lags can make it difficult to know just what effect on sales a campaign is having.

Taking measurements too close together can also give the impression that nothing is happening. However, taking them too far apart can be equally misleading. Results ought to be monitored at least quarterly. Annual results may show that brand awareness is 10 per cent higher now than it was twelve months ago but they will not show what has happened in between. Brand awareness may have been 15 per cent higher six months ago and have fallen steadily since then. Figure 8.1 shows the dangers of leaving gaps that are too long.

With some types of campaign (for example, **off-the-page** direct coupon responses) the impact is easily measured by the number of coupons that come back, but not all campaigns can have such a device built into them. A surprising number of television advertisers remain unsure as to just what it is that television actually does for them.

8.9 Research and public and press relations

In many instances the triggers that stimulate a company to do *ad hoc* research come out of secondary sources. Negative or hostile mentions in the press may be picked up through routine media monitoring. Internal records may show that the number of customer complaints has increased or that more customers have taken their business elsewhere. Alerted to the possibility that the company's image is slipping, *ad hoc* research might be set up to assess the damage. There are a variety of ways in which this could be tackled. Company salespeople could be briefed to include certain key questions in their sales interviews. Telephone interviews and personal face-to-face interviews are possible. Consumers could be questioned and even non-consumers could be included. Remember that when it comes to questions of image it is not necessary for a person to have any first-hand experience of a product or company to have an opinion about it.

Key factors checklist

Two approaches involving a checklist of key factors could be used. In the first, the company is simply scored against the items on the list. In the second, the company can be compared with its major rivals. Suppose that a supermarket chain believes that the following factors contribute to its overall image:

- The friendliness of its staff.
- The range and variety of its products.
- The cleanliness of the establishment.
- The efficiency of its checkout operations.
- The range and quality of its free literature (recipe booklets etc.).
- The overall price level of its products.
- The layout and design of the stores.

Secondary data, for example, would show that friendliness of the staff is high on most people's list. During the late 1980s, price was only fifth on the list but during the early nineties it crept up to third.

Our fictitious company could now question people using, for example, simple scale questions:

On a scale of 1 to 10 how do you assess the friendliness of the staff at your local XYZ supermarket?
Not very friendly   1 2 3 4 5 6 7 8 9 10   Very friendly

It would be useful also to find out how important the respondent thought staff friendliness was anyway. One way to do this would be to show him or her the checklist above and to ask something like:

From the following list please select the three items which you think are most important and rank them first, second and third.

Staff friendliness	—
Price	—
Checkout efficiency	—
Range of products	—
Store cleanliness	—
Free literature	—
Store layout	—

A respondent who circled 2 on the first question but selected friendliness as the most important factor on the second is sending out a very serious message.

The above line of inquiry will enable the supermarket chain to see how it stands against an agreed range of criteria. But is it doing better or worse than its rivals? (Remember that the object of the research is not to find out if XYZ staff are friendlier than Tesco's or if XYZ stores are cleaner than Sainsbury's, but to find out if people think that they are.) This would involve asking similar questions but asking respondents to answer them several times in response to different store names. To avoid respondent bias, it would be sensible not to reveal that the the survey was being done on behalf of XYZ stores.

On a scale of −5 to +5 please score each of the following supermarket chains for the efficiency of their checkout operations:

Sainsbury's	−5	−4	−3	−2	−1	0	+1	+2	+3	+4	+5
Tesco	−5	−4	−3	−2	−1	0	+1	+2	+3	+4	+5
XYZ	−5	−4	−3	−2	−1	0	+1	+2	+3	+4	+5
Safeway	−5	−4	−3	−2	−1	0	+1	+2	+3	+4	+5

Again, it would be useful to know something about the respondent's own behaviour.

When did you last visit the following stores:

	During the last week	During the last month	During the last three months	More than three months ago
Sainsbury's	−	−	−	−
Tesco	−	−	−	−
XYZ	−	−	−	−
Safeway	−	−	−	−

After carrying out research along these lines, our XYZ supermarket would be in a position to judge its image against clearly set criteria and against the image of its major rivals. Suppose that the research confirms what it already feared, that it has a bad image, how should it now proceed? This is one of those cases where the same data may mean two different things and before the company does anything it needs to know if it is dealing with a performance gap or a communications gap (see further in chapter 14).

8.10 Test markets and model building

Test marketing

Originally associated with the idea of test marketing a new product, **test marketing** soon became adapted to the idea that any aspect of marketing could be tested. New packet designs and new advertising campaigns are two of the things that can be test marketed. The idea is that a small area of the national market is selected and the new product, package or advertisement is tested there before a national (or international) roll-out is contemplated. The theory is that if the product fails in the test area then it would probably have failed in the national area as well and the cost of a wasted national launch can be avoided. There are, however, problems with test marketing and some companies have preferred to take the risk of going straight for a national launch. The problems are:

- A test market operation gives the game away and alerts the competition to the company's plans.

- Given the need to act quickly when bringing a new product (or advertising campaign) to the market the test market period may simply be seen as an unacceptable delay.
- There are genuine difficulties which affect the choice of a truly representative test area. If the test area is not representative of the national market as a whole then the results are compromised.
- Test marketing may be an expensive way of finding out what you want to know.
- It may prove difficult to contain the test within the chosen area, particularly if major retailers with their own central purchasing and distribution systems do not wish to co-operate.

Simulated test marketing

An alternative to real-life test marketing is **simulated test marketing**, using a computer model. Of course, a computer model needs some real-world data to work on and, therefore, some preliminary testing of the product, packet or advertisement will need to be done to provide this. A computer can then project this data into a model based on real-world market characteristics such as size of population, age groups, spending power and purchasing preferences and can 'predict' likely market success or failure within limits of plus or minus 20 per cent.

Models are, themselves, very complex to build and companies wishing to use such a model would probably go to a specialist agency such as Nielsen and pay to use its QUARTZ system.

The advantages of simulated models are:

- They enable secrecy to be maintained as the simulations are conducted in a confidential atmosphere.
- They enable two or more variations of the concept to be tested more or less simultaneously on the same market data. In other words they allow 'what if' questions to be asked, such as 'What if we lowered the price by 10 per cent?'
- The model could include national data and need not be limited to a prescribed 'test area'.
- The costs of 'failure' are relatively low since no real production or distribution has occurred.
- Time is compressed. In a real-world test market it takes a month to get a month's sales figures. A model can simulate a month's sales in next to no time once the model is set up and approved.

Additionally, models are seen as being useful in training young executives in a relatively cheap and risk-free environment.

Simulations, however, are not without their limitations and, like conventional market research, should not be used as the sole basis of making a decision.

8.11 Summary
- Marketing research covers all aspects of marketing.
- Market research is specifically concerned with the behaviour and motivation of consumers.
- Research should be undertaken to reduce risk and uncertainty in order to improve decision making.

- Research should not, however, be used as the sole basis of decision making but as a decision-assisting technique along with management skill, intuition and judgement.
- Continuous research goes on all the time; *ad hoc* research is set up for a particular purpose.
- Secondary research makes use of existing data and information; primary research starts from scratch collecting new pieces of data.
- There is a wide variety of secondary data including commercial reports, government and professional reports and data provided by the media.
- To discover how effective an advertisement has been in terms of its recognition or impact on consumers or to discover what sort of image a company has requires primary research.

**8.12
Assignments**

1. Discuss the pros and cons of in-house market research as opposed to appointing a research agency. Are there some circumstances where using an agency (or using in-house facilities) might always be better?

2. Explain carefully why it is thought to be better to do secondary research before attempting primary research. Are there some circumstances where secondary research would be inappropriate anyway?

3. Devise a simple questionnaire to assess the image of an organisation (other than a supermarket) against whatever attributes you think are important.

9 Advertising and the media

9.1 Introducing the media

Media is a much used word familiar to everybody. In fact, anything that carries a message is a **medium**: letters, notices on notice-boards and word of mouth are all media. But in this chapter we are concerned with the advertising media.

It is often said that the media is a game for five players. They are:

- **Media owners**   They sell time and space to advertisers.
- **Campaign planners**   They decide which media to use and when. (They may be in-house or out-house.)
- **Media buyers**   They book the space and time needed. (The same person may plan and buy.)
- **Advertisers**   They are the originators of the campaigns.
- **Audiences**   Possibly the most important. We can say that audiences are what is bought and sold.

Other ways to gain access to the media

Although our concern here is with advertising, it is important to recognise that this is not the only way to gain access to the media for publicity and promotional purposes. The other methods are:

- Press (or media) relations: see chapter 15.
- Event sponsorship: see chapter 19.
- Programme sponsorship: see chapter 5.6.
- Product placement: see chapter 5.5.
- Cause placement: this is a relatively new phenomenon where advocates of a whole range of causes and issues from Aids to race relations and from physical disability to mental impairment lobby radio and television producers to get a sympathetic treatment in programmes such as soap operas and documentaries.

Media for advertisers

For advertisers the relevant media can be classified into six groups:

The **spaced-based** media	Newspapers Magazines Posters	Collectively known as **press and print**
The **time-based** media	Cinema Television Radio	Collectively known as **broadcast**

Cinema is a time-based media but for regulatory purposes is included with press and print.

Vehicles

Each media group is made up of a number of what advertising people call **vehicles**. For example, there are many different newspaper titles each of which is a vehicle.

9.2
Newspapers

The dailies

National daily papers (the dailies) are distributed from Monday to Saturday and are divided into the qualities or **broadsheets** (because they are printed in a large format) and the popular or **tabloid** papers (printed on smaller pages). As a general rule, the qualities are read in professional, high-income households and the tabloids in non-professional, lower-income households. Qualities include *The Times*, the *Guardian* and, in Scotland, *The Scotsman*. The tabloids include the *Daily Mirror* and the *Sun*. Between the two extremes are the middle-market papers such as the *Daily Mail* and the *Daily Express*, which are also tabloid size.

The Sundays

Most dailies have a Sunday equivalent. *The Times* has *The Sunday Times* and the *Daily Mirror* has the *Sunday Mirror*. The Sunday papers are set up as separate businesses under their own management and editorial control and sell their own advertising space. British Sundays are becoming more like American papers with their multiple sections.

Local papers

Local papers are found in every town. They are usually weekly and their editorial coverage is confined to local events – births, deaths, marriages and so on. They are of limited interest to national advertisers and tend to attract mainly local companies. However, national retail chains with local branches and national manufacturers (for example, carmakers) with local distributors do use them. There are two types – paid-for, over the counter, papers sold at newsagents and free papers distributed to every home and business in the neighbourhood. Free papers rely entirely on advertising revenue. Both paid-for and free papers may belong to groups of papers serving adjacent neighbourhoods and an advertiser can often get a discount by going into two or more titles in the same group.

Regional and evening papers

Regional papers cover large parts of the country and often carry national and international news. They are very good for regional campaigns. Evening papers may be either local or regional. The London *Evening Standard* is very popular with commuters, contains a lot of national and international news and serves a population bigger than some of the smaller European nations.

9.3 Magazines   There are two main types of magazine: those sold in the consumer market and those sold in the business and professional markets (for the latter see also chapter 21). Consumer magazines usually come out weekly or monthly. They serve a different purpose from newspapers and do not try to print the latest news. This is partly because of the relative infrequency of publication – a monthly magazine is not going to be able to cover the news 'as it happens'. It is also partly to do with their production schedules.

Monthlies, for example, tend to be printed weeks before the **cover date** with the content agreed even earlier. Since a magazine with a cover date of September hits the stands in August, an advertiser planning for late August exposure will have to go into the September issue to achieve it. Many magazines circulate a list of intended features so that advertisers can plan ahead; the trade publication *Advance* summarises all this information for advertisers or press relations people to use.

Consumer magazines

There are several hundred consumer magazines in the UK and they can be grouped according to their content. Some are general interest magazines but most are special interest catering for computer enthusiasts, DIY fans, photographers, motor-bike enthusiasts, for people facing special events in their lives, such as retirement, marriage, housemoving or even coping with divorce and bereavement. Ethnic magazines are generally referred to as the black press.

Free magazines are also found; they may depend on advertising revenue for their existence but they may also be provided as a service. They include:

- Newspaper sections, usually with different editorial and advertising control from the title paper.
- In-flight magazines issued by an airline as a service to passengers but also issued by some long-haul bus and train companies.
- Give-aways at railway stations, usually targeted at a particular group such as young professional women and dependent largely on classified advertising for their existence.
- In-store magazines such as W H Smith's quarterly *Bookcase* which showcases individual authors, titles, series and themes.

9.4 The broadcast media (radio and television)   The broadcast media is split not only between radio and television but also between the public sector (the BBC) and the independent sector. The BBC provides both radio and television services, is financed by an annual licence fee and carries no advertising. It also obtains revenue from its business activities carried out under the name of BBC Enterprises, which handles everything from the sale of programme-related merchandise, such as audio and video tapes, to the sale of BBC programmes to overseas stations.

The BBC has been under threat of privatisation with the possibility that it would lose its licence-fee funding and be forced to take advertising business; but in July 1994 it was told that it would retain its current status for ten more years and that the licence fee situation would be looked at again in five years. Whilst closed to the advertiser (for five years, anyway), it is accessible to event sponsorship and media relations activities.

Independent radio (IR) is a commercial service that survives by selling advertising time. It breaks down into two national stations (INR) and about 150 local stations (ILR). Like local papers, ILR stations may belong to a larger group serving different localities. Almost all radio (BBC and IR) operates on the terrestrial system but there is a small amount of cable radio.

Independent television is more complicated. There are two ways of financing it and three ways of delivering it. The oldest operators are the Channel 3 stations collectively called ITV. These, like radio, are terrestrial and sell advertising time. ITV is largely a regionalised service with 15 stations (two of which, uniquely, share the London region). There is, however, a national breakfast time service (GMTV), also a part of ITV, which goes out using the broadcast facilities of the other stations. Channel 4 is the only national day time and evening terrestrial service available to advertisers.

Case Study

Channel 4

Channel 4 was an interesting experiment. Deliberately set up to provide for a range of interests and tastes not generally catered for by Channel 3, it was recognised from the outset that it might not be able to attract sufficient advertising revenue to enable it to survive. It was, originally, protected by a guaranteed income out of a levy paid by the ITV companies which also had to put their own sales expertise at Channel 4's disposal. It no longer receives this, but still retains some protection if its advertising income fails to reach a certain point.

In its first full year of financial independence (from 1 January 1993), Channel 4 exceeded all expectations and became something of a victim of its own success. It exceeded the revenue target set for it, took a larger than expected share of total television advertising spend and actually found itself repaying £38 million to Channel 3. Channel 3 now views Channel 4 as a serious competitor for the advertiser's money. Another indicator of the health of Channel 4 is that in 1993 it reached, for the first time, larger audiences than BBC2.

Cable and satellite are the other two ways of delivering television programmes into the home. Although they can sell advertising space, their main commercial thrust is in recruiting subscribers who then provide them with a monthly rental income. The ITC (Independent Television Commission) *Factfile '94* lists 51 satellite programme services (of which 37 were active) and 139 cable programme services (of which 80 were active).

Terrestrial, cable and satellite services are all licensed by the ITC. Terrestrial franchises are sold by competitive bidding and terrestrial programming is subject to strict ITC requirements. Cable and satellite licences are available practically on demand; there is no enforceable programming requirement and it is not even necessary for the licensee to be able to broadcast at the time the licence is granted. Homes with only terrestrial facilities are termed **terrestrial homes** and those with alternative services as well are termed **satellite homes**.

9.5 Posters and cinema

Posters and cinema, at first sight very different media, have two things in common. They are both located permanently outside the home and they are both vast in number. Each one of the thousands of poster sites and cinema screens available can be thought of as a vehicle. An advertiser can, if he wants, pick them one by one (or **line by line**), but in practice they are more easily bought in packages or **preselected campaigns**. Posters, furthermore, have no editorial surround at all and cinema advertisements are different in their surround even from television which they most resemble. For these reasons what follows is of little relevance to them and they will be discussed more fully in chapter 11 (for posters) and chapter 12 (for cinema).

9.6 Understanding how the commercial media works

Commercial media

Commercial media owners have to attract both audiences and revenue. Their revenue may come from their audiences or from advertisers (and, nowadays, from sponsors also). Individual media may be a mixture of both advertisement and editorial content or one only.

- **ITV and IR**   Deliver a mixture of advertising and editorial (programme) content. Free to audience. Depend on revenue from advertisers but programme sponsorship is increasingly important.

- **Satellite and cable**   Like ITV, cable and satellite companies offer a mixture of programme and advertising content. However, whereas ITV services are free to viewers, cable and satellite companies also raise revenue from subscription fees.

- **Newspapers and magazines**   Usually contain a mixture of advertising and editorial content. Earn money from both advertisers and readers; exceptions are free newspapers and magazines, and papers, such as *LOOT*, which give advertising space away but are priced to readers. Sponsorship of individual newspaper sections is a new development.

- **Posters**   A pure advertising medium. No editorial matter and all the revenue is earned from the advertisers. Posters are unusual in that audience size cannot be influenced.

- **Cinema**   Almost a pure entertainment medium with one advertising break usually before the feature film.

9.7 How the media attracts audiences

There is severe competition for audience size, leading to newspaper **circulation wars** and television **ratings wars**. Editorial and programme content are important factors in this competition, but there is a great deal of inter-media (one paper advertising in another paper) and cross-media (papers running television campaigns) advertising as well.

Newspapers run **editorial promotions** and tie-ins with television programmes, such as the '*Daily Mirror* – You Bet' sponsorship. Papers have recently been involved in **price wars** which became so critical that calls for official inquiries were raised. Satellite and cable companies have used both personal selling and direct-mail techniques and have offered discounted (even free) introductory periods to new subscribers.

This is all of interest to advertising campaign planners and media buyers. They will take great interest in anything that the media do to increase audience size and will be reluctant to buy space in a paper with falling sales if no efforts are made to reverse the trend.

Off-air and on-air promotions

Both radio and television use their own facilities to promote future programmes. The justifications for these on-air station ads are that they are reaching their own audience and that they are free. It is estimated that if LWT had to pay for its own on-air promotions at rate-card value the bill would exceed £40 million a year.

Criticisms raised by the advertising industry are that they compete for the viewer's attention against advertisers who have paid and add to the clutter surrounding paid-for commercials in much the same way as extended programme credits do. However, in November 1993 the ITV Network Centre published the result of its own research showing that station ads need not be a turn-off for viewers and listeners.

Nevertheless, broadcasters know that on-air promotions cannot carry the full burden of maintaining audience size. They reach only the existing audience and cannot tell anyone else what the station has to offer. Furthermore, in spite of the Network Centre's conclusions, concern about clutter still persists.

Off-air promotions, to minimise ad clutter and reach a wider audience, are now a matter of course. Radio has been at it longer and seems to do it better than television. Sales promotions, sponsorships, poster campaigns, live events, roadshows, exhibitions and direct mail are all in use. Perhaps the most colourful is character- and show-related merchandising with everything from *Gladiators* hypertonic drinks to *Big Breakfast* and *Strike It Lucky* boardgames.

The commercial broadcast stations need to attract audiences to attract advertisers and they need to offer a relatively clutter-free environment. The BBC, although shielded from the need to attract advertisers, is, nevertheless, a major player in off-air advertising, Mr Blobby merchandising being one of the successes of 1993. It is not just that the sale of licensed products brings in revenue: it reassures existing audiences and encourages new ones.

The Broadcast Promotions & Marketing Executives (BPME), a body of professional media advertisers covering satellite and cable as well as BBC and ITV, gives annual awards for the best on-air and off-air promotions and is committed to the concept of on- and off-air integrated marketing strategies.

In charge of all this effort on a paper or magazine is the circulation manager. **Circulation** refers to the number of copies sold, whereas **readership** refers to the number of readers – this being the larger number as most copies will be read by more than one person. With the broadcast media there is no such distinction between circulation and readership: there is simply **audience** size to measure.

9.8 How the media attracts advertisers

Circulation sales are overseen by the circulation manager, but space sales are overseen by the advertisement manager, supported by a team of space salespeople, or media representatives. These media representatives go out to agencies (and even to the clients) to pitch for business. On large publications the advertisement manager's role may be split between a display manager and a classified manager and, with the growth of advertorials, there may be an advertorials manager as well. Multi-section papers may have different sales teams for each section. The broadcast media employ air-time sales representatives. Media representatives are not just selling space or time but the whole vehicle. The buyer has to be convinced that the vehicle offers a suitable environment and will want to hear about not only the audience size and composition, but also the editorial position, the quality of its reporting, the balance of text and pictures, the editorial content and even the quality of the printing and paper used.

Press and print media may also advertise in specialist journals (such as *Marketing Week*) and use direct-mail shots to agencies and advertisers. They may offer so-called **space-plus** deals, which include incentives such as free copies, free run-on advertisements and even free editorial coverage. They may also offer a design and copy preparation service for the benefit of small or inexperienced advertisers.

Case Studies

1 The *International Herald Tribune*

The *International Herald Tribune*, an English-language paper which, despite its American sounding name, was founded in Paris over a hundred years ago, offers an important vehicle for UK businesses wishing to advertise worldwide. It publishes three versions daily: Worldwide, Asian only and Atlantic only, the latter covering Europe and America with the possibility existing of arranging for European advertising coverage alone.

The work of selling space in the UK is carried out by a London office with a sales team of six: three for display ads and three for classified ads. Classified ads account for about 38 per cent of total advertising revenue. The London office also oversees African sales which is done by agents. One of the interesting problems affecting an international publication is that the advertisements which it carries may come under a very wide range of legal jurisdictions making a particular advertisement (a tobacco advertisement, for example) legal in one country and illegal in another. According to the *Tokyo Agreement*, a copy of the *International Herald Tribune* on a French aeroplane is technically on French territory when the plane is in flight, even if the plane is in English airspace. Such complications, where they arise, have to be pointed out to a potential advertiser who must then assume all the consequent risks of proceeding. It is unusual for an international journal itself to be prosecuted.

International Herald Tribune does not have a monopoly of international space sales and operates in a fiercely competitive market pitching for business against such equally established titles as *The Economist* and *Newsweek*. It does, however, enjoy a reputation as a classic daily paper occupying a unique niche between specialist business publications, such as *The Financial Times*, and general interest publications, such as *Newsweek*. The *International Herald Tribune* is

ISLE COLLEGE
RESOURCES CENTRE

read both for work reasons and for general interest and is regarded as an essential read for the international business community.

A major plank in the *International Herald Tribune*'s platform is the extensive research which it does into its own readership.

A full-page questionnaire is printed in the *International Herald Tribune* every four years and in 1993 this produced over 10000 responses. Readers were 'rewarded' indirectly for their participation to the tune of one US dollar per respondent donated to a nominated charity (over $10000 was donated). The *International Herald Tribune* is published and printed in France but is also transmitted simultaneously by land-line or satellite to ten other print sites around the world. Market research returns come in to each site and are subsequently weighted to reflect the circulation by print site. The research report covers such things as the occupation, income and education of *International Herald Tribune* readers. Readers are predominantly wealthy, well-educated, in management, responsible for significant purchasing decisions and work for international corporations. They also travel a lot.

To supplement the quantitative research, the *International Herald Tribune* commissioned Research Services Ltd to carry out a small number of in-depth interviews in France, Germany, Italy and Switzerland. English-speaking expatriates were deliberately excluded from this survey which targeted *International Herald Tribune* readers for whom English was not their first language. The subsequent report (*Visibility Impact and Value of Advertising*) compared attitudes and opinions relating to the *International Herald Tribune* and other international publications such as *The Financial Times*, *Business Week* and *Time*.

In addition, *International Herald Tribune* sponsored the *1992 International Air Travel Survey* which was carried out at the international departure gates of 20 major western European airports during October and November 1992 and netted over 40000 responses.

Armed with the results of these three substantial pieces of research, space representatives were well placed to argue the merits of advertising in the *International Herald Tribune*.

Media buyers, however, can be tough negotiators and they press hard for concessions. The *International Herald Tribune* responds to this pressure with a programme of added-value incentives as do the other international titles. This may include free copies, run-on advertisements and sponsored copies.

Source: based on a lecture given by Sarah Hill, the International Herald Tribune *'s UK Classified Advertising Manager, at Schiller International University, Waterloo, London*

2 The *Independent*

When the advertising world becomes uncertain of the future of an advertising vehicle, that uncertainty is reflected in the reduced space sold. This was the difficult situation facing the *Independent* in the early months of 1994. One advertising director was quoted in the *Evening Standard* as saying: 'The truth is that we cannot include the *Independent* in any long-term plans. . . . We can't be committed to a newspaper when we don't know if it is still going to be around next month.' Another said: 'It's not just the uncertainty about the paper's future, but also its direction that is of concern.' A fear was that Mirror Group Newspapers (then seeking to take control of the *Independent*) would radically change the style of the paper. Media buyers, unwilling to commit ahead, were tending to buy (if at all) on a purely last-minute basis.

9.9 The media content (editorial, programming and advertisements)

In a newspaper there are both advertisements and editorial matter; on radio and television the programming is the equivalent of the editorial. In either case anything which is not an advertisement is either editorial or programming and it is usually easy to tell the difference. Media owners are in any case required to make it clear although the growing practice of advertorials is giving some concern. Advertisements differ from editorial not only in their purpose but also in their origin, and that distinction must be preserved.

However, the role of the editor as 'gatekeeper' must not be overlooked – an editor can insist on an advertisement being reworded and can even refuse it altogether. In 1993 Mandi Norwood, Editor of *Company* magazine, refused to carry advertisements for the controversial United Colors of Benetton campaign, even going to the extent of canvassing the opinions of *Company* staff beforehand.

It can work both ways and advertisers can withdraw their support from a publication if they do not like the way it is being handled. The *Daily Mirror* coverage of a story concerning the Princess of Wales is a case in point.

In late 1993 the *Daily Mirror* and *Sunday Mirror* printed photographs of the Princess of Wales that had been taken without her consent by a secret camera in a health club where she was a member. This was considered a serious breach of journalistic standards creating a media story in its own right and giving ammunition to the *Mirror*'s rival, the *Sun*. The *Sun* took great pleasure in devoting pages of editorial copy to criticising the *Mirror* and in a front-page feature on 9 November 1993 it listed three major advertisers (the RAC, Autoglass and the Britannia Building Society) who had issued critical statements even to the extent of saying that they were dropping the *Mirror* from their media schedules. The *Evening Standard* of the same day ran a similar feature under the headline 'Advertising backlash begins', but balanced the story with the statement that two companies (HMV and Vauxhall) had both said that they did not base advertising decisions on editorial policy.

9.10 The variety of advertising

Manufacturer to consumer advertising

Manufacturer to consumer advertising (MCA) is one of the most common types. It may be designed to promote a specific product (**brand advertising**) or the company as a whole (**corporate advertising**).

Retailer to consumer advertising

Retailer to consumer advertising (RCA) serves a different purpose. Whereas a manufacturer is interested in selling a particular brand, a retailer is interested in getting people in to the store (regardless of what they buy). The success of retailer advertising is attested to by the fact that many shoppers have a stronger sense of loyalty to a particular store than they do to a particular brand. If the brand they prefer is not in stock they are as likely to choose another brand as they are to go off to a different store.

Joint advertising

Joint advertising occurs when a manufacturer joins together with a retailer to share the cost of an advertising campaign to their mutual advantage. A provider of package holidays, for example, may join forces with a high-street travel agency to promote holidays. Two manufacturers of complementary and non-competitive products, such as washing machines and washing powders, may act together.

Industry-based advertising

Industry-based advertising looks like manufacturers' advertising but its motivation is different. When manufacturers advertise, they usually do so in competition with each other: one brand of instant coffee against another brand. Sometimes, however, firms within an industry may recognise that the real competition is not with each other but with a rival substitute product (butter producers may identify margarine as the real competition). In such cases, competitors join together against a common threat and produce such slogans as 'Butter is good for you'. Such advertising usually does not mention individual brands and is sometimes called **generic advertising** to distinguish it from brand advertising. Industry-based advertising is usually done through a trade association or industry marketing body to which member firms subscribe.

Corporate advertising

Corporate advertising may serve a wider market than just consumers and may serve non-business corporations as well. It may have its place within the context of a public relations campaign and is concerned with:

- The **identity** of the company (who it is, what it does, what its philosophy is, etc.).
- The **image** of the company (how the company is actually perceived by its audiences).

Corporate advertising is usually pro-active but may sometimes be used in a reactive way if the company has been getting a bad press.

Recruitment advertising

Recruitment advertising is used by both business and non-business organisations. It usually concerns employment recruiting, but a college may use it to recruit students or a church may use it to attract new members. The Legal Aid Board case study in chapter 11 discusses a recruitment campaign.

Non-business advertising

Non-business advertising covers a very wide field from charities, churches and political parties (**cause advertising**) to local and central government and services, such as ambulance and fire brigade. A major entrant in recent years has been educational marketing. A great deal of this is recruitment advertising, but it may also be used to promote new services or facilities.

Display and classified advertising

Display advertisements are designed to attract immediate attention and are spread throughout the editorial matter where they might be more readily noticed by the reader. Classified advertisements look more like entries in a directory such as *Yellow Pages* and are often just listed alphabetically under a variety of headings in the classified section. Publications seem to differ as to just where they draw the line and some have semi-display advertisements as well. It is not uncommon for a publication to have two separate sales departments to sell space.

A page of classified advertising can look very boring and has been called the 'graveyard of advertising'. Nevertheless, it is important and can produce upwards of 35 per cent of advertising revenue. Classified ads are really confined to print, but some radio stations run 'bulletin boards' for local announcements and Teletext on television performs a similar function.

9.11 The future of the media

It is beyond the scope of this book (not to say this author) to even attempt to predict precisely how the media will look in, say, five or ten years' time. But it will certainly be very different from today. Already there is the possibility of *The Financial Times* becoming an electronic newspaper. The previously distinct technologies of telephone and television now have the ability to merge; with the benefit of interactive technology and a camera eye incorporated into the TV set, we will be able to talk to and see our friends and business partners on screen. Hybrid media – a mixture of telephone, television and computer – are technically possible. The development of digitalisation and fibre optics promises the capacity to push hundreds, if not thousands, of signals in both directions at the same time and talk of the Information Superhighway is already commonplace. The prospect of having hundreds of channels to choose from (not forgetting BT's experimental video-on-demand movie service) is both exciting and daunting.

There is a great deal of optimism and enthusiasm in all of this, but there are still problems unresolved. Ownership rules will have to be revised to take consideration of the need for more cross-media ownership. A dominant technology will have to be accepted (possibly through government decree – with a great deal of lobbying the while) even though we may go through a period similar to that which affected the British domestic video market in the early days when VHS (the winner) battled with the Beta and Philips systems for market supremacy. (What system will the proposed Channel 5 work on?) The Superhighway will have to be put in place, possibly underground like cable television, possibly overhead like British Telecom.

The continued growth of satellite cannot be ruled out either. There are many possible distribution systems and, pessimistically, as media correspondent Torin Douglas put it in *Marketing Week* (4 March 1994), 'unrealistic ambitions, too many rivals and not enough customers'. This latter point raises another spectre at the feast. Whatever the technology will be, it will not be terrestrial and fears have been raised in the US that terrestrial television will become a second-class medium, poorly funded and poorly provided, as those who can afford it turn to the new multimedia option. Homes which either cannot afford the new technology or who are not yet wired into the Superhighway run the risk of becoming a 'media underclass'.

What might all of this mean for marketing? Home-shopping channels such as QVC will almost certainly increase and at least one writer has hazarded the view that the shopping centre with all its capacity for generating traffic noise and fumes will go into decline as more and more people choose to shop from home. The projected capacity of television viewers to preselect what they want to see and to educate their television sets to track channels looking for the right programmes could be extended to include commercials as well ('I don't own a pet, so please don't show me any commercials for petfood.' – 'I am thinking of buying a new family car so can I see all the ads for that please.'). Personalised on-screen messages (the same message going into every home but with the householder's name on screen – a sort of video mail-merge) are on the cards. Television audiences will become more fragmented as choice increases and the capacity to more accurately target a viewing audience should improve as a result.

At the business level, there is likely to be an increase in video-conferencing and a greater use of the screen to support telephone selling (easy to sell across the catalogue if the person can actually see the products on screen as well). A whole range of business functions currently possible but limited by the storage and transmission facilities of contemporary technology are going to be liberated as these hurdles are overcome.

Read the screen

'View the page, read the story. That's what you do on paper. Why not do it on screen?' So runs an advertisement for one of the latest developments in media technology – the *Evening Standard*'s electronic newspaper *Business Day*. Claiming superiority over earlier 'text-fed' electronic papers, the *Evening Standard* offers an enhanced image of the actual newspaper page exactly as it would be seen by a reader who bought it from a newstand. Subscribers can access stories on a PC by the click of a mouse and there is also an index which will take the reader directly to the required story without the need to 'turn the pages'. Each new edition (the *Evening Standard* has three editions a day and *Business Day* is a multi-page section of this) is available on screen immediately it is printed and, obviously, much earlier than it could be purchased in its traditional paper format.

9.12 Summary

- For advertisers, there are six media groups which can be further divided into vehicles.
- Media can be thought of as time-based or as space-based but for regulatory purposes they are split into press and print and broadcast.
- Media owners work hard to develop and maintain their audiences and to sell time and space to advertisers.
- There is a wide range of different types of advertisements to be found.
- There are going to be great changes in the media over the next decade, but precisely what those changes will be it is too early to say.

9.13 Assignments

1. Draw up a list of the media characteristics of each of the six groups.

2. Do an audit of the local media in your area and, where possible, indicate the type of audience that each might have.

3. Discuss where you think television is likely to be in ten years' time.

10 Planning an advertising campaign

10.1
Introduction

This chapter looks at the general aspects of campaign planning, such as developing the brief and selecting the media. Specific aspects are dealt with in chapter 11 (space-based campaigns) and chapter 12 (time-based campaigns). Practices and procedures do vary from in-house to agency and from one agency to another, but what follows is typical.

10.2
Developing the brief

The first step is developing the brief (see also chapter 4.8). The brief sets out what is to be done: the methods to be used, the time-scale involved, the budget allowed for and so on. Even if the work is done in-house there will still need to be a brief.

There will in fact be several briefs (or one main brief with several derivative briefs). Here we look at background briefs, media briefs and creative briefs. There can be others emanating from these. The media brief could give rise to a separate buying brief and the creative brief to an artist's brief. This can be seen as a hierarchy with the main brief at the top providing the overall broad picture with derivative briefs at the lower levels covering a narrower field of operations but going into more detail. To start the process we need a draft brief.

The draft brief

The **draft brief** is initiated through a process of discussion between the agency and the client. It outlines the general problem and is just a starting point which can be negotiated and renegotiated to produce the final brief. The client may have very fixed ideas at this stage or only very general ideas; ideally, the client should have very clear business and marketing objectives without being too rigid as to the ways of achieving them. This gives the agency a good basis for proceeding.

The agency representatives take the preliminary ideas back to the agency for further discussion. Ideas from the media team and the creative team can then feedback and influence the final brief. In any case, even the final brief is only the beginning of the campaign development process. Its purpose is not to tell everybody what to do but to point them in the right direction – its job is to clarify the problem rather than to specify the solution.

Account executives

It is in the development of the brief that we first meet the account executives (or account managers). Saatchi & Saatchi in *The Brief* (a guide for prospective clients) describes the account handler as 'the guardian of the entire process' and the account planner as 'the keeper of the strategy'. Sometimes one person will do both jobs.

The account executives are sometimes called the 'suits', because they are business people who dress and act appropriately, or the 'bag carriers', because they carry the proposals to the client. Account executives form part of a larger group, the account team, which also includes the marketing, media and creative specialists allocated to the account. The account team is supported by research and production.

The **account handler** liaises with the client and is responsible for the day-to-day management and running of the account. This involves such things as:

- Financial control.
- Status or progress reports.
- Providing information to key agency departments such as media planning.
- Seeing the entire project through its various stages from beginning to end.

Together with the **account planner**, the account handler also works out the basic strategy.

The account planner has responsibility for:

- Establishing the campaign objectives.
- Establishing the basic principles which lead to the advertising solutions of the client's problems.
- Developing the creative brief.

The account planner is also responsible for commissioning research and analysing and interpreting market data.

Draft brief to final brief

Getting from draft brief to final brief might involve the following steps:

- Account executives develop the draft brief for presentation to the media and creative departments.
- With these departments they develop the creative brief and the media brief.
- The media planners and the creatives then work up their own proposals and, in turn, present these back to the account executives for a roundtable critical discussion. As the creatives do not usually present their ideas directly to the client, it is really up to the account executives to represent the client's interest and to act as devil's advocate on the client's behalf.
- When the team as a whole is satisfied that its proposals are such that they can be sold to the client, then the account executives present them for client approval, albeit with some modifications.

Getting client approval is so crucial that it will pay the handlers and planners to take some time to rehearse their presentations carefully. A poor pitch can sink a well-thought-out campaign and failing to anticipate a client's questions and objections is one hallmark of poor preparation.

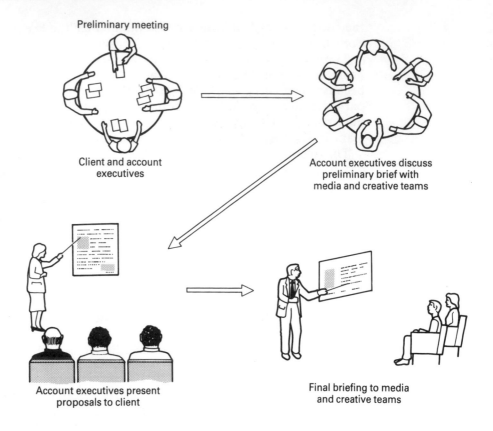

Fig. 10.1   Developing the brief

Incidentally, it is not necessary to begin with one brief only. Two or more sets of advertising proposals may be considered and it would not be unknown for two different campaign proposals to be presented to the client. It has even been rumoured that weaker proposals have been deliberately put to a client first to clear the air for the stronger proposals which the agency really wants to promote.

Figure 10.1 outlines the process so far.

The final brief

According to Saatchi & Saatchi (in *The Brief*), a good brief should be:

- **Objective**   Clearly supported by sound evidence and research.

- **Critical**   The facts should be clearly established and their relevance and importance spelled out.

- **Creative**   The client's problems should be addressed in a lively and imaginative way.

- **Analytical**   The client's needs should be clearly drawn out and objectives should be developed which meet those needs.

Of these, the last is probably the most important in driving the rest of the campaign. It is essential for the client to spell out his own objectives clearly and for these to be properly understood and addressed by the account team. Sometimes a client may need help in getting the objectives clarified and this might be another important outcome of those early meetings between client and account executives.

Signing off confirms the brief as being agreed and authoritative; all previous versions of the brief are now void and should, to avoid confusion, be destroyed. The brief can now be finalised and presented back to the media and creative teams. Although these two teams can work independently of each other, it is a good idea to bring everybody together for the final briefing session. This session is a combination of a verbal presentation (to generate enthusiasm) and the written document (for later reference).

The final briefing document will probably have three key sections:

- The background to the creative and media briefs.
- The creative brief.
- The media brief.

All briefs relating to the same account will have some information in common. If the account is for a branded product this information should include the client's name, the name of the brand and the date on which the brief was issued. There would also be a job title and possibly a job number. The names of personnel representing the different departments should also be included (the account handler, the creative representative, the media representative, etc.).

The background brief

The background brief, which may not be very long, should include the following (if the product is a new one some of this information will not yet be available):

- Key characteristics of the brand.
- Performance so far.
- An account of previous advertising and promotional support.
- An analysis of the competition.
- Any legal or other restrictions as to how the product might be advertised and what might be said about it.

The creative brief

The creative brief will include:

- The type of campaign that the client wants (for example, a sustained press campaign or a one-off TV advertisement).
- The target audience.
- The advertising objectives (for example, to build brand awareness).
- Any mandatory inclusions (such as the client's logo or any specific claim about the product which must be mentioned) and the desired brand image.
- The creative budget and the time-scale involved.
- The single minded proposition.

The single minded proposition

Perhaps the most important part of the creative brief is the so-called **single minded proposition** (SMP), together with the justification for, or substantiation of, that proposition.

The SMP is based on the idea that it is better to say one thing clearly and convincingly than it is to try to say a number of different things. The SMP must aim to do two things:

- Differentiate the product from its rivals so as to make it both memorable and desirable.
- Motivate the target audience into the desired response.

The SMP must be rooted in the factual, critical and analytic background to the creative brief. It may relate to:

- Product characteristics.
- User characteristics.
- Ways of making the product.
- Ways of using the product.
- Benefits of using the product.
- Costs of not using the product.
- Strength of the product.
- Weaknesses of rival products.

The SMP may relate to anything so long as it is true, single-minded, compelling, lively and memorable. Ideas for SMPs can come from clients, agency staff, research, testing competitors' products, brain-storming sessions or any one of a dozen different sources.

The media brief

The media brief will include:

- The specification of the target audience.
- The media of choice.
- The media budget and time-scale involved.
- The client's marketing and advertising objectives.
- The availability of current research material.

Printing and circulation of the brief

Before the work of preparing the agreed campaign begins, copies of all sections of the brief must go to all relevant departments including production and traffic control. Final copies should always be signed off by a senior executive and earlier copies destroyed.

10.3 Production and traffic control departments

Production is the task of converting the approved creative ideas into a form which can be used by the media of choice: camera-ready originals for printing, broadcast-standard sound tapes for radio and so on. Many agencies have their own production departments for printed advertisements. Radio stations offer production facilities and agencies would normally take advantage of these rather than attempt to make the commercials themselves. There are many specialist production houses for

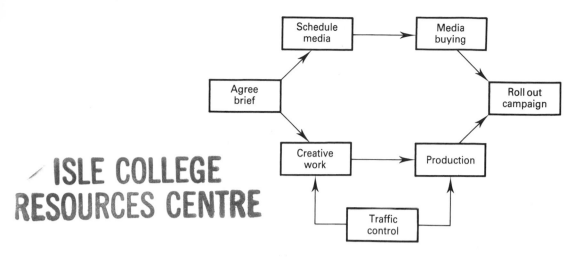

Fig. 10.2 From brief to roll out

ISLE COLLEGE
RESOURCES CENTRE

television commercials and an agency would put a television advertisement out to one of these. With cinema, a major contractor such as Rank Screen Advertising would be able to offer advice and assistance.

Traffic controllers are found not only in the agency world but also in publishing. A traffic controller, or traffic manager, needs to be single-minded and determined. The traffic controller has to make sure that everything comes in on time and to budget, and that all deadlines are met. Media people accept deadlines and budgets as a matter of course but, unfortunately, there are creatives who regard such things as mere distractions and who do need to be cajoled and even bullied. However, a traffic controller can be more than just a taskmaster and is often a tactical problem-solver doing such things as booking extra studio time if that should be necessary.

Figure 10.2 shows the process in diagram form.

10.4 The size of the campaign

There are various ways of stating the size of an advertising campaign. The concepts involved can be used to set the parameters for the campaign and also measure its effectiveness. The media planner in deciding where, when and how often an advertisement appears will have all of these concepts in mind.

The most common terms are OTS, reach and frequency:

- **OTS (opportunity to see)** It can be used to specify the number of people who get an OTS once or it can be multiplied up – each person being given, for example, four OTSs. An OTS is just that – an opportunity. Whether people do actually see the advertisement is a different question. **OTH (opportunity to hear)** is the radio equivalent.

- **Reach** Reach is sometimes also referred to as **coverage** (or even **net coverage**). It is the number of people in a target group who have the opportunity to see (or hear) the advertisement at least once. It is usually expressed as a percentage.

- **Frequency** This refers to the total number of times during a campaign that each individual target group member is exposed to the advertisement.

Generally speaking, for the same budget, reach (or coverage) gives more people fewer OTSs and frequency gives fewer people more OTSs.

Other terms to keep in mind are:

- **Frequency distribution** This is a more detailed concept than frequency alone and describes how many people in a target group saw an advertisement how many times. It could be something like 10 per cent did not see it at all, 30 per cent saw it once, 40 per cent saw it twice and the remaining 20 per cent saw it at least three times.

- **Cover** This is the number of times an advertisement is seen (or heard). **Net cover** is the number of people who see it at least once. **Four plus cover (4 + cover)** is the number who see it at least four times. **Gross cover** is the total number of times the advertisement is seen.

- **Impact** A single impact (or impression) is the exposure of one person in the target audience to the advertisement. **Total impact** summarises the total effect of a campaign, taking both reach and frequency into account: for example, 80 per cent of the target audience saw the advertisement three times each on average.

10.5 Media planning and media buying

These two functions are usually carried out by different people and are said to involve different personality attributes. Planners tend to be more deliberate and methodical, whereas buyers are often more opportunistic and intuitive. Buyers have to be good negotiators, whereas planners do not. Problems can arise, however, when the planner sets up a schedule which the buyer finds difficult to achieve or when the buyer wants to take independent action which modifies the original plan. Some commentators have even talked about 'planning versus buying' rather than planning and buying. The work may be divided between in-house and out-of-house or between two agencies with the agency handling the account putting the buying out to another. The media independent has an important role to play here as a buying house (or shop), although some media independents can handle planning as well.

Planning involves two main stages: the inter-media decision and the intra-media decision.

The inter-media decision

The inter-media decision consists of deciding which group, or groups, of media (see chapter 9.1) to use. There are single medium campaigns which stick to one group only and mixed-media campaigns using two groups or more.

Each media group should be looked at within the context of the advertiser's objectives, time-scale and budget. Even competitors' advertising campaigns can influence the decision, although here there are two different schools of thought. Some planners may go for a 'run with the pack' approach of doing what everybody else is doing, whilst others deliberately choose to be different.

The following list, though not exhaustive of the considerations, gives some idea of what to think about:

- **Permanency** One of the strengths of print lies in its relative permanency. Whereas a television commercial lasts for only a few seconds and may be missed, a printed advertisement lasts for as long as the publication lasts. A single insertion of a print advertisement may have many chances of being seen, whereas a single airing of a television commercial has only one.

- **Length and complexity of message** Because of their permanency, print advertisements can be referred back to and reread. There is no need for the reader to take in the entire message at the first reading nor is the reader required to take the message in during a fixed time slot such as television or the cinema requires. Because of this, the message can be longer and more detailed. Advertisements which make use of a questionnaire-type response coupon clearly are intended for print.

- **Audience attention** With television advertising there is the danger of lost audience attention. This often occurs because the audience uses the commercial breaks to do something else or to 'zap' around seeing what is on other channels. This is less of a problem in print because of the opportunities which exist for referring back and rereading.

- **Colour, sound and movement** Colour is now commonplace in newspapers, although magazines usually have better colour reproduction than papers. However, television and cinema will always have the edge, together with the dramatic impact of both sound and movement. Sound and movement offer far more creative opportunities including, of course, the chance to use animation. Sound permits authoritative or humorous voice-overs, the use of music and the development of memorable jingles as well as dialogue. The use of the human voice and sound effects allows additional emphasis not possible on the silent page.

- **Production lead times** As a general rule, it takes much longer to create and produce a commercial for television or cinema than it does for print. It is far easier and quicker to modify a print commercial (even to replace it altogether) in mid-campaign than it is to modify a film or television commercial.

- **Costs** Television and cinema commercials are more expensive to produce. It has been estimated that on a second-for-second comparison a television commercial costs more to make than just about anything else seen on television.

- **Advertising copy deadlines** This is the closing date for getting the commercial to the media in time for it to be printed or broadcast. Newspapers are **short-dated** and can take delivery a matter of hours before publication. Magazines are **long-dated** and may require delivery weeks ahead of publication. Television and radio stations have set deadlines but may (on payment of a late-delivery penalty charge) accept material later. In situations where it is necessary to move quickly (in a crisis situation, for example, or to stimulate the slow-moving sales of tickets to a concert) papers, with a short deadline, have the clear advantage. In fact, wherever there is a need to act quickly, or to make last-minute changes to advertising copy, media with short deadlines always have the edge over media with long ones.

- **The audience environment**   Roadside posters are seen by people on the move, whereas cinema commercials are seen in a much more relaxed environment. Radio ads can be heard in the car or as a background to some other activity. Newspaper ads might be read in the train or at home. Thinking about the conditions under which an advertisement will be seen or heard can affect not only the choice of media but the creative concepts used.

Other factors affecting the inter-media decision

Media owners (and media groups) run their own promotional campaigns. The Newspaper Publishers Association ran a series of full-page advertisements throughout 1993 extolling the virtues of a press campaign.

Media representatives themselves can affect the inter-media decision, although in practice they are more likely to affect the intra-media decision (see below). Nevertheless, in trying to sell space in say, a newspaper, a sales representative may have to present arguments as to why print would work better than television.

The wholesale and retail trade can also affect the inter-media decision, particularly in the **fast-moving consumer goods (FMCG)** sector. Retailers like to see a product well supported by advertising and may indicate that they look more favourably on a television campaign than on a print campaign. Rumours abound in the advertising world and one rumour is that some manufacturers of FMCGs throw a very small amount of television behind a predominantly newspaper campaign to impress distributors. Sales representatives can 'truthfully' say, 'Oh yes, we are giving this product television support.' A relatively cheap way of doing this for an established brand is to rerun an old commercial and buy up any time which is still available at the lowest rates. Production costs are out of the way and only air-time has to be paid for.

Single medium and mixed media campaigns

It is sometimes thought that running a mixed media campaign should be considered only if a totally successful campaign can be run in the medium of first choice and there is still enough money to move into a second or third. Splitting a limited budget between media groups may just result in two half-campaigns with insufficient impact. There is an alternative view which follows the 'multiplier' argument to the effect that a combined campaign can produce better results in total, as one medium actually reinforces the impact of the other, as in a 'hearts and minds' campaign.

Choosing between a single medium or a mixed media campaign raises a number of issues:

- **Production costs**   Will the budget run to both a print and a television commercial, for example?

- **Transfer**   Will the creative concept transfer from one medium to another? Animation requires movement and the effect may be lost with a single print image.

- **Impact**   Will splitting the budget between two media undermine the potential impact of either or both of them?

- **Reach and frequency**   Will the campaign reach different audiences through the different media or will the same people be reached both times, thus increasing the frequency of exposure to the message? Is it the intention to try to reach two separate audiences, anyway?

- **Scheduling**   Developing a co-ordinated schedule is obviously going to be more difficult the more media groups are involved.

A 'share of mind' campaign might be better in newspapers where rational arguments can be developed; television (which can appeal more to the emotions) might be preferred for a 'share of heart' campaign. Mixed television and magazine campaigns can be referred to as 'heart and mind' campaigns. Alan Smith (an international periodical consultant) told delegates to the conference Magazines '94 that the two-pronged 'hearts and minds' campaign combining television with magazines can increase sales by 14 per cent compared with a pure television campaign.

10.6 Intra-media selection

After the media group (or groups) has been selected, the next stage is the intra-media selection. If the decision is for a newspaper campaign, which papers (or vehicles) are going to be used? The following points with respect to each vehicle must be considered:

- Editorial stance and editorial coverage.
- Quality of reproduction.
- Size and composition of audience.
- Cost per insertion.
- The **cost per thousand (CPT)** of reaching the target group. This might be expressed as cost per thousand housewives, for example, or cost per thousand males.

To a large extent, the above factors are quantifiable; weights can be attached to different editorial or promotional activities and computers can be used to rank media in order of usefulness to a particular campaign. In spite of this, many planners and buyers prefer to use their own insights gained over years of media-watching and analysis and not to rely too much on computers except for the obvious time-saving tasks, such as calculating CPT and monitoring circulation and audience figures.

Media planning is not an exact science and experience and personal judgement are always important. The two extremes of trying to reduce everything to numbers on the one hand and depending entirely on hunch, judgement, flair and intuition on the other should, however, be avoided.

10.7 Cost per thousand (CPT)

It is not very helpful to think only in terms of the cost of an insertion, although the question of whether it can be afforded is relevant. The size and quality of the audience must also be considered. The size of the audience is measured, for example, by the number of readers a magazine has. The quality of the audience is measured by the proportion of those readers who are likely to at least consider buying the advertiser's product. Regardless of how low the cost per thousand of reaching the readership is, it is of no value if that readership is of poor quality.

The following case study is a simplified model of what might happen and shows how this might be looked at.

Case Study

The princesses and the frogs

Suppose that you had a target market of single women aged 30 or under and that research figures told you that in your market area there were some 500 000 such women. Your objective is to set up a magazine campaign which gives each one of these women an OTS (opportunity to see) an advertisement at least once. You want to achieve this result at the lowest possible cost per thousand (CPT).

The publication which seems most suitable has a readership of 1 000 000 and a full-page advertisement in it costs £5 000. You are informed that 20 per cent of its readership fall into your target category. You can think of the 20 per cent as good *prospects* (people who are likely to respond positively to your campaign; some advertisers call them *princesses*). The other 80 per cent are poor prospects who are not likely to respond (they are sometimes called *frogs*).

The cost of reaching 1 000 readers is £5. However, this includes the cost of reaching all those frogs. So how much is it really costing you to reach those 200 000 princesses? The answer is, of course, £25 per thousand. How do other publications compare?

A second publication might have a readership of only 800 000 and charge you £4 500 per page. However, this publication might tell you that 25 per cent of its readers are single women aged 30 or under. A simple calculation shows that the cost per thousand of reaching these princesses is now only £22.50 and the second publication is the better buy: £22.50 per thousand is better than £25.

However, neither of these publications alone can offer you what you want. You want to reach 500 000 women and each of these magazines can offer you only 200 000. If you advertised in both you would reach only 400 000 at most and, in fact, you would probably not do that. It is possible that some of these women read both publications. Suppose that 50 000 of them do this (it does not mean that they buy both publications, they may have a swapping arrangement), then to avoid double-counting you must subtract 50 000 from your total. If you advertise in both publications you will give an OTS to no more than 350 000 at a total cost of £9 500 (about £27 per thousand on average).

But you still have to find a way to give an OTS to another 150 000 people. You must look at other publications and it may be that to achieve your objective you have to go into four, possibly five altogether. The ability to rank the publications in the order in which they can make the best possible contribution to your campaign objective is vital. Go into the wrong four or five and you may be paying a lot of money to talk to a lot of frogs.

Suppose that with four publications you could reach 90 per cent of your target for £18 000 and that going into a fifth publication in the hope of picking up the other 10 per cent would cost you another £4 000. The marginal cost would be a staggering £80 per thousand and difficult to justify. (By the time you are looking at the fifth publication it is very likely that you will have reached a large proportion of its readership already through the first four.)

It might be more effective to use the extra money repeating the advertisement in one of the first four publications. The second publication, for example, might let you have two insertions at a discount. It would be worth trying a bit of negotiating and rethinking the campaign objective. Even settling for 90 per cent of your original target and saving the cost of a fifth insertion might be attractive.

The above case study is based on the (not very realistic) target of 100 per cent coverage or reach (with the option of forgoing the fifth insertion and settling for a reach of 90 per cent). However, it might have been thought that one OTS would lack impact and that it might be better to go into each of the first two magazines twice, giving 350 000 people at least two OTSs at a cost of £19 000 instead of giving 500 000 people at least one OTS at a cost of £22 000. The first option maximises reach and the second frequency. They could be expressed in percentage terms: 100 per cent getting one OTS against 70 per cent getting two OTSs.

10.8 Media schedules

A schedule is a plan using a combination of different vehicles in the chosen media group with a specified number of insertions in each vehicle on preselected dates. Computers can be used to draw up schedules and to evaluate them against the chosen target group in terms of coverage of that group and cost per thousand. The danger of depending too much on a computer is that it might throw up one particular schedule which meets all the weightings etc. fed into it without giving you an opportunity to consider alternative schedules. In practice, you might want to set up three or four different schedules and use the computer to evaluate these against your chosen numerical criteria whilst giving yourself the freedom to use your own judgement on matters which are less easy to quantify.

Media salespeople, once they are aware of your requirements, may themselves suggest media schedules (naturally favouring their own title). There is no harm in being prepared to discuss these as long as you recognise the bias.

Title	Week 1	Week 2	Week 3	Week 4	Week 5	Week 6
Daily Mail	√		√	√		√
Daily Express	√	√		√	√	
Today		√	√		√	√

Fig. 10.3   Six-week newspaper campaign

Schedules can be visually displayed using a grid. If a mixed media campaign is planned, it is better to use a separate grid for each type of medium.

Figure 10.3 shows such a grid for a six-week newspaper campaign.

10.9 Summary

- The first step in developing a campaign is the brief. This may go through several stages before getting client approval and being finalised. At this stage it may be subdivided into a background brief, a media brief and a creative brief. There may, in turn, be other derivative briefs.
- Selecting the right media group (or groups) and then, from within this group, selecting the right vehicles leads to the preparation of a media schedule which can be represented in the form of a grid.

10.10 Assignments

1. Think of a good from the FMCG sector and develop a brief for it.

2. Discuss the relative advantages and disadvantages of different media groups.

3. Draw up a media schedule for a consumer durable in the furniture range of products. You could take any consumer durable.

11 Planning space-based campaigns

11.1 Introduction

This chapter looks more closely at campaign planning for the space-based media. It should be noted that the references to the creative and production sides of a printed advertisement can also be applied to other printed matter such as leaflets and direct-mail letters.

11.2 Buying newspaper and magazine space

Space sizes

There are standard sizes which newspapers and magazines offer. Display advertisements may be quarter-page, half-page and full-page and there are also eighth-page advertisements and double-page spreads. Magazines can even offer three-page spreads (or four) with the benefit of fold-out pages.

In practice, it is possible to negotiate an advertisement of any size and shape. Half-pages may be **landscape** (occupying the top or bottom half of the page) or **portrait** (occupying the right or left side). Quarter-pages may be top-left, top-right, bottom-left or bottom-right; a quarter-page may also be set up to run from the top to the bottom of the page but a quarter of its width and so on. Figure 11.1 illustrates some of these possibilities.

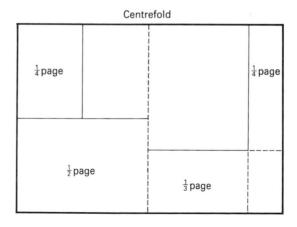

Fig. 11.1 Advertisement page sizes

Advertisement positions

Advertisements may be positioned at different places throughout most publications. Specifications include:

- **Run-of-paper (ROP)**   The editor places the advertisement anywhere it will fit in.

- **Outside back cover (OBC)**   This position is valued for the exposure it gives an advertisement even when the magazine is closed or when the magazine is being read on a train and the persons opposite can see the advertisement.

- **Inside front cover (IFC), inside back cover (IBC)**   Some magazines will even permit advertising on the **outside front cover (OFC)**.

- **Double centre-page spreads**   Double-page spreads obviously offer a larger surface. The centre spread is particularly attractive in newspapers and centre-stitched magazines because it is the only one printed on a single unbroken sheet of paper. Elsewhere it is printed on two separate sheets and true alignment does not always occur.

- **Facing matter (FM)**   This means that the advertisement will be opposite some editorial feature and not just opposite another advertisement. An FM position gives the advertisement a better chance of being read compared to one surrounded by other advertisements.

Preferred positions cost more money than ROP and are generally believed to be more effective. The higher price may, however, be just a question of supply and demand: there is only one back cover on a monthly and only twelve back covers a year. It may also be that advertisers who can pay the higher prices can also pay the best creatives so that preferred positions have the most attractive ads. Right-hand pages are also thought to be better than left-hand pages.

The rate card

Newspapers and magazines set out on their rate cards their prices for display and classified advertisements of different sizes, reduced charges for multiple insertions, higher charges for preferred positions and the special rate for 'bleeding' an advertisement (running the printed image off the edge of the paper so that there is no white margin).

Rate cards, however, are often treated simply as a basis for negotiation and an experienced buyer can secure substantial discounts (or other 'non-space benefits' such as free copies).

One situation where bargaining occurs is when a magazine is ready to go to press and one half-page of advertising space is still unsold. The magazine editor could, of course, fill the space with editorial matter but this would not bring in any revenue. A space salesperson might begin phoning round established advertisers offering the half-page at a discount. As the deadline for going to press draws nearer and the space remains unsold the price can be negotiated down to a fraction of its original level. A space buyer faced with such an opportunity may adjust the media plan to take advantage of it.

Rate cards are based on circulation figures: the larger the audience the higher the rate. Advertisers who place long-dated advertisements for 6 or 12 months ahead face the prospect that the readership may not be as big when the advertisement appears as when the space was bought. (Some buyers may buy the entire year's run of OBCs in a single purchase.) It could, of course, go the other way. Unfortunately, there have been instances of desperate media-owners being 'economical with the truth' when it comes to admitting that their sales are falling (although this is not possible when independent auditors such as ABC verify the circulation figures). A publication may try to push up the rate card to offset falling copy sales which is really trying to get the advertiser to pay more for less.

Case Study

The Legal Aid Board franchising initiative

The Legal Aid Board exists to ensure that people who cannot normally afford legal advice, assistance and representation can get it. As part of its remit, it is also responsible for assessing and paying the solicitors who carry out legal aid work.

In early 1993 the Board embarked on a franchising initiative which would accredit franchised firms of solicitors to a defined quality standard. Successful franchise holders would be empowered to make decisions autonomously without constantly referring back to the Board using powers traditionally only available to the Board itself. For this reason, it is essential to grant franchises only to applicants of the right calibre who can be relied upon to carry out the work of the Board in a relatively unsupervised way. To implement this radical development, 100 new positions were created for the people who would play the key role in setting up the franchise scheme. Recruiting these 100 people was the objective of the campaign.

Austin Knight, a specialist recruitment agency, had only nine weeks from beginning to end – not just to get the advertisements placed, but to get suitable applicants to the assessment centres for interview.

Establishing the concept

Although the main objective of the campaign was to attract recruits, it was recognised that the word 'franchising' in a legal context needed to be explained. The whole concept was new and unless potential applicants had a very clear understanding of its implications the wrong type of applicant might be attracted (or not enough of the right type). Additionally, the concept of franchising a legal service had to be publicised to a wider audience than just potential applicants It really needed to be explained throughout the legal profession. For these reasons, a print campaign was decided upon. A print campaign could be set up quickly and it allowed for a more detailed explanation. Also the use of graphics enabled the establishment of a 'logo style' stamp, or seal, with the words 'A SMOOTHER PATH TO JUSTICE' (see fig. 11.2).

Fig. 11.2   Legal Aid Board advertisement

This seal played an important part in branding the franchising system and it appeared on advertisements and documents throughout the campaign. The concept was further branded, throughout, on the basis of the Board's commitment to the provision of a quality, assured, value-for-money service.

The campaign was backed up with an information pack containing a comprehensive document explaining the franchising initiative. This was sent to all interested parties. It also contained a specially designed self-administered questionnaire which was intended to enable people to assess themselves against the job specification before applying.

The campaign

The initial advertising campaign was based on five national newspapers, two specialist legal titles and two ethnic minority publications. *The Sunday Times* and the Law Society's *Gazette* were the lead media vehicles.

Because the whole concept was so new, it was difficult to estimate the possible response. In case the lead campaign failed to produce enough response there was also a contingency media plan which would have brought in some strong regional titles reflecting the 13 area offices of the Board.

To establish the campaign with the Board's own personnel, it was first presented at a pre-launch seminar.

Response management

The contingency plan was not needed. Over 6 000 information packs were sent out and nearly 2 000 applications were received. This alone called for a major exercise in **response management**. Applicants were categorised into those who closely met the criteria, those who nearly met the criteria and those who failed to meet the criteria. Eventually, nearly 400 shortlisted candidates were invited to interviews which were held at assessment centres at five locations. The interviews lasted over ten days and Austin Knight was actively involved at all stages. All the posts were filled.

Editorial coverage

The potential for editorial exposure was seen at the outset. An article by the Board's training and development manager appeared in *The Sunday Times* a week before the campaign launch, followed by two local radio station interviews. The legal press took up the story and, when all was done, *Personnel Today* ran an editorial piece describing the success of the campaign.

Follow up

Despite the undoubted success of the campaign with all positions filled, Austin Knight was puzzled by the discrepancy between the 6 187 information packs sent out and the 1 908 applications received. Why had so many (nearly 70 per cent) not taken their applications further? Austin Knight carried out a sample survey and discovered, gratifyingly, that the self-assessment questionnaire had done its job. The majority of those who had not pursued their interest had self-selected themselves out of the race. They had effectively carried out their own preliminary screening.

Furthermore, Austin Knight discovered that many information packs had been sent for by people in the legal profession who simply wanted to know what it was all about. As one of the objectives of the campaign was to establish the validity of franchising in a legal context this, also, was a satisfactory outcome.

Source: Austin Knight

11.3 Difficult situations

In some situations the media buyer may be reluctant to buy space: for example, when an established publication is losing circulation and is rumoured to be on the brink of closing down or where a change of editorial control signals a new direction with a possible change in readership profile (see chapter 9.8). In either case the journal has an uncertain future and buyers may choose to hold back on long-dated bookings and go for last-minute bookings with the chance to negotiate the rate down. This, of course, simply adds to the publication's difficulties.

When a new publication comes out, the buyer has the problem of buying space without the benefit of circulation figures. Space salespeople may take round a **dummy** or **mock-up** of the first issue together with an indication of the proposed content of the next two issues. This gives space buyers some idea of what the new vehicle is going to be like. It does not tell them what the audience will be and for this they must rely on the estimates of the publisher. To encourage buyers, the publisher may discount the rates for the first two issues, offer free advertising in the third issue to advertisers who make firm purchases in the first two and even promise rebates if the circulation figures do not match expectations. If space is bought on the basis of sales of 500 000 copies and only 300 000 are actually sold, buyers will feel that thay have paid for something they did not get. (Getting a rebate for lower volume is possible, but not always guaranteed.)

11.4 Creating for print

The creative team

Creatives can begin work as soon as the brief has been agreed. They usually work in pairs. The **copywriter** thinks up the words (the copy) and the **art director** 'visualises' the copywriter's ideas and is responsible for the overall appearance of the advertisement.

Elements of the advertisement

The work of the creative team revolves around the various elements which make up the anatomy of the advertisement. These are the headline, the body copy, other display copy and visual elements such as logos, illustrations and photographs. These are all used together to come up with a solution to the creative brief.

- **Headline/strapline** This tells the 'big story' and aims to grab attention with only a few words. It is called **display copy** and is usually in the largest letters in the advertisement.

- **Body copy** This is the solid block of explanatory text.

- **Subheadings** These are subordinate headings to break up the body copy and provide reference points.

- **Captions** These are lines of explanatory text which appear under or near photographs or illustrations.

- **Slogans** These are designed to be memorable phrases to bring the product to mind. Slogans can be transferred from one advertisement to another even when different headlines and body copy are used.

Typefaces

Typefaces are the distinctive styles of the letters used. They are said to have different personalities and thus different psychological effects on the reader. Some are solid and reliable-looking whilst others can appear much more fragile and delicate. Typefaces may be thought of as masculine or feminine, traditional or modern. They may even suggest national differences: some typefaces can look very Germanic or Oriental even though the words themselves are in English.

The method of reproduction may influence the choice of typeface: some delicate typefaces do not reproduce well in newsprint, although they may be very effective on the higher quality paper of a magazine.

Selecting the right typeface(s) is usually the art director's job. He will wish to choose one which reinforces the basic message of the advertisement and he may choose different typefaces for headline, subheadings and body copy.

Copy fitting

Copy fitting (which can be done on a word processor) involves fitting the words required to the space available. The basic parameters are the size of the letters and the number of words. The size of the letters involves both their height (measured in **point sizes** – there are 72 points to the inch) and their width. Tall thin typefaces need more vertical space but less horizontal and short fat typefaces need less vertical space and more horizontal.

The typographer can take the space available and calculate how many **characters** (letters) will go into it or take a piece of copy and calculate how much space it will take up. Adjustments to both the point size and the number of characters may be necessary and it may be that all that is needed is to replace one long word with a shorter word of the same meaning. Subheads, captions and headlines all have to be fitted around the visuals to produce a pleasing whole and they may all be in different typefaces as well as different point sizes – they will all have to be measured for the space they will take up.

Composition

Composition is the skill of setting up the typeface taking account of the length of lines and other requirements. Some common terms are:

- **Ranged left (ragged right)**   Aligned to the left-hand margin with the right end of the lines of uneven length. Sometimes called **aligned left**.

- **Ranged right (ragged left)**   Aligned to the right margin so that the left end of the lines are of uneven length. Sometimes called **aligned right**.

- **Justified**   The space between characters and words is adjusted so that all of the lines are of equal length. Sometimes only the space between the words is adjusted and this can produce unsightly 'valleys' running down the lines of text.

- **Centred**   The space at the end of each line is redistributed between the beginning and the end to place the text in the middle.

11.5 The visual elements of the advertisement

Logos and trade marks

Logos and trade marks are the devices which a company uses to distinguish itself and its products. The logo is the emblem of the company, a badge which may consist of a group of letters such as BHS for British Home Stores or M & S for Marks and Spencer. When ICI split into two separate companies in 1993, it created a new logo for Zeneca. As Zeneca was completely unknown, the first Zeneca advertisements carried the ICI logo as well with the words 'Zeneca Garden Care formerly part of ICI'.

A trade mark is related to a particular product. A company may have one logo but several trade marks. When BMW acquired the Rover company, it also acquired the distinctive Rover marque which it continues to use. When a packaged product appears in an advertisement and the trade mark can be clearly seen on the package, there is no need to repeat it elsewhere.

Logos and trade marks are the property of the client and are protected in law. A creative cannot take it on himself to alter the client's devices. Inclusion of the trade mark may be mandatory.

Photographs and drawings

Photographs or drawings may be used and the choice may be influenced by the method of reproduction. Newspapers have come a long way since they were described as 'printed in soot on butcher's wrapping paper' but nevertheless they are still a disposable item and are not printed on the best papers using the best inks. Magazines score higher on these **production values**.

If the advertisement is for newspapers, then there is the risk that a photograph, particularly a small one, will not reproduce well and a skilfully rendered drawing may be much more effective. The mood of the advertisement can make a difference – humour can often be more easily conveyed with the use of cartoon figures than with photographs.

Other design options

Margins, white space, rules and bleeds are all design options which, if used correctly, can greatly enhance the finished advertisement.

- **Margins**   Margins are not only the empty spaces parallel to the edge of the page; they may also be left around the advertisement itself to provide a visual (and psychological) break from surrounding matter.

- **White space**   The area of the advertisement in which no text or visual matter occurs is called white space. Many advertisements are designed in such a way that 50 per cent or more of the available space is left white. The white-space concept counters the temptation to try to crowd too much into the advertisement.

- **Rules**   Typographical lines of various kinds can be used to frame copy or break it up into visual blocks of type. Rules can also be used to underline or overline a block of copy. Illustrations might be set in a ruled box.

- **Bleeds**   In planning to bleed an advertisement, it is essential not to set body copy too close to the edge. By the time the publication is printed and trimmed, ends of lines could be lost. A double-page spread designed as one complete image is 'bled into gutter' (where the adjoining pages come together) and care must be taken not to set vital matter too close to the inside as it could be pulled in and lost – a human face spread across the gutter could lose part of the nose. Perhaps worse is when the bleed does not extend far enough so that a white line splits the image.

11.6 Layouts and dummies

The layout shows the relationship between text and illustration on the page in a rough form. For the purpose of getting client approval a dummy (or mock-up) may be made. Dummies may also be used in researching the concept. Different layouts may be experimented with at this stage. With the advent of desk top publishing (DTP) and the ability to scan images, all this can be done on screen and elements of the advertisement can easily be moved around. Typefaces and point sizes are easily adjusted and the elements can be rotated to slope to left or right, or to be curved or staggered. A lot of this work is, however, still done manually and requires great patience and skill.

11.7 Researching the concept

Initial testing might involve no more than making a dummy, but it may also involve paying an artist to work the concept up closer to the real thing (or even all the way). The more the concept is worked up, the greater the cost involved, but the clearer it is to the **respondents**.

Respondents may be interviewed one at a time in a face-to-face structured or semi-structured interview or groups may be formed. The proposed advertisement could be shown in a folder (which gives this technique its name of **folder test**) or it could be pasted into a dummy newspaper or magazine. With the co-operation of the printer, it is even possible to arrange for the advertisement to be inserted into a limited run (for research purposes only) of a real magazine which, of course, makes it all the more realistic. Ideally, client approval for the concept should be obtained before large sums of money are spent researching it. A sceptical client might, however, insist on some research evidence before giving approval.

11.8 Preparing for print

Printing involves three clear stages – pre-printing, printing and print-finishing. The full process is well beyond the scope of this book but some general issues are discussed below.

- **Sizing the image**   Since photographs and illustrations are seldom supplied in the right size, the original image has to be **scaled**, i.e. enlarged or decreased, until it fits or **cropped**, i.e. unwanted areas cut away. Scaling up and down can be done by photomechanical transfer (PMT) using a process camera. The process camera can also be used for scaling blocks of copy.

- **Screening**   To avoid the severity of black and white, the black areas can be toned down by screening. This produces a printed area made up of many black dots evenly distributed over the white. The more black dots there are to the square inch the darker the effect will be and screens are graded so that different amounts of black are allowed through.

- **Other effects**   As a variation, an ink other than black can be used and a paper (or stock) other than white. Another variation would be to reverse the ink and paper to get white letters on a black surface, or **WOB (white out of black)**. Reversing the colours can also be done by PMT.

- **Assembly (paste up)** When PMTs of all the parts (headlines, body copy, etc.) have been produced, they can be cut out and assembled, or pasted up, on to a base board. Up to this point the headline, body copy, etc. are separate pieces (sometimes called the **mechanicals**) which must be carefully assembled for total accuracy is essential to produce **camera-ready copy** for delivery to the publisher or printer. Some agencies employ people who specialise in assembly.

  When the assembly is complete, it must be protected with a transparent overlay. This overlay can then be marked-up with instructions to the printer and it can even be coloured in by hand so that the printer can see the desired end product. The original itself must be protected at all times – the tiniest blemish may be picked up and printed. Damaged originals can be corrected (or retouched) by hand or electronically, but this is a very expensive process best avoided.

11.9 Colour printing

One-colour printing

In one-colour printing, one ink is used but screens allow for variations in shade and density. A non-white stock (paper) can create the appearance of a second colour at very little extra cost.

Two-colour printing

Two-colour printing enables the colours to be mixed to produce a third; using screens, different intensities of all three can be achieved. If illustrations have to appear on the same page as black copy, then one of the colours in the illustration must also be black otherwise three colours are being used. One way out of this is to print the copy in one of the colours used for the illustrations – this might be done for a leaflet.

Three-colour printing

Three-colour printing is possibly the least popular. The principle is the same, but it does not always look much better than two colour (which is cheaper) and for a little extra expense the superior four-colour process can be used.

Four-colour printing

Four-colour printing uses four **process** (standardised) colours: black, magenta (a pinkish red), cyan (a bright blue) and yellow. The colours in a coloured photograph or artwork are separated by computer into the four basic process colour values. This is called **colour separation**. Combinations of these four colours, using different screens, will make any tint needed for commercial printing (colour separation is really reversing the process of combination). The process will not handle gold or silver and these must be dealt with separately.

After the colours have been separated, four different images can be prepared. When the colours are laid down one at a time then the original reappears in all its glory.

A good printer will be able to get a perfect **register** with the colours being printed in exactly the same place one on top of the other. If the printing is out of register then the final image (the full colour of the original) will be blurred and unattractive. Accurate register is vital and when newspapers and magazines offer colour printing a media buyer will be concerned with their ability to get such things right.

11.10 Print processes

A variety of printing techniques are in use for newspaper and magazine work and for promotional work such as leaflets.

Letterpress

Letterpress is a form of relief printing. It is the oldest and by now probably the least used method. The printing is done from a raised surface to which the ink is applied and transferred directly to the paper. The original is in reverse (as you would see it in a mirror) so that the resulting print is 'right reading'. For long runs and a professional appearance the printing surfaces are made of metal. Rubber stamps are a cheap form of relief printing.

Offset lithography

Offset lithography uses a flat, planographic surface not a relief one. The camera-ready original is shot photographically on to a thin aluminium plate which is chemically treated to attract ink to those parts of the plate where it is needed and to repel ink from those parts where it is not. A separate plate is made for each colour and the ink is then 'offset' on to a rubber blanket cylinder from which it is transferred to the paper. Offset printing has been in use in the US since the 1920s but gained momentum in the UK in the 1960s when newspapers and magazines converted to it. Anything which can be photographed can be reproduced using offset lithography and it is the most commonly used method.

Gravure printing

Gravure printing is the opposite of relief printing. The image is cut, or etched, into the surface of the plate as opposed to being raised from it. The etching produces cells, or holes, in which the ink can collect and from which it is transferred to the paper. Gravure processes are particularly suitable for long runs as there is little wear to the surface of the plate. It is also very good for photographic reproduction and is favoured by quality magazines.

Flexography

Flexography is a process which is similar to offset in that it uses an intermediary blanket between the plate and the paper. It is not, however, planographic (flat) but uses a raised printed surface. There are also differences in the set-up of the blanket and the ink is water based. Flexography is very suitable for newspapers: it has a sharper image and there is less ink rub-off.

Inkjet printing

Inkjet printing, operated by computer, is an increasingly popular process. It eliminates many of the mechanical tasks such as making plates. It uses pulses of electronically controlled ink to produce the print and as many as 1 200 dots (ink pulses) per square inch are possible giving a near photographic quality. For general use, 300 dots per square inch give a satisfactory image. Inkjet printing with its computer-driven speed and sharp image is particularly suitable for mail-merge operations and would be the method of choice for personalised direct-mail promotions where the names and addresses can be changed at print-speed. If material is required for planning into a newspaper advertisement, then inkjet printing can be used to create a **bromide** (glossy print) or film for the purpose.

Screen printing

Screen printing is still referred to as **silk screen**, although for long runs nylon (or some other synthetic) is preferred. A screen is set up with solid areas to block the ink and a fine, silk-like mesh to let the ink through where it is needed. The ink is forced through the screen with a rubber squeegee. A more complicated automatic procedure is used for commercial posters and items such as T-shirts and mugs which might be used as part of a promotional campaign.

11.11 Distributing the advertisement

The advertisement may be scheduled to appear in a range of publications. Arrangements must be made to ensure that each one gets a copy of the advertisement in a reproducible form. As the method of printing will influence the nature of that reproducible form, it is essential to make sure that each publication gets the right type of original.

New technology has revolutionised the distribution of material. Typesetting can be computerised and artwork can be digitalised for electronic transmission. Fibre optics and satellite make it possible to send whole pages of type and art from one part of the world to another.

11.12 Print-finishing and the finishing touches

A media buyer should be as concerned with the quality of the print-finishing as with the quality of reproduction. Both contribute to what the reader sees and can have a considerable effect on the success of the advertisement. Apart from concern with the quality of the trimming and binding, there are other finishing touches which cannot be carried out in the printing process. Where small areas of gold or silver foil are to be applied (as on scratch cards, for example), they must be applied after the page has been printed. Special pages printed to a higher quality than the norm for a particular magazine can be ordered separately from another printer and **tipped in**. Free samples can be fixed to the page after printing and there have even been pop-up advertisements in the manner of children's pop-up books which need to be assembled after the printing has been done.

Some of this work can only be done by hand and a print-finisher may employ local labour on a casual basis to do it. Sometimes a particular direct-mail shot requires a non-standard envelope for which no machine is available and these must then be hand folded and glued. This all adds to the cost and must be taken into consideration when planning a campaign.

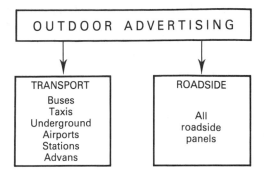

Fig. 11.3 Outdoor advertisement classifications

**11.13
Outdoor
advertising**

Poster advertising

Poster advertising is sometimes characterised as a 'message on a wall'. However, what constitutes a 'wall' is an open question and outdoor advertising includes advertising on taxis and buses as well. You can even advertise on the panel of a parking meter – probably the smallest wall of all. The poster medium is different from other media in being a pure advertising medium with no editorial content at all. This absence of editorial surround focuses the audience's attention on the message. To the extent that a poster has a surround, it will be an environmental surround rather than an editorial one. Outdoor has two main classifications **roadside** and **transport** with the latter further subdivided. Figure 11.3 shows the main categories.

**11.14
Transport
formats**

There is considerable variety of transport formats. Taxis include full livery, exterior panel (70 × 20 in) or door panel (39 × 20 in) with the opportunity for interior advertising. Buses include T-shape or L-shape panels with single-deck or bus-back options and, again, interior panels (26 × 8 in). Railway stations, airports and underground stations all make use of standard sheet formats with lift and escalator panels and Tube car panels as options. **Advans** (poster panels fixed on to mobile vehicles) are mainly 48 sheet, but there are some 6-sheet advans in London.

These transport formats have different target audiences – see Table 11.1.

Table 11.1 Transport formats and their target audiences

Format	Audience	Audience	Audience
Buses	Housewives	Tourists	Motorists
Taxis	Businessmen	Affluent tourists	Up-market residents
Underground	Commuters	Tourists	Young people
Railway	Commuters	Day-trippers	
Airport	Business travellers	Leisure travellers	

Source: Maiden Outdoor

**11.15
Roadside
formats**

Contractors are responsible for the provision of roadside poster space for which the appropriate planning permission has been obtained. The terms used are:

- **Panel**   The space for a single poster. There may be more than one panel on a site.

- **Sheet**   Posters are measured as consisting of so many sheets. Over 95 per cent of available panels fall into the four most popular sizes (4, 6, 48 and 96 sheet) but other sizes may include 12 or 16 sheets up to super-sizes in excess of 96 sheets.

- **Site**   The physical location of the poster space. This is often described in terms of its immediate environment (residential, commercial, etc.). Solus sites have one panel; many sites offer more than one. A single contractor may own thousands of sites.

Figure 11.4 shows the main poster sizes with some measurements inset.

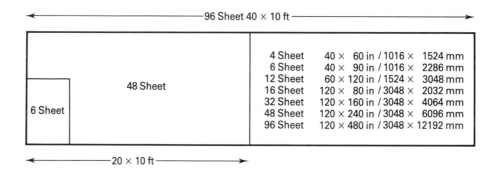

Fig. 11.4   Poster sheet sizes

Poster sites

To bring new poster sites into existence requires planning permission and the variation in the number of sites around the country may be traced to differences in the attitudes of local authorities – some see posters as a blight on the landscape. To offset this criticism, contractors often have to landscape a proposed site or offer other benefits, such as street furniture. Adshel, for example, specialises in installing bus shelters in return for the poster rights.

In 1994 the prospect of government legislation to relax poster planning laws raised questions among established major contractors about opening the market to 'cowboy' operators and the Outdoor Advertising Association (founded in 1982) called for a full discussion of the issues.

**11.16 Deemed
consent**

Deemed consent normally applies to retailers who use the walls of their own premises to advertise goods sold in their shops and they are usually excused the need to apply for permission. Even so, there is a limit to the size of poster that can be put up under this arrangement.

In the building construction industry, 48-sheet posters are technically covered by deemed consent, but there are cases where contractors, relying on the fact that councils do not have the personnel to enforce regulations, are putting up 96-sheet posters without permission.

11.17 The Poster Audit Bureau (PAB)

The Poster Audit Bureau (PAB) was set up in 1976 to remedy some of the problems which made posters less attractive to advertisers. Specifically, it addressed the twin problems of ensuring that posters were put up by the agreed date and that they were posted in the right places. The costs of the PAB were borne jointly by the advertisers and the contractors and enabled 50 per cent of sites to be checked fortnightly. This meant that during a one-month campaign all sites would be checked at least once. Today, site auditing is carried out by independent organisations such as Site Seers and Site Reports.

11.18 OSCAR and computer mapping

OSCAR

OSCAR (Outside Site Classification and Research) is a major provider of site analysis data carried out by NOP Poster Ltd on behalf of the Outdoor Advertising Association (OAA) and the Joint Industry Committee for Poster Audience Research (JICPAR). OSCAR works on the basis of using a variety of objective criteria to grade a site – every site being identified by contractor, address, number of panels and town/district code. The main criteria used are:

- **Neighbourhood factors** Location, road type, bus routes, traffic flow, speed limits, distance from town centre, nearest shopping centre, proximity of retail outlets and so on. This leads to the **gross audience figure** of the number of vehicles and pedestrians who pass the site.

- **Visibility factors** Distance from which the panel can be seen, angle of panel to road, height above ground, illumination and competition in the area (a solus site would have no competition).

OSCAR is not intended for evaluating individual panels but for evaluating campaigns of 40 plus panels. Table 11.2 gives Maiden Outdoor's evaluation for its preselected Flagship 500 panel campaign based on the OSCAR score of OTSs per week (in thousands).

Table 11.2 Maiden Outdoor evaluation of 500 panel campaign

Average OSCAR score per panel	133.3
Average net audience (OSCAR score × 1000)	133 300
Average net audience × number of panels (133 300 × 500)	66 650 000
Multiplied by 2 for a fortnight campaign	133 300 000

A two-week campaign using these 500 panels achieves approximately 1.3 million impacts.

Table 11.3   Typical cover and frequency figures

	One Week		Two Weeks	
	Cover	Frequency	Cover	Frequency
1 500 panels	40%	7	51%	10
3 000 panels	57%	10	67%	16

Typical 'all adult' figures for a 48-sheet campaign using average sites. The greater the number of panels and the longer the campaign the greater the potential build of both coverage and frequency.

Computer mapping

The poster buyer might not want to buy a preselected campaign but wish to select sites with particular features. Supermarkets, for example, may want sites on major approach roads within specified drive-times. In these cases, computer mapping can locate the target areas and specify the availability of different panel sizes within it. If a particular consumer audience is being targeted, computer mapping can use geodemographic databases such as Acorn (A Classification of Residential Neighbourhoods) to select areas such as 'affluent suburban housing' and 'council estates' to position posters at these sites where they have the best chance of being seen by the target audience. With the increase in both airport shopping and garage forecourt shopping, sites adjacent to or within airport terminals and garages may become attractive to some businesses.

11.19 Poster audience research and campaign evaluation

Campaign analysis

Pre- and post-campaign analysis using OSCAR scores can be used to calculate the cover and frequency of a given campaign for up to 210 sociodemographic groups taking account of age, sex, occupation, viewing and listening habits and so on. (See typical figures in Table 11.3.)

General observations on poster campaigns as a whole indicate that posters are more popular with males than with females and with younger people rather than with older.

RSL Signpost

RSL (Research Services Ltd) Signpost began in 1991 and is a service available in London only. It tracks campaigns for branded products by using ten sampling points within the M25 perimeter. Three hundred respondents (male and female, aged 18–60) are shown 'de-branded' photographs of real sites to assess such things as recognition and attribution. So far, 700 campaigns have been researched and norms established as a basis of comparison.

Maiden QED

Maiden QED is a form of experimental research carried out in conjunction with RMS (Retail Marketing In-Store Services) using matched samples of ten stores each. For the first sample, a 100 quality 48-sheet campaign is set up in the catchment area. The second sample has no poster support and the inference is that differences in brand performance can be attributed to the posters.

Observational research

Another approach is to use observational research to count the number of people passing a poster in a shopping centre interspersed with interviews to build up a profile of those passing.

11.20 Buying poster campaigns

Booking poster sites

Posters can be used in single medium and mixed-media campaigns. Poster sites are usually booked up for a minimum of one or two months but shorter periods can be negotiated. The contract period runs from the **in-charge** date (the first day) to the **out-of-charge** date (the last day). The same poster need not stay up for the whole period and London Weekend Television (LWT) was one of the pioneers of the weekly campaign. In late 1993 LWT ran a weekly campaign using only three words each week, the words beginning with the letters *L, W, T*. Arranging for posters in such a campaign to be changed exactly as required calls for careful planning. Some sites are booked on what is virtually a permanent arrangement and are referred to as **TC sites (till countermanded)**.

It is possible to buy sites **line by line**, picking the ones required from the contractor's list. It is even possible to buy one site only for a particular purpose. The easiest method, however, is to buy a preselected campaign. Maiden has the Flagship (see page 133), the Checkout (a 600 quality 48-sheet campaign with proximity to major grocery outlets) and the Motorpack (a network of 48-sheet posters throughout motorway service stations). All the major contractors offer preselected campaigns.

Case Study

Littlewoods

Littlewoods Pools ran a 48- and 96-sheet campaign to gain stature and backed this with a 6-sheet campaign to gain high-street presence. Their outdoor schedule for a four-week burst from mid-January to mid-February 1994 included on a national basis about 300 96-sheet, nearly 2 000 48-sheet and over 5 000 6-sheet posters.

The objectives of the campaign were to increase visibility, encourage participation by current, lapsed and potential purchasers and to maximise benefit from the advertising campaign.

RSL Signpost measured the results giving Littlewoods an excellent performance of:

- 58% recognition (against a database norm of 37%)
- 78% liking (against a database norm of 53%)
- 38% purchase intent (against a database norm of 32%)

The agency was Lowe Howard-Spink and the specialist was International Poster Management.

Source: Maiden Outdoor Posters in Perspective

See also the Scallywags case study (pages 178–9).

Figure 11.5 shows the links in the buying chain.

Poster specialists are funded by a commission of 5 per cent paid by contractors on **gross billings**. They specialise in planning and buying poster campaigns to an agreed agency brief. This arrangement is unique to the poster industry.

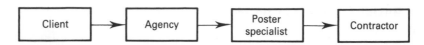

Fig. 11.5   Buying chain

11.21 Posters: the creative process

Posters, it is said, are the art director's medium. This reflects the fact that in many cases the poster is seen by people who cannot pause for long enough to read more than a few words and are more likely to be attracted by a simple clear visual image.

This view, however, is more true of roadside and overlooks the circumstances where posters can have a 'captive audience', as in many areas of transport. Underground passengers waiting for a train have time to read the cross-track posters which, in some cases, look more like pages from a magazine. There are also, of course, posters on the platform side as well, but it is the cross-track posters that give the most scope.

Underground passengers can also be presented with relatively long messages inside the car. Tube cards are excellent places for playing on the audience's problem-solving abilities as they offer something to occupy and amuse the mind during the journey.

At roadside, posters supporting a television campaign may contain no more than the slogan from a television commercial (with the words usually put at the top to avoid low-level obstruction). A good tip for the beginner is to make all the letters twice as big as you think they should be – what looks like a big letter shrinks to insignificance when posted high up. Another good tip is to allow for stretch: most posters stretch and the edges are inevitably lost, so don't put important matter too near the edge. A clever device for a developing campaign is to use **slipping** – changing the original poster by covering part of it rather than reposting the whole.

It is possible to test a concept by using a unique system (Maiden Mentor) created by Continental Research in which a proposed poster can be scanned into a computer and superimposed on to photographs of real sites for research purposes.

Not all roadside consists of printed posters pasted to wooden hoardings. J. C. Decaux are responsible for the charming continental free-standing columns which have blossomed around London and Mills & Allen's Backlights combine with More O'Ferrall's Superlites to brighten up the darkness. Maiden's Spectacolor at Piccadilly Circus in London is unique in Britain providing computer-animated advertising on a 30×15 ft illuminated display. An ultravision effectively offers three posters on the same panel by the use of revolving slats to form different faces which appear in sequence and which can each be used by a different advertiser. Another way in which an ultravision can be used is for one advertiser to book all three faces to create a 'tease and reveal' campaign in which the first face poses a problem which is resolved as the second and third faces come into view. Finally there remains the possibility of specials which can use any artistic or creative medium from hand-painting to ceramic tiles and which can be built in any shape required. Saab had one recently with a giant three-dimensional dashboard complete with steering wheel.

11.22 Poster production

Printing posters

Screen printing is good for short runs and allows special colours such as Day Glo to be used. It produces quality posters of high visibility. Litho is considerably cheaper for long runs. Inkjet printing can be used for very short runs and even one-offs (see pages 129–130). Since posters are exposed to the elements and are usually pasted over older ones, it is a good idea to insist on grey-backed, opaque, heavy paper and to ask for light-fast inks. At least 15 per cent extra posters should be ordered to compensate for weather damage, graffiti and stripping. Panels are routinely stripped back to the base and then need reposting.

The responsibility for ensuring that the printing is done to the required standard and in sufficient number lies with the agency which is also responsible for distribution (usually ten days before the in-charge (see page 135) date). The biggest cause of late posting is late delivery, but a specialist dispatch company can be hired to collate and deliver posters to the right billstores.

Case Study

Taste takes a plunge in the battle of the bras

So ran the headline in the *Daily Mail*'s Femail Forum of 24 February 1994. Journalist Louise Atkinson launched a strong attack on the latest round of underwear advertising which included a poster campaign by Playtex to promote its Wonderbra range. The poster campaign was at the heart of the struggle for dominance of a £20 million market triggered off by Playtex reclaiming from rival Gossard the licence which it had sold 30 years earlier. Gossard, with an unexpected gap in its product range, retaliated with its new Ultrabra.

Atkinson's complaint was with the whole poster, press and television campaign which she denounced as sexist. On Playtex's posters she said, 'Pictures of pouting blonde model Eva Herzigova – who incidentally looks as if the last thing she needs is extra uplift grins down from posters with an endless list of lascivious copy lines. One reads: ''Or are you just pleased to see me?''.'

Apart from the alleged offensive and sexist content of the campaign, there were worried comments passed elsewhere about the risk of such posters distracting motorists and contributing to a decline in road safety.

The power of a controversial campaign to attract media comment led not only to the *Mail*'s full-page article but also to a two-page colour spread the same week in the TV listings magazine *TV Quick* and a feature on the satirical TV programme *Saturday Night Clive*.

At the other end of the media scale, the *Croydon Post*, a local free newspaper, ran a quarter-page feature under the no less punning headline 'A storm in a b-cup' in which it discussed Playtex's £1 million poster campaign. But perhaps the biggest media coup in terms of free editorial coverage was a 3½-minute feature on the breakfast TV programme GMTV which gave Gossard a nationwide platform with a carefully produced visit to the Gossard Ultrabra factory at Gwent in Wales. Interviews with happy employees beaming that the new bra was selling so well that it gave them added job security were worth their weight in gold. Think about the cost of producing a 3½-minute commercial.

Footnote: The ASA received 536 complaints about the portrayal of women in advertising and upheld 111 in 1993 – almost three times as many as the year before.

11.23 Summary

- Press advertisements tend to follow standard sizes, but any size or shape can be negotiated.
- Positioning press advertisements varies from ROP which is left to the discretion of the editor to preferred positions which are normally dearer.
- The rate card sets out prices but is open to negotiation.
- The creative team, copywriter and art director, develop solutions to the client's problems utilising a variety of concepts such as display copy, body copy, straplines, margins, white space and bleeds.
- There are several printing processes used by newspapers and magazines and these can affect the way in which the finished advertisement is delivered for publication.
- The outdoor advertising industry has two main branches, roadside and transport.
- At roadside posters are of various sizes measured in sheets and posted on to panels located at different sites. Sheets are also used in some transport work, but there are other possibilities such as bus and taxi panels, Tube cards and so on.
- Site evaluation and pre- and post-campaign evaluation are all possible taking advantage of systems such as OSCAR and Maiden Mentor.
- It is possible to buy poster sites one by one (line by line), but it is easier to buy preselected packages built around themes such as proximity to supermarkets.
- Some sites are booked TC (till countermanded), but a normal period might be two months – the same poster need not stay up throughout the period.
- Poster specialists act as campaign planners and buyers for agencies and are financed by the contractors.

- Roadside posters often have very few words to accommodate the passing traffic but some transport posters with captive audiences (particularly cross-track) are as wordy as some newspaper advertisements.
- Poster production needs to take account of the exposure to the elements and heavy paper with non-fade inks are recommended. Printing up to 15 per cent extra to compensate for weather damage or graffiti is also recommended.

11.24 Assignments

1. Design a black-and-white print advertisement for a product of your choice – you need not be an expert draughtsman (many art directors can't draw either), but your intentions should be quite clear.

2. Discuss the advantages and disadvantages of preferred positions compared with ROP positions for press advertisements.

3. Explain carefully the printing processes available for newspaper and magazine ads and where you might expect them to be used.

4. Discuss the merits and demerits of photographs versus drawings to illustrate various types of product in press advertisements.

5. Do a local survey of the roadside poster sites within, say, half a mile of your college. Note the types of product and service provided and discuss why particular sites might be good or bad.

6. Select some television campaigns and discuss whether they might transfer easily to posters. If so, what words or images from the TV ad would you use?

7. Discuss the problems involved in researching poster sites and poster campaigns, and outline some of the research methods available.

12 Planning time-based campaigns

This chapter discusses campaign planning for the time-based media of television, cinema and radio.

12.1 Terrestrial television

Availability of terrestrial television

Channel 3 (ITV) covers the whole country, but because it is regionalised, it is difficult to set up a national campaign. Channel 4 does offer a national audience, as does Breakfast TV (GMTV), but they are somewhat limited in their attractiveness to advertisers in so far as Breakfast TV commands only the early part of the day and Channel 4 commands a relatively small audience. The ITV Network Centre plans a large proportion of Channel 3 viewing so that, for example, *Coronation Street* goes out at the same time across the country. Such networking does enable an advertiser to identify a national audience but it remains true that the advertiser has to deal with 15 different regional companies to reach it. To ease this situation from both sides sales houses came into existence (they are co-owned by the stations they serve) to handle the sales of more than one company. Under ITC regulations no sales house should handle more than 25 per cent of revenue. The takeover of LWT by Granada in 1994 brought two sales houses together, giving Granada control of 29 per cent of total sales, more than the 25 per cent allowed under ITC regulations and in contravention of an undertaking given to the Department of Trade and Industry. ITC at this time declared that although some flexibility of the 25 per cent rule might be possible the Granada situation was such that it could not consider it without government approval. Granada unsuccessfully approached the Director General of Fair Trading and was given until August 1995 to comply with its previous undertaking. In June 1994 Granada announced the creation of a new sales house to represent Granada, LWT, Yorkshire, Tyne Tees and Border and which came in at just under the 25 per cent limit.

There are also specialist buying houses (media independents) which can handle the purchasing requirements of a number of agencies thus further reducing the number of transactions that would otherwise occur. These sales and buying houses act as distributors between the suppliers and users of air-time. Some independents also plan campaigns.

Television scheduling and buying

Television may be selected on the basis of a single medium campaign or it may be part of a mixed media strategy in which case it could be the lead medium supported, perhaps, by posters or magazines. It need not be used all the time. Some companies plan for short campaigns and many companies stay off the small screen for years at a time, as the Woolwich case study shows.

Case Study

'In a changing world it's good to be with the Woolwich'

In February 1994 the Woolwich Building Society returned to television advertising after an absence of two years. In the meantime, it had concentrated on a national radio campaign using the strapline 'In a changing world it's good to be with the Woolwich' which featured the voice of comedy actor Eric Idle. The success of the radio campaign prompted an integrated mixed media campaign in which television was to play a part using the same strapline. Eric Idle's voice was used as a 'voice-over' to give verbal expression to various animated domestic items, such as a tablelamp and a camera.

The television campaign (under the wing of agency Ogilvy and Mather) was scheduled for six weeks in early 1994 and aired on London, Meridian, Anglia, STV and HTV. The television campaign was itself backed up by another burst of radio advertising and some national press coverage.

When buying television time, a choice may have to be made between reach and frequency (see pages 111–12). This may mean a choice between a thinly spread national campaign across all regions and a more concentrated campaign in one or two regions only (the 'strawberry jam dilemma' – the more you spread it, the thinner it gets).

Television rating points (TVRs)

Television rating points are so important that they have been described as the currency with which television air-time is bought and sold. A single TVR represents 1 per cent of the advertiser's target audience having the opportunity to see (OTS) an advertisement once. One hundred TVRs would, therefore, represent all the advertiser's target audience having an OTS each. (It may, however, represent 50 per cent having two OTSs.) It is of great importance in establishing the quality of the total audience for any particular programme as opposed to its mere size. A popular starting point is the concept of the 400 TVR campaign which gives 80 per cent of the target audience five OTSs each. If the target audience includes all individuals nationally, we would talk of 'national TVRs'. If the target is, however, men only, we could talk of male TVRs and if we were looking at the Granada region only we could specify Granada male TVRs and so on.

The planner may specify 400 TVRs nationwide subject to an **equal impact** requirement, i.e. that the same number of TVRs are obtained in each region. To achieve this, the buyer will look for a balanced regional distribution of TVRs which will be affected by the size and geodemographic make-up of each audience. It will certainly mean a different spend in each region to achieve equal-impact TVRs nationwide.

Preferred spots and other options

There may be good reasons for wanting to position a commercial in the mid-break of a particular programme (or just before or just after it). Buying such a preferred spot can involve the buyer in something like an auction.

If the buyer is not committed to a particular spot but simply wants to arrange for a commercial to appear sometime within a stated period, there are television equivalents of the ROP advertisement (see page 119). These are:

- **ROW (run of week)** A cheap way to buy time. The advertisement appears at any time during the week at the media owner's discretion.

- **ROM (run of month)** There are no guarantees as to which day of the month the commercial will appear.

- **ROY (run of year)** There are no guarantees as to which month the advertisement will appear.

With certain well-established fast-moving consumer goods (FMCGs) which do not have any noticeable seasonal variations in the level of demand, it may not be important just when an advertisement appears as long as visibility is maintained and the product is seen on screen from time to time. An advertiser may just buy a package of ROY spots at the beginning of the year and take a chance on when they appear. Stories have been told of media owners forgetting about such arrangements for weeks on end and then pushing out a lot of transmissions of the same commercial in a short time to catch up.

ROM and ROW offer a little more control, especially necessary where seasonal products are concerned because at least the commercial will not go out at the wrong time of the year – which is a risk with ROY.

For new products which need guaranteed television support such arrangements may prove unsuitable.

When all the above factors have been considered, it will be possible to draw up a schedule (see fig. 12.1).

The resource

The television buyer is faced with the task of trying to buy all the agreed air-time within budget, but this may not be possible and the buyer must remain flexible and open to alternative suggestions. TV buying is such a skilled operation that, unlike press and radio, the advertiser cannot buy direct but must go through a specialist buyer who has the right technology (the **resource** as it is sometimes called) and understands the intricacies of the system. Television buying is a computer-based operation and all sales are simultaneously logged by both the buyer and the seller and it is essential to have access to, and to understand, the software involved.

The pre-empt system

It is essential to understand the pre-emptive nature of television air-time buying and to see how quick judgements and decisions in trying to achieve the scheduling objectives are required.

Television schedule for: _____

Client: _____

Product: __Jan. to March 1995__

Period: _____

Area(s): __Anglia, Central, Yorkshire__

Week commencing Monday	January					February				March			
	02	09	16	23	30	06	13	20	27	06	13	20	27
30-second commercial √	√	√	√	√	X		√	X		√	√	√	√
20-second commercial X		√	√	√	X		√	X		X	X	X	X
		X	X				√	X					
		X	X		X		√	X					

Fig. 12.1 TV advertisement schedule

Pre-empting means that a buyer who has 'bought' a spot at one price may subsequently lose it to another buyer who is prepared to offer a higher price. The two main elements of this pre-emptive system are the rate card and the television rating points or TVRs.

The following example shows how the pre-empt system works.

Buying television air-time is like a sealed-bid auction. The rate cards give a range of prices and it is up to the buyer to decide what price to offer based on the number of TVRs that spot can deliver. Suppose the media buyer is aiming for a 400 TVR campaign and knows (through audience research) that the spot in question will deliver 40 of them – 10 per cent of his target. He may, then, offer a price on the rate card at or below 10 per cent of his budget. At this point, the buyer may offer a price well down the rate card. His offer will be accepted and logged – this is all done on computers at both ends. Unfortunately, another buyer becomes interested in the same spot and offers a price higher up the rate card. The new buyer obviously thinks that the spot is worth more to him and is prepared to pay more for it. Our buyer has been pre-empted and can only get the time back by going higher up the card again. He may finish up buying the same spot three, four or even five times before he gets it (if he does). But if he spends more than 10 per cent of his budget buying this spot he will have to buy other spots cheaper to stay within budget. He lives with the constant tension of paying too much and going over budget and not paying enough and not being seen on television – not a job for the faint-hearted. The only way absolutely to guarantee a spot is to offer the top price on the rate card before anybody else does.

12.2 Cable and satellite television

Cable and satellite operations give access to specialised markets through such themed services as the Children's Channel and the Cartoon Network (aimed at the younger market), Japansat and TV Asia (aimed at the ethnic markets) and Sky Sports and the Movie Channel. Audiences, however, are relatively small and geographically unevenly distributed. Sky television, for example, which came on air in 1989, reached 1 million UK homes by 1990 rising to 3 million by January 1993. However, the total number of satellite homes increased by 56 per cent between March 1992 and March 1994, pushing at an independently forecasted near 6 million UK homes by the end of 1995. Sky currently holds 18.1 per cent of the combined satellite-ITV viewing in the Midlands but only 4.5 per cent in the North-East.

Buying air-time on non-terrestrial systems is quite unlike buying terrestrial time and it is advisable to approach each licensee separately to see what is available. Sky television, for example, has no rate card as such but negotiates each contract separately with the advertiser/agency taking account of the target audience, commercial length, channel, time of day and month. It sells air-time on seven different channels and an advertiser can go into all seven or as few as needed to suit the campaign. They are:

- Sky One　General entertainment.
- Sky News　24-hour news service.
- Sky Sports　Sports from the UK and around the world.
- Sky Movies Plus　24-hour blockbuster film channel.
- The Movie Channel　24-hour blockbuster film channel.
- Sky Movies Gold　Classic movies, ancient and modern.
- Nickelodeon　Kids' programming, fast and furious.

Time is sold on a first-come, first-served basis, subject to availability.

An interesting feature is that, unlike ITV and C4, commercials are shown only at the beginning and end of films on the film channels and not in the middle of them.

Once the campaign is booked, it is logged on a computer and the client gets a printout of all spots by channel, date, time and programme (subject to a clause that the time may vary by up to eight minutes either side). There are two sales offices – one in London for London and the Home Counties and one in Manchester for the rest of the UK.

However, even if an advertiser decides to ignore satellite for advertising purposes, he cannot ignore the effect that it has on his terrestrial audience. Terrestrial-only households do not have the alternative of switching to satellite, whereas satellite households (roughly one in six) obviously do. (A satellite household has terrestrial television as well.) Research shows that satellite households typically watch less ITV than terrestrial-only households, particularly in the important 15–34 age group. The mathematics of incorporating this knowledge into campaign planning remain unresolved. A new research system STEER (Satellite Television Equivalent Expenditure Reports) is monitoring this area to help advertisers and agencies to plan more effective satellite–terrestrial mixes.

Satellite and cable companies do not, however, have the same dependence on advertising revenue as Channels 3 and 4 and attach as much importance to recruiting subscribers.

ISLE COLLEGE
RESOURCES CENTRE

12.3 Cinema campaigns

The contractors

Buying a cinema campaign is possibly easier than buying any other sort of campaign. Although there are many hundreds of individual screens, there are only two sales contractors. Rank Screen Advertising (RSA) control about 85 per cent of the UK market and Pearl & Dean control the rest. They offer similar services – the difference between them is mainly that of size. A particular screen will be either an RSA screen or a Pearl & Dean screen and if that is the screen an advertiser wants then he must go to the company whose screen it is.

Cinema and television compared

Although the same advertisements can be, and often are, screened on both media, there are considerable differences between them. Television is often dubbed the 'small screen' and cinema the 'large screen', and cinema's large screen impact can encourage a more ambitious treatment of a creative idea with some film commercials several times longer than the typical TV ad. They differ not only in size but also in shape, with the height/width ratios different from each other. Films made for the wide screen are often cropped for television although a growing practice is to televise them in 'letterbox' format (with the top and bottom of the TV screen left blank) and wide-screen televisions are now on the market. These factors can influence the creation and production of screened advertisements.

The viewing situation is also obviously different. Cinema is seen in a dark auditorium with all the panoply of theatre; television is seen at home with all the comforts (and distractions) of domestic and family life. People make a conscious effort to go to the cinema, whereas stopping in to watch television is often a default decision (there is nothing else to do). Audience attention is better at the cinema (to some extent, the advertisements are part of the entertainment) with less than 15 per cent of the audience leaving their seats and, of course, there is no zapping. Recall of screened advertisements is better than of television ads, but the coverage build is slower. This reflects both the fewer exposures of a cinema commercial and the smaller proportion of the population who are regular cinemagoers compared with regular television watchers. The same advertisement can be shown several times in one evening on TV but once only during a cinema programme.

Buying a cinema campaign

- **The Audience Discount Package (ADP)** This is the most popular campaign option and provides mass cinema audience coverage across one or more regions up to a nationwide campaign. It offers no opportunity for selectivity which fact is reflected in the rates with RSA quoting a typical CPT of £29 for a national campaign.

- **Line by line** The minimum requirement for a cinema campaign is one screen for one week. Like poster sites, screens can be bought on a line-by-line basis (one at a time) and this might suit advertisers with a specific niche market. Rates vary from screen to screen with location and seating capacity affecting the rates (seating capacity indicates the maximum audience any screen will have). RSA offers different types of line-by-line campaigns – for example, one screen, all the screens at one site (the Leicester Square Premiere has four screens), all the screens in one city (Birmingham has 44), all the screens in one conurbation (Wolverhampton has 109). Again, there is a parallel with posters in that both contractors can offer preselected campaigns.

- **Film packages**   These allow an advertiser to tie a campaign to a particular film and to follow that film around the country. The appeal of film packages rests on the ability to profile the audience each film will have. CAVIAR (see page 84) has a library of such profiles and builds expected new release profiles on an analysis of old releases. This is obviously easier for sequels, with the projected profile of *Wayne's World 2* based on the actual profile for *Wayne's World*.

- **Art screen packages**   These give advertisers access to a niche market with, to quote RSA, 'a quality environment to reach the élite consumer'. Art screens show films of a minority interest which are seen typically by people with low ITV viewing habits. RSA can offer a package of 25 London art screens and Pearl & Dean 13. Outside London, they offer 36 and 12 respectively and both offer national packages.

- **Others specialist packages**   Both contractors offer children's packages (see chapter 13). RSA can even offer a 'service cinema' package covering members of the British armed services (described as 'predominantly male, upmarket and aged between 18 and 44') stationed abroad in western Europe (12 screens) and Cyprus (two screens).

- **Pre-prepared ads**   It is possible to make use of pre-prepared ads which are so general that they could apply to any business in a specific trade. The client pays to impose a logo or other on-screen message, possibly with a voice-over, and then has a screen commercial at very little cost. Such ads are very suitable for local campaigns for businesses such as garages, car showrooms, hairdressers, restaurants and even local colleges.

12.4 Creating a television (or cinema) advertisement

Television commercials have often been described as 30-second theatre. A good place to begin is with the different types of story-line.

Reality-based story-lines

Originally called 'slice of life', such advertisements often deal with a very specific event – young Jason's first day at school, proud parents at their daughter's graduation ceremony and so on. They have developed into full-blown serials with a story-line stretching over several episodes and taking months, if not years, to develop.

Story-lines based on reality should have clearly defined characters, well-established settings and a good story. Some of the best known ones have been with us for years.

Oxo, the beef-cube manufacturers, have been exploiting this technique since 1957 with its now classic 'Katie' series which ran for nearly 20 years and its more recent 'Family' series which began in 1983. By placing the product in topical situations reflecting changes in social and family trends, Oxo has repeatedly updated its image. The campaign remains a favourite with consumers and professionals alike and picked up the 1992 IPA (Institute of Practitioners in Advertising) Silver Award for Advertising Effectiveness.

While Oxo commercials tend to tell a complete story-line each time, the serial commercial develops a story-line over a series of episodes with something of a cliffhanger at the end to keep viewers guessing. Perhaps the most famous is the Nescafé Gold Blend commercial which, built around a developing love affair between a handsome young man and a beautiful young woman, so captured the imagination that it became the subject of much editorial comment and created the concept of 'Gold Blend Man'. The first Gold Blend series ran for 12 episodes over six years until 1993 when the original cast was replaced and a new story-line was introduced. In the new series, the presence of two handsome young men, both attracted to the same woman, provide dramatic and romantic interest.

The *Yellow Pages* advertisements each take a totally different story: the elderly author tracking down a second-hand copy of a book he wrote many years ago, the small boy searching out a special item as a birthday present for his model-train enthusiast father and the slightly manic John Cleese commercial in which he finds a specialist to get himself and his parents back into the car from which they had been locked out.

Documentary style story-lines

The documentary approach to television advertising divides into two main concepts, although they can work together – **demonstrations** and **testimonials**. Car-makers use the demonstration approach when they show us how much protection the driver (and passengers) will get if the car is involved in a crash. Tyre manufacturers show us how much better their tyres can hold a wet road, smoke-alarm manufacturers show us the tragic consequences of not having an alarm fitted when a fire breaks out (one example of the use of grief and death) and John Cleese (again) gives a Monty Pythonish performance on behalf of the Health Education Authority in which he points at a pile of ash, comments that this is the amount of ash a cigarette smoker makes and observes that, of course, they do not all get cremated. Television and cinema are clearly the best media for demonstrations – print is too static and radio lacks the visual quality needed.

Testimonial type documentary commercials frequently make use of well-known figures from public life to sing the praises of a product or service but may make use of an unknown person whose occupation provides the authority required. Unknown firefighters or nurses (suitably uniformed – it is the uniform which gives the authority) can be used. One shampoo commercial featured a testimonial from an unknown trainee beautician.

Surrealism

This is an approach that takes a situation with which the viewer is basically familiar and distorts it through deliberate and bizarre changes in subject matter, perspective and time. The moving image allows the creator to show the process in action so that things change before the viewer's eyes. Surrealism on screen owes much to the skills of the computer genius, the special effects whizz-kid and the film editor who cuts and joins in the right places. In surrealist advertisements we have seen a mountain road turn into a snake to be carried away by a soaring eagle and a small boy walking across the kitchen ceiling so as not to muddy his mother's recently washed kitchen floor. When the departure from reality is only slight, the point is easily taken by the viewer. However, if the departure is too great, the result may be visually stunning but the message may be lost in the process. The Guinness commercials with actor Rutger Hauer coming alive out of a famous painting or ending up in the belly of the whale attracted a great deal of comment, although, ironically, Guinness decided to drop them because research showed that people did not really understand them.

**12.5
Personalities
and characters**

We can use the word *personalities* to discuss individuals from any walk of life (entertainment, sports, politics, etc.) who appear in commercials as themselves to endorse a product or service. Endorsement is a similar concept to testimonial and the term **celebrity endorsement** is sometimes used in this context.

Characters, on the other hand, can be defined as fictitious people often specifically created for the purpose of a television commercial who may, nevertheless, be played by famous personalities. Sometimes characters are 'borrowed' from another context; in which case, to avoid copyright problems, they may be slightly modified – given a different name for example or just not named at all. Fictitious characters may be played by unknown actors and actresses and the advertiser may well generate a great deal of publicity out of the search for the right person.

Real-life personalities who represent themselves

Joanna Lumley, star of television shows *Absolutely Fabulous* and *Class Act*, is seen as often in television commercials as in television programmes. She appeared in the British Gas campaign which used the strapline 'Don't you just love being in control?', the Fairy campaign for Glazeguard dishwasher powder and Gaymer's Olde English Cider among others. In an advertisement for Cellnet phones (in which she did not actually appear) she was impersonated by, among others, John Cleese (again) queuing to take part in a spoof Joanna Lumley lookalike contest.

Irish football manager Jack Charlton has even more advertising credits to his name. Mitsubishi, Shredded Wheat, Mars and Guinness are among the companies and products he has promoted. In fact, Guinness simply borrowed an Irish Tourist Board commercial and tagged on an extra five seconds for the Guinness slogan. The Irish Tourist Board was happy to co-operate.

Agency Abbot Mead Vickers (AMV) created the 'celebrity recipe' concept for Sainsbury's in 1991. Selina Scott, Wendy Craig, and Ian McShane were used in three separate commercials in which each demonstrated how to make a particular dish. Every commercial ended with the campaign strapline 'Sainsbury's – everyone's favourite ingredient'. The stated purpose of the campaign was to portray Sainsbury's as a practical, friendly and helpful ally in the kitchen.

Characters created for a commercial and played by a famous person

A now famous character specifically created for a television campaign and brought to life by the talented comic Rowan Atkinson is Barclaycard's Lathom. The commercials have acquired a cult status, but the point here is that it is not Rowan Atkinson endorsing Barclaycard but Rowan Atkinson playing a character who is central to the Barclaycard series. The nice irony in this series is that the Rowan Atkinson character is typically dismissive of Barclaycard and claims to be able to handle things without Barclaycard's help. He always, in the end, has to acknowledge that Barclaycard's help is needed.

Characters played by unknown performers

The Milky Bar Kid is a fictitious character whose role is played by an unknown child selected after a series of auditions which, themselves, are a source of much publicity for the manufacturer (but with some negative publicity last time when Nestlé's declined to interview a black boy for the part).

Fictitious characters 'borrowed' from another context

Two actors who have featured in commercials as 'lookalikes' of characters which they originally created in television series are Richard Wilson who played cantankerous senior citizen Victor Meldrew in the BBC's *One Foot in the Grave* and George Cole who played the lovable rogue Arthur Daley in ITV's *Minder*. The former has appeared in commercials for the Abbey National Building Society and the latter in commercials for the Leeds Permanent Building Society. They do not, of course, appear as Victor Meldrew and Arthur Daley, but the suggestion is too obvious to be missed and most viewers will make the connection.

12.6 Voice-overs, hands and feet

It is not always necessary to use the whole of the actor or actress and in some cases the voice alone is enough. Termed **voice-overs**, voices can be specified at the creative stage as MVO (male voice-over) and so on. Many professionals earn a great deal of money doing a large number of voice-overs without ever being seen on the screen. There are hand models for nail varnish advertisements and close-ups in washing-up liquid commercials (with a different person providing the voice?). The Dove soap commercial is an effective, low-budget job using close-ups of a woman's hands with a male voice-over – the only props being a bar of Dove soap and a piece of litmus paper used to demonstrate its purity.

12.7 The use of animals

Animals can appear alongside humans, but perhaps the best remembered animal commercials are those in which the animals replace the humans altogether. PG Tips with its chimpanzees (human voice-overs) is one of the best known and is the longest running UK television advertising series of all. They first appeared on British television in 1956 (pipping Oxo by one year) and Francis Wheen (writing in 1985) tells us that by then one of these, 'The Furniture Removers', had already been shown more than 1 000 times – and it is still appearing. Digby, the Old English Sheepdog for Dulux paints, and Arthur, the cat which ate with its paw for Kattomeat, are both traditional figures. Training animals is, of course, a highly skilled job and specialist animal agencies have to be used.

12.8 The use of animation

The creator may decide to dispense with people and animals all together and to go for animation instead. Animation can also be combined with live people (the film *Who framed Roger Rabbit* is a classic example of this technique). Again, there are animated characters created specifically for a commercial, such as the little men in the Tetley teabag campaign. Established cartoon characters such as Tom and Jerry can be used under licence.

Animation techniques

The production of an animated commercial is quite different from one using live people. The techniques include:

- **Frame by frame drawings** Allows the characters to move by changing the position of legs, arms, etc. very slightly in each successive frame (usually using transparent acetate 'cels' overlaid on a static background). It is very time-consuming and expensive and sometimes senior artists draw the beginning and end of each movement and junior artists ('the in-betweeners') provide the middle frames. There are as many as 16 frames to the second.

- **Stop action** Uses three-dimensional articulated puppets. The film is advanced frame by frame and between each frame the puppet is moved very slightly – it can take all day to get a few seconds of movement.

- **Claymation** Uses models made of clay which can be used to give a more natural and fluid movement.

Some advertisements manage to dispense with movement altogether, whether human, animal or animated, and just use voice over a shot of the product – very cheap but very uninteresting. Direct response advertisements for gadgets, records and videos (usually shown on Channel 4) fall into this category.

12.9 Different treatments

We can now look at some of the various treatments the stories can be given.

Death and grief

The John Cleese commercials on behalf of the Health Education Authority treated death in a black-humour way whilst aiming to make the very serious point that smoking kills. Campaigns which make a similar point – that speeding kills – have treated death in a much more dramatic and serious light: so much so that one particular announcement was pushed back behind the 9 o'clock watershed after viewers complained that it was too frightening for early evening airings. The £1.5 m Ministry of Transport campaign features a 16-year-old girl knocked down and killed who then rematerialises as a ghost looking down at her own dead body and screaming at the motorist, 'You killed me. You were going too fast.'

Adventure and mystery

In 1994 Yorkie chocolate bars abandoned a 17-year campaign featuring a lorry driver in favour of the fugitive, man-on-the-run series under agency J Walter Thompson. Ingredients of the story-line include the mystery of why the man is on the run, who is after him and will he ever get caught.

Kronenbourg, a premium-brand lager, used a continental setting even to the extent of French dialogue with English subtitles in the '*Que Signifie 1664*' series which by the time the third episode was aired was credited with a 12 per cent increase in market share. The series features hero Henri attempting to solve the disappearance of his glamorous neighbour.

Humour

Two of the best-known humorous commercials are those for Barclaycard featuring Rowan Atkinson and the Vauxhall Astra advertisements featuring Tom Conti as Atkins the somewhat inept anti-hero. In one of these, with all the appearance of a love-sick young man, he rapturously recites the virtues of the car then turns to his, until now ignored, girlfriend with the three words, 'I love you.' 'Say that again,' she responds and Atkins obliges by repeating all the virtues of the car.

Nostalgia

It is sometimes thought that nostalgia appeals only to those old enough to have been there in the first place. If this is true then the use of nostalgia in advertising can be a dangerous tactic because, by definition, most of those watching would not have been there. In fact, many people who are too young to remember can still be positively affected. Perhaps the most famous campaign is that for Hovis bread which takes the viewer back to the world of cobbled streets and delivery boys on pushbikes when the local bakery was at the heart of the community. The campaign for Werther's Original sweets plays on nostalgia in a clever, history-repeating-itself scenario with grandfather reminiscing about the time he received his own first Werther's Original from his grandfather and then giving one, in turn, to his own grandson.

12.10 Researching the creative idea

Testing at the earliest possible stage has the advantage of getting some feedback before too much money is spent. It has the disadvantage of testing something that is not yet in its finished form. The closer the concept is to the finished form at the time of testing the more reliable the results are likely to be, but the more money will be spent.

There are four possible methods which usually involve a group of respondents and may take place in small groups, in a theatre or a hall.

The scenario

This involves having the creator talk (without any visual aids) to the group, taking them through the story scene by scene and explaining the action sequences, the settings, the dialogue, etc. Where more than one group of respondents is used, there is the danger that the presenter may unwittingly vary the presentation, first stressing one point and then another. To avoid this, a tape-recording might be used. Following the presentation, there would be an in-depth discussion. Group members could explain how they felt about the characters involved, whether they liked them, identified with them or whatever. The way in which the product or service is presented could also be discussed.

The storyboard

This uses a device like a comic strip to take the group members visually through the commercial scene by scene (see fig. 12.2). The lapse of time can be indicated showing how many seconds each scene would last and dialogue can be written under each frame or picture. The use of colour can be exploited in a storyboard presentation. Because TV is itself a visual and colourful medium, there may be a built-in preference for storyboards over scenarios.

The message: The Xeikon hi-tech computer-driven printer is suitable for in-house print operations. The Xeikon is capable of being run by a trained secretary and has the ability to produce large runs of high-quality business documents such as reports and prospectuses.

The original rough was drawn in match-box sized frames to produce a 24-frame storyboard looking rather like a page from a comic. Each frame was then individually worked up to a 4in × 5in black-and-white image, and it is these that are reproduced in fig. 12.2. Subject to client approval they would next be worked up into full colour and these would provide the basis for an animatic.

The animatic

This uses an on-screen presentation in the form of a series of still photographs rather than a moving picture. It is a sort of on-screen storyboard except that, of course, only one picture is visible at a time.

The simulation

This is put together fairly cheaply using a hand-held video camera, studio mock-ups and lookalike actors and actresses instead of the highly paid stars who will appear in the real thing. These dummies can be shown in a **hall** or **theatre test** to an invited audience.

1   The monitor

2   The computer chip

3   Close up of machine feeder

4   The operator

5   Printing a large run

6   The Xeikon logo

Fig. 12.2 Key frames from a professional storyboard (Ronald J. Wootton Associates)

Theatre and hall tests

A theatre test uses an ordinary cinema and can take up to three hours. Audience members may not know that they are there to test the commercials and may be told that it is the films which they are reviewing. At the end of the session, they will be asked to fill in questionnaires. A hall test may last for only 15 or 20 minutes and involves inviting people in off the street to see video presentations on an ordinary television screen. Again questionnaires are used. Theatre and hall tests mainly give quantitative results, but the method can be used on smaller groups followed up with group discussions to give qualitative information.

12.11 Producing the commercials

Commercials can be made for television and cinema using 16 mm or 35 mm film. For television transmission, they are then transferred to videotape. Videotape, once thought of as a poor relation to film and used primarily for news purposes where immediacy was more important than production values, has improved so much that some television commercials are now being shot directly on to video. Video has its own advantages: instant play-back is standard (no anxious waiting to see what the film will look like) and it is also easier to edit.

In the early days of television advertisements, some were actually broadcast live. There were, however, too many instances of things going wrong – not the least of which was actors forgetting their lines or using the wrong name for the product. Today, most advertisements are pre-recorded using film.

The script

The scriptwriter's job goes beyond writing the dialogue. Even if no dialogue is used (as with Levi's campaign 'Stitching' where a marlin fish is caught on a length of Levi's thread to demonstrate its strength) the talents of the scriptwriter are still needed. The script is in fact a set of instructions co-ordinating front of camera activities (action) and off-camera activities (music, voice-overs, etc.).

The script is written in two separate but parallel columns – one for all the visual aspects, headed 'PICTURE' or 'VISION', and the other for all the voices, sound effects, music, etc., headed 'SOUND'. These two sides of the script must exactly correspond to each other so that voice-overs follow the action precisely. For production purposes, they are treated separately and integrated afterwards. On-screen dialogue may be recorded simultaneously, but if the commercial is to be translated for a foreign market it is better to treat it separately. (See the script for Castlemaine XXXX reproduced on pages 157–9.)

Directors and production companies

Before anything can start, a director and production company must be selected. There are many good production houses available and given the nature of the commercial the agency may already know who it wants to direct it. Otherwise the way forward is to ask to see some directors' reels. These are collections of advertisements directed by one person and compiled on to one reel (or more) for the purpose of evaluation. The chosen director may well be tied into a production company so that question can be resolved at the same time. Alternatively, two or three production companies can be given copies of the script and asked to pitch for the work by presenting their ideas as to how it ought to be shot together with a set of estimates. There will be many decisions to be made.

Locations

One of the reasons why people like to work on television and film commercials is the opportunity to go on exotic locations – sometimes. The location is just as likely to be somebody's kitchen or garden as the Bahamas or California. Wherever it is, a suitable location has to be found and this can be a costly and time-consuming process. Torin Douglas in his *Complete Guide to Advertising* tells how for Levi's 'Stitching' commercial experts were consulted to pinpoint places in the world where marlin could be caught in November (the scheduled filming month). The list included Panama, Kenya and Mexico. Information then had to be gathered about weather forecasts and the clarity of the water (for underwater filming). At a more domestic level, when the charming and award-winning National Dairy

Council's 'Milkman' campaign needed a location, it found in north London a new development with a street which matched its requirements exactly. However, when the weather is a factor, it might turn out better to create a garden in a studio. The film crew would, no doubt, rather go to Florida.

Casting

Another reason why people like to work on television commercials is the opportunity to work with the stars – unless the star is a chimpanzee.

Unknowns are, of course, also used. Sometimes unknowns are chosen as a matter of preference. Where there is an open competition for the part then auditions will be held at which the agency and client will be present. Some agencies have their own casting departments.

Whether a star or an unknown is to be used, it should be made clear if the commercial is a one-off or one of a planned series stretching out over several years. People may not wish to take the risk of being typecast nor may they wish to tie themselves to a long-term contract. There is no such problem with the Milky Bar Kid who is routinely changed when the incumbent becomes too old for the part. Using people as icons or symbols for the product is not limited to Milky Bars. Rutger Hauer was chosen by Guinness because with his pale complexion, blonde hair and broad shoulders he could be dressed in black to personalise a glass of Guinness.

Props

The most important prop in most commercials is the product itself, the packet of breakfast cereal, the tin of dogfood, the car or whatever. If the package is to be shown, then a sample must be used which is entirely free of any blemish or damage (the package may even be touched up by hand). In commercials where the product is 'destroyed' multiple specimens must be available in case a scene has to be reshot. An advertisement showing a champagne bottle being opened may be the end product of 20 or 30 takes, each requiring one more unopened bottle. The product is not the only prop: in a washing-up liquid commercial plates, pans, glasses, etc. will also be needed and great care must go into choosing them. If the plates are obviously very expensive, they may give the product the wrong sort of image and alienate a lot of potential buyers. With financial and insurance services, there is often no product as such to show and in these cases the non-product props play an important part in establishing the product benefits. A commercial for a pension scheme filmed in a nice garden (location) with good quality patio furniture (props) creates the image of a decent lifestyle to which the consumer can look forward.

Lighting

This is a major contributor to the mood and impact of the commercial. A low, blueish light angled to leave half the face in shadow or a back-lit silhouette can create an air of mystery. Light flickering on faces as though from a television set can create a domestic mood even if the television set is never actually seen.

ISLE COLLEGE
RESOURCES CENTRE

**12.12
Production**

This stage involves the two most powerful and influential characters in the production of the commercial – the director and the editor. Although they are working to the creator's brief, they are each of them, nevertheless, creators in their own right and the finished version owes no less to their talents than it does to the creator who had the idea in the first place. The director and the editor make the creator's ideas work.

Filming

When production begins in earnest, the commercial becomes the director's property. If they are lucky, the creators may be allowed to watch but a common opinion is that by this stage they ought to be back at their desks creating somebody else's commercials.

The amount of effort that goes into filming a 30-second commercial is unbelievable and by the time the advertisement is complete a whole hour of film (sometimes two or three hours) may be lying on the cutting-room floor. This is partly because a director may choose to set up several camera units to take the same scene from different angles and partly because the same shot may have to be taken over and over again to get it right. To facilitate all this activity a **call sheet** is prepared telling everybody where they are expected to be at any given time of the day.

When animals are being used, they can, of course, be trained to perform as required but there are times when the easiest course of action is just to shoot a great deal of footage and go through it later looking for usable shots – perhaps only 1 per cent of the footage taken.

With all the time required for such things as setting up the lighting and moving props around there may, at the end of an extremely busy day's shooting, be no more than 15 to 20 minutes footage actually in the can. That might, eventually, become only a few seconds of the final print.

Editing

The following day everybody will gather round to see the **rushes** (a quick, cheap, unedited print of the previous day's takes). A lot of footage will be eliminated at this stage, but eventually there will be sufficient footage to complete the assignment and from this a **rough cut** will be made. Two or more versions could be made, but the most important, at this stage, would be the **director's cut**: the director's selection of the takes he thinks work best and linked together to tell the story as he sees it. A point to remember here is that the director (and the editor) may be absorbed by the filmic qualities of the work whereas the agency and the client will be more concerned with whether or not it will actually sell anything. It is perfectly possible to produce a brilliant commercial, even an award-winning commercial, that makes very little impact on the client's profits.

Eventually, the commercial will be **fine cut** and all the finishing touches put in, including synchronising the sound track with the film, dissolves (which allow one scene to change into another without a sharp break) and graphics (words which are overlaid on to the film). Words can be made to **crawl** across the screen (bringing the letters up one at a time).

12.13 Post-production

When the final cut is made, it is necessary to arrange delivery to the ITV companies or cinemas where the commercial is going to be screened. If **bulk prints** are made then each ITV region may require six copies which, if a national campaign across all ITV regions plus Channel 4 is intended, would involve the manufacture and distribution of over a hundred bulk prints – an expensive exercise. A cheaper alternative is to transfer the film to video before sending it to the stations, in which case only one copy need be sent. It is even possible to send the commercial by landline using a company which has such video distribution facilities. Again, always check with the media owners. Sky requires two SP Betacom tapes and one VHS tape (PAL) for each separate piece of copy and has a handling charge per copy – Sky will also make the commercial subject to the provision of a script.

For cinema, of course, bulk copies of the film must be distributed and depending on the number of cinemas booked this also can prove very expensive. Meeting copy deadlines is important here as it is for print. ITV companies usually want their copies a week before the first transmission and cinema ten working days.

Case Study

Castlemaine XXXX (TV campaign)

Title: Experienced Storytellers
Client: Carlsberg-Tetley

May 1994
Forty seconds

Campaign Requirement
- Build on XXXX status as a huge national brand particularly amongst younger beer drinkers

Campaign Success
- Still early days ... but massive media enthusiasm at its launch [N. B. The comment about 'early days' was made in June 1994]

Television Script

PICTURE	SOUND
Open on a young girl, a farmer's daughter in the outback. She is wearing a floral print dress as she sort of skips through the field down to the lake in front of the farm.	
She is a bit soppy as she says hello to the sheep.	GIRL: Hello sky, hello birds. Hello sheep ... isn't it a beautiful day.
She arrives at the lake and looks out across the water and sighs at the beauty of it.	GIRL: Sigh ...

Fig. 12.3 Castlemaine XXXX TV campaign

A frog at her feet croaks, she looks down and smiles in delight.

GIRL: Hello Mr Frog . . . I bet if I was to give you a kiss, you'd turn into a handsome sheep shearer . . .

She picks up the frog in both hands and blows it a kiss.

There is a small bang and the frog turns into a handsome muscular sheep shearer. She is only temporarily taken aback.

She stands on tip-toe, closes her eyes and puckers her lips to be kissed.

He dutifully kisses her, somewhat tentatively.

There is another bang. She disappears and he finds she has turned into a can of XXXX and a glass which he is holding.

He pours the beer from the can into the glass. It catches the sun.

MVO: Castlemaine is made with golden cluster hops.

He takes a long satisfying drink from the glass.

He looks admiringly at the beer in the glass.

SHEARER: You haven't got any sisters, have you?

CU pint of XXXX.

SUPER: EXPERIENCED HOPPERS WOULDN'T GIVE A CASTLEMAINE XXXX FOR ANY OTHER LAGER.

MVO: Experienced hoppers wouldn't give a Castlemaine XXXX for any other lager.

Source: *Saatchi & Saatchi*

12.14 The development of commercial radio

Originally, radio broadcasting was initiated for the purpose of selling radio sets – obviously a difficult thing to sell if there are no programmes to receive. (The present policy of satellite companies buying the television rights to major sporting events and even the dispute between pop star George Michael and records giant Sony are contemporary examples of the same phenomenon – it is easier to sell the hardware if you control the software.)

By the 1920s some 200 independent stations existed. In 1922 the British Broadcasting Company was formed by an amalgamation of many small independents and the idea of a national network evolved. In 1926 the British Broadcasting Company's licence expired and the present BBC (British Broadcasting Corporation), a national service, was set up by royal charter to replace it.

The wheel began to turn full circle in 1967 when the BBC opened its first local radio station at Leicester and by 1983 there were 30 BBC local stations. Today there are 40. These BBC local stations do not accept advertising.

In 1972 commercial radio in mainland UK was established by the Sound Broadcasting Act which set up 30 independent local radio (ILR) stations. Over the years more and more licences to operate commercial radio stations have been granted. In some cases this has led to a growth of smaller and smaller stations serving local neighbourhoods and in others it has led to the parallel provision of separate and competing stations serving the same neighbourhood. The existing 150 ILR stations are virtually all controlled by larger groups such as GWR, Capital and Emap.

The most recent development has been the creation of national commercial stations such as Classic FM and Virgin Radio. The Radio Authority is proposing a third national service and five new regional services may soon be in operation. National stations offer opportunities for national campaigns and many advertisers who had not previously used radio came into the market for the first time. Classic FM, as the name suggests, is for the lover of classical music and offers a more up-market editorial surround for advertisers, whilst Virgin Radio appeals more to a younger popular music audience.

The development of commercial radio, a long way yet from being a major player in the advertising world, has posed a problem for BBC Radio. There is an ongoing battle for audiences which independent radio seems to be winning. Bad news for the BBC is that it holds a larger share of older listeners and a smaller share of the under forty-fives relative to the independents.

12.15 Radio and television audiences compared

People tend to use radio and television in quite different ways. These differences can be explained, in part, by the visual nature of TV which makes it more demanding. This is not to say that television viewers give their undivided attention to the small screen; they do not, but there are things that a viewer cannot do which a radio listener can. Driving a car, washing and shaving, putting up a shelf and gardening are examples. In all these cases, the radio can become a sort of companion, talking away in the background or providing musical accompaniment. This can, of course, be a minus factor for advertisers with the fear that the message will become so much background noise and be lost. Listeners do, of course, also settle down to listen to a concert or a play much as they would to watch a television programme, but the tendency is for radio to be on as an accompaniment to some other activity.

Radio listeners tend not to zap from programme to programme as viewers do. This may be partly because television sets have remote controls which make zapping easier, but the explanation seems to be rather that radio listeners find a service which they like and then stick to it. Lisa Buckingham writing in the *Guardian* (24 December 1993) quotes Capital Radio commercial director, David Mansfield, as saying, 'Radio has a unique relationship with its audience. It is very personal: listeners feel it is their radio station and advertisers are becoming aware that they can buy into that relationship which they can't get elsewhere. Radio is not like television, where people have a relationship with programmes rather than the companies which make them. Radio listeners are far less promiscuous than TV viewers.' Putting it another way, listeners are not so curious about what is going on on other services. This feature of radio audiences makes the job of the radio air-time buyer easier. Instead of being so concerned, as the television buyer is, with the audience for each separate film, soap opera or documentary, he can concentrate more on the simpler question of what kind of people listen to a particular station. In the USA this is more developed than it is in the UK and one station will do nothing all day long but play Country and Western music. Such a station will appeal to a loyal, albeit small, audience whose tastes can be fairly easily researched. Advertisers know exactly what they are getting for their money. With around 150 ILR stations already broadcasting and more still to come, the Americanisation of independent radio may not be so far off and London may, for example, be on the verge of getting its first women's station.

In general, radio audiences tend to be smaller than television audiences but more homogeneous. One important factor affecting audience size is the fact that radio listening is more of a solitary activity whereas television viewing is more of a group or family activity. The larger television audiences are much more varied and diverse in make-up.

12.16 Using radio advertising

Radio advertising has been regarded as the Cinderella of the advertising world characterised by poorly made commercials suggesting that the only advertisers who would use radio are those who could not afford to use television. It is rapidly shedding this image. It has, in the past, attracted only about 2 per cent of total advertising revenue compared with 10 per cent in the US. This is projected to rise to about 5 per cent over the next few years and radio is, obviously, becoming more attractive. This increase in popularity among campaign planners is partly attributed to the increased sales efforts of existing ILR and INR stations and partly to the existence of new stations. The entry of national commercial radio clearly played an important part. Contrary to early expectations, it did not simply eat into the advertising revenues of the ILR stations but attracted more advertisers and encouraged existing advertisers to spend more. An equally vital factor is the increased interest placed on improving creative and production values.

Another important factor has been the provision, through RAJAR (the relatively new joint industry audience research system), of a credible, well-funded and regular supply of secondary data to the advertising industry. In fact RAJAR's first year-on-year results showed commercial radio gaining at the expense of the BBC to the tune of about 2 million viewers – good news for radio air-time sellers and buyers alike. The Radio Advertising Bureau (RAB), an industry-sponsored body which liaises with advertisers, has not only worked to promote the benefits of radio advertising but also to help new advertisers to understand a media which many felt was difficult to use. For example, some potential advertisers did not appreciate the extent to which radio can be used for direct response campaigns tied in to a direct-mail operation to the trade. Capital Radio features these possibilities in its promotional literature and offers advice on setting up such campaigns. Both air-time costs and production costs are equally important for an advertiser with the radio CPT (cost per thousand) often running at as little as one-third of the television CPT with even more dramatic differences in production costs.

Radio can be used in a similar way to posters. It can be first choice in a single medium campaign, but it can also be used in conjunction with other media – poster campaigns can be selected to match ILR areas. Manufacturers of nationally branded goods may use radio to boost sales in selected areas (possibly tied in with local distributors) and the relative speed with which radio commercials can be made and radio-time bought facilitates its use in such a tactical way. Local businesses, for whom television advertising is either too costly or inappropriate, may turn to radio instead. Indeed, local businesses may combine local radio with local press advertising which, with the possibility of deemed consent posters (see page 132) outside their own premises, can make a good local mixed media campaign.

Radio advertising is not confined to consumer goods. Many of the products and services advertised in so-called drive-time advertising (when the audience will be heavily weighted with business people driving to and from work) can be business goods. Office stationery, personnel recruiting services, mobile telephones and business travel are some such goods. The drive-time audience is largely confined to the early morning and early evening travel peaks and gives way to a more house-bound audience during the day and at evenings and weekends.

In general, any product that can be advertised in other media can be advertised on radio. But radio is less suitable for products for which there are lengthy mandatory inclusions. Financial products, for example, require some lengthy disclaimers and warnings which can be tucked away in small print at the bottom of a printed advertisement but which would sound extremely boring if read out on air.

12.17 Buying and selling radio air-time

Radio buying is now becoming a specialist function with large organisations (such as Zenith Media – the largest broadcast media buyer) having separate radio buying departments. National Network Radio is a relatively new, and still small, initiative which gives buyers an opportunity to buy around the country on different stations on a themed basis (for example, gardening programmes) and, of course, where companies like Capital and Emap own a group of local stations that can be exploited to make buying easier.

Larger advertisers, particularly those planning a regional or national campaign, find it easier to buy air-time through sales companies such as Independent Radio Sales (IRS). Air-time sellers often prefer this route as such an arrangement reduces the number of buying and selling points and gives some economies of scale and operation.

IR stations employ their own sales people who, strongly competitive with local press advertising, scour the local papers to identify potential leads to follow up by telephone or personal visits. Many IR stations use on-air advertising to attract advertisers and one tactic is to feature satisfied clients endorsing the effectiveness of radio advertising. Slogans such as 'Radio advertising sells faster than the speed of sound' may be heard.

Capital Radio, for example, offers some interesting services: **spot plans** enable a commercial to go out at a time that best fits the product; **thermal packs** are used for temperature-related products so that commercials are aired more often when it is hot (for ice-cream) or cold (for cough mixtures); **time spots** tie the commercial to relevant on-air announcements.

Kiss FM (another London station) offers advanced booking incentives of 15 per cent for a campaign booked at least 28 days in advance and has a special **test market** package for new products or services. For local businesses (defined as those which derive 90 per cent of their turnover from the Kiss FM listening area) there is a special rate. Kiss FM builds its rate card around a 30-second fixed-rate spot with rates for shorter or longer commercials geared to this (minus 50 per cent for 10 seconds, plus 30 per cent for 40 seconds, for example). Kiss FM also operates a system of surcharges for preferred spots – a surcharge of 20 per cent guarantees a specific hour and 30 per cent a specific hour and day. Other IR stations around the country offer similar services. Small local businesses may need advice and help with setting up a radio campaign. Giving such advice, right up to writing the script and producing the commercial, is part of the service offered to attract advertisers. In such cases, of course, the cost of production is additional to that of the air-time bought.

12.18 Creating and researching the concept

If posters can be characterised as messages on a wall then radio can be characterised as images in the mind. Radio is often thought of as a poor sister to television because it lacks any visual quality, but this is to ignore that what we do not have put before our eyes we create for ourselves in our imagination. Indeed, the concept of closure in Gestalt psychology presupposes this (see page 72).

The entire script of a TV commercial may transfer well to radio (as did the Vauxhall Astra campaign starring Tom Conti), but sometimes an entirely different campaign is developed (compare the Castlemaine XXXX radio and television scripts reproduced in this chapter). Note that the radio script, having no visuals, is divided into dialogue and sound effects.

If posters are an art director's medium then radio is a copywriter's medium. Where there is no art there would seem to be no need for an art director. Nevertheless, it is a good idea to attempt to visualise the proposed advertisement. A little artwork (however elementary) can greatly assist the copywriter's imagination. Indeed, some professionals go so far as to create a full storyboard.

Radio drama works best when you can 'see' the people involved: when they are believable, have personalities and backgrounds and, even when you are not told about their backgrounds, you find yourself building up a picture of them. This involves a process called characterisation which means that you can believe that the characters have a real life which takes place outside the confines of the commercial. One way to achieve this in testing out an advertising concept is to get people to act out the commercial as though they were doing it to camera or in front of an audience making full use of facial expression and body language. If the concept is being researched using a group of volunteer consumers they can be asked questions such as 'What do you think the relationship between these people was before this incident took place?' or 'How do you think the relationship between these people will be affected by what you have just heard?' But too often radio commercials sound like what they are – people just reading words off pieces of paper.

It is not only the characters that need to be credible. The setting has to be established and, in the absence of visuals, this is where music and sound effects come into their own. Although voice-only commercials are cheaper to make, it can be a false economy in terms of effectiveness.

Silence on radio can have the same effect as white space on the printed page. It can highlight the text and be used to provide a barrier between one commercial and the next. In practice, advertisers are, naturally, reluctant to pay good money for silence and a preferred alternative way of buffering the advertisement is by the use of sound effects or music. With visual advertisements, it is usually simple to tell where one item ends and another begins. With sound alone, the margins are not so clear unless they are positively signalled in some way. Whether to provide these signals by silence, music or sound effects is a creative judgement. Speech can, of course, be used to lead in and out of the commercial as long as the core message is not compromised in the process.

Length and timing are also important. A radio commercial can be made in the same lengths as for television (usually a multiple of 10 seconds up to a maximum of 60 seconds) and one very good reason for acting out the script is to get the timing right and to pace it correctly within the chosen length. At the very least, the script should be transferred to an ordinary tape recorder and played back to get a feel of the pace and structure before proceeding further.

Like other advertisements, radio commercials are subject to a degree of control. Proposals which may be judged controversial in any way should be cleared by the Broadcast Advertising Clearance Centre (BACC) – see page 47.

12.19 The production process

In theory, with a good quality tape recorder, it is possible to make your own radio commercial. In practice, the likelihood of producing anything of real broadcastable quality is low and the job is best left to the professionals – independent stations usually have good in-house production facilities. The cost of making a professional commercial is a **fixed cost** and the more often it is aired the lower the average cost of each airing. As one of the virtues of radio advertising is the capability for frequent repetition (it's possible to hear the same commercial three or four times in three-quarters of an hour) spending money on production is not wasted.

Once into the production studio, with the exception of cameras and outdoor locations, you are treading on similar ground to the television commercial. You will need the skills of a producer and director, with all the necessities of script, performers, music and sound effects, etc.

On radio the quality of the voice is paramount. But it is not always worthwhile paying star names for their voices alone: a specialist voice agency may have what you want at considerably less cost. In any case, voice auditions should be held.

It is often said that getting the music right is harder than getting the voice right. In the cinema, the soundtrack is often written after the scene has been filmed so that the music matches the action. The same principle can apply in radio. If the budget will run to it, it is worth approaching a specialist composing agency.

Finally, the temptation to book a studio for a whole day and to go on recording and re-recording a 30-second commercial until it is right should be avoided. The production should be properly rehearsed and planned to cut expensive studio time down to a minimum.

12.20 Distribution

After the commercial has been produced, it has to be distributed to the various stations on which it is going to be aired. A professionally produced commercial will probably be on a cartridge for transmission purposes. A cartridge is a closed continuous loop sealed within a cassette-type case. A bank of such cartridges can be set up in advance within the broadcast studio and each one can be pressed into action when required. It loops round and automatically resets itself for the next airing. A self-made commercial may be delivered to the studio on the original cassette, but in this case it would be transferred to a cartridge before it could be broadcast. An alternative to delivering the commercial on either cassette or cartridge is to send it by landline from the agency to the studio in much the same way as a telephone call is made. Advances in radio technology may make the use of cartridges obsolete very quickly.

When a company, say Capital Radio, makes a commercial for a client, it charges for the writing of the script and the production of the finished article. In the process, performers and musical accompaniment will also have been used and the artists concerned will have been paid a fee. This fee is for Capital Radio usage only and if, subsequently, the client wishes to use the commercial on a national campaign, say on Virgin, the performers are entitled to an extra **usage fee**. The same applies to the music arrangers whose interests are protected by the MCPS (Mechanical-Copyright Protection Society). For the purely local usage, the script will have been cleared through Capital's own copy clearance office but for the national usage it will have to go through the BACC. No additional fee is payable to Capital since no extra writing or production costs are involved.

Case Study

Castlemaine XXXX (Radio campaign)

Title: Bank of Beyond September 1993 – November 1993
Client: Carlsberg-Tetley Thirty seconds

Campaign Requirement
- National radio promotion with direct mail
- Win Australian dollars, 25p-off coupon, flights to Australia
- Primarily targeted at housewives, but to promote overall awareness of XXXX

Campaign Success
- Winner of 1993 Institute of Sales Promotion Gold Award for best use of paid-for media. Platinum Award for best overall promotional campaign
- 62% of radio winners were female
- Voucher redemption 5.5% (4% expected)
- Excellent radio station feedback

Radio Script

SOUND EFFECTS DIALOGUE

MAN 1: (with sentiment and feeling) Have you seen this XXXX 'Bank of Beyond' promotion, Snowy?

You can win real Aussie dollars . . .

SFX: Waltzing Matilda played on strings.

SNOWY: Lovely crisp little things they are.
MAN 1: You can even win flights back to Oz.

SNOWY: Ah, I can see the little wallabies frolicking in the bush right now . . .

SFX: Music stops abruptly.

MAN 1: And there's no purchase necessary.

SNOWY: Ek, I knew there'd be a catch.

VO: The XXXX 'Bank of Beyond' Promotion Cards will be coming through your door.

Source: Saatchi & Saatchi

12.21 Summary

- Terrestrial and non-terrestrial television sell air-time differently. Terrestrial TV is sold on the basis of rate cards, TVRs and a pre-empt system similar to a sealed-bid auction. Sky television, in contrast, has no rate card as such and negotiates with each advertiser or agency separately through two regional offices. Sky air-time is sold on a first-come first-served basis.
- Terrestrial TV requires specialist buying skills to set up a campaign which is usually done through specialist selling and buying points.
- Cinema campaigns are different again. There are only two contractors and screens are controlled by one or the other. Screens can be bought line by line, but there are various packages, such as the art screen package, which are tailored to meet specific needs. It is also possible to lock into a particular film with the film package and follow it from cinema to cinema.
- Television commercials use story-lines, involving real or fictitious people, based on social reality or with a documentary appeal. Surrealism can also be used as long as the audience can still make some sense of it. Animals may be used with or without people (or even to represent people) and animation offers further scope for the imagination. The story-lines may be treated with humour, adventure, nostalgia and, if properly handled, even with grief and death.

- Concepts for TV commercials can be tested in halls or theatres using scenarios, storyboards, animatics and simulations before going to production. The choice of directors and production houses is important as are the different stages from script to location, casting and choice of props through to editing and the final finished version.
- Independent radio (IR) is available on two (soon possibly three) national stations with about 150 independent local stations (ILR). Regional stations may be operating by the end of 1994.
- Radio is the only non-visual media group and this fact affects both the creative and the production aspects of running a campaign.
- Still relatively small at less than 5 per cent of total advertising spend, radio advertising is increasing in popularity and its usefulness in conjunction with such things as a sales promotion or direct-mail campaign is now much more recognised.
- Radio can be used on its own, but radio and poster campaigns, for example, can be matched up with poster sites selected within a given ILR area.
- Radio audiences tend to be more loyal than television audiences, forming an attachment to stations or services rather than to individual programmes. This special relationship is something which advertisers can exploit.
- Radio is not confined to the home and can be used as an accompaniment to other activities such as driving and gardening.
- As an advertising medium radio can be used for both consumer and user goods and the drive-time concept is important for the latter.

12.22 Assignments

1. Discuss the relative merits of the ITV and Sky methods of selling air-time.

2. Think about some cinema commercials which are not normally seen on TV and discuss what it is about them, if anything, that makes them more suitable for the big screen.

3. In what ways might creating a commercial for the big screen be different from creating one for the small screen? Would all TV commercials be equally effective in the cinema and vice versa?

4. Develop a script for a 30-second TV commercial. Act it out in front of a group for evaluation and constructive criticism.

5. Draw up a list of about twelve consumer goods and discuss which treatments you would give each one (humorous, nostalgic, etc.). Do you think that every product could be given every treatment or do you think that some treatments would not always work?

6. Think of a product which could be sold in either the consumer or the user market (airline tickets, for example) and try to develop two different concepts with a suitable 30-second radio script for each. Present the concepts (and/or scripts) to a group discussion and evaluation.

7. Radio is a copywriter's medium. Discuss.

8. Consider the ways in which radio advertising could be used in conjunction with another media group or a below-the-line activity.

9. Compare and contrast the separate treatments given to Castlemaine XXXX in the television and radio ads.

13 Advertising and children *

**13.1
Introduction**

In this chapter our main concern is with selling things to children but this is hard to disassociate from selling things through children – it depends on who makes the purchase decision. As far as selling things through children is concerned, the issue is made more complex by the fact that some of the things sold in this way are not children's products at all. There is a sort of matrix with fuzzy boundaries (see fig. 13.1) of child products and adult products on the one hand and appeals to children and appeals to adults on the other. The boundaries are blurred: a breakfast cereal may be either an adult or a child product (although some are more obviously designed for kids) and some appeals may strike responses in both adult and child alike. Incidentally, the word 'kids' is quite widely used as in 'kid-appeal' and its use, in this context, is neither sloppy nor patronising. A third dimension which cuts across all sectors of the matrix is the use of children in the advertisements themselves. Children are often used in advertisements for products such as Oxo and services such as the AA within the context of a social or documentary dramatisation and very young babies are used to sell baby-care products to young mothers. We are less concerned with this aspect in this chapter (except where children are used in advertisements to sell products to children) but that does not mean that the use of children in this way is of no interest at all. The ASA and ITC, not to mention concerned parents groups, are anxious not to see children wrongly exploited for commercial gain.

**13.2
The structure
of the
children's
market**

According to James McNeal, in his book *Kids as Customers*, children constitute a three-layer market. The first layer, or **primary market**, is concerned with the child's own discretionary income arising from pocket money, earnings and gifts. Children do not spend all their money immediately and some do save. Savings, therefore, swell the discretionary income at key purchase points when children 'dis-save' to finance a larger than 'pocket-money' purchase.

American and British research reveal high levels of savings. McNeal estimated that about a third of American pocket money is saved and the Halifax report showed 68 per cent of surveyed children claiming to save something, mostly for a special reason. Twenty-nine per cent saved for holidays, 15 per cent for large toys and 14 per cent for computer software and equipment.

---

* This chapter was co-authored by Doreen Stone, Marketing Manager of the London College of Printing and Distributive Trades, whose research archives for her MA thesis 'The Extent and Effect of Child-Directed Advertising with Particular Reference to the Under 12s in the UK Market in the 1990s' provided both the inspiration and the stimulus.

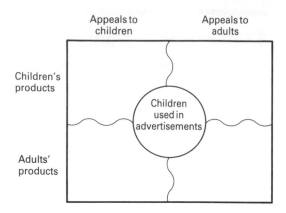

Fig. 13.1   Matrix of child and adult products and their appeal

The second layer, or **secondary market**, represents the influence that children have on the purchasing decisions of their parents. This may be related to the purchase of children's products, such as clothes, toys and games, but may also relate to the purchase of other items, such as furniture and holidays. It even extends to the parents' own clothes – 'You're not really going to wear that are you, Mum?' The influence may be direct – a straightforward request for a new pair of designer-label trainers – or indirect where the parents take account of what they perceive the child to want without actually involving the child in the decision-making process.

The relationship between the primary and secondary markets is determined to a large extent by the attitudes of adults. Some parents may give only a little pocket money and pay for more things themselves, thus keeping more purchase decisions in the secondary area. Other parents may give larger amounts of pocket money with some statement to the effect that 'If you want a new pair of trainers, you can buy them yourself' – this shifts the purchase into the primary field. Grandparents, aunts and uncles, traditionally givers of gifts, have tended to become givers of money (or at least givers of gift vouchers) as they bow out of the attempt to keep up with children's changing tastes and fashions. The extent to which this takes place is obviously of interest to marketers.

Until he was about six years old my youngest son, now a successful businessman in his own right, had no discretionary pocket money. If he wanted something he asked for it and, if it wasn't unreasonable, he usually got it. It was decided to give him pocket money and to make him responsible for his own purchases – basically, he was told: 'You can spend it how you like, but once it's gone, it's gone, and you won't get any more.' The following week we were in the local newsagent's and he saw some new model soldiers in the display rack. 'Dad,' he said, 'can I have one of those, please?' 'It's up to you,' I replied. 'It's your money.' He looked again at the soldiers, shook his head and said, 'No, I'm not wasting my money on that rubbish.' The purchase had shifted from the secondary to the primary market with a different outcome. I probably would have 'wasted' my money (or let him waste it for me).

The third layer, the **tertiary market**, can be called the future market. Children grow up to be adults and their adult purchasing patterns will be affected by their childhood experiences and perceptions. The concept of 'a customer for life' can take on almost Jesuitical proportions (give us the child and we will give you the man) when applied to wooing this element of the child market. Banks and building societies encourage the saving habit, restaurants encourage the eating-out habit, publishers encourage the book-reading habit and so on in the hope that tomorrow's adults will be savers, diners and readers (ideally as customers of the same business but, at least, economically active in the market). It goes further than this, though; children take in the images of adult products such as alcohol and tobacco which they are not yet allowed to buy but to which they may, nevertheless, form an attachment. Children often cite among their favourite commercials Red Rock cider, Heinneken beer and Guinness stout. The packaging and advertising of Camel cigarettes have often been criticised for their use of a cartoon-character camel which children quite clearly identify with and like; Hoffmeister's streetwise George the bear faced similar criticism. Advertisers of adult products may deliberately seek to exploit images which they know will appeal to children and which may shape their future adult preferences.

13.3
The growth of the primary market

The primary market is not small. Office of Population and Census figures (1992) projected a growth of 5 to 14-year-olds in the UK from 7.16 million in 1991 to 7.91 million by the year 2001 – much bigger than the entire population of Denmark (just over 5 million) and almost as big as the populations of Belgium or Greece (nearly 10 million each). The interest in the size of the market is indicated by the number of articles in trade journals ('There will be 10 per cent more children in Britain in 2000 than in the late 1980s,' *Travel Weekly*, 9 September 1992) and reports ('by the year 2000, the number of children will rise to 11.9 million keeping the market buoyant for toys and other children's products', *Retail Intelligence Report*, Vol 5 1988).

It is not small in purchasing power either, as companies as diverse as the Halifax Building Society, Tetley and Wall's, which have all produced estimates of children's spending power, testify. The Halifax Building Society's 1992 report on children's spending and saving showed an average pocket money of £1.48 for the under-twelves augmented by earnings to bring it up to £2.09. Older groups do better: the Halifax quoted £7.90 per week discretionary income for 12 to 16-year-olds. The Henley Centre for Market Research (quoting Gallop) gives an average for 5 to 16-year-olds of £3.86 per week discretionary income. Stone (1993) summarising answers from 271 7 to 11-year-olds across London showed 41 per cent receiving under £2, 25 per cent between £2 and £4 and 34 per cent over £4, with an average of £3.05. There are difficulties in reconciling all these figures with different base years and different age-bands, but a very simple (and almost certainly understated) model would give a minimum of £2 × 52 weeks × 7 million 5 to 14-year-olds = £728 million a year. Add in the under-fives and the over-fourteens and allow for a higher average of, say, £3.50 and you could be looking at something in excess of £1 250 million. As James McNeal says: 'Kids pack an economic punch.'

Social and demographic factors have played a part. Even in these times of high unemployment there are still many two-income households with both parents out at work and as Selina Guber, President of Children's Market Research Inc (USA) says of the American scene, 'Mom and Dad, too busy making money to spend it, are surrendering the purse-strings to children.' Some supermarkets in the USA are so used to seeing the kids doing the shopping that they have introduced scaled-down versions of the shopping trolley to suit these smaller customers. The divorce rate, high on both sides of the Atlantic, is also a contributory factor with many children enjoying the phenomena of receiving money (or gifts) from two sets of parents who may be seeking to compensate (or over-compensate) the children.

Technological changes with the acceptance of the television set as a standard piece of household equipment (it is barely 25 or 30 years since television sets stopped being regarded as luxuries and became household necessities) and improved ways of manipulating on-screen images have exposed children to a wave of media communications to which their grand-parents (and perhaps their parents) were not exposed. This, in turn, may have had a significant effect on the expectations of today's young people, almost all of whom have been born into television homes.

Changes in the size and purchasing power of children as a primary market have gone along with changes in the pattern of things bought, partly as a result of increasing autonomy (fewer things bought for them, more money given to them) and partly as a result of the development of new products. The stalwarts among pocket-money purchases remain sweets, toys, maga-zines and comics. There are, however, differences between the sexes and between age groups. Stone found that video games rated second (after sweets) for boys but only ninth for girls, whereas clothes rated first with girls and eighth with boys. Books ranked higher for girls than for boys, sup-porting the findings of Mallory Wober (author of several special reports commissioned by the IBA before it became the ITC) that 'Girls more often read books than do boys' (perhaps because the boys are too busy with their video games). In fact, toys which rated highly for both sexes in the younger (7 to 8-year-old) group seemed to be replaced by clothes for girls and video games for boys in the older (9 to 11-year-old) group.

Clothes and shoes did not feature at all in Carrick James's 1977 survey of 7 to 10-year-olds' expenditure (Carrick James Market Research report, cited in the 1982 OECD report, 'Advertising directed at children'). McNeal, how-ever, found that expenditure on clothes and trainers had gone from 0 per cent to 11.5 per cent of children's discretionary income in five years (1984–9) and Stone found girls of 7 to 8-years-old rating clothes second and girls of 9–11 rating clothes first. This does not necessarily mean that boys have no interest in clothes but, possibly, that they have no interest in clothes shop-ping. Many adult men have no interest in clothes shopping either and are content to let their female partners buy their clothes for them.

Table 13.1   Children's influence on adult purchases

How often does your child have any influence on deciding your purchases?	
Food	82%
Children's clothes	79%
Holidays	50%
Furniture	30%
Parents' clothes	20%

13.4 The development of the secondary market

The above figure takes no account of the value of the secondary market which is no recent phenomenon, as a quote from Harvey Lesser, in *Television and the pre-school child* (1977) shows: 'children were once considered to have little influence on product purchase decisions. They are now viewed as having considerable influence even on products that are consumed by adults.' How much influence, in economic terms, children have on their parents' spending is hard to measure, but it is generally regarded as being much greater than the value of their primary spending and a wide range of industries takes it very seriously:

- Children are exerting an influence across a range of product categories . . . beyond traditional children's markets (*Marketing Week*, 21 August 1992).
- Children certainly play an important part in the decision-making equation . . . children have highly developed opinions of where they want to go and what they want to do (*Travel Weekly* 9 September 1992).
- The Henley Centre's findings conclude that children are 'a persuasive influence behind the scenes' (*Super Marketing* 15 April 1993).

McNeal, in the US, gave food and drinks as by far the biggest area of influence but also included toys, clothes, cars, electronic goods and health and beauty products. The Henley Centre's UK results on this issue aroused considerable editorial comment (see Table 13.1).

The figures in Table 13.1 were based on the parents' perception. Stone asked the children how they perceived it and obtained 354 replies (see Table 13.2).

13.5 Pester power and parental yielding

'Parental yielding' is a fairly well established concept that goes beyond acquisition and purchase to include such things as bedtime and television-viewing. It is, in any case, a natural part of the growing-up and socialisation process as parents gradually yield greater autonomy to their children. The trend seems to have been, however, to yield to children at a much earlier age and over a wider range of issues so that parents appear in some cases to be disempowered (the children always get their own way) and children are seen to be growing up too soon (loss of childhood). Sally Ford-Hutchinson of agency D'Arcy Masius Benton & Bowles says that agency research revealed two different kinds of parents: ' "Controllers" who need a good reason for giving something (the educational or nutritional value, for example) and "indulgers" who are much easier going and may give in on grounds like, "You can't stop kids eating sweets, they all do it." ' A knowledge of child–parent relationships is obviously useful to advertisers.

Table 13.2   How children perceive their influence on adult purchases

Do your grown-ups listen to your views when they buy:

Drinks	75.0%	Toothpaste	39.0%
Shoes	65.5%	Holidays	35.5%
Clothes	65.6%	Soap	33.0%
Sweets	62.0%	Parents' clothes	30.8%

Associated with this phenomenon is the concept of 'pester power' – the pressure that children can put on parents to get their own way. It starts as early as the age of two when the child rides around the supermarket in the trolley, pointing out products featuring well-known cartoon characters, and proceeds through the toddler stage when the child triumphantly brings goods back to the trolley. By 5 or 6 years old they have usually developed persuasive techniques which include a repertoire of appeals to love, pride, duty, guilt and indulgence. Phrases such as 'I need', 'Everybody else has got one' and 'I'll pay you back later' are all part of it. Galst and White, writing in their book *The Uneasy Persuader* (1986), claimed that children make an average of about 15 requests per shopping trip. A recent HMSO report *Your Food: Whose Choice* (1992) stated that 85 per cent of children made requests or demands and that 'two-thirds get what they want'.

Television advertising influences the pattern of things asked for, as Stone found. In answer to the question 'Do you often ask for things advertised on TV?', 65.5 per cent said yes. A question about the children's expectancies of getting their requests met confirmed the view of Elizabeth Sweeney of the Children's Research Unit that children soon learn that only a limited number of requests will be met. Only 28 per cent said that they 'usually' expected to get what they asked for, 55 per cent said 'not very often' and 17 per cent actually said 'never'. Not surprisingly, yielding is more likely to occur when the purchase price of the thing asked for is low and when the thing asked for is more easily perceived as a child product such as toys, soft drinks and breakfast cereals.

A variety of phrases have been used in connection with this – goods are said to rate high or low on the 'nagging scale'. 'Passive dictation' occurs when the parents buy what the children want without asking because 'they already know'. Judith Van Evra in her book, *Television and Child Development* (1990), uses the concept of PIAs (Purchasing Influence Attempts) to describe the pressures that children put on parents and phrases such as 'uneasy persuasion' and 'the unhealthy persuader' describe the pressures put on children by advertisers in general and television in particular. 'Shopping conflicts between parents and children can often be linked to the child's demand for something advertised on television' reported Robert Liebert and Joyce Sprafkin in their study of the effect of television on child behaviour (*The Early Window*, 1988). Perhaps a more disturbing phrase is Foxall's 'reverse socialisation' (in his *Consumer Behaviour: A Practical Guide*, 1980) with the notion that it is the children teaching the parents. Nick Park of Aardman Animation (the creator of the 'Creature Comforts' electricity commercials) is quoted as saying that children 'may be the best targets for certain adult products, especially when adults do not have brand loyalty. They can be induced to serve as very effective lobbyists.' In other words, the adult decides to buy breakfast cereal but the child dictates the brand.

13.6 The battle for the child consumer

Competition for the child consumer takes place on three fronts:

- **Between widely different industries competing for a share of the child spend** For example, toys versus clothes. Mat Toor, a manufacturer of electronic toys, writing in the 9 April 1992 issue of *Marketing*, contrasted the world of the pre-1980s when mothers chose children's clothes and the children were not much interested in who made them with the 1990s where children are more fashion-conscious, choose their own clothes and will often prefer a new item of clothing to a new toy: 'Kids are leaving the toy market at an earlier age.'

- **Between sectors of the same industry** For example, confectionery versus snack foods. The Mintel Report *Sugar Confectionery* commented that 'children are being steered to other food sectors' and that the snacking habit is eating into confectionery sales as children turn to crisps, biscuits, popcorn and new products such as Pop-Tarts. Mat Toor, again: 'The unsuspecting toy industry hasn't been Tango'd, it's been Nintendo'd and it really should have seen it coming.' Apparently, once a child has a Sega or Nintendo console, he'll spend all his spare cash on games for it at the expense of traditional toys.

- **Between brands** For example, Nintendo versus Sega, Barbie versus Sindy. In the run-up to Christmas 1992, Sega's Sonic the Hedgehog knocked Nintendo from the UK market-leader position with a wild, fast-moving and anarchic advertising campaign. In the six-week run-up to Christmas 1993 Nintendo, with new agency J. Walter Thompson, fought back launching a £1 million a week television campaign starring comedian Rik Mayall. In one ad he wanders around a futuristic laboratory where research scientists are producing ever more complex Nintendo games. It is estimated that Sega and Nintendo spent £30 million in a brand war for a market worth £700 million. In the girls' concept toys market, manufacturers of Sindy and Barbie (fashion dolls) and Sylvanian Families and My Little Pony (collectables) can spend between £0.3 million and £1 million each on maintaining their place in the market.

Computer product placement

A curious development is the practice of placing products such as Penguin Biscuits and Quavers into computer games. For fees of between £13 000 and £50 000, a manufacturer can get a 20-second animated sequence featuring the product and can even have the game developed around it. A Consumers' Association spokesman expressed concern about this way of targeting youngsters and described it as 'sneaky to say the least'.

Table 13.3   Analysis of 381 advertisements screened on Saturday morning TV

Product category		Product category		Product category	
Toys	17.5%	Toiletries	5.2%	Videos/music	2.4%
Cereals	13.0%	Drinks	4.0%	Shoes	1.8%
Snacks	8.3%	Cosmetics	2.6%	Finance	1.5%
Retail	6.0%	Milk/meat	2.6%	Other	9.6%

13.7 Children and advertising

There is very little doubt that the modern child's first exposure to advertising is usually on television. 'Television has emerged as the dominant experience in the lives of most children, monopolising more time than any other single activity apart from sleep and school.' (Organisation for Economic Cooperation and Development (OECD) 1982). 'Television is a pervasive presence in children's lives. Nearly every child watches some television every week,' said Dr Barrie Gunter in 'Critical Eyes' (*Spectrum*, Winter 1991). 'Young children are undergoing a television-dominated childhood,' said Conrad Lodziak in *The Power of Television* (1986). Television has even been dubbed 'the electronic babysitter'.

Not surprisingly, television is the medium of choice for most advertisers targeting the child market (at either the primary or secondary level). There is a fair amount of choice: ITV and Channel 4 both run various programmes under the overall umbrella of 'children's television' and cable and satellite services like Nickelodeon and the Children's Channel provide other, albeit smaller, audiences. However, it does not end with children's television. Many, even quite young, children watch adult programming and are consequently exposed to advertisements nominally aimed at adults. A 1991 BARB/AGB report on the children's top ten included *Coronation Street, Beadle's About, Blind Date* and *Strike It Lucky* as amongst the most popular and an IBA report of 1985 showed that, even then, out of 533 4 to 13-year-olds just over half watched at least one programme after 9 pm and 27 per cent claimed to watch as many as three. Including the BBC's *Neighbours* and *EastEnders*, it is obvious that adult soaps are very popular with children and commercial soaps provide useful slots for the child-directed advertiser. Nor are advertisements during children's television programming confined to children's pocket-money products. Stone analysed 19 hours of Saturday morning TV over several consecutive weeks and found that the 381 advertisements (about 20 an hour) broke down into the product categories shown in Table 13.3.

So children may see advertisements for products which they would not normally buy for themselves during children's TV and they are certainly exposed to adult-directed advertisements at other times. In the course of a day's viewing children may see advertisements aimed directly at them (the pocket-money primary market), ads which will feed their tendency to pester (breakfast cereals etc.) and ads which might shape their future preferences and purchasing habits (finance, retail, cosmetics, etc.). A point of concern with some critics is that some of the ads for genuine child products (some toys, video and music goods, for example) are outside the normal pocket-money range and seem clearly intended to encourage pestering.

When it comes to children's perceptions of television advertising, it is clear that very young children see television in a conceptual vacuum in which they cannot distinguish between a programme and an advertisement. At age five or six, they may be able to distinguish one from the other and know that an advertisement is trying to sell them something. They are, however, unlikely to have any useful information base, or concept of price and value, by which they can make valid judgements. When an exasperated mother says 'No. You can't have that, it's too expensive', or 'I can't afford it', it is unlikely that the average five to six-year-old will really understand that either (Mum is just being mean). Children may be as old as 9–11 before they can begin to 'see through' the rhetoric of advertising and to see that the goodies are not all as good as described or to develop an understanding that the goodies on offer do not stem from a benevolent source but from a commercial enterprise out to make a profit and that Mum and Dad are not just being difficult when they say no (some of us never learn).

Another of the reasons why television is so important, apart from its 'window on the world' position as one of a child's most important sources of information, is that it allows for the use of all the effects that appeal to kids. 'Children have a low boredom threshold, a penchant for images and bright colours and an ability to absorb more detail than adults in a shorter period of time.' (*Travel Weekly* 9 September 1991); 'The boredom threshold of a child is frustratingly low.' (*Marketing Week* 21 August 1992). 'Continuous action', 'constant excitement and suspense', 'striking visual effects', 'psychedelic, fast talking and frenzied' and 'attention-grabbing' are all ways in which child-directed advertisements have been described (and also, incidentally, ways in which some children's programmes have been described). A 30-second Amiga advert featuring a monstrous android and a computer whizz-kid had 36 different edits (more than one a second) and no dialogue, only the words 'Have you got what it takes?' coming up on screen.

However, ads aimed specifically at boys (Transformers, Air Blasters, etc.) are somewhat different from ads aimed specifically at girls (Sindy, Barbie, etc.), with the latter, whilst remaining colourful and attention-getting, being considerably calmer and less frenetic than the former. Advertisements for boys' products tend to be more outwardly orientated (adventurous and aggressive) and those for girls' products more inwardly orientated, creating a private inner world. The difference is particularly noticeable in some of the sound tracks with both words and music reflecting the visual content. An interesting feature of the sound tracks in all cases is the predominance of male voices. Out of 331 speakers in 320 commercials taken from five Saturday mornings, Stone noted that just over 80 per cent were male (and most of these adult male at that) reinforcing a perception of the adult male as 'the voice of convincing authority' (Barcus, *Children's Television*, 1977) and in line with the finding of the American pressure group Action for Children's Television (ACT) that 90 per cent of voice-overs are male.

There are also differences in the ways in which different products are represented. Traditional toys such as Scalectrix and Lego or Barbie and Sindy are often featured in advertisements using live children and close-up shots of the products. Video games might be featured in a more fantastical way using live children actually inside the game as opposed to playing with it. Sweets, cereals and snacking goods may make more use of cartoon characters and animation.

Creators are looking for 'kid-appeal' and 'kid-ness', trying to see the world as kids might see it or creating images that appeal to kids. Companies which value the importance of the child influence have their own research teams keeping them up to date on child trends and tastes and helping them to avoid the cardinal error of 'talking down to kids' – children do not like to be patronised.

Of course, television is not the only medium. Many newspapers have children's sections (the *Daily Mirror*'s Mega mirror, for example) and there are comics and magazines clearly intended for the younger reader in which advertisements can be placed. Comics are generally differentiated as nursery comics, for very young children of either sex, boys' comics which are often sport, war and adventure orientated and girls' comics which tend to be romance and fashion orientated. Up to the 1950s or sixties the norm was that comic reading stopped at about age 12–14; but the impact of first the American industry and more recently the Japanese has popularised the reading of comics at a much later age with comics quite deliberately produced for the older reader. Comics are themselves often given away by manufacturers as a sales-promotion stunt, sometimes using established titles and characters, as when Kellogg's Golden Crackles gave away a 2 × 3 in 12-page mini version of the *Beano*, and sometimes with characters specifically designed for the company, as with Wall's 1994 *Chill* comic featuring 'The Ice Team' (Sparkle, Twister and Sunsplash).

Radio commercials aimed at children are also used and both the cinema contractors (RSA and Pearl & Dean) offer children's packages. Children's packages offered by Pearl & Dean run for 18 weeks throughout the year, specifically targeting the school holidays which are obviously going to be the times for children's films to be shown and for new releases ('U' certificate animations etc.) to appear. The packages can be upweighted to include other mainstrean family releases such as *The Addams Family* or *Wayne's World*. RSA's Disney package is sold on the same 18-week basis with the message to advertisers, 'With children today developing increasing brand awareness and exerting more influence than ever before on family purchasing, *what better way to reach parent and child simultaneously*.' CAVIAR research results show that Mum is twice as likely to take the kids to the pictures than Dad. An RSA network campaign will reach 10 per cent of all 7 to 14-year-olds in week one rising throughout the 18-week duration of the campaign to nearly 50 per cent of 12 to 14-year-olds and around 63 per cent of 7 to 11-year-olds.

Poster advertising also has a part to play. The Scallywags campaign shows how a manufacturer with a limited budget can use posters to very great effect.

Case Study

Scallywags

Hall & Associates, the manufacturers of Scallywags, appointed agency Leagas Shafron Davis Chick Ayer to launch their Scallywags bathcare range in 1994. The brief stated that there was no previous advertising experience for the brand and that the budget was limited. The campaign objectives were:

- To create brand awareness amongst the core target audience of housewives with children.
- To generate sales across the Scallywags product range.
- To provide a springboard with which to attract distribution of the range.

The media solution was a national solus poster campaign. With no previous advertising and no other media involved in the campaign this was an excellent opportunity to measure the effectiveness of posters in the child-product market.

The campaign activity involved the period 15 March to 30 April 1994 using roadside and cross-track posters with the message 'Scallywags Bubblebath for kids who get into hot water'.

- 900 48-sheet posters were posted at roadside.
- 100 48-sheet posters were posted cross-track.

The campaign was tracked by RSL Signpost across a four-week period and by Nielsen data from January to May. The Nielsen data gave pre-campaign figures as well as looking at the figures for the immediate post out-of-charge period. The results were encouraging.

- 36 per cent awareness with 67 per cent positive rating and 40 per cent intention to purchase amongst housewives with children.
- 48 per cent awareness amongst 18 to 24-year-olds and 44 per cent amongst Tube travellers.
- Peak market share of 11.5 per cent (equivalent to 26 per cent share where stocked).

The campaign seemed not to have drawn business away from rival children's bubblebath brands but to have expanded the overall marketplace.

Source: Maiden Outdoor

Sales promotions

Sales promotions are, of course, widely used and manufacturers are quick to take advantage of any craze that kids might have. Dinosaurs and Teenage Mutant Hero Turtles have been used to sell anything from clothing to breakfast cereal through straightforward character merchandising to the giving away as gifts of posters, models, stickers and the like. Every new film offers opportunities for this sort of treatment and it is already estimated that *The Flintstones* might earn as much from such spin-offs as it will at the box office. Joint promotions are often attractive to advertisers. Heinz and Little Chef in mid-1994 ran a joint 'Kids Eat Free' campaign featured on the labels of Heinz Chef's Specials range of

Fig. 13.2   Scallywags advertisement

goods in which a child accompanied by an adult could eat up to £2.50 worth of food in exchange for two tokens providing that the adult spent at least £5. When, in July 1994, Ready Brek offered Corgi toy cars (which changed colour after being dipped in hot water) the *Daily Mirror*'s Mega Mirror ran a competition to give away 100 of the cars in answer to the qualifying question 'From which cereal is Ready Brek made?'

13.8 Criticisms of child-directed advertising

There has been a wide range of criticism of child-directed advertising and bodies like the ITC and the Radio Authority both have codes to limit its worst excesses. That these codes do not go far enough for some critics will undoubtedly fuel further debate. In reading the following paragraphs it is important to recognise that they represent the views of critics, some of whom are strongly committed to the view that advertising to children is wrong. Counter arguments are not given below but that does not mean that no counter-arguments exist.

- **The effect on unhealthy eating habits** The HMSO report *Your Food: Whose Choice* (1992) devoted a whole chapter to the harmful effects of food advertising on children, and in 1993 a Channel 4 survey of 250 10 to 15-year-olds revealed that 59 per cent ate no fruit and 53 per cent ate no vegetables whereas 88 per cent ate snacking food at least once a day and 74 per cent drank soft drinks at least once a day. The survey findings (based on diaries kept by the children) featured in the Channel 4 series *Eat Up*. More damning was the OECD report which stated that 'Persuasive commercial forces work unremittingly to encourage unwise eating habits . . . They promote over-salted, over-sugared snack foods that distort diets' and lead to tooth decay, obesity, diabetes and heart problems. The American Medical Association said, 'Advertising on television is counter-productive to the encouragement of sound eating habits.' The National Food Alliance, which has the backing of the British Dental Association and the British Heart Foundation, has called for an advertising-free zone for children's television and has criticised the ITC for being too soft on advertisers.

- **Increased child–parent conflict** The obvious conflict arises when the child wants something and the parents say no. This makes many parents feel that they are being pushed into adopting negative attitudes as a response to advertisement-stimulated pestering. A frequent example arises from the child's desire to buy a dearer branded product in order to obtain a gift when the parent (usually Mum) really feels that a gift-free cheaper product will do just as well or, at a dearer level, when the child wants a designer-label garment because 'all my friends have got one' and the parents believe that a cheaper item will be just as nice. The practice of most supermarkets of placing sweets next to the checkout points became a public focal point for conflict, and pressure has resulted in supermarkets (for example, Azda) removing sweets from all checkouts or, as with some others, from some checkouts. An aware child may, however, know that it is being led through a sweet-free checkout and this solution is not enough for some parents.
  To balance the argument, it should be noted that many parents do not mind saying no and accept it as part of the developing process and that

many children do not really expect to have all their requests met. Nevertheless, conflict, where it exists, is very real and very painful.

- **The exploitation of peer-group pressure**   Peer groups are part of any society and in themselves are not alarming. Everybody belongs to a group, be it based on age, religion, occupation or on status and fellow members of the same group are one's peers. Peer-group pressure occurs when a 'price' is exacted for membership of the group and acceptance in it. The 'price' in the child market is seldom cash but usually involves the performance of some deed or the ownership of some property. At its worst, it may involve some act of petty theft or joy-riding. But here we are concerned only with the extent to which, in order to belong, a child has to have a particular branded product.

  The emphasis on brand is important. Many modern youngsters feel that to belong they have to wear the right label. The label defines who they are: it is the badge of membership. The concern expressed here is that children are drawn into value systems based on material possessions rather than on personal qualities of liking and respect. Furthermore, they are drawn into an uneasy dichotomy where loyalty to the group comes into conflict with loyalty to the parents and they are too often persuaded that their peers are more important to them. The extent to which advertising exploits this peer-group pressure is seen by some critics as potentially harmful.

- **Disappointment**   Advertisements can raise expectations that the product may ultimately be unable to satisfy. Most adults can cope with the hyperbole and rhetoric of advertising that promises a better social life, increased career prospects and improved sporting ability for using this or that toothpaste, shampoo or soft drink. We accept the hype and the 'puffery' for what it is, but young children are often unable to separate the gloss from the reality and are subsequently very often disappointed. Advertisements for collectable items, construction kits and electric train or road-racing sets often show a child surrounded by what might well be hundreds of pounds worth of items in a problem-free environment. The reality of opening up a fraction of what might be seen on screen and of putting together self-assembly items which somehow never seem to want to fit in a situation where somebody else wants to use the same floor space or table-top is very different. The disappointment may be fuelled when the manufacturer launches Mark II and the child is stuck with the now out-moded Mark I and becomes subject again to peer-group pressure and child–parent conflict until Mark II is bought. Football clubs which make a considerable amount of money from selling child-sized team strips are often accused of feeding this problem when they too often redesign the strip leaving young Johnny running around in last season's colours.

ITC and Radio Authority codes

Both the ITC and the Radio Authority Codes address the issues raised in this chapter and do give very clear guidelines. Account must be taken of the limited ability of children to distinguish between fact and fantasy and advertisements must not raise unrealistic expectations with respect to size, ease of assembly or performance (ITC clauses 2 and 3). Advertisements must not encourage children to pester their parents or make unfair appeals to loyalty or make a child feel inferior for not owning the product (ITC clauses 5, 6 and 7). Advertisements must not encourage children to eat frequently throughout the day or to eat near bedtime or to suggest that confectionery items are a good substitute for meals (ITC clause 11).

13.9 Summary

- Advertising to children is mainly concerned with the primary market of selling pocket-money goods which children can buy out of their own discretionary income. Some items sold in this way are higher in price than the term pocket-money would suggest, but evidence shows that children are capable of postponing present consumption to save for such larger items.
- The secondary market represents the influence which children have over their parents' purchasing decisions and in this regard their influence often extends beyond their own needs to include furniture, cars and even their parents' clothes.
- Children can also be seen as tertiary consumers in so far as their adult purchasing preferences can be shaped by their childhood experiences.
- Issues like pester power and parental yielding have attracted much comment with some critics saying (in spite of codes to the contrary) that advertisers play on this element of parent–child relationships even to the extent of targeting children for the sale of goods which the children themselves would not normally buy. Other criticisms have included the encouragement of poor eating habits, the exploitation of peer-group pressure and the raising of false expectations.
- Television has become the main medium for exploiting the children's market, partly because of its accessibility (most children watch television) and partly because, as a medium, it offers all the features of colour, movement and excitement that children like. Print, radio, cinema and posters, however, have all been used.
- Advertising to children is regulated by such bodies as the ITC and the Radio Authority, but some critics feel that these codes do not go far enough.

13.10 Assignments

1. Discuss your own recollections and perceptions of the extent to which you feel that you influenced your parents' purchasing decisions.

2. Discuss the extent to which you either applied or were subject to peer-group pressure.

3. In either or both of the above cases discuss the extent to which the issues could (or should) influence the creative effort in putting a campaign together.

4. Do you agree with the proposition that there should be an advertisement-free zone for children's television? What difficulties would you foresee in setting up such a zone?

14 Public relations

Public relations (PR) is often taken to include press relations. Here they are treated in two separate chapters. For a full understanding, chapters 14 and 15 should be read together.

Any organisation has a great number of **publics** with which it will have a variety of relationships. Some of those publics will be of very great significance and able materially to affect the success or otherwise of the organisation. Some will be less significant. Some of the relationships will be of a steady and unchanging sort and others may be more volatile and even hostile. Every organisation needs to be aware of the nature and extent of its significant publics and of the quality and status of its relationships with them.

Public relations can be defined as the development and maintenance of positive relationships between an organisation and its publics. The word *development* places the responsibility on the shoulders of the organisation and the word *maintenance* identifies public relations as an on-going and continuous process.

Publics are sometimes referred to as audiences, but this implies an interest on the part of the publics which they may not always have. They are sometimes reluctant audiences and the organisation may have to work hard to secure their interest. Publics are also sometimes identified with consumers and consumers are certainly an important public. Consumers are not, however, the only public.

Public relations is a communications activity that is unusual in being both a professional, highly skilled function on the one hand and something which everybody in the organisation can do on the other. In this chapter we are concerned with the profession of PR, but we should not ignore the other aspect.

14.2 Public relations as a non-specialist activity

Everyone in an organisation performs some sort of public relations function whether aware of it or not. To this comment can be added that every act of communication performs some sort of public relations function as well. Public relations as a separate specialist business function can succeed best if these two propositions are properly understood by everybody. In fact many external PR campaigns have to begin with changing the attitudes and behaviour of people inside the organisation and getting their support. The poor attitudes and behaviour of some people inside an organisation may actually be thought of as 'bad public relations' and be contributory causes to any PR problems the company has.

Every message sent out (whether oral or written) has a PR dimension regardless of its actual purpose – it may be well or badly written, well or badly designed, or both. Poorly designed sales literature, impolite receptionists, trucculent deliverymen, offensive advertisements – all create bad impressions. Professional PR cannot take the responsibility for all these failures, but neither can it be seen in isolation as though everything else that is done or said has no impact on the company's image and reputation. People not directly involved in PR might well be reminded that 'everything you do and everything you say tells somebody else something about what sort of organisation this is'. The formal recognition of this fact is seen when companies include public relations in the policy and decision-making process.

14.3 Public relations and corporate and business policy

Policy decisions always carry with them public relations implications. Some decisions can be anticipated to be unpopular and public relations can be of assistance in such situations in both pointing out the source and strength of possible resistance and in proposing ways of neutralising it. 'Public relations problems' are identified and 'public relations solutions' are proposed at the policy-making stage.

On the other hand, the policy decision may create 'public relations opportunities' of which the decision makers are unaware. In this case, public relations has the role of identifying such opportunities and proposing ways of exploiting them. The appointment of a new marketing director, the installation of new machinery, the launch of a new product and the decision to relocate the company head office all offer public relations opportunities.

Where public relations expertise is involved at every stage of the decision-making process, PR problems and PR opportunities can be identified early and PR solutions and programmes put in place in a thoughtful and systematic way. This is what we call pro-active public relations: thinking ahead and defusing trouble or planning for maximum beneficial publicity.

Unfortunately, some companies have not always thought so positively about the public relations function and have tended to treat it more as a 'fire-fighting' function to be brought in to deal with problems if and when they arise or as a 'window dressing' operation designed to make the company look good regardless of the facts. This attitude to public relations is not acceptable.

It is not the role of public relations to make corporate or business policy decisions nor to sort out business problems and crises. These are management functions which must be carried out by those in charge. The role of public relations is to develop and protect the company's image during the policy- and decision-making stage and subsequently throughout the implementation period and beyond.

Managers may make decisions of which public relations practitioners do not approve, but beyond making their reservations clear and pointing out the public relations pitfalls they can only carry out their client's or employer's wishes unless, of course, they feel strongly enough to resign.

14.4 The variety of publics

As we have observed, consumers are an important public. But there are other **marketing publics** to be considered. Suppliers at the backward end of the value chain and wholesalers and retailers at the forward end are also important. The necessity of developing and maintaining good relationships with these is self-evident and **relationship marketing** which emphasises supplier and customer retention over the long term recognises this. It takes time and it costs money to develop a customer or a supplier and to lose them through poor relationship management is inexcusable.

Throwing a wider circle around the organisation, we can identify as publics the community at large, groups such as trade associations, trade unions, government departments and consumer associations and individuals such as members of Parliament, local government officials and the media.

The company's own employees form a significant internal public. Their co-operation and goodwill also needs to be developed and they also will, from time to time, need to be persuaded and reassured about company policy.

14.5 Hostile, friendly and neutral publics

A simple distinction is between **friendly** and **hostile** publics. A manufacturer should be able to regard such publics as consumers, suppliers and so on as friendly, although their goodwill should never be taken for granted. Any manufacturer, however, may also arouse, however innocently or unwittingly, the hostility of publics. Manufacturers of cosmetics have attracted the hostility of animal rights groups, tobacco companies have lived with hostility for decades now and some manufacturers of children's products, particularly electronic games and confectionery, have attracted the anger of some parents, educationalists and some of the medical profession.

Generally speaking, if a survey showed that 70 per cent of parents thought well of your company and its products you could say that, on the whole, parents were friendly. However, you would still have to think carefully about the other 30 per cent, particularly if later surveys showed the tide of opinion moving in their direction so that six months later only 65 per cent were favourable and 35 per cent were now against you.

The terms friendly and hostile are a bit extreme and are not the only possibilities. Publics may be **neutral** in their attitudes and indifferent to what the company is doing. They may even be ignorant of the company's existence altogether. This does not mean that they should be ignored – they may be indifferent to you (or ignorant of you), but that does not mean that you should not be interested in *them*.

When we talk about publics as being consumers, shareholders, suppliers, etc., it is easy to forget that no real person is ever just a consumer. Some of the company's consumers could also be among its suppliers, its shareholders and even its employees. It is not, therefore, possible to tell different stories to different publics and get away with it for very long. One of the advantages of a mission statement (see chapter 3) is that it focuses all sorts of messages in the same direction.

It is also important to recognise when a particular public is so adamantly hostile to you that you can never win it round and it is a waste of time trying. The point here is that you do not always need everybody on your side. In a contested take-over bid, all you need is a majority of the shares (not all of them) and in a general election a political party does not need all the seats (just more than the others).

	Friendlies	Hostiles	Neutrals
Local councillors	friendly councillors	hostile councillors	neutral councillors
Local residents	friendly residents	hostile residents	neutral residents
Local businesses	friendly businesses	hostile businesses	neutral businesses

Fig. 14.1 Attitude matrix

Taking different types of publics and different attitudes a company could develop a matrix. A property developer, for example, could finish up with something like fig. 14.1.

Instead of treating all councillors as hostile or all businesses as friendly, the contractor could do some research and find out who is in each box. In PR terms, it might pay to treat the hostiles as a single public (regardless of whether they are residents, businesses or councillors) and see whether the grounds of their hostility are sufficiently alike to be dealt with by similar measures. For example, they might all have the same environmental objections to a new development – loss of civic facilities, increased traffic congestion, etc.

We can now see that publics:

- Can be made up of individuals (consumers or workers, for example) or of organisations (suppliers, retailers or agencies).
- Can be either very large (consumers may be numbered in tens or hundreds of thousands, even millions) or relatively very small (how many local councillors are there?).
- Can be internal or external to the organisation.
- Can be friendly, hostile or neutral.
- Can represent a wide variety of relationships with the company giving rise to different areas of public relations such as consumer PR, trade PR, supplier PR and internal PR.

We may also encounter product PR (to support an existing product or a new product launch), financial PR (aimed at shareholders) and PR which specialises in particular areas such as fashion PR.

Public relations crops up in different forms in non-business areas as well. Politicians and other public figures may have their own PR advisers. Local government utilises PR in communicating with residents and central government departments are among the biggest producers of press releases to publicise their decisions. Service organisations such as the police, ambulance and fire services also use public relations.

First sort out your objectives

Identify your target publics

Find out what they think of you

Decide what tools to use

Fig. 14.2   Developing a PR approach

14.6 Developing a PR approach

There are four factors to consider in developing a public relations approach.

The public relations objective

First, the public relations objective must be clear. It could be to get a decision made in the company's favour – permission to go ahead with a new development, for example. This objective should then, ideally, be linked to one single proposition – 'the proposed development will benefit the community in the long run'. The objective could, however, be to raise name-awareness (see the Cornhill case study in chapter 19) or to improve the image of the company (corporate PR).

Identifying the target public (or publics)

Secondly, it is necessary to identify the strategic publics. Whose support do you need to get that shopping centre through? Suppliers become a very significant public if your company is revising its purchasing policy, whereas in the run-up to a new product launch wholesalers, retailers and consumers would matter most. In a merger or take-over the shareholders of both companies are strategically important publics.

The target public's perception

The third consideration is how do your target publics currently perceive you? Are they currently friendly, hostile or even indifferent?

Developing the PR plan

Finally, the PR plan has to be developed. What public relations tools should be used to overcome negative feelings, harness positive feelings and achieve the objective? (For planning in general, see chapter 22.)

14.7 Public relations tools

There is a wide range of tools available to the public relations practitioner. None of these is, in itself, exclusive to public relations and any of them could be just as easily used in the context of a direct-mail, sponsorship, sales-promotion or advertising campaign.

The list includes:

- Competitions.
- Exhibitions.
- Demonstrations.
- Lectures.
- School and college visits.
- Direct mail letters.
- Open days.
- Leaflets.
- Posters.
- Information services.
- Sponsorships.
- Press releases (see chapter 15).
- Press information packs (see chapter 15).
- Press conferences (see chapter 15).

These need not all be used in any one campaign, but they should all be considered. On a limited budget, trade-offs may have to be made between, say, open days and college visits.

14.8 Reactive public relations

All organisations exist within an environment of controlled and non-controlled publicity (see chapter 2). When the organisation becomes a focus for unsought negative criticism, PR has a reactive role to play.

Sometimes the criticism is of a very public and high-profile form as when a member of Parliament criticises an organisation in the House of Commons or when an advertisement is publicly criticised by the Advertising Standards Association. At other times the negative feelings expressed towards the organisation are less easy to spot and may persist for some time before being noticed. Some research might be commissioned to establish the full depth of any negative feelings towards the company. It is the job of reactive public relations to respond to all negative comments and to repair the damage.

Constant monitoring of public opinion is an essential part of this process so that the public relations practitioners are aware of what is being thought and said. This monitoring might depend on the co-operation of others. Salespeople can report back on anything that they pick up from customers; the consumer complaints department should make sure that persistent and repetitive complaints are passed on. Anybody in the organisation from the deliverymen to the receptionists can act as a conduit when customers are not happy.

Monitoring the media for unfavourable mentions of the company, its products, policies and personnel is also essential. Such comment could be in the form of a major article or feature or nothing more than a letter to the editor. Specialist **cuttings agencies** monitor the media for a range of clients (a client may specify 'press only', 'all media', 'UK only', 'Europe' or 'worldwide').

Dealing with, or reacting to, negative attitudes may involve a major exercise such as calling a press conference or, in an extreme situation, threatening legal action. It may involve no more than a 'letter of reply' to the editor (most editors will print a reasonable letter of reply) and, at the simplest, just a letter to a single dissatisfied customer. This need not all be done by the public relations department: in the latter case, the letter could be sent out from the consumer complaints department.

Of course, in reacting to such negative attitudes it is essential to establish whether or not they are based in fact. This makes a very important difference to the way in which they are dealt with and gives rise to the distinction between **performance gaps** and **communications gaps**.

In chapter 8 we saw that by using market research techniques a supermarket might discover how it compares with rivals on such image factors as the friendliness of its staff or the cleanliness of its premises. The supermarket might learn that it is perceived as being less friendly than others – but what does this mean?

14.9 Performance gaps and communications gaps

Performance gaps

Put simply, this means that the criticisms aimed at the company are based in fact and are an accurate reflection of the company's current practices.

- Suppliers complain that the company is a slow payer because the company is a slow payer.
- Animal rights groups complain that a cosmetics company experiments on animals because it does.
- Guests at a hotel complain that it is old-fashioned because it is.

In each case, the criticism is justified and it cannot be dealt with by public relations alone. Indeed, it is a maxim of good public relations that you cannot solve poor management performance by throwing public relations at it. The only way to deal with justifiable criticism levelled at a performance gap is to take steps to remove the cause of the criticism.

Two high-street companies, one a bank and the other a building society, ran advertising campaigns designed to meet criticisms made by their customers. In one the claim was made that 'You are always greeted with a friendly smile' and in the other 'We never let the phone ring more than three times before it is answered.'

Unfortunately, both companies forgot to tell their employees who continued not smiling and letting the phone ring (and ring). Both these campaigns attracted hostile criticism and featured on consumer-based television programmes such as *That's Life*. Rather than making their customers feel better they made them feel worse. The performance gaps had not been properly addressed.

This does not mean that the performance must be completely revised before public relations can begin. There is a public relations opportunity in recognising the problem before taking steps to put it right.

Another strategy, of course, would be for an organisation to decide to defend its performance against its critics.

Case Study

What's wrong with McDonald's?

That was the title of a leaflet distributed in June 1994 by two environmental campaigners. McDonald's, describing the leaflets as containing 'numerous highly defamatory statements' and a wholesale attack on almost every aspect of its business, took the campaigners (quickly dubbed 'The McLibel Two') to court to defend its performance. The leaflet, containing 25 allegations linking McDonald's products to cancer, heart disease and the destruction of rainforests, used such terms as McCancer, McGreedy and McGarbage. It was quickly announced that as many as 150 witnesses would be called and that the case would last into the autumn. In fact, the case is now expected to last until late 1995 and has already been called the most costly libel case in British legal history.

McDonald's had only recently announced its plans to double its UK outlets with a deal that would take it into colleges and hospitals as well as canteens and racecourses. Any time would be a bad time to be criticised in such a way, but the timing of this particular attack was doubly unfortunate from McDonald's point of view. As a McDonald's spokesman said, the criticisms would do untold damage to the company's interests if not publicly refuted.

Communications gaps

In these situations criticisms arise out of misunderstanding. The people who make the criticism may believe that they are right but, in fact, they are wrong. They have, somehow, got hold of the wrong end of the story.

What is happening here is that the company is failing to communicate properly. It may be that the people who complain of the hotel being old-fashioned have not stayed there since it was modernised and simply do not know that it has been refurbished. The failure to let them know can be seen as a lost public relations opportunity. It could be that the people who hold the negative images of the hotel have never been there but have only spoken to somebody who was there before it was improved.

Figure 14.3 shows the development from the initial research to the PR solution and subsequent research.

Case Study

Maximising public relations opportunities

There are some events in the life of a firm that occur very rarely and one of these is the relocation of the company to new premises. When

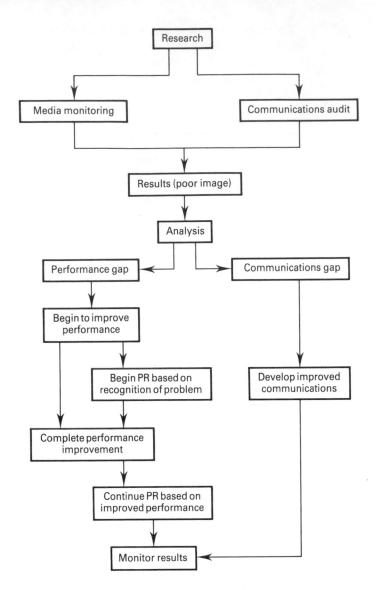

Fig. 14.3   Flow diagram of PR plan

Crabtree Vickers (a maker of printing equipment) relocated in 1981, they left behind premises which they had occupied for over 100 years. Factory relocations cause anxiety for several publics – suppliers, customers, the local community and, of course, the workforce. The natural inclination is to keep as low a profile as possible until it is all over. However, marketing manager John Peet recognised some PR opportunities and persuaded the board to bring PR consultancy Pielle in to maximise these. Peter L. Walker, head of Pielle, visited the existing plants (two in Leeds and one in Otley) to assess the task. There was a need to act quickly as suitable new premises had been spotted and a prompt decision was needed. His report was accepted within a week.

There was some bad news. Twenty-five per cent of the workers were to lose their jobs and the move would take Crabtree Vickers out of Otley where it was the last major employer. Crabtree had been having difficulties and presenting the move as saving 75 per cent of the jobs would have been a fair point. Employees and the local community were targeted first to hear the news in the best way. Customers naturally anxious about the completion to schedule of long-dated orders (it can take a year to finalise the purchase of heavy printing equipment worth as much as £1m) were targeted next with a combination of personal letters, a special edition of the company newsletter and paid-for reports in the trade press.

A key factor throughout was the personal involvement of management at every grade. This was particularly important in arranging personal visits of customers to the new site in Leeds. The central message was the advantage of one single, modern site as opposed to three separate old-fashioned sites. Getting people to the new site was considered so important that money was diverted from the planned attendance at DRUPA, the Dusseldorf trade fair, to finance it. Disappointed visitors to Dusseldorf were actually flown to England in the company's executive jet to see the new factory. In a trade 'open week' no less than 400 customers visited the site.

Pielle staff spent a total of 118 days on the campaign which was judged to have met both its double-pronged objectives on the industrial and the marketing fronts – attracting in the process considerable favourable comment in the trade press. Commitment to the campaign by individual Crabtree managers in preparing and disseminating information was a major contributor to its success.

All this happened some time ago, but the lessons are still there for any contemporary firm. Be imaginative, maximise the PR opportunities to the full, if necessary rearrange priorities to provide finance and, above all, get everybody involved.

Source: based on 'Surviving a Factory Move' Marketing *19 May 1983*

14.10 Summary

- Every organisation will have a wide range of publics which may be friendly, hostile or indifferent.
- Friendly publics may turn against the company and hostile publics can be won over.
- Developing and maintaining good relationships with as many publics as possible is at the heart of PR.
- Pro-active PR involves setting PR objectives and working towards them using a variety of PR tools.
- Reactive PR is responding to the hostile and negative criticisms of others. If the criticisms are justified, it is essential that performance is improved so that PR can do an honest job. If the criticisms are not justified, then the company is not communicating itself effectively and PR can be put to work straight away.

14.11 Assignments

The assignments for this chapter are grouped together with the assignments for chapter 15.

15 Press relations

15.1 Introduction

Press relations is often undertaken by the person responsible for public relations. But large organisations often have a press and public relations department or even a separate press office.

Media relations, in fact, would be a more accurate term, since press relations covers radio and television programmes as well. Organisations may, of course, make use of an external agency.

The media differ from other publics in that they are not the end of the communications effort but a part of it – **communications targets** rather than **final targets**. Taking the overall view, press relations is inseparable from public relations. The point of developing the former (press) is to gain access, through the editorial sections of the media, to the latter (publics). The operational objective of press relations is to get the client mentioned beneficially; the ultimate objectives are to raise the visibility and the credibility of the client. The media is an intermediary public in a two-step model of communication (see chapter 6).

The selection of media vehicles to reach specific target publics should be made with the same attention to detail as goes into the selection of media for advertising purposes. Indeed, in product PR the media groups and vehicles which are ideal for an advertising campaign will also be ideal for an editorial campaign.

15.2 The media as independent third-party endorsers

Press relations is not simply a question of getting the clients mentioned, but of getting them mentioned beneficially. In other words, you want journalists to act as endorsers of a product or company. You want them to recommend – and thus to influence the opinions and decisions of the target public. But you also wish that recommendation to be perceived by the public as genuinely independent. The client and the public are the two main parties in the transaction and the media is a third (and independent party), so we can say that what is being sought is **third-party endorsement**.

Third-party endorsement lends weight to the product in two ways – one is the weight and authority of the media vehicle and the other is the weight and authority of the writer. When both writer and newspaper are respected, the endorsement gains in value. Advertorials (see page 46), which some people see as compromising the difference between advertisements and editorial content, may (if allowed to get out of hand) compromise the independence of editorial opinion. Particularly if it resurrects the cynical belief that any positive reference to a product has been bought and paid for somehow.

15.3 The independence of the media

The independence of the media can be seen in the three following scenarios, familiar to any experienced press relations officer (PRO):

- The journalist takes no interest at all in what is offered and makes no attempt to follow up the story.
- The journalist takes an interest, follows up the story, and writes a nice piece which the editor subsequently spikes to make room for another story thought to be more important.
- The journalist smells a 'good story' but takes an opposite view from the one offered and writes a negative review (an adverse credit) – in such a case a PRO would be grateful to an editor who spiked the story.

A PRO soon learns that the media are under no obligation to write about the company and, if they do choose to write about it, they are under no obligation to be nice. That is what being independent means. And it is really only in the light of this independence that a positive mention has any real value.

15.4 Varieties of mentions

Obviously, the best outcome for a PRO would be to get a full article devoted entirely and beneficially to the client – better still if pictures accompany the article. Not so good but still acceptable would be a shared beneficial mention with rival companies. Several PROs representing clients in the same industry might all be targeting journalists at the same time and the outcome might be a a feature mentioning all of them. Lower down the scale of achievement would be a mention with a purely descriptive, or neutral, comment or a name-only mention with no accompanying comment at all. This might occur in an article on, say, fixed-rate mortgages where a bank, such as Barclays, might simply be mentioned as one of the suppliers. Front-page beneficial mentions or credits are better than inside mentions, but if the mention is adverse the deeper it gets buried the better. In the case of product PR the best place to get a mention could be alongside the preferred position for the advertisements.

15.5 Monitoring the media

Just as the media can be monitored for negative comments so also can it be monitored for positive comments. The vehicle (tabloid, broadsheet, national, local, etc.), the size (number of column centimetres), position (front page, sports section, etc.) and tone (beneficial or not) can be noted as also can the presence or absence of photographs. When a particular editorial campaign has been run (to announce the opening of a new superstore, for example), the success of that campaign can be measured – in this case, local media coverage rather than national can be expected. Such monitoring can give an indication of the visibility and the credibility given to the client by the campaign.

One of the main differences between an advertising campaign and an editorial campaign is that with the former you know in advance the exposure you are going to get, while with the latter you just have to wait and see. However, there are steps which can be taken to improve the prospect of getting the desired exposure. This takes us into the practice of press relations and controllable inputs.

15.6 The practice of press relations

The independence of the media can be seen as an uncontrollable element, but that does not mean that the media cannot be influenced in the client's favour. Some ways of improving a company's (or client's) PR performance are outlined below.

Event scheduling

Events designed to raise the visibility and credibility of the client can include sponsorships, competitions, open days and demonstrations. In preparing a schedule for such events their news value must be considered. Very few events can expect to get national media coverage but the possibility of local media and trade press coverage should not be overlooked. Unusual events have a better chance of being covered but they should not seem ridiculous, inappropriate or in poor taste. Events such as open days, not in themselves unusual, can be made more interesting by being opened by some local or national celebrity, just as sponsoring something close to the heart of the community (for example, the local craft fair) can get more attention.

Timing is important. If your event clashes with somebody else's then media attention is diluted. At national level, planning something to take place on the same day as the London Marathon, for example, is to risk being ignored. Other events could be in the political arena, such as a visit of a foreign head of state, or it could even be a society wedding. Awareness of the social and political calendars as well as the sporting and arts calendars can help to avoid a clash. There are directories such as *Foresight* which give event listings and you should make sure that your own events are included.

The media contact list

Who are you going to tell about your event? This can be looked at in two ways: (i) which journalists and (ii) which newspapers. Avoid the temptation to tell everybody: it is a waste of time and money and will only serve to undermine your own credibility as a PRO. A fashion writer will not wish to be told about the latest computer software for accountants. This does not mean that you should not attempt a little ingenuity: a new treatment for lawns might get a mention on the sports page at a time when the quality of the playing fields is an issue – you have to make the right pitch!

You should develop a list of journalists known to be interested in your clients and their products. There are recognised associations and groups of all sorts of journalists: sports writers, fashion writers, gardening columnists, etc.; organisations such as CARMA International provide lists of journalists together with their professional interests. (CARMA International is a company which tracks the articles written by different journalists on various organisations and even gives a rating as to each journalist's attitudes and biases. Using a computer database a PR specialist is able to check a journalist's profile before dealing with queries or sending out information.) A good PRO will have these lists in place and will keep them up to date. It could be fatal to approach a financial journalist with a story about fixed-rate mortgages if he or she is known to have a low opinion of them. If your client manufactures chemical weed-killers and you know that a particular gardening columnist absolutely loathes chemical treatments of any sort then leave him off the list (journalists can be divided into hostiles and friendlies as well).

It is equally foolish to send your story to every media vehicle. Some vehicles are known for their coverage of particular topics such as sports but they may never have a gardening feature. If you were publicising a revolutionary lawn mower you would be targeting gardening magazines, papers with a regular gardening column and programmes such as *Tomorrow's World* which regularly feature new products. However, there may be less obvious opportunities and it would be worthwhile consulting a directory such as *Advance* which gives notification of the editorial intentions of media vehicles. Many magazines have their main features planned months ahead of publication date, so it is of great value to know as early as say, November, that the March issue of *Homes and Gardens* is to run a feature on lawn care.

It is essential to keep records up to date. Journalists move around from title to title and from media group to media group; some are freelance and write on any subject for any paper or magazine they can sell an outline to. New titles come into existence and old ones die out.

Take the trouble to meet journalists and to develop personal relationships. Depending on the field you are in, you may find that there are not so many top journalists involved.

Contacting the media

It is important to remember the editorial copy deadline by which a media vehicle must receive copy if it is to be included in the next issue. Copy can be sent by post, telephone, messenger or fax. Things happen in the City on a Friday which make ideal copy for the Sunday papers and City-based press officers may spend a great deal of time on Friday evening and into the small hours of Saturday morning (and even right through Saturday) on the telephone talking to financial journalists on the Sundays.

Provision must be made for *inward* contact as well as outward contact, so that journalists can contact the press office to follow up on a press release. Sometimes a journalist may make the first contact or ask for an interview and the press office needs to be able to handle this. Journalists do not work normal office hours and it is necessary to give an out-of-hours number as well so that queries can be dealt with late at night.

Press releases

Press releases are written statements, sometimes called **news** or **media releases**, issued whenever anything newsworthy happens. Avoid the temptation to send out a routine weekly press release – there is nothing routine about the incidence of newsworthy stories.

There are a few stylistic conventions involved in writing a press release, but they are not universally followed. It is important, however, for a press office to be consistent so that all releases are written and designed in the same way. This enhances the credibility of the press office and helps busy journalists to spot releases from a good source.

Press releases should be issued on specially designed press-release stationery. Sending out press releases on standard company notepaper is not acceptable.

Makepeace and Thackery : Solicitors
Domestic and Commercial Conveyancing

PRESS   **10/94**
RELEASE   **12th August 1994**

Makepeace and Thackery to take on Matrimonial Work

Makepeace and Thackery, established in 1982 to undertake domestic and commercial conveyancing, has taken on a new partner to handle matrimonial work.

This will enable the firm to offer a more complete service to those clients whose matrimonial and property problems are inevitably interlinked.

The new partner is Jane Haworth and the firm will, in future, be known as Makepeace, Thackery and Haworth.

—oOo—

Note to editors

Jane Haworth is 29 years old and qualified in 1988. She has six years of experience in matrimonial work with Farrell and Baldwin. She is married to Geoffrey Haworth, a Barrister, and they live in Sittingbourne, Kent. Jane and Geoffrey Haworth have no children.

A photograph of Ms Haworth is enclosed.

---

569 South End, Maryport MA2 6AB   Tel 031 0297 : Fax 031 3399
Contact : Sally Fairing   Ext 35

Fig. 15.1 Press release

Millions of press releases are sent out each year and the majority of them are ignored. There are many reasons for this. The press release could have been:

- Sent out too late or to the wrong journalists.
- Poorly designed, badly written, or too long.
- A newsworthy story but overshadowed by the events of the day.
- Boring and uninteresting.

There is always an element of luck present: an excellent campaign may miss out because some disaster overshadows it and forces it off the page, whereas a mediocre campaign may get more coverage because there is nothing much happening and the editors are glad of any story.

Press information packs

Press information packs (sometimes simply called press packs) are similar in purpose to a press release but include more information which may be

---

Makepeace and Thackery : Solicitors
Domestic and Commercial Conveyancing

569 South End, Maryport MA2 6AB   Tel 031 0297 : Fax 031 3399

NEWS RELEASE

10/94   **Embargoed 15th August 1994**

Makepeace and Thackery to Take on New Partner

Makepeace and Thackery, specialists in domestic and commercial
conveyancing, is to take on a new partner to handle matrimonial work.

This will enable the firm to offer a more complete service to those clients whose
matrimonial and property problems are inevitably interlinked.

The new partner is Jane Haworth and the firm will, in future, be known as
Makepeace, Thackery and Haworth.

—End—

Note to editors

Jane Haworth is 29 years old and qualified in 1988. She has six years of
experience in matrimonial work with Farrell and Baldwin. She is married to
Geoffrey Haworth, a Barrister, and they live in Sittingbourne, Kent. Jane and
Geoffrey Haworth have no children.

Makepeace and Thackery has been established since 1982.

A photograph of Ms Haworth is available on request.

—oOo—

Contact No. during office hours 031 0297 Ext 35 (Sally Fairing).

Fig. 15.2 News release
An alternative treatment of the story in fig. 15.1. There are no absolutely fixed
rules about the layout of a press release but it is important for a press office
to adopt a house style so that all press releases coming out of that office look
alike and follow the same conventions.

contained in a specially designed card or plastic folder. They contain
material which the company particularly wants to publicise, or which
journalists might be expected to ask for anyway, such as photographs and
product illustrations. They can be sent out by mail or courier or distributed personally at a press conference or preview, in which case they
might also include a programme for the day's events and gift pencils or
pens bearing the company logo or product trade mark. Press packs might
be used for new product launches (car makers use them when launching
new models) or for major events like the opening of a new supermarket
or hotel. All manner of promotional literature, diagrams, product

specifications, leaflets, booklets (a short history of the company, perhaps) and even product samples can be included. They are obviously more expensive to produce than simple press releases but this cost should be balanced against the potential benefits of obtaining greater media exposure. Photographs and illustrations must be suitable for reproduction but since they may be scaled (reduced in size) or cropped (parts of the picture cut away) to suit editorial preferences the published result may not be what was hoped for.

- **Embargoes**   Unless it is stated to the contrary, it is assumed by journalists that stories contained in press releases and information packs are for immediate publication. Some releases make this clear by bearing the legend 'For Immediate Publication'. There may, however, be situations where it is necessary (to meet editorial deadlines, for example) to get information to the press earlier than you want it released to the public. In such cases the practice is to embargo the information by putting on the press release the date when it can be made public. The embargo may specify a time as in 'Embargoed until 12.30 pm 15 July 1994'. Editors usually respect an embargo and the number of incidents when information is published before its official date are very few.

Press conferences

Press conferences are usually called for major events where impersonal means will not suffice. New product launches may require a press conference, particularly of large items such as a new car model: photographs sent in a press pack are not the same as seeing the real thing and motoring correspondents will want to see it and test drive it for themselves. Launches of blockbuster films are good candidates for this sort of treatment and the conference can become a major event in its own right. A well-organised press conference can reposition a product to a more prominent place in the media, taking a new film off the film-review page and on to the front page, for example, or taking a new car out of the motoring page and into the main news.

Having decided that enough journalists would be sufficiently interested to attend, the timing and venue for the conference must be agreed upon. The question of hospitality (the provision of suitable refreshments) must be considered and arrangements made for setting up facilities such as telephones and modems in sufficient number so that journalists can make immediate contact with their papers.

At most press conferences arrangements have to be made to accommodate photographers, both still and film, together with sound recording technicians and all their equipment. In some cases a 'photo-opportunity' can be set up apart from the conference itself. 'Interview opportunities' can be similarly stage managed.

Press invitation lists

There may be occasions when the number of journalists wishing to attend is greater than can be accommodated. It might be possible to repeat the event, perhaps on a regional basis. Some events, however, cannot be repeated, journalists have to cover the event as it happens, and a decision must be made as to who to invite. On such occasions it might not even be so much a question of sending out invitations as sorting out applications from the press for tickets to attend. In such cases there are likely to be some significant writers who must be invited and they will be earmarked for a priority invitation. In the upper echelons of the fashion business top journalists are not only prioritised for a seat but given numbered seats.

However, for most publicists, the fought-for invitation to a press conference is the dream scenario. For most press conferences it is more important to check that key influential journalists have not inadvertently been overlooked and that invitations are accurately addressed and sent in good time.

News conferences

News conferences are sometimes so called to distinguish them from press conferences. They are usually called in some emergency or crisis situation (see chapter 16).

Writing for the media

It is often said that the trick in writing press releases is to write them in such a way that they can be reproduced exactly as a ready-made article. Some journalists, of course, do prefer to research and write their own pieces using the press release as a starting point, but local papers particularly will often use a press release just as it is.

There is also the possibility of offering a ready-for-print article to a magazine, subject, of course, to normal editorial practices. When work is accepted in this way, there are usually some golden rules. The piece should be of a generally factual and informative nature rather than promotional. Criticising competitors is not permitted, neither is the use of self-adulatory phrases such as 'we are the best'. The name of the product or company can be included but, perhaps, not more than once or twice throughout the piece. Press officers who have themselves been journalists are often well placed to exploit such opportunities which tend to crop up more frequently in the trade press and should be considered as another aspect of business-to-business communications.

15.7 Press relations and advertising

Press relations differs from advertising in a number of ways.

- Advertisers deal directly with the advertisement departments of the media and negotiate with media representatives. Press officers deal with the editorial departments of the media and negotiate with journalists.
- The advertising message is controlled by the advertiser (subject to the law and media policy). The public relations message is controlled by the media which may change it or abandon it entirely.

- The timing and incidence of advertising messages are controlled. The advertiser chooses both when and where the messages appear. Public relations messages are uncontrolled both with respect to their timing and the places where they will be seen. Again, it is the journalists who have the final word.
- Advertising space or time is bought and paid for. Editorial space and time arising out of a public relations campaign have to be worked for.
- Advertisers work to advertising copy deadlines. Press officers work to editorial copy deadlines. The deadlines are rarely the same.
- A press relations budget may allow access to more media vehicles than an advertising budget alone. The cost of advertising on television may be prohibitive but a small-scale editorial campaign may get some TV coverage.

15.8 Summary

- Developing editorial campaigns to obtain media coverage in the form of beneficial mentions involves developing relationships with journalists and observing editorial requirements such as copy deadlines.
- The independence of the media means that they are under no obligation to mention a company and may, in any case, mention it in a critical way.
- A press office will have lists of relevant media and named journalists together with a profile of their writing interests and attitudes.
- Press releases, press information packs and press conferences are the main tools of the profession but writing articles for the media can also be undertaken.
- There are significant differences between the way in which advertising uses the media and the way in which press relations uses it and the two disciplines can be used together in a combined advertising–editorial campaign.

15.9 Assignments

1. Select a firm (or an industry) and maintain a cuttings file over a four- or six-week period. Analyse your cuttings – what sort of an image does the firm have? It need not be a business – you could select a charity or a band.

2. Choose an organisation and draw up a list of the publics which that organisation might have. Try to profile these publics – are they predominantly friendly, hostile or neutral? Try to explain why they might hold the views they do.

3. Draw up a public relations plan for your course (or your college). What tools would you use and why?

4. Think of a newsworthy event (perhaps in the life of your college) and design and write a press release for it.

5. With a particular product in mind, develop a media list showing key journalists and journal titles, with dates and frequency of publication, editorial interests and editorial copy deadlines.

16 Crisis communications

**16.1
Introduction**

Many organisations experience a crisis at some time or another and it has become increasingly obvious that the ability to cope with crisis situations is one of the hallmarks of good management. This chapter discusses how crises come about, the setting up of management procedures for coping with a crisis and, last but not least, the communications implications. But first, we need to consider the range and variety of crises.

**16.2
Financial,
operational
and
reputational
crises**

In practice, financial, operational and reputational crises often overlap. A financial crisis can easily become an operational crisis and either can develop reputational overtones.

A financial crisis involves the money side of an organisation, and could be a cash-flow difficulty, rumours of poor results or fraud. Suppliers, customers and investors are all nervous of doing business with a company with a suspected financial crisis.

An operational crisis is one that threatens the day-to-day running of the organisation. A factory fire, a strike, a shortfall in the supply of components are all examples.

A reputational crisis is anything that undermines the reputation of either the company or its products.

Accidental and deliberate crises

A factory fire can be either accidental or deliberate. So can product contamination: powdered glass in baby food, anti-freeze in wine, acid in hair shampoo and salmonella in spicy sausages have all been recent examples. A faulty bottling plant or a careless operative may be the accidental cause, but when such things are deliberately brought about there is an extra, frightening, dimension.

Such deliberate actions have given rise to the expressions **product sabotage**, **product terrorism** and **product blackmail**. A blackmailer may simply threaten to do such a thing unless the company pays a large ransome. Sometimes the saboteur or blackmailer is a member of the organisation.

Slow build up and sudden impact crises

Accidental crises may have a slow build up: they can be 'disasters waiting to happen'. A factory fire, for example, may be traced back to inadequate safety control systems, to a practice of allowing flammable waste to accumulate in store-rooms, perhaps. Other crises, however, provide no warning signals and can be called sudden impact disasters. Natural disasters such as hurricanes and floods can come about without warning so that the organisation has no time to recognise the danger and protect itself.

**16.3
Unwanted
attention**

Whenever a crisis occurs, the first questions asked are 'What went wrong?' and 'Whose fault was it?', followed by 'What are you going to do about it?' These are important questions and management will prefer to be left alone to sort them out. Unfortunately for management, crises attract the unwanted attention of the media.

The organisation is, for the time being at least, under the spotlight and will need a very good communications strategy to deal with it.

**16.4
Management
responsibility**

Managing a crisis does not consist simply of waiting for the unexpected to happen and then dealing with it. It consists just as much of anticipating what might happen and putting in place contingency procedures for dealing with it when it does. A good motto for crisis management might be: 'Hope for the best but prepare for the worst.'

Every organisation should be able to identify a list of things that could occur. For an airline, this could include the possibility of a terrorist hijack, for a processed-food manufacturer deliberate product contamination, for a hotel group a major fire and so on. Thinking about what can possibly go wrong is a good place to begin. To prepare for what might go wrong an organisation can put in place a variety of measures, such as setting up a crisis management team, preparing a crisis manual and crisis training. Some people prefer the use of the word *response* and talk of response teams, response manuals, etc. instead.

Crisis management teams (CMTs)

A crisis management team (or response team) is a group of people trained to take charge of a crisis. Team members must have strong personal characteristics, be decisive, calm, quick-thinking, good organisers and leaders. Crises do not happen to order and CMT members can expect to be on a 24-hour call out.

In addition to the personal qualities, team members should have the necessary administrative and technical skills that any given crisis may require.

Crisis manuals

A crisis manual (or response manual) is an in-house document setting out what needs to be done and by whom. Each manual has to be written with a particular organisation in mind but a typical manual should include at least the following:

- The objectives to be aimed at in a crisis situation.
- The membership and duties of the crisis management team.
- Procedures for key personnel such as receptionists, telephone operators and secretaries.
- A list of key contacts outside the organisation with addresses and telephone numbers. The list could include emergency services, government departments (Health & Safety Executive, for example), trade associations and journalists.

- Stand-by statements on issues which might arise such as the company policy on product recall in a product contamination situation.
- Fact sheets on the company's structure, organisation, products, safety policies, marketing, sales and distribution, etc.
- A list of anticipated questions (from suppliers, customers, the media) and official answers.
- Procedures for dealing with the media, including the names or positions of key personnel who are specifically authorised to be media spokespeople. These may be public relations executives or senior management.
- Follow-up procedures such as letters and personal visits to dealers, debriefing company staff at all levels so that they know that everything is in hand and writing to affected consumers.

The crisis manual should be easily available. All communications managers (advertising, public relations, etc.) should be fully conversant with it so that they act in accordance with agreed company policy.

Crisis training

Training is also essential and simulations are a key method. Airline crews, for example, regularly practise emergency evacuations as do crews on passenger ships and ferries. Every organisation which has a periodic fire-drill is, in fact, using a crisis simulation technique.

Many companies send members of staff on crisis-management courses and crisis management conferences have been well supported in recent years.

Crisis agencies

Crisis agencies (product recall agencies, for example) specialise in trouble shooting and in a major crisis, or a particularly unusual crisis, it might be as well to call in a specialist. The advantage of this approach is that the agency staff can cope with the crisis leaving company managers to carry on with their ordinary everyday responsibilities.

16.5 Crisis communications

Any crisis has the potential to damage the reputation of an organisation. The job of crisis communications (crisis public relations, in particular) is twofold:

- **Damage limitation**   To confine the story to as limited an audience as possible and prevent further damage to the image of the company.

- **Image restoration**   To take steps to restore the image of the company to its pre-crisis level.

If other parties already have knowledge of the problem, or if it can be anticipated that they will find out about it anyway, then it makes good sense to include them in your list of target publics and talk to them. However, it also makes sense to try to prevent the bad news from spreading any further.

There is a legal and moral dimension to this. A firm with severe cash flow problems (and no real hope of surviving) which attempts to trade out of its difficulties by continuing to do business with suppliers it cannot pay or to accept advance payments from customers for goods which it cannot deliver is behaving unethically and risks prosecution in attempting to conceal the truth. However, if the firm resolves its cash flow crisis so that it can continue to trade it may feel entitled to keep that information to itself.

What should be done if a crisis becomes common knowledge and the media get wind of it? Two fictitious case studies (based on a variety of real experiences) show what might happen (see pages 207–12).

16.6 Crisis and the media

In this section we want to emphasise 'working with the media' rather than 'dealing with the media'. It is a mistake to think of the media as the enemy. Journalists have a vital role to play in putting across the company's story and it is pointless to antagonise them. Of course, you always have to remember that the prime motivator for any journalist is the prospect of a good story and you are unlikely to get much sympathy if the company is caught out in some fraudulent activity or act of sheer incompetence. Neither will you get much sympathy if you deliberately try to keep away from them information which they feel their audiences have a right to know.

You cannot prevent others from talking to the media and if journalists cannot get from you the story they are looking for they will get it from somebody else (a disgruntled ex-employee, for example). In fact, evidence suggests that media interest in a crisis is relatively short-lived once journalists have got all they can out of it. If they are still picking away at a problem weeks later, it may be something you are doing (or failing to do) that keeps them interested.

The basic ground rules for working with the media in a crisis are:

- Tell the media what has happened. Do not give the impression that you are hiding something.
- Tell the media who is responsible. Don't offer up scapegoats or sacrificial lambs and don't create the impression that you are covering up for somebody.
- Tell the media what you are doing about it. Be specific and be prepared. The media will ask hard questions and they will expect hard answers.
- Keep the media up to date. Hold regular media briefing sessions and give out new information as it becomes available.
- Aim to 'kill' media interest as soon as you decently can. As a general rule, the media will move on of their own accord when they tire of the story or something better comes along. But you can help this process by letting them know that there is nothing else worth saying.

If the crisis is of such a nature that it generates official inquiries, questions in the House of Commons or legal proceedings, then the media will stay around. In these cases, you still have to work with the media and it is essential to establish proper channels of communication.

Communicating with the media

Crises require that you act quickly. Posted press releases are too slow: speed and personal interaction are of the essence.

- **Call a news conference**   Set it up quickly and invite people by phone. Use all possible means, including fax and couriers, to let journalists know where and when the news conference will be. Choose a location for the news conference carefully. It should be near the scene of the crisis or at head office. Don't choose a venue so far from the scene of the problem that the media feel that that they are being kept away from it.

- **If necessary, set up a newsroom**   Remember that journalists will want to get their stories back to their papers etc. as quickly as possible and it may pay you to install temporary extra outbound telephone units (reserved for outgoing calls only). There will also be extra incoming calls from journalists unable to attend the conference or simply ringing up to see if there is anything new on the situation. Set up a separate unit to handle these calls and ensure that personnel who talk to the media on the phone know what they are doing. It is usual in a major crisis to reserve some phone numbers exclusively as media hotline numbers to be issued only to the media and to no one else.

- **Appoint a media spokesperson (or spokespersons)**   Make it clear that nobody else is to talk to journalists. Media spokespersons should be people who have been trained in talking to the media; addressing a large group of eager journalists in a crisis situation is an unnerving experience.

- **Use a prepared statement**   Journalists are usually better at asking questions in a crisis than people are at answering them and a poorly prepared spokesperson is at a disadvantage. It is a journalist's job to catch the spokesperson off guard and it is the spokesperson's job not to be caught off guard. Another advantage of prepared statements is that copies can be made available to attending journalists and sent out by fax or courier to others. They can be circulated to other company personnel not at the news conference and they become a matter of record. This avoids disagreement later as to what was actually said.

- **Allow time for questions**   As far as possible try to limit questions to those arising out of the prepared statement. The better prepared you are and the more open and frank you have been the easier it will be to do this. Never say 'No comment': if you cannot answer a question, or do not wish to, say something like 'I am unable to answer that particular question at this moment. As soon as I am in a better position you will be informed.' 'No comment' on its own always sounds as though you are hiding something.

Case Studies

1 The case of the faulty kettle

Patterson & Drew (P&D) produces a range of electric kettles, one of the most popular of which is the Pride, a cordless, jug kettle in stainless steel. Despite good quality-control procedures, a batch of 5 000 units with faulty switches was distributed. This raised the prospect of a serious accident and called for prompt action. The fault came to light when three kettles from the same batch were returned. One problem was the time-lapse between the distribution of the kettles and the complaints coming in.

A product recall exercise was set in motion. Procedures for product recall were set out in the company's response manual. There were also fact sheets ready, detailing the accident-free record of the company's products and describing P&D's excellent quality-control procedures and its commitment to customer safety. A stand-by statement detailed the steps the company would take in the unlikely event of a recall being necessary (as in this case it was).

The affected publics were wholesalers and retailers on the one hand and consumers on the other. A problem was that the retail purchaser might not be the actual user. Pride kettles were popular as birthday, Christmas and wedding presents.

Dealers were expected to be very annoyed. They had their own businesses to think of and would not like the idea of selling potentially dangerous goods. Neither would they appreciate the inconvenience of a product recall. On the other hand, they had enjoyed good relationships with Patterson & Drew in the past and might be fairly easily placated.

Only one batch was affected and the batch number on the kettles made it possible to identify the dealers to whom they had been sent. Only these were contacted. If any other dealers got wind of the situation they were to be sent a prepared letter with the appropriate fact sheets and stand-by statements but otherwise they were not, at this stage, to be contacted.

Where stocks remained on wholesale and retail shelves the recall was easy. Wholesalers were able to identify the retailers to whom they had sold stock. Where goods had been sold direct to the central purchasing office of a retail chain they had been dispersed throughout the branches but were retrieved with the minimum of fuss. Nevertheless, the number of people who knew of the problem increased.

About 4 000 kettles were retrieved in this way. This left the prospect of tracing about 1 000 from the public. Retailers keep records, and where customers make use of a credit card or charge acccount it may be possible to trace them through this. However, when customers pay by cash they are often much harder to trace. Some buyers registered their purchase by returning the warranty card enclosed with each kettle. However, all of this takes time and there was always the risk of a serious accident. Another method would have to be employed. Reluctantly the company decided to go public. It realised, of course, that dealers from whom they had so far kept the problem would be bound to find out. They wondered what the media might make of it but felt that that was a risk they had to take.

An 'advertising' campaign in the form of a series of product-recall announcements was devised. Because of the need to act quickly a newspaper campaign was used. Radio was considered but ruled out because it was thought that a verbal message might be either missed or misunderstood.

PRIDE CORDLESS STAINLESS STEEL JUG KETTLE

SAFETY WARNING

Serial Number PD/d34/94

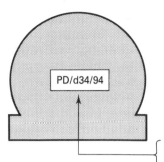

There have been a few incidents involving the failure of the switch fitted to the Patterson & Drew 'Pride' stainless steel cordless jug kettle. Only those models with the serial number PD/d34/94 are affected and if you own a Pride kettle with any other serial number or any other Patterson & Drew product there is no cause for concern.

The serial number can be found on the base of the kettle as shown in the diagram.

If you own a Pride cordless kettle with this serial number you should

(A) Disconnect it immediately and stop using it. (B) Complete and return the coupon below to:

**FREEPOST P&D, PO BOX 57,
Hanson, Rutland RU9 1BR**

Upon receipt of your coupon you will be sent a pre-paid container to enable you to return the kettle. This will be fitted with a new switch and returned to you without delay.

We apologise for any inconvenience and hope that owners of Patterson & Drew products will appreciate our concern to ensure the continued satisfactory performance of all our products.

If you have any queries please phone FREEPHONE (0773) 58585 and ask for Customer Services quoting the serial number above.

NAME _____
ADDRESS _____
Patterson & Drew Pride Stainless Steel Cordless Jug Kettle: PD/d34/94

Fig. 16.1 Product recall notice

At the same time, the rest of the trade were advised. It was felt better that they should not learn of the problem by reading about it in the papers. There was also a need to assure them that they had not received any faulty goods themselves.

The product-recall announcements published in the newspapers emphasised that only one batch (identifiable as PD/d34/94) was at fault and that all other Patterson & Drew products were perfectly safe. It advised owners of Pride kettles with that batch number what they should do and assured them that they would be fully compensated.

Production and quality-control procedures at the factory were carefully checked to ensure that such an event would not happen again. Arrangements were made for the tagging and storing of recovered units to ensure that they did not get back into circulation.

Members of the sales force were briefed as to how to handle wholesalers and retailers when next they called on them. It could be anticipated that some dealers would take it out on the sales representatives and it was important that representatives understood the very important public relations role which they had to play.

Fortunately for Patterson & Drew the media took very little interest in the story. Apart from the paid-for announcements there were only a few lines in the local paper. Of course, if Patterson & Drew had not acted promptly and if a user had suffered severe shock, or even death, then the media would have had a real story. On the whole, the company came out of it quite well.

On the negative side, however, was the cost of the product-recall exercise. A post-mortem analysis showed that it had cost more to retrieve each kettle than it had cost to market it in the first place. On the positive side, later research showed that all affected publics, wholesalers, retailers and consumers, were impressed with the professional way in which the situation had been handled.

Patterson & Drew learned a valuable lesson. The advertising campaign and the direct-mail letters to the trade generated far more telephone calls than the switchboard could handle. It was decided that, should such a thing happen again, an inbound telephone bureau would be briefed to handle the work. The crisis manual was duly updated.

2   The case of the missing schoolboys

Vector Holidays was set up in the early 1940s to organise adventure holidays for schoolchildren in the 12–16 age group. In the early days schools were often less adventurous than they are today but now Vector takes its young charges into Europe on a range of adventures, including mountaineering and white-water canoeing for which it has to recruit highly skilled specialist instructors.

Vector uses a direct-mail approach to headteachers and, recognising the power of decision-influencers, it also targets form tutors and significant subject tutors such as sports teachers. Non-teaching school governors are also targeted. Participating schools need the permission of parents and Vector supplies schools, on request, with explanatory leaflets for children to take home.

In September of last year three 16-year-old boys on a mountaineering holiday in Austria went missing. The boys were high spirited and given to playing jokes and the first reaction of the team leader was that they had absented themselves deliberately as a 'lark'. It was only after night had set in and the temperature had fallen that the team leader began to be worried. He notified local authorities and a search was set in motion. Believing that the boys would turn up, he decided that there would be no point, at that time, in notifying either the school or the parents. Those decisions were, however, taken out of his hands when another member of the party phoned home and let the matter slip. Before long, the headteacher had been roused at his home and was very annoyed to learn of the problem in such a way.

One of the fathers also phoned the local newspaper and a reporter on the local paper acting as a stringer for a national passed the story on.

Within hours the team leader back in Austria was dealing with phone-calls from an angry headteacher and distressed parents. He was also faced with the physical presence of an Austrian journalist who was covering the story for the British newspaper. The boys still being missing, the story found its way on to breakfast television and radio news in the UK. Media interest escalated and before long there were several journalists at the Austrian mountaineering centre and interviews with parents were appearing in later editions of the daily press and in local and regional evening papers. The editor of one paper had offered to pay all the costs of taking the three sets of parents to Austria in return for exclusive interviews.

After 48 hours the boys turned up. It was, as the teamleader suspected, a prank. The boys had made a reckless bet that they could survive on their own for two days and nights. Although the boys were safe, it was not all over for Vector.

James Morgan, Vector's chief executive, decided to meet with the headteacher and the affected parents at the company's expense and he booked accommodation in the boys' home town for this purpose. He hoped to limit the damage done to Vector in particular (but also to the whole concept of adventure holidays for young people) by persuading the parents that the boys had acted in a way for which the team leader and his colleagues could not be held responsible. A harder task was to justify the decisions of the team leader not to involve local rescue services earlier and not to inform the parents themselves. He succeeded in his first objective but failed in the latter. Subsequent to the publication of the parents' admission that the boys had behaved badly and the dismissal of the team leader for poor judgement the media lost interest. The dismissed team leader called his own press conference at which he said that he had been 'thrown to the wolves' and made a scapegoat. This received very little media attention, but he did get on to one breakfast TV show where he criticised Vector's management quite bitterly. Vector arranged private and undisclosed financial compensation for all the parents on the grounds that everybody's holiday had been spoilt. No legal actions ensued.

In the aftermath, Vector lost four bookings which were on the verge of being agreed and for two months afterwards new enquiries were very much down on previous figures. To offset this, Vector intensified its direct-mail activities making far more use than previously of customer endorsements and including a new section in which it spotlighted some of its key instructors pointing out their excellent qualifications and experience.

Other companies in the same industry had watched the Vector story unfold with varying degrees of apprehension. Publicity of this sort was bad for the whole industry and there were fears (groundless as it turned out) that an enterprising journalist might do a feature on what went wrong with school-age adventure holidays. Such a feature would not have been welcomed by anybody in the business.

POSTSCRIPT This case is fictitious and based on a variety of incidents but in May 1993 a schoolgirl died after an inexperienced instructor took a 'short-cut'. What were described in a November court hearing as 'lamentable emergency procedures' caused a three-hour delay in getting her to hospital. The managing director of the adventure centre and the company itself were each fined £15 000 plus £15 000 costs. The managing director was told that had the law allowed it he would have gone to prison.

16.7 Crisis situations and non-media publics

In the cases of Patterson & Drew and Vector we meet with other publics apart from the media. These include, in the case of Patterson & Drew, the external publics of wholesalers and retailers on the one hand and consumers on the other. As Pride kettles were often given as gifts, a distinction had to be made between the purchaser of the kettle and its eventual owner and user. People who give gifts like to feel confident in the gifts which they give and this very important segment of the market could have been damaged. Internally, we meet the salespeople who would at some point have to call on the dealers and the telephone operators and receptionists who might have to deal with angry callers and visitors. All these internal publics need training in dealing with a crisis.

In the Vector case the range of external publics is more diverse, from schoolteachers and governors on the one hand to parents and the children on the other. In both cases prospective as well as actual customers or consumers had to be considered. Vector lost four accounts which were on the verge of completion and general enquiries were down. Another Vector public turned out to be their own competitors who were naturally worried about the effect of the Vector crisis on their own businesses and watched with interest how Vector would handle it.

Apart from the paid-for announcements which Patterson & Drew caused to be inserted in the national press and attempts by Vector to cope with the media, what other methods of communication were used? Both companies made extensive use of direct mail, Patterson & Drew to its dealers and Vector to its client schools and other publics. Both companies used the personal element, notably, in the case of Vector, in the personal visit of its chief executive to the headteacher and parents involved. Both cases involved the necessity to keep all personnel informed and internal memos and reports would have been used.

One point to bear in mind is that the problem is not necessarily finished with when the media lose interest. By and large, the media lose interest when they judge that their readers have lost interest. Other publics, however, will have a more enduring relationship and their interests may cause them to be involved not only weeks but years after. It may, for example, have taken Vector months to sort out the details of the financial compensation to the parents. When the crisis leads to a public inquiry or to legal action things can go on for a very long time. When the results of an inquiry or a legal action are made known, public and, therefore, media interest may well flare up all over again.

16.8 Summary

- Crises of different sorts can affect any business. When they do they have to be dealt with promptly to limit the damage they can do to the company.
- Every company should have crisis management procedures, such as CMTs and crisis manuals, in place.
- Crisis communications to limit the damage done to the company's reputation and to restore it to its pre-crisis level involve dealing with the media and other affected publics.
- Public relations has an important role here making use of news conference, pre-prepared statements, personal meetings and newsletters. Paid-for advertising can also be utilised.

16.9 Assignments

1. Monitor a crisis situation as it unfolds in the media – keep a cuttings file.

2. Think of a particular business (an airline, a fast-food business or a cosmetics company) and try to identify what could go wrong and what would need to be included in a crisis (or response) manual.

3. Draw up an outline plan for a product-recall exercise.

17 Direct marketing

17.1
Introduction

Direct marketing is a method of approaching the consumer without going through the indirect routes of mass-media advertising. In its most common forms it includes both **direct mail** and **telephone marketing**. Personal calling, letterbox leafleting, handing leaflets out in the street and even sticking them under the windscreen wipers of stationary cars can all be included.

Getting the message directly into consumers' homes may be a first step to getting them into the retail outlet by advising them of special offers, sales promotions and new lines. It may be an invitation to request more information or it may be a straightforward sales pitch soliciting a purchase. **Home shopping** carries the exercise as far as it will go, cutting out not only mass-media advertising but the traditional retailer as well. The purchaser does not even have to go to the shops but orders either by post or by telephone or through agents who call at the door.

Currently, **mail order** (buying by post) accounts for 5 per cent of retail sales. When ordering by phone is included, this figure rises to 8 per cent. (This takes no account of the effect of direct marketing on over-the-counter sales.)

The story of the princesses and the frogs (chapter 10) is relevant here also. In any large group of people there are going to be both potential buyers and those who have no interest at all. If the latter (the frogs) greatly outnumber the former (the princesses) then mass-media advertising becomes less attractive. To use a very simplified model:

If you pay £2 000 per advertisement to market a new product to an audience of 10 000 people of whom 9 000 are frogs, then the cost of reaching the 1 000 princesses is £2 each. If each princess is given four OTSs (see page 111) this bumps the cost up to £8 each. If 250 (25 per cent conversion rate) of the princesses buy the product, this bumps the cost up again to £32 per purchase (or £2 000/1 000 princesses × 4 OTSs × 25 per cent conversion rate = £32 to gain a new consumer).

The argument for direct marketing is that by approaching each of the princesses direct and ignoring the frogs altogether the cost of winning each sale can be greatly reduced. If the cost of acquiring a mailing list, producing the letter and distributing it produces new consumers at a cost of less than £32 each, then direct mail is obviously better.

Other analogies have been used. Mass-media advertising has been likened to taking a scattergun to the market and firing it indiscriminately in the hope of hitting the right target. Direct mail, in contrast, has been likened to a sniper carefully picking off targets one at a time. A less military metaphor sees conventional advertising as **broadcasting** (scattering the message very wide) and uses the relatively new buzzword **narrowcasting** to describe direct mail.

The scattergun approach is most suitable for products with a very large market appeal where the proportion of a mass-media audience which might buy the product is high. But where there is more of a **niche market**, direct marketing may be more effective. However, big name producers in the branded FMCG sector are increasingly turning to direct mail.

17.2 Direct mail

Almost everybody has received direct mail letters at some time. Many of these are perceived as being of no interest and are dismissed as **junk mail**. A lot of direct mail is inappropriately targeted with happily married men being invited to join a dating agency, dead people being invited to take out an insurance policy and those with money to invest being invited to take out a loan. Sometimes the letters themselves are poorly designed and printed.

To offset these problems, the direct-mail industry has had to do two things:

- Target people more selectively.
- Stimulate interest with better designed and more appealing letters, inserts and envelopes.

17.3 Selective targeting

The mailing list

The basis of accurate targeting is a well researched and constructed mailing list and a good place to begin is to think about a particular product: for example, a fairly expensive garden toy, a swing perhaps, for children between the ages of three and seven. You would be looking for:

- Households containing at least one child in that age group.
- Households with access to a garden where such a swing could be permanently erected.

This would rule out most flat-dwellers, young couples who had not yet started a family, families where the youngest child was eight years old or over and so on. Bearing in mind the cost of the item you might also rule out families on a limited income. Furthermore, if you were a London-based firm, you might want to limit your campaign geographically. You might add to the specifications:

- Families living in the South-east.
- Families with a disposable income of over £10 000 a year.

Where are you going to get an accurate and up-to-date list of families living in the South-east, with gardens and children and income to match your requirements? There are a variety of sources.

Internal company records

Enquiries and orders come from people who match the specified characteristics and this can be used to compile a **first-party list** (a list built from company sources). These are often thought superior to lists acquired from other sources (or **third-party lists**), but they can take time to build up. Direct response advertising can be used to generate new names (see below, page 220).

Swapping lists

You could swap your list with another company but, preferably, not one with whom you are in competition. A manufacturer of children's clothes, for example, would be interested in the same households. If your company has 2 000 names and the swapping partner has 2 000 names you might finish up with 4 000 names altogether. But beware, some names may appear on both lists and would need to be weeded out (**de-duplicated**). Even so the list size would be significantly increased at little expense.

Buying lists

Another possibility is to buy the list of a rival manufacturer going out of business. A mailing list is an asset and the people responsible for winding up the other company will certainly be interested in selling it. In fact, a mailing list can be such an asset that one company may go as far as buying another company out just to get its list.

Case Study

Park Foods

In June 1994 Park Foods, Britain's largest food-hamper firm, paid out £10.5 million for thriving Heritage Hampers. The only assets which changed hands for this vast sum of money were a team of 12 000 agents and the Heritage list of customers. The enhanced Park Foods customer list now includes 1.6 million buyers of Christmas hampers to give Park Foods a £120 million share of a £300 million market. Christmas food hampers are typically paid for over the year with the money being collected by agents of whom Park Foods now employs 90 000.

Source: Daily Mirror 11 June 1994

Renting a list

A common practice is to rent a list from a **list-broker** or **bureau**. Like the advertisement department of a newspaper, these brokers issue rate cards and, again, there may be the opportunity to negotiate. The rates are set at so much per thousand names and you can rent as few or as many thousands as you wish. If the broker had 100 000 names in the computer to match your requirements, but you wished to use only 5 000, then the 5 000 names would be extracted at random and supplied on self-adhesive preprinted labels. You are paying for only one use of these labels and you are not permitted to photocopy them. To prevent fraudulent use of its property the bureau might plant the list with a small number of control names. If the control names receive a second mailing from you then the broker will know that you have been cheating.

To get the best out of a list bureau it is advisable to prepare a proper brief and to give the bureau time to meet it. Tell them what field characteristics are wanted (children between three and seven, garden, etc.), what the product is, what other promotion you might be doing to support the product and so on. Given time the bureau should be able to make you a good proposal. If you have any reservations it is possible to test-market the broker's list with, say, 500 names to see what response you might expect from a larger mailing.

List maintenance

The list has to be kept up to date. Old addresses have to be deleted, new addresses have to be added and the list has to be de-duplicated to make sure that each name occurs only once.

There are a few definitions which you might find useful. You would be the **list user**. The **list broker** would work for you, for a fee, arranging the rental of whatever lists you want to use. The **list owner** is the organisation which owns a list and is prepared to rent it out. A **list manager** is the person who maintains the lists and enhances them so as to further exploit their commercial usefulness. Finally, a **list compiler** is responsible for collating the information and turning it into a form which makes it accessible to you, the list user.

17.4 Omnibus and solus mailings

You may prefer to find a **bureau**, or **lettershop**, to handle the enveloping, addressing, franking and posting for you. You will need to supply them with sufficient copies of your letters and other inserts (a full-service bureau will research, write and print for you as well). A cheaper option would be to take part in an omnibus mailing where your letter goes out in the same envelope as other companies' letters. The disadvantages are that your mailshot might go out with a rival mailshot, the lack of impact and the timing. Omnibus mailings usually have a fixed dispatch date which may not suit your needs. The dearer, but more effective, option is the solus or sole mailing which can be sent out alone exactly at the time you specify.

17.5 Piggy-backs and card decks

Piggy-backs

A **piggy-back** (or third-party insert) allows you to get a cheap mailing for your letter by riding on the back of somebody else's mailing. Service utilities and credit-card companies send out regular statements and a manufacturer of domestic water-softening equipment, for example, could pay the water utilities in hard-water areas to include a leaflet.

Card decks

Card decks are sets of high-quality cards each featuring a separate product and designed as a prepaid postcard for easy turnaround. The recipient receives a pack of, perhaps, 30 cards and simply returns those in which he or she is interested. A card deck might feature a wide variety of goods, but some business-to-business decks might focus on related goods such as office supplies.

17.6 Preparing the letter and envelope

Addressing, mailing, etc. are front-end activities. In this section we are concerned with the back-end activities of preparing the letter and envelope. (See also chapter 11.4 on creating for print.)

Personalisation

Early attempts at personalisation involved leaving a space for the name to be inserted later. Names were often out of alignment, too short or too long for the space provided or lighter or darker than the surrounding matter. Today, with computer-driven inkjet printing, the name and address can be changed for each letter (anywhere in the mailshot and as often as required) at print-speed and the space can be automatically adjusted for names of different length. Personalisation can be applied to the envelopes, to the salutation at the beginning of the letter ('Dear Mr Milner' rather than 'Dear Householder') and to selected places within the body of the letter ('Now, Mr Milner, what do you need to do to take advantage of this amazing offer').

This is not to say that there is no place at all for the older non-personalised 'Dear Householder' style of letter. For a direct-mail shot to advise every householder in a five-mile radius of a new hypermarket it might work very well and would certainly be quicker and cheaper to organise.

Teaser copy

Teaser copy is anything that is printed on the envelope to arouse curiosity and to encourage the recipient to read the contents. There is a need to be careful as misleading copy may lead to a complaint to the Advertising Standards Authority.

Case Study

Universal Stores

In May 1994 the ASA upheld a complaint that a mailing from Universal Stores with the copy 'You really are a winner in our 1994 Super Prize Draw' was open to misconstruction as it could be taken to mean that the recipient had won a major prize rather than that the recipient was being invited to enter a prize draw in which every entrant would receive a small gift just for entering. The company recently used a window envelope revealing a real car key with the on-envelope message 'You could already have won a Ford Fiesta LX' – the words 'could have' are not misleading in the way that 'really are' were held to be.

Plays on negatives are sometimes used – 'Don't bother to open this letter unless you are really interested in cutting your household heating bills.' Transparent heat-sealed envelopes do away with the need for teaser copy on the envelope because the contents can be clearly seen. In such a case, the teaser copy may be printed on the visible part of the letter with the 'pay-off' out of sight in the inner folds.

A well-designed envelope can be disfigured by the post-office franking system and, if you are mailing in sufficient quantities, you may be able to use a **printed postage impression** (PPI) which allows you to incorporate a 'postage paid' symbol into the design of the envelope.

Involvement devices

Involvement devices give the recipient something to do. A simple device is a self-administered questionnaire which may lead readers to an awareness of their needs. A gift may be offered in return for a request for more information. 'If you send for our catalogue within seven days we will send you, entirely without obligation, a free travel clock' and a popular device is the 'scratch-off' which invites the reader to disclose a hidden message by removing a layer of foil. A straightforward gift may be preferred: 'Enclosed with this letter is a complimentary key-ring for you to keep, even if you decide not to take advantage of this once-in-a-lifetime offer.' This is obviously dearer than just giving a gift to people who qualify in some way but can be offset by making the gift less expensive (a key-ring rather than a travel clock) and by the knowledge that a key-ring can be a constant reminder of the product.

17.7 Mailing and remailing

Postage is a major cost and it is a good idea to keep the weight of each mailable unit below the level at which it would pass into a higher postage band. First-class post should only be used if there is a good reason – for most mailings second class is acceptable. The cheapest but slowest method is the bulk rebate system which may take up to seven working days. Discounts are available on presorted (into counties or towns) quantity mailings. Simple addressing systems produce names in strict alphabetical order and it may pay to use a system which can presort before the letters are printed.

Remailing involves minimising postage costs by taking advantage of cheaper overseas rates. The principle is that a mailing for the home market is shipped abroad in bulk and remailed back as individual items. This works because of a complicated way of settling international balances between the national postal authorities – exaggerated, in some cases, by internal subsidisation to force overseas rates even lower. It is believed, at the time of writing, that France and Germany, among others, may refuse to handle remail from low-cost remailers such as Panama and the Dominican Republic.

Mailers determined to exploit cheap overseas opportunities may move their entire operation (including printing) to a low-cost country as this would no longer count as remailing. Such a solution is fraught with problems. Lists may be pirated, political instability may disrupt the postal service and there are even stories of upwards of 20 per cent of names being deliberately left off a list by unscrupulous overseas operators.

**17.8
Post-campaign
reviews**

After the campaign it would be appropriate to carry out a review. How many letters sent out, how many 'gone-aways' (letters returned because the addressee has moved), how many positive replies and so on. A high rate of gone-aways would indicate an out-of-date list and an unusually poor level of response would indicate an inaccurate list. Some agencies will offer a refund on wasted postage if gone-aways exceed an agreed limit or the response is poor.

**17.9
Direct-res-
ponse
advertising**

Mass-media advertising of the direct-response type can be used to generate either sales or new leads. The two main forms are **off-the-page** print and **off-the-screen** TV ads. Off-air radio ads are also possible.

The principle is that a media ad campaign is used to stimulate initial interest and that the audience will preselect themselves by making use of one of two response mechanisms: a cut-out reply coupon or a reply phone-number. Where cut-outs are used care should be taken to ensure that they are not printed back to back with other cut-outs as the use of one destroys the other. The response may be made free by the use of a Freepost address or a Freephone number. Some print ads contain both.

Radio and TV cannot use a cut-out coupon but can still give an address. The difficulty for the broadcast media is that of allowing the viewers/ listeners enough time to take an address down and some TV campaigns have been criticised for not leaving the information on screen for long enough. For these reasons the print media is often preferred to the broadcast.

The omnibus reply coupon is a feature in some magazines where each advertisement is coded and all the interested reader has to do is fill in one coupon on which several different codes can be entered. The responses can then be sorted and dealt with centrally.

Response management, follow-up and evaluation

Direct-response advertisements are the easiest to monitor. Advertisements can be coded (the first to go into the *Daily Express*, for example, can be coded DE1 and a record of all DE1 returns analysed). Sales or leads can be counted and credited to precoded advertisements and the subsequent conversion rate of leads into sales can also be measured.

The form of follow-up may vary from sending a brochure to making a phone call or a sales visit. The respondent may be offered the option of requesting a sales visit in which case the words 'No salesperson will call unless requested' may be included. In other cases the advertisement may contain the words 'you will not be troubled with any other unsolicited material or sales calls.'

Where the purpose is to sell, then instructions as to the method of payment must be included. Paying by credit card is increasing and buyers may be asked for their card numbers. Sellers (who can keep all other information for future mailings) should not keep any record of such numbers. Many advertisements say 'Allow 28 days for delivery' and both the ASA and the ITC expect an advertiser to have set up sufficient fulfilment facilities to enable all orders to be dealt with in that time.

Direct-response advertisements can contain a great many inclusions from clip-out coupons and telephone numbers to payment details and mandatory disclaimers: all reasons why print campaigns may be preferred to television or radio which are more limited in their ability to handle such details.

Interactive television

Selling into the home through the use of interactive TV is now a reality. The extension of the advertisement into full-scale channels devoted to this aspect of home-shopping is seen in satellite and cable channels such as QVC (Quality, Value, Convenience). As long as television and telephone technology remain separate, this type of service operates through the telephone response mechanism. With fibre optics and digitalisation pulling these two technologies together, the prospect is now very real of most homes being able to buy what they see on the screen using their remote controls to send messages back down the television wire to the seller. More than this, the screen will become a sort of moving catalogue where the viewer will be able to see products on demand and to alter their specifications and angle of view at will. The one-to-one nature of direct marketing may be further developed by the prospect that viewers will be able to dictate the type of advertisements which they wish to see.

Revenge shopping

Both Grattons and Littlewoods (two of the biggest mail-order companies) recognise what they call 'revenge shopping'. Apparently, when their husbands are glued to the television screen watching football or racing, wives get their own back by turning to their mail-order catalogues and buying something. During big events such as the Cup Final, companies are deluged with extra orders – so much so that they have to lay on additional response management facilities. Littlewoods with 600 regular staff to answer calls brings in another 50 when a big match is on.

Fig. 17.1   Revenge shopping

**17.10
Telemarketing**

Telemarketing, that is direct marketing by telephone, consists of the out-bound call, commonly referred to as **telephone selling**, and the inbound call from the customer. To operate efficiently, it needs the same attention to research, data collection and list-building as direct mail. Where direct mail uses a carefully written letter, telemarketing may make use of a carefully produced script.

Unfortunately, too many outbound calls have become labelled **junk calls** with telephone sellers failing to show sufficient care. At its worst, outbound calling has the image of untrained, financially exploited people working from home and using their own telephones to sell products of which they have very little knowledge. There is an image of telemarketers working their way through the phone-book, cold-calling householders and reading the same tired script. Quite often, the only purpose of these callers is to generate leads which they then pass on for a fee to a specialist salesperson who pursues the prospects further.

An annoying practice is to claim to be conducting market research. This not only damages the image of telemarketing but of market research also. Another annoying practice (developed in the US) is the auto-dialled recorded message player (ADRMP) which calls numbers at random and plays a prerecorded message. The best professional view is that such pre-recorded messages should be played only after a live caller has obtained permission from the callee and established that the message is acceptable.

Inbound calls and response management

The inbound side of the industry has its own problems. The most critical of these is the inability of the advertiser's telephone system to handle large numbers (or bursts) of calls in a short period of time when a Freephone direct-response campaign has proved particularly effective. This results in annoyance to a prospect faced with an engaged signal and a loss of good-will to the advertiser. A second problem is the sometimes poor telephone manner of the telephonist so that when callers do get through they are met with indifference or rudeness.

Firms moving into telemarketing for the first time could avoid these problems by engaging an inbound bureau. These bureaux receive the calls on behalf of the advertisers, capture the necessary information such as names and addresses and pass the orders or enquiries back for processing. With a major national campaign a series of regionally based inbound bureaux can be used and the calls passed on to a local branch of the client company. A mixed in-house/out-house operation allows bureau staff to operate from within the client's premises so that the client's own database can be used and its security preserved. In-house systems can be linked to out-house bureaux if the situation requires.

Systems technology

The most basic systems technology is the provision of enough trained staff and telephone equipment to cope with the volume of business. Companies such as Littlewoods and Grattan are able to identify the peak 'burst' periods and to ensure that staff are in place to cope. Particular spots in the television schedules have been identified as periods of high activity – the mid-break in *Coronation Street* (the 'three-minute Street market') and just before and after *EastEnders*, for example.

At a more advanced level, there is technology for data capture and database enhancement with the possibility of using such systems as QAS's QuickAddress with which the operator has only to ask the caller for a postcode to be able to raise the street name, town, district, etc. on screen; then it is necessary only to ask the caller for the house number and the system does the rest. An American device now available in the UK is able to recognise the telephone number from which a call is being made at such a speed that the telephone subscriber's personal details are on screen before the conversation actually begins.

Freephone numbers and customer service

A 1992 Gallup survey for British Telecom showed that over 60 per cent of 1 000 people interviewed regarded companies offering free calls as being caring and wanting to do business. The free call service offers the three As of *accessibility*, *affordability* and *availability* to people who might otherwise not have time to shop around and the survey showed that many consumers take advantage of Freephone numbers to check out several companies. This underlines the positive aspects of telemarketing as providing a customer-care service dealing with customer enquiries as carefully as with orders. American hotels have developed this concept, the inbound calls being answered by operators who immediately identify themselves by name and take trouble to find an alternative booking if the caller's first preference is unavailable. In the UK, Forte Hotels offer a similar approach, but generally speaking the UK is well behind the US where half of all inbound calls are free.

In practice, there is a great deal more to telemarketing than just telephone sales. It includes the whole process of dealing with customers, handling their enquiries, getting out estimates, monitoring dispatch and delivery dates and overseeing such things as after-sales service. Terms such as **up-selling** (encouraging the customer to buy more) and **cross-selling** (drawing the customer's attention to other product categories) have entered the jargon of telemarketing.

17.11 Other aspects of direct marketing to the consumer

Personal selling is not widely used but there are a few organisations which rely on it. Betterware, a company which describes itself as 'the leading UK housewares retailer in direct home shopping', uses local agents who letter-box catalogues with a note that they will call again to take orders. Avon uses a similar technique to sell both men's and women's toiletries. Although Betterware and Avon products are different, they have one thing in common in that they are the type of goods that every home will consume. There is no need for selective list-building and the blanket approach works well. Selectivity may, however, come into the choice of neighbourhood (there are neighbourhoods where the response to home selling is low); but once a neighbourhood is entered then every household can be canvassed.

Letterbox marketing works on the basis of dropping unaddressed, and usually unenclosed, leaflets through letterboxes. It is often done through the local free newspaper publisher who will drop leaflets along with the paper. Typical users of this approach are fastfood outlets, minicab companies, estate agents and home-improvement companies. Leaflets seem to have more success when they are dropped before the morning postal delivery as they get picked up and looked at with the post. They lose impact when, as sometimes happens, six or more are all forced through at the same time, frequently suffering damage in the process.

Leaflets may also be handed out on the street or placed under the windscreen wipers of parked cars – both practices that can lead to complaints of littering and disputes with local authorities, some of whom forbid them.

**17.12
Summary**

- Direct marketing is a one-to-one approach to the consumer that cuts out mass-media advertising. It may, however, be linked to media advertising when the latter is used to generate leads which can then be used in future direct-mail campaigns.
- The commonest forms of direct marketing are direct mail and direct telephone. They both require up-to-date technology and the proper construction and maintenance of lists. Badly handled, they attract criticism and become labelled 'junk mail' and 'junk phone calls'.
- Home shopping is an important part of this industry and interactive television shows the extent to which this can go.

**17.13
Assignments**

1. Collect over a period of about two to four weeks all the promotional literature which comes through your letterbox. Divide it into posted and non-posted and analyse it by type of company/product, purpose, nature of appeal and so on.

2. Watch and listen for television and radio direct-response ads. What did you like or dislike about them? Do you think that they would have worked better in print? If so, why?

3. Write and design a mailshot suitable for announcing the opening of a new 24-hour petrol station with forecourt shopping facilities. This will be distributed by post over a five-mile radius.

4. This leaflet (badly printed, unenclosed and unaccompanied by any other material) comes through my letterbox about three times a year. (The name of the company is withheld to protect the guilty.) Critically evaluate it and identify its purpose. Try to write one that might work better.

PRIVATE & CONFIDENTIAL

Dear Sir/Madam

First of all let me apologise for addresing you in this manner. The reason is that what I am about to offer you is something **we cannot** make available to the general public.

Through our research department we have identified a few properties in your road, one of which is yours, that would be suitable for us to use in our advertising campaign.

For the first selected homeowner to respond from your road we are prepared to install our award winning range of windows and doors for only the **cost price**. This will mean heavily subsidising our normal prices and offering vast savings.

We would then pay you to rent the front of your property for a period of 10 weeks, during which we would place a small advertisement board on the outside of your property. We would also take before and after photographs of your windows for use, with your permission, in our next brochure.

A one year nothing to pay scheme is also available for these properties.

This offer is available as a one off only and is limited to one selected property in your road. Therefore we request, if this is not of interest to you, not to pass on the details as this may affect our normal marketing. Thank you.

If you would like more details please ring me **now**! on FREEPHONE 000 00 00 00

Yours faithfully

(Customer Relations Manager)

ALTERNATIVELY CUT ALONG THE DOTTED LINE AND FREEPOST YOUR DETAILS TO US

Name _____ Address _____

_____   _____ Tel _____

Please contact me with further details ☐ Please tick relevant box.

Please arrange for my home to be
viewed for suitability   ☐

Please send written details to me   ☐

18 Sales promotion

It is sometimes said of sales promotion that its purpose is to be there during the final stages of the purchase decision process, either carrying the customer over the line between purchase and non-purchase or affecting the characteristics of the purchase, such as its size or timing. In the latter case, sales promotions may affect people who would have bought the product anyway: it is just that they buy sooner rather than later or more rather than less.

A professional buyer may be dealing with a salesperson or, as in a self-service retail outlet, the consumer purchaser may be alone. In the first case, sales promotions can work on the motivations and behaviour of both the seller and the buyer, rewarding the salesperson for making the sale and rewarding the buyer for making the purchase. In the second case, there is only the buyer to consider and, in the absence of a salesperson, all the emphasis, at the point of purchase, is put on offering the buyer an incentive. These relationships between rewards and selling (creating a **push** for the product) on the one hand and rewards and buying (creating a **pull** for the product) on the other are at the heart of sales promotion. The emphasis on sales in the term **sales promotion** is, perhaps, one-sided. Some aspects of sales promotion are really **purchase promotion** and it is interesting that what we call **point of sale (POS)** the Americans call **point of purchase (POP)**.

In fact, even in a self-service outlet, there are still push elements at work. Shop displays, the position of the product on the shelf, or at or near the checkout can all stimulate sales: they act as 'silent salesmen' doing the work that a salesperson might otherwise do. Such things are normally the province of the retailer rather than the manufacturer and come under the heading of **merchandising**. In this chapter we will think of sales promotion as what the manufacturer does and merchandising as what the retailer does. Merchandising and sales promotion can work together but they can also conflict when the manufacturer's interests are not shared by the retailer.

There are moral dimensions to this. A retail customer seeking impartial advice as to which washing machine to buy may be unaware that the retailer may have particular reasons for pushing certain models. Where sales promotions are targeted at children, parents may be pestered into making purchases which strain the family budget (the expensive breakfast cereal with the free dinosaur as opposed to the cheaper, gift-free, own-brand).

Many practices are included under sales promotions: for example, premium offers, free offers, editorial promotions and charity-linked promotions. Sales promotion schemes are widely recognised to be complex to set up and administer. Sales promotions offered to the consumer come under the ASA and have the same requirements to be legal, decent, truthful and honest as any other form of advertisement.

**18.2
Short-term
and long-term
considerations**

Sales promotions were once thought of as having only a short-term tactical value in stimulating the sales of a slow-moving item. Today, it is recognised that they can have a longer-term strategic value. The spend on sales promotions now matches conventional advertising. This is due partly to manufacturers' desire to find a cheaper alternative to expensive television advertising and partly to their wish to have more control over the fate of their products in the retail stores. The ability to tie sales promotions in with other activities such as sponsorship, direct mail or public relations has also played a part.

The development of sales promotion techniques to secure long-term goals, such as building customer loyalty, deseasonalising the demand for seasonal products, blocking off competitors and increasing market share, is now well recognised. Any promotion that requires the participating consumer to provide a name and address can also be used to build a mailing list and this might actually be its major purpose.

Sales promotion can occur at three levels:

- **Sales-force incentives** The internal use of sales promotions aimed at the manufacturer's own sales force.

- **Trade promotions or trade incentives** The external use of sales promotions aimed at wholesalers and retailers.

- **Consumer promotions** The external use of sales promotions aimed at the consumer.

Figure 18.1 illustrates the relationship between these elements.

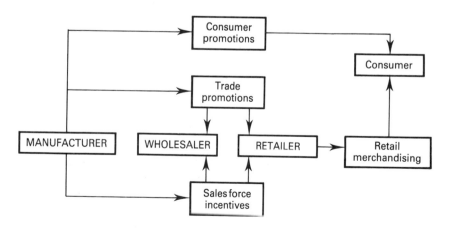

Fig. 18.1 The relationships between the manufacturer's various sales promotion activities and the merchandising activities of the retailer

18.3 Internal sales promotion

Motivating the sales force

Both financial and non-financial rewards are used either separately or together to motivate the sales force. The purpose of these rewards is to focus the salesperson's efforts on the **close of the sale** and, for this reason, the rewards given are performance related. If no order is taken, no extra payment or reward is given.

Financial incentives

There are three methods of remuneration: salary only, salary plus commission and commission only. We are concerned with the commission element, particularly where it forms part of a package with basic salary. The basic salary guarantees a minimum income regardless of performance and contributes to the building up of a loyal relationship. Commission systems – payment by results – should be easy to understand and immediate so that a salesperson can readily see the benefit.

The design of incentive schemes varies from employer to employer. Some prefer a high basic salary with a low commission element and others a low basic salary with a high commission element. Some begin paying commission on the very first sale of the week (or month) and others begin paying only after a minimum sales target has been reached. Some use a standard, unchanging, percentage rate of commission and others use a stepped rate with the percentage commission increasing as certain target levels are passed. There are even companies who pay different levels of commission on different products. Yet again, some give rewards for specific tasks, such as introducing new products or opening new accounts. Some systems are so complicated that they become costly to administer and difficult for staff to understand.

Three kinds of problem can arise. The first is that if the system is too complicated, it can actually fail in its purpose and can even result in salespeople concentrating on the wrong activities. The second is that, after a while, salespeople may settle into a pattern of income that they know they can live with. These so-called **target workers** set themselves personal income targets and as long as these are met they do not strive much harder. Target workers having a better than average week have been known to keep orders 'up their sleeves' by post-dating them to the following week. The third is that, in the end, money is only money and in itself does little to build a long-term relationship between salespeople and employer. An employer who relies on money alone risks losing star performers to other employers with deeper pockets.

Non-financial rewards

Non-financial rewards offer another approach. They are sometimes called **psychic rewards** because they enrich the workers' perception of themselves as good workers whose efforts are truly appreciated. Such rewards can create memorable occasions in the life of both the salesperson and the company and may have more enduring value than merely money. They may serve to build loyalties, bonding salespeople and company together. An example is the holiday paid for by the company on which successful salespeople can take their partners. This 'incentive travel' can have the added dimension of building a relationship into a saleperson's home by involving the partner in the reward process.

Annual company dinners, where all salespeople (and their partners) are invited regardless of performance, do not generate a spur to action as such but again can build loyalty. However, they do offer a platform for making annual awards such as 'salesperson of the year' and the opportunity to be rewarded publicly can act as an incentive (particularly if the prize winners and their partners get to sit at the top table). Some companies have 'salesperson of the month' awards and 'salesperson of the region' awards as well as annual, national awards. This increases the number of prizes and acts as a greater incentive. Even things of no monetary value such as having one's photograph in the company house magazine as salesperson of the month count as psychic income.

Sales-force incentive schemes are complex and can, if badly thought out, produce unwanted results. Unless closely tied in with specific targets and other performance indicators, they can encourage salespeople to make very short-term decisions aimed at maximising their own benefits without regard to the tactical and strategic consequences for the company of what they are doing.

| 18.4 External sales promotions: trade | **Motivating the trade** |

Motivating the trade

The historical concept of independent middlemen buying from whom they chose (and as and when they chose) and taking responsibility for selling their own stock does not sit well with the modern manufacturer. Such a concept was all right in the production-orientated stage of market development when the problems of selling were scarcely recognised, but today's manufacturers, in a fiercely competitive market, know that it is unwise to rely entirely on the motivation of middlemen alone. After all, independent middlemen owe no particular loyalty to any one manufacturer: as long as customers are coming in to the shops it makes no difference to them which manufacturer's goods they are selling.

Manufacturers were faced with the problem of breaking into that independence and, somehow, involving wholesalers and retailers in their own business objectives so as to gain more control over the fate of their products as they passed through the distribution channel. One solution lay in forward integration, with manufacturers taking on the wholesaling and retailing functions, and another was the use of restrictive practices. A third solution lay in **trade promotions** where the basic philosophy is to give the trade a reason for buying and selling your goods rather than somebody else's.

Initially, these practices were rooted in the idea of getting the manufacturer's goods 'sold in' to the middlemen and they were put in place to support the *push* tactics of the sales force. However, to the extent that they operated on the middleman's motivation to buy they created demand at that point in the distribution chain and can be seen to have a *pull* effect also (that is, if we see push as operating on the sales side and pull as operating on the demand side).

So, just as consumer promotions encourage consumers to buy, trade promotions can be used to encourage the trade to buy. These pull incentives include:

- Offering longer periods of credit (two or three months instead of the traditional one).
- Sale-or-return schemes (whereby retailers can return unsold stock to manufacturers for a full refund).
- Annual rebates given when a wholesaler or retailer passes a critical level of purchasing.
- Discounts for bulk purchases.

Such (non-psychic) incentives carry their own problems. Extended credit affects the manufacturer's cash flow. Sale-or-return encourages reckless ordering. Annual rebates lead to last-minute panic buying as tradespeople rush to qualify. Quantity discounts encourage the trade to advance their purchasing cycles rather than to buy more. Furthermore, they only work to get the goods into the shops, whereas a manufacturer really wants them sold on.

After all, it is a maxim that no product is ever sold until it is in the hands of the final consumer. Goods sitting on wholesale and retail shelves represent no future income for the manufacturer until they move off the shelves and generate the cash to finance more orders. Manufacturers soon learned that it was not enough simply to **sell in** to the wholesalers and retailers. They had also to develop ways of helping the trade to **sell out**.

Schemes which rewarded middlemen for buying came to be accompanied by schemes which rewarded middlemen for selling. Top dealers (or their top salespeople) can be invited to partake of corporate hospitality in the form of a day at Wimbledon or a visit to the Grand National (see chapter 19). They can be given prizes such as gold watches in the same way that a manufacturer's own sales force can and they can be honoured by having their photograph in the manufacturer's house magazine. There are psychic as well as financial benefits here also.

The provision of luxury display stands and cabinets at the manufacturer's expense enhances the appearance of a retail outlet, thus increasing both the shopkeeper's pride in the premises and the sales potential.

In pursuit of this goal of assisting retailers to sell out, manufacturers began to develop material and schemes to entice the retail customer at the point of purchase. Point-of-sale (POS) material came to be commonplace, so much so that some shopkeepers complained about the volume of it. POS material includes mobiles to hang from shop ceilings, cardboard cutouts to stand on floor or counter, dispensing units and window posters. Explanatory leaflets and booklets, colour cards and sample swatches all add to the scene.

Such activities led to a sort of sales promotion war as manufacturers came increasingly to value the extra exposure that display stands and POS material gave them in the shops. They vied to supply retailers with ever more luxurious stands and usually put restrictions on their use to prevent retailers using them to display rival brands as well. Small grocers and newsagents still complain that the free (but restricted) display refrigerators provided by the larger ice-cream manufacturers take up too much room and limit their freedom to seek alternative and cheaper sources of supply. Both cigarette companies and newspaper publishers have paid for the outside of a newsagent's to be refurbished (showing the manufacturer's name prominently in the process).

Manufacturers even go to the extent of training retail sales staff at their own expense. This is particularly useful when the product is of a technical nature such as stereo equipment or when a customer may want expert advice (for example, with skin and hair care products). The salesperson benefits from the extra training (and the psychic income of a certificate of training), the retailer benefits from having better trained staff and the manufacturer benefits by increasing the potential for its products to be recommended and sold.

Fitting the shop (inside and out), providing display material and training the retail staff are all ways of 'integrating' forward to support the product without actually going to the expense of buying the shop outright.

Small retailers sometimes complain of the loss of independence they feel as manufacturers seek increasingly to attain **channel dominance**. Large retailers, such as Sainsbury's and W H Smith, are not so powerless. When it comes to channel dominance it is often they who call the tune. They are not so easily persuaded to give floor space to a manufacturer's stand or prominence to a manufacturer's product. They usually prefer to control their own retail environment and manufacturers who want special attention have to negotiate, and often pay, for it. In such situations the manufacturer's sales promotions play second fiddle to the retailer's merchandising.

18.5 External sales promotions: consumers

Motivating the consumers

This section deals with consumer promotions. In a well-integrated plan we might expect to see the whole process of promotions running through from sales-force incentives, to trade incentives, to this final stage of consumer incentives. Here we consider consumers who are currently using the product and potential consumers who may be using rival brands.

Consumers

Consumers can be looked at in various ways. Some are very loyal to the brand and will buy it anyway, regardless of whether there is an offer or not. If there is an offer, they are getting a 'free ride' and the benefits they obtain are being funded by the manufacturers – these **free-riders** are sometimes called **free-funders**.

It is different, of course, if the existing brand-loyal consumers take advantage of the offer to increase their level of consumption: although there is always the possibility that they will revert back to their pre-offer level when the promotion has run its course. Permanent increases in the level of consumption are, obviously, a long-term pay-off.

If consumers simply buy ahead (**advance their shopping cycle**) without actually increasing their level of usage, they affect sales now at the expense of future sales. This will probably be the case with items like shaving cream. A man can only shave so often; he will not shave more simply because he has bought three cans of shaving cream for the price of two; it will simply be that much longer before he buys shaving cream again (but at least he won't be buying a rival brand either, so the offer may block a rival out of the market for a few weeks).

So with brand-loyal consumers there are those who:

- Take advantage of the offer without increasing either their purchase or usage of the product.
- Increase their consumption short term, for as long as the offer lasts.
- Increase their consumption over a long-term period.
- Advance their purchase decision and buy for future usage.

Potential consumers

When the market is relatively new and undeveloped (for example, the market for vegetarian meat substitutes such as Quorn), potential consumers are likely to be people who have never tried meat substitutes at all. In a mature market (for example, instant coffee), potential consumers are probably already drinking rival brands. Potential customers tend to fall into the following groups:

- Those who will ignore the offer because they are loyal to a rival brand or a substitute product (dedicated meat eaters may ignore a Quorn offer). They are sometimes called **unmovables**.
- People who will buy the product only as long as the offer lasts and then switch back to their pre-offer brand.
- People who will form a liking for the product and will continue to use it on a long-term basis. Some of these may be **slow movers** in that they are unlikely to respond to a one-off promotion but may, over a period of time, respond to a sustained campaign.
- People who flit about from offer to offer like butterflies and have no loyalty to any brand, but will just take advantage of any offer. They are sometimes called **promiscuous nomads**.

Figure 18.2 shows some possible outcomes.

18.6 Different types of consumer promotion

Consumer promotions may be aimed at first-time trials, retrials or repeat purchases. They may be designed to win new consumers, win back old consumers, encourage brand loyalty or encourage increased consumption. They may even be used to encourage a different use of the product (for example, deseasonalising the demand for holidays or ice-cream or repositioning a breakfast cereal as a late-night snack).

Some of the most popular forms of sales promotion are those which adjust the price–volume ratio in some way to give the purchaser 'better value for money'. In this context, the free sample can be seen as having a **zero price**. It is important when offering standard packs at promotional prices to make the purchaser aware that it is a special price for a limited period and not the regular price. Otherwise, when the offer is over, the consumer may see the reversion to the normal price as no more than a price increase.

Free samples

Free samples (given away in store, posted or letterbox dropped) are frequently used. They may even be attached to a complementary product: a new brand of fabric softener being given away with a popular brand of washing powder, for example. Tasting sessions in supermarkets are one way of giving a free sample with, for example, bite-size pieces of cheese being handed out. Free samples, however, may not give the recipient

ISLE COLLEGE
RESOURCES CENTRE

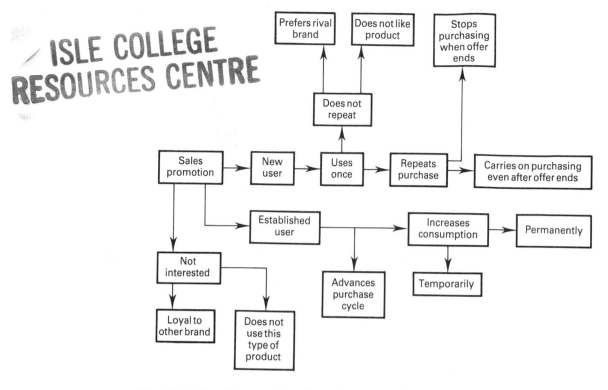

Fig. 18.2 Possible results of a sales promotion

enough experience of the product; some shampoo samples distributed to households are barely sufficient for more than one or two washes and this may just not be enough. Television rental, cable and satellite companies offer free at-home trial periods and car-dealers offer test-drives as ways of allowing the consumer to sample the product.

Money-back offers

In a money-back offer, the consumer buys the product first at the normal price and then reclaims some or all of the money from the manufacturer. Such offers enable the consumer to have more experience of the product than a free sample allows, but they put the buyer to some inconvenience. They are normally limited to one per household to prevent abuse of the offer.

Redeemable coupons

Promotional price offers may be tied in to a direct-mail or letterdrop campaign in the form of redeemable coupons (10p off your next jar of . . .) and coupons may be included as part of a press advertisement or even handed out in the street as sometimes happens with fastfood chains. One advantage of redeemable coupons is that special labels do not need to be printed. This makes them very useful where large stocks of pre-labelled products are already on hand, but they are often thought of as a nuisance at the checkouts.

Next purchase coupons

A form of redeemable coupon is the one which the consumer gets only after buying a standard pack at the regular price. The coupon is redeemable at a subsequent purchase for the duration of the offer. Redeemable coupons work best with consumers who already know that they like the product and will be more successful in encouraging brand loyalty through repeat purchases and winning back lost supporters. Next purchase coupons are often **on-pack** (perhaps because the packs were already in stock at the time the scheme was introduced) but these are sometimes removed by shoppers who put the product back on the shelf. It is better to put the coupon **in-pack** to frustrate such dishonesty.

Coupons are designed to be redeemed only against a genuine purchase of the specified product. In spite of this, some major retailers risk the wrath of manufacturers by redeeming coupons without bothering to check that the product was bought and some even redeem coupons for products which they do not sell. Manufacturers sometimes find that their coupons are being used as a weapon in inter-store rivalry and thus undermining the purpose of the promotion. Coupons (rightly or wrongly administered) are, in any case, perceived by many retailers as a nuisance; they slow down the checkout process and involve considerable work in reclaiming the money.

Banded packs – multiple packs

Packs offer a way of adjusting the price–quantity ratio by fastening, for example, four bars of soap together and selling the pack for the price of three. Such packs are usually made up by the manufacturer and delivered to the retailer ready banded. Modern barcode technology has removed the need for physical banding and is able automatically to make the adjustment when the fourth bar goes through the checkout. This technology makes it possible for retailers to introduce their own promotions (merchandising) – making it clear to the consumer that it is the store and not the manufacturer who is the benefactor.

Collections

Any promotion that appeals to the collecting instinct is likely to succeed – petrol stations have been exploiting this appeal for decades. Tobacco companies were once famous for their (still collectable) cigarette cards and many other products from sweets and ice-cream to tea have followed with what are now called **trade cards**. Not surprisingly, child-related products such as breakfast cereals are among the biggest users of collections. Sometimes the gift is in-pack, but otherwise the scheme may depend on collecting coupons redeemable when enough have been collected. Collectables of relatively small value are usually free.

Self-liquidating promotions

Self-liquidating promotions require the consumer to pay towards the cost of the gift, but usually the price asked is a great deal less than would normally be charged in a retail outlet. If the money taken from the consumer does not exceed the costs of postage and packing, the gift may still be described as free.

Prize promotions

Prize promotions include lotteries, free draws, contests of skill and games of chance. They should be accompanied by clearly set out conditions, including the closing date, the criteria for winning and a description of the prizes. In other words, competitors should know what they have to do and what they will get if they win.

Charity-linked promotions

Charity-linked promotions set out to raise a specific sum of money for a specified charity (or charities). The consumer contributes through making the purchase (or multiple purchases) and the reward to the consumer is the self-satisfaction derived from supporting a worthy cause.

Editorial promotions

Sales promotions wars between rival national newspapers range from price wars to competitions for quite extravagant prizes. Front-page flashes announcing the promotion (details inside) have sometimes been criticised as misleading the consumer by not making the qualifying conditions clear enough. The ASA upheld no fewer than six complaints in one month in 1994.

18.7 Redemption problems

Misredemption and malredemption

Misredemption occurs when the person claiming the prize is not the person who bought the product – a claimant may simply have collected coupons from family and friends. More serious is the practice of **malredemption** which is a large-scale misredemption engineered by syndicates out to make money at the manufacturer's expense where schemes involving cash payouts are involved.

Under-redemption and over-redemption

Managers have a responsibility to ensure that sufficient promotional packs are made available to meet expected demand and that (where gifts are claimed by post) the facilities exist to turn round all requests within 28 days. **Under-redemption** occurs when the promotion fails to attract interest with the consequence that the manufacturer is left with a large amount of unwanted stock, either of specially labelled or banded products or of gifts. **Over-redemption** occurs when the manufacturer is unable to meet demand with the loss of a great deal of goodwill into the bargain. Gifts offered must not seem to the public as too trivial to be bothered with nor as 'too good to be true' but as reasonable in the circumstances. Hoover paid the price for making a 'too good to be true' offer.

Fig. 18.3 The free burger system

Case Study

Students 'cash in' on building society's free chips offer

In October 1993 the Alliance & Leicester Building Society ran a pro-motion aimed at holders of Link cards, of whom there are more than 18 million. Anyone using a Link card to withdraw money from an Alliance & Leicester cash machine automatically received a token which could be exchanged for a free burger, drink or chips at Burger King, the fastfood outlet. Crafty students soon realised that all they had to do in order to qualify was to withdraw £10, which they could immediately take inside the society's offices and pay back into their accounts. One student said: 'It's no trouble. You can stick your money in and take it out again as often as you like.' Another student, found with 14 tokens in his pocket, was questioned by police but no charge was brought because he had not broken any law. A spokes-person for the building society observed that it had shown a lot of initiative on the part of the students. A Burger King spokesman said that his company did not mind as most users of the tokens bought other things as well. Both companies agreed to continue the offer until March 1994.

18.8 Merchandising

In general, merchandising carried out by retailers is similar to sales promotions carried out by manufacturers. A retailer and manufacturer can work together to run a joint promotion, although the possibility exists that what retailers want to do on their own premises may leave little or no room for manufacturers' initiatives. Generally speaking, a retailer is concerned with drawing customers into the store to spend money and may use staff training and incentive schemes, store layout and special offers to achieve this – the retailer may not really care whose products are bought. The manufacturer, in contrast, may not really care where his products are sold as long as somebody is buying them somewhere.

18.9 Summary

- On the face of it, sales promotion sounds easy: give the sales force a bonus, offer the trade some free display stands and knock something off the price of a product. In practice, sales promotions need very careful planning and administration with carefully selected objectives and methods.
- The company may find itself motivating the sales force to sell the wrong thing, giving away benefits to free-funders without any significant increase in sales or running up against the retailer's own merchandising plans.
- Misredemption, malredemption, under- and over-redemption can all occur.
- On-pack gifts and next-purchase coupons are sometimes separated from their packs by shoppers who leave the pack behind.
- Some retail stores redeem coupons without checking that the goods have actually been bought.
- Sales promotions can go brilliantly well, but they can also go wrong and when they do they can cost a company far more than when any advertising campaign goes wrong.

18.10 Assignments

1. Produce a report on the sales promotion activities currently taking place in your local supermarket (or other store). Distinguish between those which are manufacturer-based and those which are retailer-based (merchandising).

2. Discuss some of the ethical problems involved when business interests conflict with the desire of the consumer to be given impartial advice. Is sales promotion any different in this respect from any other branch of advertising?

3. Take a specific objective, such as getting first-time trials of a new product, and discuss which type of sales promotion might work best.

4. Discuss how you would use sales promotions to develop brand loyalty.

19 Sponsorship

19.1
Introduction

Sponsorship has links with many other areas of promotion. It is seen sometimes as a public relations exercise designed to raise the image of the organisation as a whole and sometimes as designed to promote the virtues of a specific product. It may even be seen as part of a sales promotion campaign or as an exercise in corporate hospitality. At the local level sponsorship can be part of a 'good neighbour' policy. In whatever way it is seen it has come to play a very large part in business affairs. Many organisations see sponsorship as a distinctive tool of promotion in its own right and have a separate sponsorship department with its own sponsorship director in charge.

Historically, sponsorship stands in a line of succession from private patronage, through government subsidy, to business sponsorship. In earlier times, painters and musicians worked for rich patrons. In the present century, the philosophy of government subsidy emerged with grants to theatres, opera companies and orchestras. The Thatcher years with its emphasis on the market place saw a reduction in such government aid. At the same time, the demand for financial assistance from the worlds of sport and the arts increased as more groups found it harder to survive. Business sponsorship, already a reality, found more and more scope for involvement. One characteristic of sponsorship is that it often enables events to take place that might otherwise not occur. Where it differs from patronage and subsidy is the extent to which it is used to publicise the benefactor.

Sponsor and sponsee

Sponsorship is an arrangement between one party (the **sponsor**) and another party (the **sponsee**) whereby the sponsor agrees to support, by financial or other means, some event or activity of which the sponsee is the organiser and which, without the support of the sponsor, often would not otherwise take place. It is not, however, an act of charity as far as business is concerned. Whether it is seen as advertising, sales promotion, public relations or corporate hospitality, sponsorship must have a pay-off to the sponsor. This return on investment is usually measured in terms of the publicity or goodwill it generates.

Sponsorship as a business arrangement

Sponsorship is a business arrangement and as such is subject to the same criteria as other business arrangements:

- The suitability and acceptability of the proposed event must be scrutinised. Does it fit in with the image of the firm and its products? Will it offend or disquiet any key public which the company wishes particularly to impress?

- The feasibility of the event must be examined. Can it realistically be achieved? Are the sponsees, as the event organisers, up to the task?
- The cost to the sponsor and the eventual pay-off must be assessed and this is not such a simple matter (as will be shown later).

19.2 The range and scope of sponsorship activities

Sports sponsorship

The main area for business sponsorship has always been sport: football, cricket, snooker, darts, car and horse racing, rugby, the London Marathon have all been the subject of a great deal of television coverage and the names of their various sponsors popularised thereby. Not all sporting sponsorship opportunities, however, have national television appeal and many of them are of purely local interest.

Sports sponsorships range in scale from the international and national down to the regional and local, and they may differ in status from the amateur to the professional or from the senior to the junior. An individual player or athlete, a team, a specific event, a league tournament or a competition might be sponsored.

Sponsorship is not always financial: sponsorships in the form of equipment, team strip or clubhouse facilities are quite common.

Arts sponsorship

Sponsorship of the arts is wide ranging: from the performing arts such as opera, concerts and theatre to non-performing arts such as painting and sculpture. A company may, for example, sponsor a retrospective of a famous artist's work or offer prizes to young musicians by staging open (and televised) competitions. As with sport, there are questions of scale and status, and events such as a world tour of the London Philharmonic Orchestra take their place alongside the sponsorship of a local junior school band.

There remains also the possibility, where both sports and the arts are concerned, for any sponsor to create its own event if the sort of event in which it might be interested does not already exist.

Other forms of sponsorship

- **Education** Companies offer scholarships for individual students, endow chairs (or professorships) at universities, finance research projects or even an entire college.

- **Media** Sponsoring television programmes (see chapter 5, particularly section 5.6) is growing fast in the UK and sponsored book publishing offers yet other opportunities. The most recent development in publishing is the sponsorship of newspaper sections – sports sections and fashion sections are popular choices.

- **Environment** Sponsorship opportunities range from 'plant a tree' or 'adopt an animal' to much more ambitious schemes.

19.3 Matching the sponsor to the event

Sponsor and sponsee must be suitably matched so that the event does not seem inappropriate in the eyes of the intended publics. The event should fit into the overall promotional plans of the company and have the potential to contribute to the company's goals. A company should always consider the purpose of the sponsorship and the target publics involved.

A brewery, particularly of lagers, has a very strong masculine image (tarnished at times by the stereotype of the beer-bellied lager-lout). The purpose of a sponsorship campaign could be either to improve the image of lager and lager-drinking generally or to stimulate sales of a particular brand. The former objective, if achieved, could benefit all lager firms and might be better pursued by an industry-wide body rather than an individual brewery. An individual brewery might decide to use sponsorship to promote a particular brand; it might be seeking to hold on to its existing market share or to increase market share at the cost of rival brands. Research might show a strong correlation between lager-drinkers and particular sports, for example darts, and this would suggest that sponsoring a darts tournament would be a good strategy. Such a strategy would generate a certain amount of late-night television coverage. Drinkers returning home at eleven o'clock might well settle down to watch a darts tournament and, although the audience for such a programme at that time of night would be small, the quality of the audience could be high in terms of the proportion of lager-drinkers in it.

A manufacturer of toys or children's confectionery, on the other hand, would be careful to avoid such sponsorship opportunities as horse-racing (good for a brewery or a tobacco firm) because it might be accused of encouraging children to gamble. If it was aiming at the pocket-money market it might sponsor something with which children could identify such as a painting competition. This could be tied in with a sales promotion using on-pack or near-pack entry forms.

A large oil company, sensitive to a negative image as a despoiler of the environment, might look for sponsorship opportunities with an environmental angle. Ecological concern is a major issue today and protection of the environment offers companies a wide range of sponsorship opportunities from the World Wide Fund for Nature (WWF) to the Royal Society for the Protection of Birds (RSPB). Some companies marketing eco-friendly products may back away from events such as motor-racing because they may be thought of as environmentally unfriendly and contradictory to the company's desired image.

A manufacturer of up-market furnishings might seek an association with style and the good life by sponsoring an orchestra and a manufacturer of computers might seek a more intellectual association by sponsoring its own version of *Mastermind*.

So far we have assumed that the major publics to be targeted are consumers. Other publics, however, might just as easily be targeted. Shareholders might like to be reminded that they have their money in a lively and imaginative organisation and sports-sponsorship offers considerable opportunity for the corporate hospitality of wholesalers and retailers. A company that knew that many of its major customers were keen on golf might sponsor a golf tournament.

In the early days of sponsorship, too many deals were rushed into with disappointing results for both sides. The management of a firm entering sponsorship for the first time would be well advised to do some research first. If the purpose is to impress the trade, then find out what people in the trade think about sponsorship in general and specific events in particular. If it is to raise public awareness of the company, then the knowledge that a high proportion of the target market watch TV detective series might point in the direction of programme sponsorship.

19.4 Joint sponsorships

Generally speaking, it requires a big firm with a substantial promotional budget to undertake a major sponsorship, and some events, such as the Olympics, might be beyond the reach of even the biggest firms. Smaller firms cannot easily get into this league and are usually left to sponsor the smaller events with lower publicity potential. This does not, however, prevent smaller firms from joining the big league as a joint or co-sponsor and such joint-sponsorships are fairly common. There are, additionally, situations where the sponsee cannot find one single sponsor to meet all the costs and in such cases will actively seek out joint sponsors. Whenever joint sponsorship is arranged great care needs to be taken over both the financial arrangements and the resulting publicity so that both (or all) sponsors benefit proportionally to their input.

19.5 Big firms and small events

Big firms can also be interested in small events. A large firm may, as a matter of policy, share its sponsorship budget around a package of small events and may even choose to support small projects as training grounds for its own managers. Managing a sponsorship deal enables a manager to develop social awareness and relationship and negotiation skills that can be put to good use elsewhere. The local branch of a giant supermarket chain can run such events and a supermarket chain may actually prefer to sponsor a variety of local events rather than one national event. A large company, unfamiliar with the world of sponsorship, may take on a small event as a sort of pilot project.

19.6 The sponsorship initiative

It may be the sponsee who takes the initiative in approaching the sponsor, and the sponsor who makes the decision. This puts a sponsee in the role of supplicant. The sponsor may have many sponsorship applications to consider and it is up to the potential sponsees, in competition with each other, to make the most convincing case. This is not always so and there are some major sponsorships (in cricket, for example) which might be considered as prize catches for the companies that land them. In such a case, the sponsor may take the initiative in making the approach and the sponsee gets to make the decision – and is in the happy position of having two or more potential sponsors competing. In either case, there will be undertakings and benefits on both side which can be understood by looking at how a sponsee might make the approach.

19.7 Making the approach

When it is the sponsee who makes the first move there are a few simple rules to remember. Organisers of small-scale local events are often not aware of them and their efforts to raise support suffer as a consequence.

Spell out the benefits

The first rule to remember is that sponsorship is not a charity. Businesses do, of course, participate in charitable giving but not, as a rule, through sponsorship. Sponsorship is a business contract from which the sponsor will want a return and the sponsee should always take care to explain the potential benefits from association with the event in question. These must be realistic. The sponsee should not promise what cannot be guaranteed and vague references to the possibility of television coverage are unlikely to impress. In any case, media coverage is not the only benefit the sponsee can offer and for a small event local goodwill might be just as attractive in an area where the company recruits many of its employees or finds local suppliers and customers.

The sponsee should try to pinpoint specific advantages. If the event is a local golf tournament, point out how many of the firm's customers play golf. If the sponsorship is to raise money for the school orchestra, play on the managing director's interest in classical music (do some research!).

Justify the event

The second rule is to convince the sponsor that the event has been well thought out. This is easier when the event, like the London Marathon, has been going for some years and has a proven track record. If the event is a one-off or the first of a proposed series, any sponsor will need to be convinced that there is sufficient public interest to generate publicity.

The event needs to be well thought out in terms of timing (does it clash with other events, such as the Grand National, which would reduce its potential audience), its location (is the venue sufficiently accessible and attractive) and the rules and regulations which govern it, if it is of a competitive nature. Events conducted under nationally agreed rules (those supervised by some ruling sports council, for example) need to be cleared with the ruling body. Independent events need to have rules which are easy to understand and are fair.

Demonstrate management competence

Not only should the event be well thought out but it should be well managed. The sponsee will need to convince the sponsor that the organisers and managers of the event are competent. Previous experience with similar events goes a long way. It is not merely with the running of the event from a technical point of view that a sponsor is concerned. The sponsee will need to show that it has the ability to market the event and handle such aspects as press conferences should such opportunities arise. In particular, the sponsee will have to show competence in handling the money involved.

Money is at the root of sponsorship deals; even if the support is non-financial it still has to be paid for. In asking for support, the sponsee should be able to give a clear indication of how much is needed overall with a good breakdown of how and when the money is going to be spent. The sponsee should be able to demonstrate ability in budgeting, accounting and cash flow management.

The initial approach

It is always sensible for the sponsee to approach a potential sponsor with a good reason as to why that particular firm has been singled out. 'You are big, disgustingly rich and £20 000 won't kill you' is not a good reason. Neither is 'We are poor, desperately in need of money and thousands of small children will be heartbroken if you don't pay up.' The initial approach should be made in writing with a concise orderly statement as to what is wanted, when and why. Above all, the pay-off to the sponsor should be stressed.

The approach should be by name and title to the person in the organisation in charge of sponsorship funds. It may be the marketing manager, the public relations manager or the managing director. The company may have a sponsorship manager or it may even be that different types of sponsorship are handled by different people.

The sponsee should offer to be available for a meeting and if a meeting arises go to it fully prepared.

19.8 Benefits and how to assess them

The sponsee

It is relatively easy to summarise the benefits to the sponsee. With sponsorship, whether in cash or in kind, the event takes place; without the sponsor's support, it probably would not.

But, even for the sponsee, the arrangement is not without its drawbacks. Sponsors, anxious to protect their investment, may seek to become involved in the actual running of the event when the sponsees would far rather be left alone. We might talk of 'arm's length sponsorship' where the sponsor does not interfere and 'hands-on sponsorship' where the sponsor increasingly seeks to take charge. Sponsors who see themselves as investing money in what is essentially a publicity exercise are more likely to want to run things themselves. Sponsors may seek to take over the marketing of the event and its financial management. Sponsees may not object to this and may even see it, not unreasonably, as additional support and help which leaves them free to do what they know best. However, sports sponsors have been known to try to change the rules, or the date or the venue to fit in with some business activity such as a new product launch or to maximise television audience size or to fit in with the television programmer's schedules.

The sponsor

For the sponsor, the benefits are more complex and largely depend on the particular marketing or corporate objective in mind. It may be that the sponsorship was intended to create interest in a new product: in which case, not only consumers but wholesalers and retailers have to be considered. Sports sponsorship offers splendid opportunities for corporate hospitality with dealers being invited to Wimbledon or Wembley for a day out at the company's expense. Moreover, sponsorship also offers the opportunity to reward the company's top salespeople, or other employees, in a similar way.

Whatever the reason for the sponsorship, its main purpose is to gain beneficial publicity for the company. This can be monitored, measured and evaluated. Indeed, as with any campaign, sponsorship ought not to be undertaken without a clear statement of its communications and publicity objectives and an understanding of how to assess them. There are two methods of measuring the success of, or response to, a sponsorship: the first uses market-research techniques and the second involves monitoring the media.

Audience research

Audience research can help the sponsor discover if the people attending the event are, in fact, those whom the company wishes to impress. Communications research will help the sponsor assess the extent to which the sponsorship campaign has improved such things as corporate recognition. This research can be carried out among the public at large and need not be restricted only to those attending. Subtle changes in the perception of the company can also be monitored. Is the company seen as more caring, for example, or more adventurous and exciting? Is it shaking off a stick-in-the-mud image?

Monitoring the media

The sponsor can monitor media response by maintaining a clippings file of newspaper and magazine articles and measuring the column-centimetres; it can also monitor radio and television programmes. The sponsor should be realistic: there are thousands of sponsored events each year and only a small proportion have any chance of national television and newspaper exposure. However, a small local sponsorship might do well in terms of local press and radio coverage and a sponsor ought to be very pleased with that.

Two important aspects of media monitoring are:

- **Mood or tone of the coverage** If the event is reported in a lively, positive way then this rubs off on the sponsor. If the reporting is negative and dismissive, the sponsoring company may well wish it hadn't bothered. In the late eighties many firms backed away from football sponsorship because of the negative association with football hooliganism.

- **Position of the report** A motor-car manufacturer sponsoring a football team is hoping to get the product 'off the motoring page' and 'on to the sports page'. There may be many football fans who do not routinely read the motoring columns and getting the product on to the sports page is a positive plus.

Sponsored events have two different audiences. There are those who actually attend and those who rely on media coverage. It is unlikely that an event effective only with the first group will prove to be worthwhile. It is necessary to reach the wider audience.

Sponsorship versus advertising

The sponsor will need some rule of thumb to assess the sponsorship deal. A simple check would be to ask whether the amount of media coverage obtained could have been obtained more easily by spending the money on a conventional advertising campaign. Any sponsor who ends up feeling that he could have had as much or more exposure by simply buying it is unlikely to be happy with the result. On the other hand, paid-for advertising space does not yield any of the other benefits of sponsorship, such as customer goodwill and employee and community relationships, and these need to be put into the balance as well. It is a fact that many companies have tried and abandoned sponsorship either because they found it too difficult to handle or because they were dissatisfied with the measurable results. Many others, of course, have been delighted.

19.9 The costs and revenues of sponsorship

Sponsorship fee

Sponsorship may be for anything from a few hundred pounds to over £1m. The value of a sponsorship, as it might be reported in the media, is usually referred to as the **sponsorship fee** and represents the sum of money handed over to the sponsee. It does not, however, end there. The sponsor may also incur a whole range of hidden costs which cumulatively can bring the cost of the sponsorship up to 50 per cent or even 100 per cent more than the original sum. A company which is not aware of the potential extent of such costs is liable to find itself not only considerably out of pocket but also to discover that the publicity generated by the event is inadequate when compared to the whole cost and not just to the original fee.

Additional costs

A careful assessment of the project before any contracts are signed should bring to light where such extra costs are to be found. If the contract is then carefully drawn up, these costs can become a matter of record and need not lead to any bad feeling as has sometimes happened.

- **Publicity** The cost of publicising the event is an obvious factor. There is little point in sponsoring an event and then not doing everything possible to put it in the public eye. Press conferences, poster campaigns, associated sales promotions, etc. all cost money to run. Souvenir T-shirts and the like need to be designed to feature the sponsor's logo or trade mark and the designer has to be paid.

- **Tickets and programmes** If the sponsor wishes special souvenir programmes to be printed on a higher quality paper or using more sophisticated printing techniques this also has to be paid for.

- **Hospitality** If the sponsorship offers the opportunity for corporate hospitality then the catering costs have to be met, and so on.

- **Administration** The administrative costs include a proportion of the sponsorship director's salary, the typing and telephone costs generated, the costs of meetings between sponsor and sponsee before, during and after the event and the legal costs of drawing up the contract and arranging for insurance.

Sponsorship revenue

The event may also generate revenue – for example, from the sale of tickets, programmes, T-shirts, food and drink in the stadium or theatre bar – and the clear title to this has to be resolved. Where an official team strip has been designed, the sale of such strips, possibly in children's sizes, can generate thousands of pounds. Some sponsors may take the view that this revenue is legitimately theirs, but this view need not be shared by the sponsee. If the sponsor is standing the full cost of the event, its claim to such revenues is strong, but if the sponsee is putting up some of the cost the sponsor's claim is weakened.

Where joint and multiple sponsorships occur, the questions of costs and revenues can become more complex. In all cases it is essential for there to be a clear understanding at the outset between all parties and this should be incorporated into the contract.

19.10 The sponsorship contract

The contract is not only concerned with costs and revenues but with the wider issues of the rights and responsibilities of both sides. It should:

- Confirm the official name of the event. This usually includes the sponsor's name.
- Confirm dates, times, and venue.
- Commit the sponsor to giving full support to the event and the sponsee to running the event in such a way as to maximise goodwill and publicity for the sponsor.
- Require the sponsee to keep good and accurate accounts.
- Where the event is of a sporting nature, require key sports personalities to make themselves available for public appearances or to meet the sponsor's guests.
- Set out procedures and arrangements concerning cancellation. A usual clause requires the sponsee to return to the sponsor the unspent portion of the fee together with an account of expenditure. In the event of cancellation a sponsor would be very fortunate to get back all the money laid out.
- Anticipate any future arrangements by, for instance, giving the sponsor the first opportunity to consider the next event.

19.11 Sponsorship and television coverage

The percentage of sponsored events given national exposure on television (including the BBC) is extremely small – there simply is not enough television time available and, in any case, the majority of events would not make good TV. A company banking on television coverage as part of the pay-off for its sponsorship fee cannot afford to leave it to chance. (There may, of course, be chance coverage, if a record is broken or something equally newsworthy occurs, but even this might get only a few seconds at the end of a news bulletin.)

To guarantee television exposure, the television programmers have to be brought in at an early stage in the negotiations and certainly before the contract is signed. The negotiation then becomes a three-way deal, with any agreements written into the contract.

If for any reason (bad weather etc.) the event is not televised, then it is possible to get compensation provided that the right insurance cover has been taken out. A sponsor cannot, however, take out insurance against the non-televising of an event if televising was not written into the contract in the first place. When television programmers are brought in, they might have an effect on both the timing and the location of the event to fit in with their own schedules.

Buying into a guaranteed television event, such as the London Marathon or the Grand National, can also have its problems. The Grand National is worth about £4m over seven years in sponsorship fees, but it is unlikely that sponsor Martell would have felt satisfied with its association with the 1993 fiasco when, after a false start, the whole race was abandoned in disarray.

Case Study

Cornhill Insurance: from twelfth man to first team

Cornhill Insurance can be regarded as one of the veterans of the sponsorship industry with what must be one of the longest relationships with a single sport. That sport, as most people will now know, is cricket and it is through cricket that Cornhill has become virtually a household name. It was not always so and back in 1978 when the first sponsorship contract was signed very few members of the public even knew that Cornhill existed. It is not that Cornhill was small as insurance companies go (it was already the twelfth largest in the UK) but that it lacked **name recognition**. This was because it did (and still does) most of its business through insurance brokers rather than directly with the public. Today at number nine in the industry Cornhill is definitely in the first team. Sponsorship has played no small part in its success.

Name recognition

Name recognition (or name awareness) is important. Members of the public need to feel confident that they are in good hands when their brokers sign them up with an insurance company and this is undermined if they do not recognise that company's name.

After considerable research into ways of achieving name awareness, Cornhill decided on sponsorship as the best approach. The opportunity arose to sponsor Test cricket at the international level and £1m was committed over five years. The contract was extended several times and by 1993 the sponsorship fee had grown to £1.6 m a year. Cricket sponsorship currently takes up 60 per cent of the total Cornhill promotional budget.

Cornhill chose cricket because of its universal appeal and extensive media coverage. Cricket is covered on television and radio as well as in the press and, through name association, the public was soon used to seeing and hearing the Cornhill name. Name association did not come automatically. Test cricket had not been sponsored before and for more than a century it had been referred to as simply 'the Tests'. To achieve their name awareness objectives, Cornhill had to persuade the media to talk about the 'Cornhill Insurance Test' instead. A planned programme of press relations was undertaken with Cornhill both providing important information and aiding in the writing of reports. Currently, all Tests played in the UK are officially designated 'Cornhill Insurance Test Series'. In practice, the word 'Insurance' tends to get left out by the media which generally refer simply to the 'Cornhill Tests'. This omission does not seem to have done much harm as research has shown that as many people identify the name Cornhill with insurance as they do with cricket.

At ground benefits

The opportunities for 'at ground' and 'corporate hospitality' benefits were also a factor in choosing cricket. At ground Cornhill is allowed to erect seven large nameboards in prime sites and to display the company name on the outfield at all Test venues. These boards prominently display the word insurance (see fig. 19.1). The contract further entitles Cornhill to complimentary tickets to use in entertaining important business contacts.

The battle for sponsorship visibility

The suitability of cricket as a sponsorship vehicle was not long lost on other companies and Tetley and the National Grid are now in the field sponsoring other aspects of cricket. Tetley, for example, sponsors the England team and the National Grid sponsors the umpires. There are also sponsored grounds – Foster's sponsor the Oval. This has raised the interesting challenge of different sponsors (as many as four) competing for visibility at the same event. Cornhill has responded to this possible dilution of its sponsorship involvement with heightened exposure at ground and sophisticated merchandising strategies.

Another development, affecting all sponsors of cricket, has been the fragmentation of cricket coverage through the media explosion of increased terrestrial and satellite services offering smaller but more narrowly defined audiences. Geoff Mayhew, publicity manager for Cornhill, describes this as a 'bitter-sweet pill' offering both advantages and disadvantages.

Cornhill's sponsorship programme

In spite of the competition for visibility with other sponsors and the fragmentation of media audiences, Cornhill remains satisfied, through awareness·surveys and media monitoring, that cricket sponsorship remains a vital contributor to its recognition – it is now one of the best-known insurers. Its 1993 fee of £1.6 m (plus all the extra costs of promotion, administration, etc.) was regarded as money well spent.

For Cornhill, cricket is a corporate sponsorship, indeed its only corporate sponsorship. However, at the local level in Guildford, where Cornhill is the largest employer, there are also a number of community initiatives including the sponsorship of the Guildford Kings, the leading UK basketball team.

Fig. 19.1   Cornhill's 'at ground' advertising

**19.12
Summary**

- Sponsorship is a means by which a company can generate beneficial publicity through name association with a sporting or artistic event or through the sponsorship of television and radio programmes, published works, educational or environmental projects.
- The media publicity generated will usually be relative to the scale and importance of the event, with major coverage having to be negotiated and worked for.
- One basis for evaluating the publicity would be a comparison with the advertisement space which could have been bought with the same money, but there is also goodwill and image enhancement to consider and these may be less easy to measure.

- Sponsorship may be tied in with other promotional activities such as public relations or sales promotion.
- The event should be carefully chosen in the light of the company's objectives and its various publics.
- The event should be well organised. Badly managed events (or poor television programmes) will reflect negatively on the sponsor.
- The cost to the sponsor is a combination of the sponsorship fee and the 'hidden costs' which may add 50–100 per cent to the final bill.
- Costs and other details, such as title, date and venue of the event, should all be covered by a carefully drawn-up contract as should the disposition of any revenues.
- With joint sponsorships, the rights and responsibilities of all parties need to be worked out.

**19.13
Assignments**

1. Put yourself in the position of an event organiser (be specific) and draw up a letter aimed at a chosen target company to solicit sponsorship support.

2. Think of a specific company and define some target publics you might want to impress. How would you go about deciding what sort of event you would want to sponsor?

3. Draw up a checklist of the pros and cons of sponsoring different types of events: for example, sporting events compared with arts events or major national events compared with local events.

4. Some companies have tried sponsorship and decided not to continue. What reasons do you think they might have for quitting the field?

20 Conference and exhibition management

20.1 Introduction

This chapter looks at what are generally called **events, shows** or **meetings**. Specifically, we consider conferences and exhibitions which are sometimes collectively abbreviated to **confex**. CONFEX is, in fact, an annual trade fair held in London for people on all sides of the meetings industry.

Events are sometimes run as products in their own right and sold for a profit; a conference on the impact of European directives on UK marketing practice would be an example. Our concern, however, is with events as promotional tools and the way in which these events can be used to enhance the image and improve the performance of an organisation. The words *shows*, *events* and *meetings* are interchangeable.

20.2 The meetings/ events market

The event

We are mainly concerned with conferences and trade fairs. The former may be sales-training conferences aimed at the sales force or trade conferences aimed at dealers or suppliers. The latter may be trade fairs set up to enable manufacturers to demonstrate their goods to prospective buyers. Often elements of both are combined in a single event (see pages 254–5).

The venue

There are many different types of **venue**. Some of them are purpose-built: for example, the National Exhibition Centre (NEC) in Birmingham and the Queen Elizabeth II Conference Centre in London. Others, such as cinemas, theatres and universities, were designed for a different purpose but are suitable for events as well. There are open-air venues, unusual venues (for example, stately homes) and very unusual venues (for example, the London Dungeon) – in fact, an event can be held just about anywhere. Hotels fall into two categories: there are purpose-built 'business hotels' and non-dedicated hotels which take holiday business as well. A single venue may accommodate two or more events at the same time.

The sellers

The **sellers** are the owners and operators of the venues. What they are actually selling is limited access to their facilities for a stated period of time and for a stated purpose, subject to a wide range of contract conditions. The contract time spreads from the **get-in** time to the **get-out** time and the buyers have legal access only between these times.

Venue-sellers have to promote their venues and may use sales representatives, brochures and leaflets which can be sent out on request or as a direct mail exercise. Brochures are possibly the most important promotional tool for most venues.

Advertisements can be placed in magazines such as *Meetings* and *Incentive Travel* and press conferences held to publicise the opening of a new venue or the refurbishment of an old one. Press releases and press information packs can also be sent out.

Facility visits whereby prospective buyers can make a personal inspection are widely used and buyers can also be met at trade fairs (for example, CONFEX).

Groups of venues, particularly privately owned hotels in a conference town, may get together to share the cost of a promotional campaign. A conference town is one which has developed conference work as a service industry: Blackpool and Eastbourne are among the best known. They have their own association: the British Association of Conference Towns (BACT).

The buyers

Buyers include any organisation (or individual), whether business or non-business, which wishes to hold an event. Political parties, trade unions, charities, professional associations: all enter the market as buyers. Many business organisations hold so many events a year that it pays them to have a full-time events buyer (variously called a meetings planner, conference organiser, exhibition co-ordinator, etc.). Such people may have their own departments or they may be part of another department such as the marketing department or the public relations department.

A venue-buyer has to select a venue as carefully as a media buyer selects media vehicles. The wrong venue can have a damaging effect on attendance or, even if attendance is not damaged, the event itself may be marred and participants may go away with bad feelings. To get the venue right the buyer needs to remember:

- The event is intended to serve an organisational objective and must, therefore, have all the necessary facilities to support that objective.
- The event also has a social dimension and the choice of venue must reflect this. People who attend events want more then just a business experience so the organiser must be sure that there are suitable social facilities both within and around the venue.

Generally speaking, the larger the event and the more specialised the requirements, the fewer venues there will be to meet the buyer's needs. There may be thousands of venues that can cater for a conference for 50 delegates requiring nothing more sophisticated than an overhead projector, but only a small number that can accommodate 3 000 delegates or have load-bearing floors capable of supporting a brand-new fire engine. The former type of venue might be available at no more than a few days' notice; the latter may be booked up for two years or more ahead. The earlier the booking is made the greater the choice is likely to be. There is one golden rule:

- **Inspect the venue before booking it**   It is unwise to book a venue without inspecting it first. Brochures can mislead and the place may be

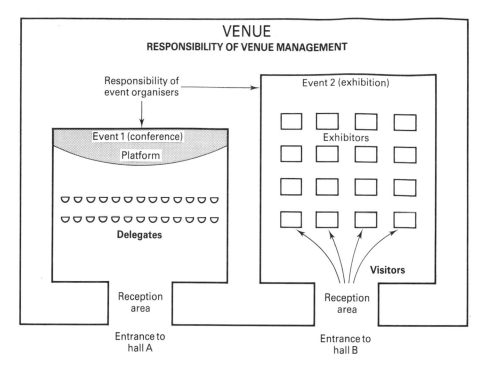

Fig. 20.1   Venue management

much shabbier than you expected or have other disadvantages which the brochure or sales representative might not mention. If possible, visit it when there is something going on: venues always create different impressions when they are full of activity than when they are quiet.

To assist the buyer there are a range of agencies from **venue finders** to **full service**. The latter will do everything from beginning to end. There is also a wide range of support services from catering agencies to script writers, and from entertainments agencies to security firms.

Figure 20.1 shows some of the relationships involved. The largest rectangle represents the venue. The two next largest represent two separate events which may each be under different organisers but which will, in any case, be in separate halls (which may be of different sizes). Within event 1 (the conference) the small semicircles represent the delegates and within event 2 (the exhibition) the small rectangles represent individual exhibitors and the arrows represent the visitors. The venue managers deal with the event organisers and the event organisers deal with the delegates, exhibitors and visitors. It is desirable to have two separate entrances from the street, one for each event, but this is not always possible.

20.3 Conferences

Typically, a conference is characterised by having a more or less passive audience being addressed by a speaker. The passivity, or otherwise, of the audience (the delegates) depends on the nature and purpose of the event. If it is an information disseminating conference, then the delegates may be

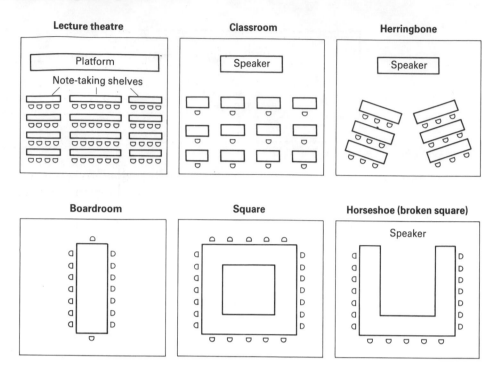

Fig. 20.2 Typical room layouts

quite happily accommodated in theatre-style seating with no note-taking facilities – vital information can be distributed in the form of reports, leaflets, fact sheets, etc. If the delegates are expected to participate in some way, then a minimum requirement might be a simple notetaking shelf attached to the seating. Purpose-built conference halls (and some university lecture theatres) have notetaking shelves as standard fittings. If the role of delegates is fully participative, it may be necessary to sit them at tables so as to give them room to work – care must be taken in arranging such a room so as to avoid too much similarity with a conventional classroom. Roving microphones might be necessary so that questions and comments from the floor can be heard more easily.

A feature of many conferences is that the delegates are split up into smaller groups for certain purposes (project analysis, for example) in which case smaller syndicate rooms must also be booked. Figure 20.2 shows some typical room layouts.

Dealer or trade conferences

Dealer conferences are events to which a manufacturer invites its customers – wholesalers, retailers, distributors, agents, etc.

The main purposes of a dealer conference might be:

- Inform.
- Train.
- Reward.
- Motivate.

Some facility for inspecting and trying out new products might be required, in which case a conference venue with some exhibition or display facilities would be needed. In some cases a simple tabletop display is sufficient. If the conference is to support a new product launch, the event would need to be organised before the new product became available to the general public and, indeed, early enough to enable the dealers to place their own orders.

Venue selection is very important. Dealers cannot be forced to attend a conference (unless attendance is an agreed condition of the dealership or agency contract) and will be disinclined to travel a long way or to visit a place which has no appeal to them. They may have to be motivated to attend.

One approach to the venue problem is to regionalise the event by having several small events at different venues around the country. This solution cuts down the dealers' travelling time by taking the event to them. It also allows for more intimate events where a more personal touch can be applied.

Overseas venues can also be used – the prospect of an overseas trip might be an additional attraction to delegates. It depends a lot on the importance to the manufacturer of the dealers it wishes to invite. In reverse, a UK manufacturer may hold a conference in the UK for the benefit of its overseas dealers.

Sales-force conferences

Sales-force conferences have the same basic motives – to inform, train, motivate and reward – as dealer conferences. Because delegates are employees rather than customers it is easier to enforce attendance. Sales-force conferences are also discussed in chapter 18.

Conferences offer the opportunity for corporate hospitality. This is usually extended outwards to important customers or suppliers but can be directed inwards to sales staff.

Corporate hospitality

A conference is a social as well as a professional event and may be designed primarily to reward dealers. When this is the main motive, we are in the realm of corporate hospitality, or 'formal fun'. The business aspects of the conference are given a lesser role and the fun factor is given the greater role. It is usual to extend the corporate hospitality to the dealers' partners so that if 100 dealers are invited hospitality might have to be provided for 200 people. Of course, the partners would not be interested in the business sessions and other arrangements (a so-called 'partners programme') would have to be made for them. For example, if a formal business session was to be held in the afternoon followed by a dinner and dance in the evening, an afternoon theatre visit might be put on for the partners. Sponsorship provides another opportunity for corporate hospitality (see chapter 19).

Setting up a conference

The main points in setting up a conference are:

- Be clear as to the precise purpose of the event.
- Decide who to invite and why. Think about how to get them to attend.
- Identify special requirements such as load-bearing floors, high ceilings, access for handicapped people and special dietary requirements.
- Choose the venue carefully and book it in good time.
- Give delegates sufficient warning of the date of the event.
- Give delegates very clear joining instructions so that they know how and when to get there.
- Establish efficient registration procedures so that delegates and their partners are checked in pleasantly and promptly.
- Prepare the programme carefully. Book guest speakers in advance and make sure that they are properly briefed.
- Pay as much attention to the social side of the event as to the business side.
- Give the venue management confirmation as soon as possible of the exact number of delegates expected and how many meals, bedrooms, etc. will be needed.
- Don't forget to allow for the conference team, guest speakers, their partners and retinue, and delegates' partners when calculating the number of meals and bedrooms needed.
- Arrange all services such as on-site reprographics, cloakrooms, lost property, first-aid, etc. in advance.
- Take proper security measures and arrange adequate insurance.
- Get the maximum promotional value out of the event: send press releases to the trade press, arrange for photographs to be taken, send follow-up letters to delegates thanking them for attending, etc.
- Make proper arrangements for visiting reporters – if the budget will run to it, set up a press room.
- Remember the golden rule of event management: *pay attention to details*. Delegates do not really notice that the coffee is hot – they do notice when it is cold. It is often what you forget to do that attracts comment.

20.4 Trade fairs

Trade fairs are a type of exhibition where manufacturers and suppliers of goods and services can display their products to potential buyers. They are microcosms of the outside world and provide a market place where the exhibitors (the manufacturers) can meet the visitors (potential customers). Not all business originating from a trade fair is concluded at the fair itself. Some of it may not be finalised for many months afterwards.

It can take a year or more to organise a trade fair. With annual fairs next year's fair may be being planned before this year's fair is over. The duration of such fairs is usually three to five days (less than three is hardly worthwhile), but they may be of any length.

A trade show is a game for up to five types of player:

- **Originator** This may be a trade association acting on behalf of the industry as a whole.

- **Organiser** Working for the originator, the organiser is responsible for everything from production to promotion. (The originator and organiser may be the same organisation.)

- **Exhibitors** The individual companies who book stands at the show to display their products are the exhibitors. At a big show there may be several hundred of them.

- **Visitors** The most important visitors are the decision makers who will decide what to buy on behalf of the companies they represent. Decision influencers are also very important visitors. Unless they make it clear (or are asked directly), it is impossible to know whether a visitor is the former or the latter. Depending on the type of show, members of the public may also be admitted but usually only on the last day when all the serious business is over.

- **Sponsors** Many shows, some fashion shows are examples, would not survive without sponsorship. The revenue generated by exhibitors' stand fees and visitors' entry fees do not always cover the full cost of the show and higher fees may scare off both exhibitors and visitors. Sponsorship is discussed fully in chapter 19.

There are two main types of trade fairs. Industry-based fairs and region-based fairs.

Industry-based fairs

The London Printing Equipment Show (LPES) serves the needs of one industry. At LPES the exhibitors are manufacturers of printing machinery and related supplies and the visitors are professional printers looking to update their capacity or to seek out new suppliers. The twice-yearly International Spring Fair and International Autumn Fair at the NEC is a similar example, but here the exhibitors are all manufacturers of craft goods such as silverware, jewellery, fine art, candles, picture frames, cushions, wooden carvings and the like and the visitors are buyers from craft and gift shops seeking to improve the range of goods they sell. In the first case the visitors are manufacturers seeking out industrial goods and in the second the visitors are retailers seeking out finished goods for resale. This is all part of business-to-business marketing (see chapter 21).

Region-based fairs

The second type of trade fair does not concentrate on the product of a particular industry such as printing or the craft industry but concentrates instead on all the products of a particular region or country. As the motive of this type of fair is often to boost exports they may be held in a foreign country and may, additionally, be subsidised by (sponsored by) the government of the producing country.

Trade fairs based on countries may be targeted at retail outlets to encourage them to carry those goods or at potential consumers to encourage them to demand those goods in retail outlets. After all, it is the demand from the general public that will pull the goods through the retail outlets.

Manufacturer-to-consumer shows, such as the Ideal Home Exhibition, work in a similar way.

20.5 Marketing a trade fair

No firm will want to exhibit at a fair that is not well marketed. There are, in fact, two different markets: exhibitors and visitors. For the fair to be successful both must be attracted.

A good place to begin, if the show is a regular one, is with previous attenders. The organiser should have two complete lists showing:

- **Previous exhibitors**   Name, title, address and size of company and the products and/or services it provides.

- **Previous visitors**   Name, title, address and size of company and its typical purchasing requirements.

The lists can be summarised in what is called an **exhibitor profile** and a **visitor profile**. If the event is a one-off or is being held for the first time, such profiles will not exist but may be estimated on the basis of previous similar events, market research or executive judgement.

Exhibitor profiles and visitor profiles have two main uses:

- They provide mailing lists for the organiser.
- They act as promotional appeals. Potential exhibitors can see what sort of prospects they are likely to meet and potential visitors can see what sort of suppliers they are likely to meet.

There is a parallel here with the media industry. Exhibitors are like advertisers, except that they are buying floor space not space in a newspaper and visitors are like readers, the audience which the exhibitors are hoping to reach. A major difference, of course, is that advertising is impersonal whereas trade fairs give buyers and sellers a chance to meet face to face.

Of course, the organiser will not expect the profiles to do all the promotional work. Other promotional activities can include:

- Direct mail to companies which have never attended before, either as exhibitors or visitors.
- Trade press advertising and press relations: many trade magazines will devote the entire pre-show issue to the event or publish a special show issue.

20.6 Exhibiting at a trade fair

It can take a great deal of time and cost a great deal of money to exhibit at a trade fair, so what does the exhibitor get out of it and how can the benefits be maximised?

Reasons for exhibiting

- Showcase new products.
- Display existing products.
- Meet with existing clients.

- Meet potential new clients – exhibitions are a good place to meet both existing and new overseas buyers.
- Generate new business.
- See what competitors are up to. They will be doing the same – before the show is over all the exhibitors will have had a look at their rivals' stands.
- As a public relations exercise: exhibitions are a good place for senior executives to meet many important buyers in a short space of time.
- Because your rivals will be there and you cannot afford to be absent.

Generally speaking, the exhibitor's aims will be either sales orientated or PR orientated. An important point to remember though is that orders taken and confirmed during the show may be a poor indicator of the value of attending. It may be that no sales are made straightaway but that sales confirmed three, six or twelve months later can all be credited to a contact made at the show. Many buyers, in any case, go to a show with a clear intention not to place orders. They want to investigate, discuss, collect catalogues and price lists and then go away and think.

Deciding which shows to attend

There are sometimes so many relevant shows that a company cannot afford either the time or the money to attend them all. If trade shows are like a media group and individual shows are like media vehicles, then the criteria would include the following:

- **Budget**   Some shows may be completely outside your reach however much you want to be there.

- **Effectiveness**   Is it better to spend your entire exhibition budget on one major show or to attend two (or more) smaller shows?

- **Past experience**   If you attended the shows last year would you want to go again?

- **Visitor profiles**   These should be studied if available.

- **Venue**   This would include the cost of getting there and the suitability of the venue for your type of product. You may need high ceilings, load-bearing floors, extra large access doors, etc.

- **Organiser**   Some organisers build up a reputation in certain areas (for example, looking after the exhibitors' interests or smooth registration procedures). They may be known for their success in publicising an event or for just generally being good organisers. From time to time an organiser can get a bad reputation and exhibitors may become wary of any events in which that organiser is involved.

Planning to exhibit

Planning to attend a show can be a twelve-month process. The decision to attend should be taken as early as possible because this will improve your chances of getting a good position, or site. As in a magazine, there are premium sites and if you want one of these you must act quickly (and be prepared to pay more). Otherwise, you may get the exhibition equivalent of ROP – having to accept whatever place is left whether you like it or not. Show organisers will provide a floor plan with numbered sites for selection. Some sites are **floor space only** leaving you to decide what to put on the floor, others are pre-erected modular shells which can save you time but limit your creativity. It is up to you to ensure that the site you book is serviced with such things as lighting, power supply and running water. If, for example, you need running water and this is not part of the standard package, you must get permission and arrange for it to be connected.

A useful planning checklist would include the following:

- **Product**   Do you want to show a full range of items or just a selected range? Do you want to focus entirely on new products or to take along some old faithfuls?

- **Site**   Do you want a corner position or a centre position? How much headroom do you need? Do you want floor space only? There are many such questions.

- **Stand**   You can have one designed, built and erected on-site at considerable expense or you may be able to use more economical portable modular constructions. The former are usually one-off and non-reusable but the latter can be taken from show to show and used over and over again.

- **Stand personnel**   The people who staff the stand should be carefully selected and properly briefed. They should know how to handle enquiries, demonstrate the product, keep proper records and how to dress and behave. At a travel show staff representing airlines can wear the company livery. If there is no company livery a simple dress code such as dark suits and white shirts for the men might suffice.

- **Stand hospitality**   You may plan to offer drinks and refreshments to visitors to your stand. If you do, then remember that this can cause a mess and make sure that the stand is kept clean at all times. If alcoholic drinks are offered, make sure that stand personnel do not over-indulge – the drinks are for the guests.

- **Stand literature**   Always make sure that you have adequate supplies of catalogues, price lists and so on. It is frustrating and self-defeating to run out of these halfway through the second day. Consider having material designed especially for the show although this is not essential.

- **Promoting your presence at the show**   It is up to the show organiser to publicise the show itself. However, it is your responsibility to publicise your presence there (see below).

20.7 Promoting your presence at the show

Promoting your presence at the show can be done at three stages: before the show, during the show and even after the show.

Pre-show publicity

Let the particular buyers you want to meet know that you are going to be there and where you can be found – tell them your stand number.

Encourage them to come to your stand. Set up an appointments diary with the people you really want to meet and give a member of staff the specific duty of organising it.

Complimentary tickets are also a good device. Most shows allow each exhibitor so many free tickets and will sometimes supply more at a discounted rate. These can often be supplied with a blank back (or at least a blank space) on which you can print your invitation message.

Keep the on-ticket message short and simple: for example, 'Your free entry ticket with the compliments of Insurex Expo-Sure at stand No. 64' or 'Please come and see us at stand No. 64.' You can send it out with a covering letter in which you can go into more detail, if you wish.

Whether you include complimentary tickets or not, the direct-mail letter is another useful tool. This gives you an opportunity to describe the new products you intend to show, with diagrams and photographs as appropriate. You may also use it to introduce special offers such as a 5 per cent discount over and above the usual trade rates on orders placed at the show.

Advertising in the trade press is essential. The space sales people will be working hard to sell advertising space to all exhibitors in the pre-show edition and by this time you should have your stand number confirmed and will be able to include it in the advertising copy. Another way of using the trade press is through press relations. If your new products are sufficiently interesting and you do a good job with your press releases you may get editorial coverage as well.

Finally, do not forget the important role that your own sales representatives can play. Brief them to make sure they tell all the customers they call on about your stand and the new products they will see there.

In-show publicity

All shows have a show catalogue in which you will get a free listing. Although some catalogues are sent out in advance, they are often so heavy that it is now common practice to issue them (or sell them) at the door. Buyers often keep them as a sort of trade directory to which they can refer over the following year. It is worth considering buying additional advertising space – it can pay off over the long term. Another option is to buy perimeter advertising which is usually in the form of large banners attached to the interior walls around the show. By arrangement with the organisers it may also be possible to have somebody paid to stand near the entrance or to walk around the arena extending printed invitations. Some exhibitors run raffle-type competitions to entice visitors to the stand.

Exhibiting is expensive and not to put considerable effort into making sure that you get to meet the right people is foolish.

Post-show publicity

Post-show publicity can be considered under two headings:

- **Follow-ups** You may not get many (or even any) orders at the show itself. But you should get a list of leads and enquiries. It is essential when the initial contact is made to keep a careful record of the person making the enquiry, the nature of the enquiry and the firm which that person represents. Tactfully find out if the visitor is a decision maker or not – if not, try to find out who the decision maker is. After the show, all such contacts should be followed up. It may be months before an actual sale develops, but the simple rule to keep in mind is 'no follow-up, no sale'.

- **Absent friends** It should be possible, using the process of elimination, to identify those buyers you had hoped to meet but did not. Perhaps they never came to the fair, perhaps they just never came by your stand. It cannot do any harm, and may pay off, to send them a 'Sorry we missed you at the show' letter. Try to use this letter to arrange a meeting anyway.

  In the case of both follow-ups and absent friends, you can always consider some sort of post-show newsletter with such items as photographs of the stand and quotes from satisfied clients.

20.8 The logistics

Exhibiting involves several logistical problems. These can be summarised as:

- Getting the stand and stand equipment to the show.
- Getting the products to be exhibited to the show.
- Getting the on-stand promotional literature to the show.
- Getting the stand personnel to the show.

All the above are controllable factors, but as they may all begin their journeys from different places the logistical problems are considerable. A non-controllable but absolutely vital additional factor is:

- Getting the people you want to meet to the show – and not merely to the show, but to your stand.

20.9 Some technological aspects

Overhead projectors (OHPs), film and slide presentations are commonplace. The multi-media revolution makes it possible to combine several elements into a single presentation incorporating sound, lighting effects, slides, video and film. Audience interaction is possible using remote control and computer graphics to analyse audience responses and present them visually on stage in a matter of seconds. It is even possible to design a conference theatre with individual screens in front of each delegate. All this calls for good preparation with a carefully worked out script, good stage management and (absolutely essential) rehearsals. Some venues have a reduced rate for set-up and rehearsal time and venues such as the Brewery in London offer stage management support. Video-conferencing allows simultaneous multi-site events using video and audio links to other venues.

It is a common practice to produce printed conference papers for post-event distribution to delegates (and even to non-attenders) and it is now possible to produce video-recordings of the proceedings which can be very useful where new product demonstration is a key feature. Mobile **road-show** exhibitions are expensive to set up but invaluable for taking the message to the audience and it is even possible to book an exhibition train and schedule it to arrive in major city stations around the country.

Case Studies

1 Taking the conference to the delegates

In November 1993 about 800 delegates turned up for a one-day conference organised by the Charities Aid Foundation to discuss ways of raising funds and running charities. Five hundred went to the Queen Elizabeth II Conference Centre in London; the others attended at the Stormont Hotel in Belfast, the Caledonia Hotel in Edinburgh and the Copthorne Hotel in Cardiff. The decision to regionalise the event was a response to the difficulties which would-be delegates would face in both time and money coming to London.

Home Secretary Michael Howard gave the keynote address and newscaster Martyn Lewis chaired the question-time session in which delegates at the outlying venues were able to take part. British Telecom landline links sent out vision and audio from the QEIICC and brought audio responses only back (a two-way visual link was possible but ruled out for budgetary reasons). A hair-raising moment occurred ten minutes before the event started when a BT technician had to strip a wire with his teeth to enable the control phone to be linked up.

Simon Lugrin from the QEIICC's presentation facilities department and Nikki White, CAF's conference organiser, planned the presentation over a three-month period beginning with a script and developing a running order and timetable for the event. Outlying venues were resourced locally using hired equipment, but two QEIICC technicians visited each site the day before to ensure that everything was set up correctly and the rooms laid out properly.

The event was also filmed by a TV crew for a programme which went out in December on BBC Television and the TV cameras had to be integrated with QEIICC cameras. For Brent Smith, presentation facilities manager at QEIICC, the most rewarding aspect of the day 'was the successful introduction of our Beta SP edit suite and multiple live-relay suite. This allowed cameras from the event room to be linked to the suite via Triax cables and mixed to allow broadcast-quality footage to be sent to the other locations. The new facilities enabled us to make use of frame stores for multiple graphics together with character generation of rolling scripts.'

Source: adapted from 'A New Vision for Charities', Conference and Exhibition Factfinder, *May 1994*

2 Insurex Expo-Sure: a niche market insurance company

The experience of Insurex Expo-Sure can be contrasted with that of Cornhill (see pages 248–50). The latter, one of the biggest insurers in the country, relies largely on sponsorship to keep its name in the public eye. Insurex Expo-Sure, on the other hand, operates in a niche market, selling insurance to the events industry, and has little need to be known as a household name. The people who matter to Insurex Expo-Sure are the insurance brokers through whom it transacts a lot of its business and the events organisers themselves, some of whom prefer not to go through a broker.

A key problem was that of convincing event organisers (whether they dealt direct or through a broker) of the wisdom of taking out specialist insurance. Many organisers believed (usually wrongly) that they were either covered automatically by their normal business insurance or that the venue management would have full insurance cover if anything went wrong. This is one of those areas where it is necessary to be clear about the duties and responsibilities of each party to a contract. The venue management must, of course, be insured but its cover is usually limited to the building itself and any subsequent damage arising from, say, fire or flood. It does not automatically cover any property belonging to the event organiser which might, for example, be stolen. For that the event organiser needs separate insurance cover. The same applies, incidentally, to individual exhibitors – they are not automatically covered by the event organiser's policy. Organisers simply were not always aware of the sorts of things which they could insure against, from a failure of the guest speaker to turn up to an outbreak of food-poisoning at a conference, from a rail strike damaging attendance at an event to snow-bound roads preventing vital exhibits from getting through.

There was no need to educate brokers in the mechanisms of insurance (that, after all, was their business) but they needed to be informed of the reasons why organisers should take out event insurance in particular to improve their ability to operate in this niche market. They had the incentive, of course, of the commission they received on each policy sold.

Insurex Expo-Sure decided to target the brokers first and a combination of trade press relations and advertising was embarked upon. Because of a limited promotional budget the emphasis was on the press relations side and here Insurex Expo-Sure found that they had a distinct advantage. In contrast to companies that specialised in, say, life insurance they had some very interesting stories to tell, airlifting an exhibit by helicopter rather than leaving it stranded on the motorway was just one (which reflected Insurex Expo-Sure's 'the show must go on' philosophy that they would rather pay out to ensure that an event did go ahead than simply pay out for one that didn't). Editors of insurance trade magazines needed little persuading to run stories which were quite obviously different and dealt with things like carnivals, sports events and concerts. Additionally, taking advertising space to run in key positions in the same issues as the stories paid off.

A bold tactic was that of developing a generic campaign, offering editors' totally unbiased copy explaining the benefits of event insurance but without pushing Insurex Expo-Sure. This 'push-free' copy created a great deal of interest but left the company with the problem of turning that interest into business. Albert Kemp, Chief Executive, decided to strengthen his personal links with the event industry by becoming more involved with associations and committees and giving seminars to businessmen (and extending this by

Fig. 20.3   An outdoor event insured by Insurex Expo-Sure

ISLE COLLEGE
RESOURCES CENTRE

giving lectures at colleges). This enabled him to get first-hand views on what worried organisers and the type of cover they needed.

Attendance, as an exhibitor, at both insurance exhibitions and events industry exhibitions (such as CONFEX) also helped to develop such personal contacts.

On the whole, Insurex Expo-Sure is in a niche market concentrating largely on exhibitions and conferences and on brokers and organisers. To the extent that it breaks out of that niche it does so in very strongly related areas, offering insurance to venue management and to individual exhibitors, for example, or covering different events such as weddings, fêtes and group travel. Exhibition contractors (stand builders and designers, etc.) are also covered. The double-barrelled approach of targeting both brokers and organisers clearly works with new enquiries coming from each source in almost equal proportions and editors continuing to show interest in stories that educate the readers.

Source: based on interview with Albert Kemp conducted by Steven Newman, Director of GAIA communications

---

**20.10
Summary**

- Events can be produced and marketed in their own right at a profit.
- Events can also be used within the context of a promotional campaign where they serve a variety of purposes from introducing new incentive schemes to showcasing new products and from entertaining valued customers to rewarding and training the sales force.
- In setting up an event, a dealer conference for example, the choice of venue is crucial and both the social dimensions and the business and functional dimensions have to be catered for.
- In deciding to exhibit at a trade fair, the exhibitor needs to choose the fairs where the visitor profile matches the sort of people the exhibitor is trying to reach.
- In the case of both conferences and exhibitions the logistics are important: stands and equipment, products, literature and personnel all have to be co-ordinated and delegates and visitors motivated to attend.
- Every effort should be made to maximise the promotional benefits of the event – trade press advertising and press relations, newsletters and personalised invitations can all be included.
- The chapter has focused on business events but the same basic principles apply to consumer events such as the Ideal Home Exhibition.

**20.11
Assignments**

1. Try to arrange, as a group activity, a facility visit to a conference hotel or purpose-built exhibition hall.

2. Prepare a report showing how attendance at a trade fair could be integrated with other promotional activities to support a new product launch.

3. Draw up a plan for a one-day sales training conference to introduce a new computerised system for handling customers' accounts.

21 Business-to-business promotions

21.1 Introduction

Business-to-business communications spread across what are generally called **user markets** to distinguish them from consumer markets. The term *user* reflects the fact that organisations buy things to use in order to achieve their organisational objectives. Manufacturers buy raw materials to make goods, retailers buy finished goods to sell in their shops and so on. Businesses also buy travel facilities to get their executives from one place to another and they pay printers to print their price-lists and catalogues. There are also non-business user markets such as charities, service organisations and political parties. In user markets, the buyers are organisations rather than individuals but, of course, the buying has to be done by people. These people may be called:

- **Industrial buyers** They buy industrial goods such as machinery, raw materials and component parts for manufacturers.

- **Retail purchasers** They buy finished goods for resale in the **reseller** market. Wholesalers also purchase finished goods for resale.

- **Requisitioners/Requisitions officers (sometimes called procurement officers)** They usually buy for non-profit-making organisations such as local government.

Different names may, of course, be used. Buyers who buy equipment such as cash registers for retailers are not buying for resale but for use and it might be better to call them requisitioners also. The main point is to recognise different sorts of buying situations reflecting different sorts of buying motives. Selling to businesses is not the same as selling to non-business organisations, although a supplier of computers, for example, will find customers in both business and non-business user markets.

21.2 User goods and consumer goods

The goods (and services) sold in user markets are called **user goods** (industrial goods, resale goods, etc.). The same product may be a consumer good or a user good depending on who it is sold to and the purpose to which it is put. A personal computer is an example which may be priced differently in each market. Sometimes the product is packaged differently – the same instant coffee can be packed in 5 kg catering packs or 200 g consumer packs.

21.3 User markets, consumer markets and market research

In a consumer market there are usually a very large number of individual purchasers with very small individual purchasing requirements and purchasing power. With user markets the situation is often very different. The number of purchasers may be relatively small and their individual purchasing requirements may vary from very little to very large amounts – the differences between user firms can be considerable. This is significant when carrying out market research. In consumer research sampling works because we have reason to believe that what we can learn from a small number of respondents can tell us something valid about the much larger number of consumers as a whole. In user market research this assumption frequently does not hold. There may be no such thing as a representative sample – and the only way to get a picture of the market might be to abandon all attempts at sampling and research every organisation. A compromise might be to survey all the big firms but sample the smaller ones.

Selling companies need to research the peculiarities of the buying companies with whom they deal so as to build up a profile of the purchasing requirements and policies of each one. For instance, a particular customer may have a policy that no supplier is to be given more than 40 per cent of the company's business. Another customer may have a purchasing policy requiring the professional buyer to get at least three competitive quotes before issuing an order. A third company may deny the professional buyer the right to open new accounts. All these differences mean that customers in the same industry may have quite different purchasing policies. They may all have different plans with respect to product and market development and these will affect their purchasing requirements in different ways. These differences can affect the way in which the business seller approaches different organisations in the user market.

21.4 Derived demand and consumer market research

The demand for user goods is a function of, and derived from, the consumer market. Usually the relationship is direct and measurable. Motor-car manufacturers buy windscreen wipers because they expect to sell cars. The demand for new houses affects the demand for bricks and a fall in retail sales leads to a fall in the demand for packaging. A supplier of user goods should, therefore, monitor the **end market** to establish a relationship between what is happening there and how this might affect the derived demand for user goods in the future. Manufacturers of both industrial and resale goods have sometimes been able to spot consumer market trends before their own customers and to use that knowledge to improve the service they offer. In effect, they spot a customer's potential problems and opportunities before the customer does. The concept of derived demand is, of course, not limited to the business sector.

There is, supporting the end market (without which all the rest is pointless), a rich mix of business-to-business activity and, naturally, this will produce a whole range of business-to-business communications. Suppliers, manufacturers, wholesalers and retailers all interact with each other in the value chain (see page 17) and along the way a variety of supporting services such as those of advertising and public relations agencies are involved. The services of printers, haulage contractors, travel agencies, office suppliers and contract cleaning and security organisations all come into play. **Relationship marketing** has entered into the discussion with its emphasis on building long-term commitments rather than having an opportunistic eye to the main chance. Business-to-business communications should reflect this 'customer for life' thinking.

**21.5
Professional
buyers and
the purchasing
decision**

A large organisation will support a separate buying department with senior buyers and assistant buyers under a director or senior executive buyer. In a smaller organisation the work of buying may be part of another job, the production manager's, for example. Buyers may specialise: for example, a large organisation may employ a specialist print buyer and a designated person in the office may be the purchaser of office supplies; large retail chains have specialist toy buyers. Practices vary and it is absolutely essential, especially for personalised communication such as direct mail and telesales, for sellers to make sure that they are talking to the right person. It is also essential to establish the decision making powers of that person – a lot of time can be wasted talking to somebody who has no power to authorise a purchase and buyers can be severely limited by their own terms of employment with respect to who they can deal with and how much money they can spend.

Professional buyers are buying solutions to their employers' problems. To this end, they should behave rationally, considering all the pertinent facts and spending their employers' money in an economical and efficient way. They are sometimes called **rational buyers** to emphasise this systematic approach. If this were entirely true then communicating with professional buyers would be simplified and only rational and logical appeals would be made. Unfortunately, research has shown that many professional buyers proceed on less rational and thoughtful grounds and that, contrary to the 'rational buyer' theory, they are just as capable of giving in to irrational impulses and being swayed by psychological appeals as any typical consumer. There are buyers who never trouble to keep informed about new products or services unless these are pushed under their noses by an aggressive seller. There are buyers who continue to patronise a supplier out of loyalty to a representative and who will change to a new supplier only when that representative changes. There are buyers who lack the ability and determination to bargain over prices even when it is known that the representative has the power to negotiate. This can lead to a situation where two buyers of equal purchasing power pay different prices to the same supplier.

**21.6 Hidden
buyers and
DMUs**

The **hidden buyer** is the person behind the official buyer, a decision influencer (and sometimes even the decision maker) who affects what is bought and/or who it is bought from. It may be the production manager influencing the choice of suppliers or the accountant who draws up a list of prescribed and proscribed suppliers. It may be as simple as somebody in the office saying that X's printer ribbons are superior to Y's. Sometimes these hidden buyers are formalised into a purchasing committee or **decision making unit (DMU)** of which the buyer may or may not be a member. A DMU may be formed, for example, when the company is upgrading its computer system and in such a case it may be subsequently disbanded. The company buyer may play no more than an administrative role carrying out the decisions of the DMU.

Communicating with hidden buyers and DMU members is clearly vital. In fact, one could go so far as to say that focusing all the promotional communications on the buyer alone could prove to be an impoverished strategy.

So now we know that:

- The influence of the professional buyer varies. There are key situations where the buyer may have no influence.
- Hidden buyers and DMUs should also be targeted for business communications.

In addition, we have established that buyers are:

- Looking for solutions to problems.
- Relatively few in number.
- Individually high in purchasing power.
- Different in their purchasing requirements.
- Different in their purchasing policies.
- Capable of non-rational behaviour.

21.7 Personal selling and personal relationships

Because of the above factors, personal selling plays an important part in business-to-business communications. It is the sales representative who is often best placed to discover a client's peculiarities and it is the sales representative who is usually in the best position to talk through a client's problems and to proffer solutions. Personal relationships between a sales representative and a buyer can be crucial in building and maintaining long-term customers.

Personal selling also plays an important part in the winning of new accounts. Sales representatives frequently have it as part of their job descriptions to prospect for new customers. The effort which goes into opening a new account and getting the first order is substantial and the cost of getting that first order may be three or four times the cost of getting any subsequent order. Opening new accounts only to get one order never to be repeated is obviously a costly exercise and the emphasis should always be on getting and keeping new accounts with a view to long-term profits.

The recognition that in some cases the nominal company buyer may have very little real decision-making power and may be the front for a hidden buyer and DMU elsewhere in the organisation has led to some sales representatives making the mistake of underestimating the buyer's role. Even if buyers do not make all the decisions this does not mean that they are entirely without influence. The buyer may not have the authority to sanction a new account but his recommendation may be crucial to getting it. Furthermore, even if the buyer is under an instruction that at least three suppliers must be used he may still have the freedom to decide which three and how the business is to be shared between them. In other words, buyers always have some power and research has shown that in the exercise of that power they frequently favour those representatives with whom they have a good personal relationship. In any case, the buyer does have access to the hidden buyer and decision-makers and may, at least in the early stages, be the only direct line to them that the sales representative has.

There is, however, a need to keep things in perspective. Not all businesses are large and there are many thousands whose individual purchasing power is not great and whose needs may not justify the regular attention of a visiting salesperson. Indeed, the average cost of a sales visit may be so high that some calls simply cannot be profitable. In these situations telemarketing (somewhat less personal but still interactive) may be a suitable alternative.

21.8 Telemarketing

Telemarketing is widely used in both consumer marketing and business-to-business marketing (see also pages 221–3).

Telemarketing and small clients

In business-to-business communication telemarketing has an important role to play in connection with small clients. There is still a degree of personal contact, albeit voice only, and this can be enhanced by having the same telephone salesperson handle any given account so that a personal relationship can be established. The customer has the assurance of knowing that one person is looking after the account. If the customer ever makes a factory visit then the telesales person who looks after the account should be introduced. Relationships usually improve when people can attach faces to names. Sometimes telesales personnel can be given the opportunity to represent the company at a trade fair and this also can provide an opportunity to meet customers who previously had just been voices on the phone. Telesales, properly conducted, can release valuable sales representatives' time for concentrating on bigger customers and can, additionally, reduce the size of the sales force required.

In fact, if the company specialises in providing a service to small firms and has no large accounts, it may consider dispensing with a sales force altogether and concentrating entirely on its telemarketing operation. If it is not prepared to go as far as that then it could use a small sales force just to prospect for new accounts which can then be dealt with by phone. Such a sales force could also make courtesy calls from time to time.

Telemarketing and large clients

Telemarketing need not, however, be confined to small customers. It could be put in place to support the sales force in its dealings with large customers. Queries can be processed, complaints dealt with and suggestions put forward over the phone during those weeks between sales visits. New product launches could be supported by a telemarketing campaign, thus paving the way for the next scheduled sales visit and special offers could be made over the phone.

In these cases, the telephone caller needs to remember that he or she is providing a support service and that the account is, after all, somebody else's. It would be unfortunate, to put it mildly, if a sales representative lost an account because of the indifferent attitude of the telephone support staff. The concept of the internal client (see page 26) is useful here. The telephone caller is contacting a sales representative's client (the external client) and should act on behalf of, and in the interests of, the sales representative (the internal client).

Telemarketing support

An example of how support might be given would be:

> 'Hello, Mr Jackson? ... This is Andrew Makepiece from Pyramid Office Supplies. You may not realise it, but our

financial year closes in two weeks and your orders over the year are just £100 short for qualifying for our end-of-year bonus. Mary Wallace, your usual representative, is not scheduled to call on you again for three weeks and we don't want you to lose out on the opportunity for qualifying. If there is anything you need I would be pleased to look after it for you.'

For all telemarketing activities a script should be worked out in advance. Where Mary Wallace has a right to commission there should also be consideration of how that right is affected by Andrew Makepiece's involvement. The commission could be split between them, for example.

It might be thought that customers would take exception to the tele-marketing approach and think that they were getting a second-rate service. In fact, many customers prefer it. They don't have to wait for a representative to call and they don't have to feel apologetic when the order is only a small one.

21.9 Field sales forces

Field sales forces are trained sales people who can be hired from a specialist field agency. A company may make use of a field sales force permanently but the more normal use might be on an *ad hoc* basis when a company feels that extra representation is required. This might, for example, be during a new product launch or in the early days of a new market entry. Another situation could be when sales are seasonal: a full-time sales force large enough to cope with off-season sales could be increased during the high season with agency personnel. (Employing permanent and temporary personnel side by side may cause some pro-blems, and there is the possibility that agency staff will not be as familiar with company procedures, but the concept is very well established and widely used.)

21.10 Share of mind and front of mind

Retaining share of mind

In pursuit of either new accounts or repeat business the concepts of share of mind and front of mind should be remembered (see page 55). If the prospective customer has never heard of you, then you are not in mind at all. If you are in mind, then efforts should be made to ensure that the buyer thinks of you at least as often as he thinks of your competitors. It is better still if your company is constantly in the front of the buyer's mind so that you are the first supplier thought of when there is a decision to be made.

Research suggests that this is one of the key factors in decision making. It may prove difficult, however, to retain share of mind and front of mind awareness when a sales call is made only once a month (remember the old saying: 'out of sight, out of mind'). Telephone calling between personal calls, trade press advertising and direct mail all help to preserve awareness and effectively 'keep the door open' for the salesperson's next visit.

21.11 Direct mail

Business-to-business mail

Direct mail is an important part of business-to-business communication (see also chapter 17) and good mailing lists are essential. Sources include trade associations, professional bodies and the subscription lists of trade magazines.

Personalised lists are preferable, but they are dearer to prepare and likely to date more quickly than non-personalised ones. Non-personalised lists use a distinguishing job title rather than a name.

Personalised mail has more chance of arriving at the right person's desk and of being taken seriously. Nevertheless, non-personalised, title-only lists are quite widely used. In the educational sector many companies are satisfied to send out mailings addressed simply to 'The Careers Teacher' or 'The College Librarian'. Businesses might write to 'The Managing Director', 'The Personnel Manager' and so on.

Some list-brokers provide title-only lists but they can backfire. Imagine a company with 14 manufacturing sites and a centralised buying department. A title-only list could result in 14 letters going out addressed to 'The Buyer'. These may or may not be rerouted to the central buyer's office, but if only four of them are the central buyer will finish up with multiple copies and, what is worse, a poor opinion of the sender.

A mailing could be sent out to support a product launch, to publicise a special offer or to announce a change in the company's methods of doing business. It may even be used to send out a company newsletter to keep both suppliers and customers informed about the company's activities or to send invitations to the company's stand at the next trade fair.

It is essential to get the timing right: sent out too early and the knowledge of the event could 'decay' before it occurs; sent out too late and the recipients do not have time to respond.

The use of joint mailings, omnibus mailings, piggy-back mailings and card decks should not be overlooked (see chapter 17).

21.12 Direct faxing

Direct faxing is a relatively new activity which began in the US. The advantages to the seller are that it is often quicker and cheaper than post. Recipients, however, complain that their fax machines are needlessly tied up and that their salespeople, suppliers and customers cannot get access. The waste of the recipient's paper is also a sore point: companies complain of leaving the office fax machine fully loaded overnight and next morning finding all the paper used up by junk fax. Some companies have gone as far as making their fax numbers ex-directory.

Properly used, fax does have an important role. A telephone conversation can be switched to fax at an agreed point in the discussion so that, for example, details of a special offer, difficult to take down over the phone, can be faxed through and verbal orders can be confirmed. In this context the same distinction of inbound and outbound fax should be made, as it is with inbound and outbound telephone calls. Direct fax is often used to distribute copy for black-and-white press advertisements.

21.13 The trade press

The magazines generally referred to as the trade press, or trade and technical (T&T), provide advertising opportunities in the business-to-business sector. Some are to be seen on sale in newsagents such as W H Smith (*Campaign*, for example), but usually only in branches frequented by business people such as at London's mainline railway stations. The majority of them (there are about 2 000) are available on subscription or through the membership of a trade or professional body and are delivered by post. The official subscriber may be a business rather than an individual and many businesses build up an in-house library of trade magazines and other sources of information. Some magazines (for example, *Personnel Today*) serve a profession and will find readers across the full spectrum of industry, others serve a particular industry or trade.

Advertising in trade magazines can keep the company in buyers' minds between sales calls and provide access to hidden buyers and DMUs. It can also be used to generate leads or to dispense information such as attendance at a trade fair. Promotional literature can be piggy-backed with a mailing of a trade magazine to its subscribers or inset (bound into the magazine after it has been printed).

21.14 The consumer media

Advertising in the consumer press

Traditionally, the view has been that there is no point in advertising user goods in the consumer press as only a very small proportion of the audience will be professional buyers. There are, however, three counter arguments. The first is that some goods (portable phones, for example) are so widely used across industry that the number of potential trade buyers is very high. Secondly, the consumer press may be a good way of reaching decision influencers. Thirdly, the product has a consumer application as well as a business use. Any product with some or all of the following characteristics might qualify:

- **Non-industry specific** It should be capable of being used in any industry.

- **Relatively low value** It should be capable of being sold to small businesses as well as large.

- **Wide appeal** It should have appeal for a wide range of decision influencers, hidden buyers or DMU members thus increasing the potential audience size.

- **Consumer appeal** It should be the sort of product that can also be sold to consumers.

Personal computers, recruiting and temporary staff agencies, insurance and legal services, mobile phones, travel facilities, photocopiers, fax machines and light goods vehicles are all types of business-to-business products which have featured in the consumer press and which meet most if not all of the above criteria.

Advertising in the broadcast media and on posters

A similar argument has also been applied to the broadcast media (television and radio) and to posters. However, all the product types listed above have also been featured in these media. The radio sector, for instance, recognises 'drive-time' when business people are driving to and from work as a good time to advertise user goods.

21.15 Other promotional considerations

Press and public relations

Using the conventional tools of trade press and public relations, including such things as press releases, newsletters and open days, is all part of business-to-business promotion (see chapters 14 and 15).

Sales promotions

The importance of sales promotions to motivate the sales force and strengthen relationships between suppliers, manufacturers, wholesalers and retailers should not be overlooked (see chapter 18).

Sponsorships and corporate hospitality

Sponsorship offers the opportunity to entertain important business guests (see chapter 19).

Conferences and exhibitions

For the importance of the events industry see chapter 20.

21.16 Business-to-business campaigns

Setting up a business-to-business campaign is just as complex as setting up a consumer campaign and involves all the same elements of the marketing and communications mixes. Nevertheless, business-to-business campaigns do have their own distinctive features and many agencies recognise this by having separate business-to-business divisions. Creatives and media planners may choose to specialise in the business-to-business area.

Case Study

Oracle Corporation UK: computer services as a strategic business issue

The relationship between top-down strategies and bottom-up strategies has already been outlined in chapter 3. The dangers of emerging bottom-up strategies diverging from top-down strategies coupled with the dangers of departmental bottom-up strategies diverging from each other have been discussed. How is a company to maintain a total holistic view and to develop an overall strategy that will enable it to integrate across departments without stultifying management initiative and creative thinking? This was the problem which the Oracle Corporation UK sought to address and which it summed up in one of its advertisements (see fig. 21.1) with the following copy:

> Computer systems tend to be used differently department by department.
> Try to bring together the information controlled by these different departments, and you run into a barrier as much to do with human nature as technology.
> So how is management to get the information it needs?

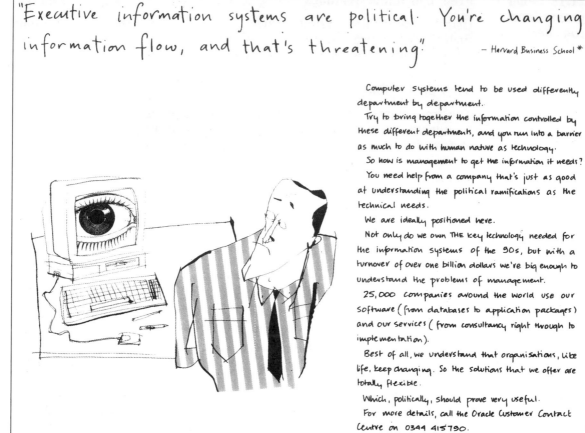

"Executive information systems are political. You're changing information flow, and that's threatening." — *Harvard Business School* *

Computer systems tend to be used differently department by department.

Try to bring together the information controlled by these different departments, and you run into a barrier as much to do with human nature as technology.

So how is management to get the information it needs?

You need help from a company that's just as good at understanding the political ramifications as the technical needs.

We are ideally positioned here.

Not only do we own THE key technology needed for the information systems of the 90s, but with a turnover of over one billion dollars we're big enough to understand the problems of management.

25,000 companies around the world use our software (from databases to application packages) and our services (from consultancy right through to implementation).

Best of all, we understand that organisations, like life, keep changing. So the solutions that we offer are totally flexible.

Which, politically, should prove very useful.

For more details, call the Oracle Customer Contact Centre on 0344 415790.

ORACLE®

OUR PURPOSE IS COMMON KNOWLEDGE

Fig. 21.1 Oracle advertisement (Saatchi & Saatchi)

Traditionally, information technology (IT) systems were designed to serve departmental needs and thus tended to have bottom-up considerations built into them. Individual departments were well served, but what about the organisation as a whole?

An additional dimension to this thorny problem was the well-documented suspicion and hostility that is sometimes observed between the organisational suppliers of IT inputs and the line managers in, for example, production, sales and marketing departments who make the operational decisions of how much to produce, sell, etc. Line managers have, at times, tended to treat IT specialists as boffins with no real business experience and IT specialists have often felt misunderstood and ignored. Strategic planners, no less than line managers, are often uncertain as to the benefits IT can deliver and how to get the best out of it.

Oracle, with the analytical and creative inputs of agency Saatchi & Saatchi, saw an opportunity to position itself as an IT company uniquely placed to provide a strategic influence in bridging the gap between the needs of management and the ability of IT departments to deliver. Its claim to understand the human and political dimensions of information management no less than the technological dimension was central to this effort. The decision was taken to focus the promotional effort on the audience which it was felt would appreciate the benefits of working with Oracle most (i.e. senior management rather than IT professionals) and to relaunch the company as the 'genuine strategic information systems partner' providing relational databases (and everything associated with them) – effectively storing, formatting, accessing and distributing information.

The campaign

Using the strong platform 'We are more expert in making information work than any other company in the world', Oracle embarked on an integrated campaign devised by Saatchi's Business Communications arm and built around the following solution:

> 'A visually distinctive corporate campaign, raising issues in a manner which demonstrates Oracle's understanding of management's needs.'

The structure of the integrated campaign is shown in fig. 21.2.

A series of print advertisements using cartoon-type illustrations and making effective use of a small amount of red to lift an essentially black-and-white campaign was devised (in the example reproduced here as fig. 21.1 the trade mark Oracle, the rule around the advertisement and the stripes on the shirt were in red). The copy varied from advertisement to advertisement – the one illustrated here carried the statement quoted in the opening paragraph above and others carried the following statements:

> But what the departments are not able to give you (because each sees the business from its own angle) is the global view that management needs.
>
> Yet with the right global information management can spot new opportunities, reshape services, and seize the competitive advantage.
>
> We've many years experience in helping our customers build or adapt their corporate informations systems – regardless of the hardware they have, regardless of the software they use.

All the advertisements carried variations of the following:

> 25,000 companies in 92 countries use our software (from databases to application packages) and our services (from consultancy right through to implementation and training).

Fig. 21.2   Corporate campaign

The results

The campaign was judged to be very effective. Tracking studies over the period 1991 to 1993 showed:

- Spontaneous awareness of Oracle as a provider of computer software and services improved from 7 per cent to 13 per cent.
- Familiarity with Oracle improved significantly with the proportion of respondents prepared to rate Oracle across all dimensions probed increasing from 25 per cent to 65 per cent.

Additionally, the campaign won the Best Software Advertisement award in the Computing Awards for Excellence.

Source: Business Communications Division of Saatchi & Saatchi

---

21.17 Summary

- Business-to-business campaigns can use all the same tools as consumer campaigns.
- There are significant differences between the make-up of a user market and the make-up of a consumer market. These differences affect the market research function and also the balance between different elements in the marketing mix.
- There is a much greater element of personal selling in the business-to-business communication mix, although some of this might be transferred to telemarketing.
- The differences between consumer campaigns and business-to-business campaigns are such that some agencies prefer to specialise in business-to-business campaigns or to have business-to-business divisions.

21.18 Assignments

1. Draw up as complete a list as you can of the differences between a professional buyer and a consumer.

2. Argue for and against using the traditional consumer media to promote user goods.

3. Explain fully why personal selling is generally more widely used in business-to-business marketing than in consumer marketing.

22 Planning

**22.1
Introduction**

The ability to plan is a transferable skill and once mastered in one context can readily be applied in another. That is why it is being dealt with in a separate chapter in which reference will be made to several different areas. To give the chapter a focal point and to develop a simple model we will consider the problem of a new product launch in the FMCG sector.

22.2 Planning a new product launch

A reference point is needed and a useful one is the launch date itself. If we assume that all the production problems are out of the way we can set our launch date three months from now. We can call the launch date t (for time) and this is when all our plans are going to come together. Setting our minds on t, we can count back from the launch date. One week before launch date t will be called $t - 1$ (one week to go) and two weeks before will be $t - 2$. We are presently at $t - 12$. By t we will want some things to have happened:

- The advertising campaign to announce the new product rolled out.
- The product itself on the retailers' shelves.
- Point-of-sale material on display in the shops.
- Consumers primed to ask for the product or stimulated to buy by in-store sales promotions and the like.

How is all this to be achieved? Figure 22.1 illustrates the discussion so far.

In fig. 22.1 the goods are to be on the retailer's shelves by t. This means that the retailer has to be given warning of the new good's availability, otherwise he will not have time to order it. He will certainly be annoyed if the first he hears of it is when a customer asks for it. The retailer, therefore, needs to be advised of the good before the consumer is. He also needs to be advised in enough time to allow him to make his plans, place his orders and so on. If we want to give the retailer about a month's advance warning, then we should be notifying him no later than $t - 4$ (four weeks before launch date). Assuming that he will order the good through a wholesaler, then we need to give the wholesalers time to stock up in anticipation of the demand from the retailers. If we assume that the retailers will begin placing their orders not earlier than $t - 4$, then that can become the deadline for stocking up the wholesalers. To give the wholesalers time to make their plans, perhaps we should begin to sell to them by, say, $t - 8$. Figure 22.2 illustrates these points. If figs. 22.1 and 22.2 are considered together, we can see that by counting down from t we are beginning to build up a picture of what needs to be done to ensure a successful launch.

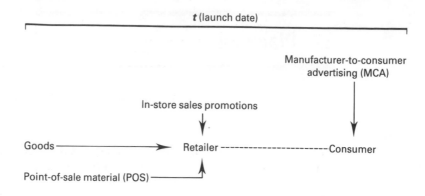

Fig. 22.1 Four things that should be in place on launch date t

22.3 The role of the sales force

We have identified $t - 8$ as the deadline for informing wholesalers. One of our most important tools is going to be our sales force and we have one month left ($t - 12$ to $t - 8$) to train our salespeople in pushing the new product. We should really start making plans to train the sales force now. We could do the training in a week (for example, we could bring 25 per cent of the sales force in for training on each of four consecutive days). We could do this in week $t - 9$, which gives us three weeks to set up the training scheme. We could start that now. Figure 22.3 shows this phase of the plan and fig. 22.4 pulls everything together.

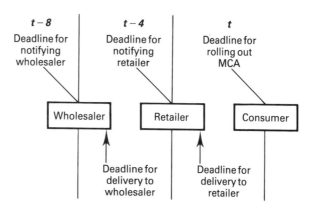

Fig. 22.2 The relationship over time of a series of interdependent deadlines
NB In this model we are going to assume that delivering the goods to the retailers is carried out by the wholesalers. This may not be the best approach. To ensure the goods are actually on the retailers' shelves, we may undertake direct delivery whilst still crediting the business to the wholesalers.

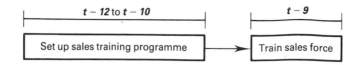

Fig. 22.3 Fitting the sales training programme into the timetable

22.4 The relationship between MCA and trade promotions

With this as our basic model (fig. 22.4) we can begin to see other relationships. For example, we see that we have to start promoting to the trade before we advertise to the consumers. However, one of the things the trade will want to be told is the extent to which the new product is going to be supported by manufacturer-to-consumer advertising (MCA). The trade like to see both the media schedules and the advertising copy as this gives them confidence that the new product will sell. This means that those two things have to be resolved first. As we have a deadline of $t - 8$ for notifying the wholesalers, we might decide to begin rolling out trade promotions in $t - 10$. And that gives us (remember we are still in $t - 12$) only a fortnight to prepare the media schedules and advertising copy. And that is just not long enough. (In fact, if we allow only 12 weeks to set up the launch, we are going to run into just this sort of problem.)

We could try adjusting some of the lead times to push the deadlines closer to t. For example, we could delay the deadline for notifying wholesalers until $t - 5$, and begin notifying them in $t - 6$, giving ourselves five weeks for setting up the MCA. To be on the safe side, we should set the

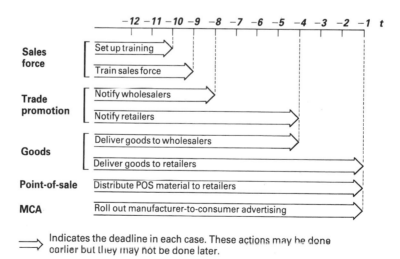

Fig. 22.4 Bringing the elements together into a single plan
NB We are assuming that our own sales force will be used to launch the product. It would be possible, however, to contract the work out to an agency which could supply a field sales force specialising in new product launches.

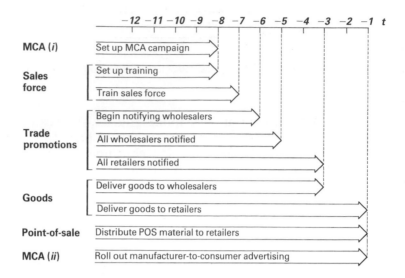

Fig. 22.5   Revising the plans to take account of preparing the MCA campaign
NB If we leave it this late then we are going to be stuck with a newspaper campaign because (*a*) print advertisements are quicker to prepare and (*b*) newspapers have short copy deadlines.

deadline for setting up the MCA campaign to $t - 8$ which gives us four weeks which is better than two.

22.5 The relationship between MCA, trade promotions and the sales force

As the sales force will also need the details of the MCA campaign, the deadline for training the sales force will need to be put back until $t - 7$ (after the plans for the MCA are complete).

Figure 22.5 shows this revised schedule with the preparation of the MCA campaign built in.

The model in fig. 22.5 is highly simplified and, like all simplified models, it is not particularly realistic. We could make it more realistic but only by making it more complicated.

This simple model makes four points:

- Actions must be done in their proper order.
- Sufficient time must be allowed for them.
- Deadlines must be established (and kept).
- Different parts of the same campaign must be integrated with each other. The MCA has to be finalised before the sales force can be trained and the sales force has to be trained before the trade promotions can begin.

22.6 Other promotional considerations

In the launch of the new product we could decide to include public and press relations and attendance at a trade fair. If we did that, then they, also, would have to be integrated into the model. As the trade fair would be aimed at wholesalers and retailers, we should choose one which is dated

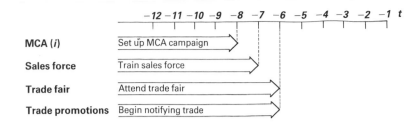

Fig. 22.6 Integrating the trade fair into the plan
NB In some industries, such as the toy and car industries, the importance of trade fairs is such that the overall plan may be geared to them anyway.

around the time when we want to start notifying the dealers. That way we can combine the effects of the trade fair with the efforts of the sales force and the details of the MCA campaign.

If we stick to the schedule in fig. 22.5 we can now include the trade fair. This is shown in fig. 22.6 with the timing of the trade fair integrated with the preparation of the MCA and the training of the sales force.

If we want to begin notifying wholesalers before we begin notifying retailers, then trade fairs may not be a good approach as both will attend – the same applies to trade press advertising (both will see it). With direct mail and sales force representation these two publics can be kept separate.

We may not want to give away any of the details of our new product before the fair. But we will certainly need to invite the dealers to come and see us at the fair. A little teaser copy could be used: 'Come and see us at the fair when our new product will be revealed for the first time.' Figure 22.7 includes the invitation – they should be sent out four weeks in advance.

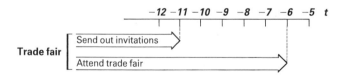

Fig. 22.7 The timing of the trade fair invitations

22.7 Master plans and sub-plans

So far, we have been concentrating on a master plan – launching a new product. However, what we really need is not one big plan but a series of sub-plans: one each for the MCA, sales force, trade fair, etc. The master plan is still important in integrating all the others, but we cannot get all the detail we need into it. Nor is it necessary to – the master plan should be a broad picture.

Figure 22.8 shows all the sub-plans we will need so far.

Master plans have sub-plans and sub-plans have even more sub-plans of their own. The trade fair, for example, would produce a sub-plan for

```
              -12 -11 -10 -9 -8 -7 -6 -5 -4 -3 -2 -1 t
Point-of-sale
MCA
Sales force
Trade fair
Trade promotions
Distribution
```

Fig. 22.8   A set of sub-plans needed for the product launch. NB By this time it will be apparent that twelve weeks is not enough. Twelve months might actually be better.

the design and construction of the stand. If direct mail were to be included, this could lead to one sub-plan for getting the direct-mail letter designed and printed and another for compiling an up-to-date mailing list. The key date here would be the time you wanted the letter to arrive at somebody's home or on somebody's desk.

Figure 22.9 shows some of the thinking involved in getting this sort of detail right – if the letters arrive late their purpose could be seriously undermined.

22.8 Paying attention to detail

If fig. 22.9 is compared with fig. 22.5, it will be obvious that the latter paints a very broad picture and the former is concerned with very small details such as posting the letters. Nevertheless, it is precisely these very small details that can make or break a master plan. Conferences have been wrecked because nobody made sure that the invitations were posted. One of the best arguments for using specialist agencies for a direct-mail shot, for example, is that they have got planning in their own areas down to a fine art. They understand only too well the consequences of not sending something out on time. But they cannot work miracles if you do not approach them early enough.

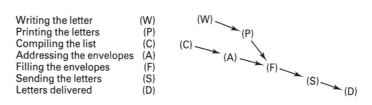

Writing the letter	(W)
Printing the letters	(P)
Compiling the list	(C)
Addressing the envelopes	(A)
Filling the envelopes	(F)
Sending the letters	(S)
Letters delivered	(D)

Fig. 22.9   Sub-plan for direct-mail letter

22.9 Effective planning

There is more to planning, however, than just getting the timing right. We can now look at some of the other elements of effective planning.

Objectives

It is useful to think about two different types of objectives:

- Business objectives.
- Operational objectives.

Business objectives have to do with such things as increasing market share, entering a new market, diversifying into a new line of production and, even, preserving the status quo (as in a 'do nothing' strategy, for example). They are, of course, essential because if the company does not have any business objectives it has no real reason to plan anything.

Business objectives are what the operational plans are designed to achieve. They should be:

- **Specific**   'Increasing sales' is not a specific objective. 'Increasing sales by 10 per cent within twelve months' is.

- **Measurable**   How else will the company know if they have been achieved if they cannot be measured?

- **Realistic**   They should be supported by clear research and analysis that justifies their acceptance.

- **Achievable**   They should be within the capabilities of the company which should have the resources and know-how to bring them about.

Operational objectives are those things that you have to achieve as the means of getting to the business objectives. For example, in support of the new product launch it may be decided to hold a trade conference as one means of notifying the trade. Holding a conference is not a business objective in itself, but the *objective* of running a successful trade conference is perfectly sound – providing, that is, that it can be related to a business objective and is not just being held for its own sake.

Holding the trade conference can be seen as one of the operational tactics used to achieve the business objective of launching the new product. Launching the new product can be seen as a strategic objective (part of a product development strategy) and holding the conference can be seen as a tactical objective.

In a client–agency relationship the business (or strategic) objectives are more likely to come from the client, whereas the operational (or tactical) objectives may come from the agency. So, if the agency is thinking of proposing a sponsorship package, a direct-mail promotion, an editorial campaign or an advertising campaign, it has to be able to answer the question: 'How does the proposal advance the client's business objective?' None of the above proposals is a business objective in its own right from the client's point of view. All of them, however, are perfectly good ways of spending the client's money and keeping the agency in business. (For business planning as such, see chapter 3.)

Targets

Setting targets has been likened to first throwing a dart at a wall and then drawing a ring round it: dead centre every time. In practice, it makes

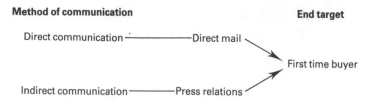

Fig. 22.10 Direct and indirect communication

better sense to draw the ring first and then see if you can hit it. Otherwise, we are back to the problem of setting up operational objectives (throwing darts) without proper regard for business objectives (hitting targets).

Depending on the type of campaign, we can aim to reach the target directly. Direct mail, to home or office, and sales representatives calling on the trade are examples. Otherwise, we may aim to reach our target indirectly through what might be called intermediary targets or communications targets. Press campaigns aimed at journalists are the obvious example, but campaigns aimed at opinion-leaders can also be included. Figure 22.10 illustrates direct and indirect ways of reaching the same ultimate target. (See also chapter 6.)

Budgets and budgeting

One of the commonest reasons for clients and agencies to fall out is money. Too many clients have come to suspect that too many agencies are just finding ways of spending their money to keep themselves going – a situation not helped by the fact that some agencies are not renowned for their ability to account for every pound of the client's money that they claim to have spent. To be fair, some clients have not been particularly insistent in asking for itemised accounts either. Some of these comments are equally valid, by the way, when dealing with in-house work as well.

The **money-led approach** begins with the client deciding how much he is prepared to spend. There are various ways in which the decision might be made: a fixed percentage of last year's sales (with or without an allowance for inflation); the same as last year adjusted for inflation; as much as can be afforded in the present economic climate; matching competitors' spend and so on.

Within this budget the agency has to come up with sound proposals for a year's promotions. The difficulties arise when the money runs out before the year does.

The **task-led approach** is, at first sight, more realistic. With this approach, the task (or project) is clearly defined, broken down into its constituent parts and costed out. The agency can then present the client with an estimate of the cost of doing the work. The problem with this sort of approach is that it is genuinely very difficult to cost out a major project in advance. It may be necessary to buy in more time, the message may need to be changed – any one of many unexpected things can happen: so once again the agency may have to go back to the client for more money. However, at least with the task-led approach the client is committed to the task (as opposed to being committed to the budget) and may come up with the extra money, whereas with the money-led approach the client may take the view that he has paid for a service and can see no reason to pay out more.

Whether the client is money-led or task-led, it is going to be easier to get more money if the money already spent can be accounted for.

Sound budgeting procedures

- **Itemise expenditure** Make as complete a list as possible of all the items you expect to have to pay for.

- **Get competitive estimates** Printers can give very different estimates for printing the same posters. Production companies can give very different estimates for producing the same television commercial. Shop around.

- **Don't be afraid to negotiate** Good negotiating skills are essential.

- **Don't give in to sudden whims** It may seem like a good idea to buy flowers for all the delegates' wives – but did you budget for it beforehand? Stick to your original plans.

- **Avoid penalty payments** Items such as cancellation fees, late-booking charges, failure-to-vacate penalties and so on can all erode your budget. For example, Capital Radio has a sliding scale for cancellations: 40 per cent of the original fee for at least 28 days notice, 60 per cent for under 28 but at least 14 days. A one-day delay in cancelling can cost 20 per cent of a £2 000 fee for every spot cancelled. With five spots that is £2 000 wasted.

- **Take advantage of any prompt payment or early payment discounts available** You may get a 5 per cent or 10 per cent discount for settling a bill within, say, 28 days.

- **Invest any surplus funds in easy access, risk-free accounts** Don't let money not needed for immediate purposes just sit around.

- **Manage cash flows** Know when cash-in is going to arrive (for example, is the client going to put all the money upfront or pay it out over the year?). Try to get money in as early as possible. Know when cash-out is leaving the account and don't pay earlier than you have to (this is not a recommendation to keep suppliers waiting for money to which they are legally entitled). If two conference venues are equally attractive and equally priced, then choose the one which asks for the smallest deposit.

- **Distinguish between fixed costs and variable costs** Making a television commercial is a fixed cost – airing it is a variable cost. Is it worth making a television commercial if you can then only air it a few times? Would it be better to spend less on producing a print advertisement and having more money for insertions? Pre-printing operations for leaflets (platemaking, setting up, etc.) are fixed costs, but the length of the print run is a variable cost. Ordering two runs of 20 000 leaflets will cost much more than one run of 40 000 because you will have two lots of set-up costs to pay for. Booking a venue is a fixed cost, but feeding your delegates is a variable cost. If you book a conference for 200 delegates and you know that only 190 will actually come, you can save the cost of ten meals if you take the appropriate action.

- **Allow for charges such as VAT**   If dealing with foreign suppliers or foreign customers, don't forget also to allow for changes in the exchange rate.

- **Keep accurate records**   Set up budget control sheets. These list the planned items of expenditure for photography, printing, etc. and allow expenditures to be deducted from the budgeted totals as they occur. In this way it is always possible to know how much money is still left under each heading.

- **Set up a contingency budget**   However careful you are there will always be unexpected outlays for which extra money has to be found. To meet such eventualities a contingency budget is called for. This might be about 5–8 per cent of the total budgeted cost. One client might expect an agency to set aside part of the agreed fee for contingencies; another client might agree to meet contingencies over and above the agreed fee. Misunderstandings over this can lead to bad feelings so it is as well to settle it beforehand. By the way, contingencies are not crises. If a real crisis blows up, the cost of dealing with it might double the original budget.

Project teams and their responsibilities

Together with a master plan for launching the new product, clearly defined objectives and targets and an agreed budget, we need project teams with clearly defined responsibilities. In practice, the project teams are likely to be agency personnel; with a full-service agency they may all come from the same one. If the work is spread around several agencies with some of it, possibly, kept in-house, then the different teams will have different locations and the task of integrating their efforts will be somewhat greater. It is essential that each team member has clearly defined duties and responsibilities. For example, it cannot be left to chance that the letters of invitation are sent out or that the copy is proofread for accuracy before anything is printed. Every detail should be assigned to some person who will be responsible for it.

Deadlines

Deadlines are so important that they should be included in a planning grid of the sort set out in figs. 22.11 and 22.12, which show the same schedule at different stages of completion.

Documentation and reports

All plans must be properly documented. Campaign briefs, media schedules, budget control sheets and planning grids have already been discussed but reports are also an important part of putting an operational plan into effect. Some typical reports are:

Job Title	Direct Mail Campaign				
Project Manager	Marian Kaplan				
Date Approved	10 March 1994				

Task description	Person responsible	Budget Agreed Actual		Deadline Agreed Actual		Comments
Printing direct mail letter	D. Smythe	£1000		10/6		
Posting direct mail letter	F. Arani	£200		15/6		

Fig. 22.11 Planning grid for direct-mail campaign: before

Job Title	Direct Mail Campaign				
Project Manager	Marian Kaplan				
Date Approved	10 March 1994				

Task description	Person responsible	Budget Agreed	Actual	Deadline Agreed	Actual	Comments
Printing direct mail letter	D. Smythe	£1000	£1050	10/6	8/6	£50 over budget
Posting direct mail letter	F. Arani	£200	£200	15/6	15/6	—

Fig. 22.12 Planning grid for direct-mail campaign: after

- **Routine reports**   These should be issued, perhaps once a month, on a routine basis to keep everybody informed and up to date. There may be routine reports for each part of the master plan (e.g. sales force, trade promotions and so on).

- **Meetings report**   This should include the purpose of the meeting, who attended, what was discussed and, most important, what was actually decided. Where a specific course of action is decided the report should also say who is to be responsible.

- **Event report**   Where some special event is part of the overall campaign then a report as to how successful or otherwise the event was is desirable. Special events would include such things as open days, press conferences and trade fairs.

- **Incident report (contingency report)**   If some contingency arises then a report should explain what happened, why it happened, how it affected the plan and what action was taken as a consequence.

- **Mid-term report**   This is like a routine report and is issued at the halfway stage in the life of the plan. It may draw all the parts of the plan together at this point in its execution.

- **Final report**   As the name suggests, this is the report that is produced

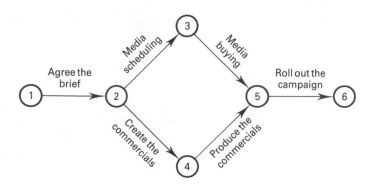

Fig. 22.13   Basic network plan of advertising campaign

when all the parts of the master plan have been carried out – in our example when the product is actually launched. In this context the final report is an operational one. It is not, of course, the last word. From a business point of view it does not stop there: the progress of the product will have to be monitored and its sales tracked.

22.10 Network planning

This chapter began by looking at the countdown approach to planning, setting a date in the future for some event such as launching a new product. An alternative approach is **network planning**. Looking at plans in terms of networks can provide a new set of insights into the planning problem.

If we consider the planning of an advertising campaign, we already have the basis of a network. Figure 22.13 illustrates this. Note that the numbered circles represent 'events' and the arrows represent 'activities'. Events simply represent the point in time at which activities can begin or end. Event 2, for example, marks the end of the activity 'Agree the brief' and the beginning of the two activities 'Media scheduling' and 'Create the commercials'.

Dependencies

In fig. 22.13 events also act as **control centres** in that it is impossible to begin either activity beginning with event 2 until the activity ending with 2 is complete (it would not make any sense, for example, to start creating advertisements until the brief was signed off). Similarly, it would not be possible to begin producing the commercials (which begins with event 4) until the creative work (which ends with event 4) is done. This relationship between activities, where one cannot begin until the other has finished, is called a **dependency**. We saw an example earlier (fig. 22.3) when training the sales force was dependent on first setting up the training programme. Deadlines tell us when activities must be completed, but dependencies tell us when they can begin. An understanding of dependencies can be just as vital as an understanding of deadlines.

Non-dependencies

There are also **non-dependencies**. For example, media scheduling has no dependent relationship with creating the commercials – they can both

Table 22.1 Activity numbering

Activity	i, j*
Agree the brief	1,2
Media scheduling	2,3
Create the commercials	2,4
Media buying	3,5
Produce the commercials	4,5
Roll out the campaign	5,6

*i, j is just the general expression for any pair of event numbers which define the beginning and the end of an activity.

happen at the same time and it does not matter if either one is started or finished before the other.

Using event numbers to identify activities

Event numbers can also be used to identify activities as in Table 22.1. Note here that creating the commercials, for example, can be referred to for networking and planning purposes as simply (2,4).

The technique involved in creating a network is beyond the scope of this book, but briefly it involves listing all the activities, putting them in logical order, drawing the network and numbering the events. Drawing networks requires a lot of practice and there are computer programmes which produce what are called **activity-orientated** networks, which don't use events, as opposed to the **event-orientated** networks used here. For our purposes event-orientated networks are easier to explain.

Networking sales force activities

The small network in fig. 22.13 corresponds to MCA(*i*) in fig. 22.5. We can expand it to include the sales force. Setting up the training scheme can be seen to have a dependency on agreeing the brief. Unless the brief is agreed, there is no reason to train the sales force. And, of course, the actual training is dependent on setting the training scheme up. Note that, when fig. 22.14 is compared to fig. 22.13, that some of the events have been renumbered to make room for the new events – this is why, normally, we should always leave event numbering until the network is complete.

Completing the network

We can now take all the information in fig. 22.5 and transfer it to a network (fig. 22.15). To complete the network, some new activities have been invented, such as the **end activity** – 'Begin to sell' (which, after all, is what this has all been about). In fig. 22.15 note that the dotted lines are **dummy activities**. Dummies are used to link up parts of the network to avoid confusion. The dummy activity from event 3 to event 4 shows that notifying the wholesalers is dependent on setting up the MCA campaign as well as on training the sales force. Note also that the point-of-sale

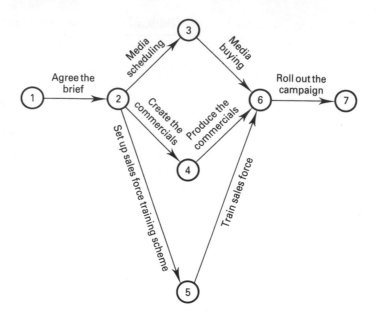

Fig. 22.14   Expanded network plan

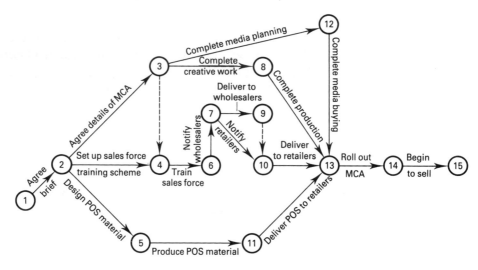

Fig. 22.15   Completed network plan

activity has no dependency with anything else in the network. Apart from the fact that it must start after the brief is agreed and finish before we start selling to the consumer it can be done at any time.

22.11 Critical path analysis (CPA)

Network planning is a useful device in its own right. It can, however, be extended into a technique called critical path analysis. CPA is beyond the scope of this book, but its advantages are that it can be used to assess the completion time of the whole project from beginning to end, to establish critical points in the network where delays (should they occur) would be particularly damaging and as a basis for costing and cost control by identifying the points in time at which costs are going to be incurred.

**22.12
Summary**

- Every promotional activity has to be carefully planned and budgeted for.
- Good budgeting practices enable a tight grip to be maintained on the whole planning process.
- Attention to detail is important – it is the small things that can ruin a plan.
- Where a mixed media campaign is planned or where, for example, planning to attend a trade fair is to be used in a product launch, integration of all the activities is essential.
- Every task should be assigned to a named individual.
- Proper reports should be maintained.
- A plan is an 'intention' which only becomes a fact after it has been executed.
- It is a good idea to have contingency plans and contingency budgets.

**22.13
Assignments**

For these assignments you should refer back to the relevant chapters.

1. Draw up an outline for attending a trade fair in six months' time.

2. Draw up a preliminary budget for a direct-mail shot (or any other promotional activity).

3. Explain the relationship between MCA, sales force training and the movement of goods through the distribution channel.

4. Draw up a draft timetable for creating and producing a television campaign.

Glossary

ABC (Audit Bureau of Circulation) Audits the sales and circulation of some 2 000 publications.

Account executive Works for an advertising agency and is sometimes called an account manager. He/she liaises with the client and looks after the development and running of the account. There may be two, the account handler (responsible for the day-to-day running of the account) and the account planner (responsible for the development of the campaign) but one person can do both jobs.

Ad hoc fee Fee paid to an external agency or consultancy for the performance of a specific task.

Ad hoc research Research carried out on a one-off basis (e.g. researching the potential of an overseas market before entry).

Adoption model (Rogers 1962) A description of the adoption process beginning with awareness and going through interest, evaluation and trial to eventual adoption.

Advertisement manager A media manager responsible for the sale of space or time to advertisers and agencies.

Advertising copy deadline The final date by which the advertisement must be delivered in an acceptable form to the media of choice. Failure to meet an advertising copy deadline may incur penalties and possibly result in the advertisement not appearing at all. Short-dated media have deadlines very close to the actual publication or transmission date and long-dated media insist on receiving copy a long time in advance.

Advertorial Advertisement which is designed to copy the editorial style of the newspaper or magazine and which looks like editorial matter. It should always, however, be clearly identified as an advertisement.

Advertorial manager A relatively new position in the media. A person responsible for the sale of advertorial space to advertisers.

AGB (Audits of Great Britain) Carries out market research into the purchasing habits and consumption of representative households.

AIDA A model of communications and consumer behaviour which emphasises the four steps of Attention, Interest, Desire and Action.

Animatic A preliminary version of a television or film commercial using a series of on-screen static pictures and often used for research purposes or to get client approval.

ASA (Advertising Standards Authority) The body set up to regulate all press and print advertising (anything that is not television or radio) and sales promotions. The ASA implements the codes prepared by the Committee of Advertising Practice (*CAP*).

Assembly Putting together all the various parts of a print advertisement such as graphics and body copy to make the finished 'print-ready' article. Sometimes called 'paste-up'.

BACC (Broadcast Advertising Clearance Centre) An advice centre for broadcast advertisements which can also issue clearance certificates for radio commercials.

Background brief The document which provides all the background information such as market share and the state of competition to the media and creative departments of an advertising agency.

BCAP (British Code of Advertising Practice) A code set up for press and print advertisements by the Committee of Advertising Practice (*CAP*).

BCSPP (British Code of Sales Promotion Practice) A code set up by the Committee of Advertising Practice (*CAP*).

Behaviourism A study of behaviour which focuses on the observed relationships between external stimuli and responses without reference to any mental and intellectual processes.

Black box A term used to express the idea that we cannot know what goes on within the human mind.

Bleeding Carrying the printed matter over the edge of the page so as not to leave a margin.

Body copy The solid blocks of explanatory text in an advertisement, direct-mail letter, etc.

Brief A statement agreed between two parties where one agrees to perform certain duties on behalf of the other in pursuance of agreed goals and objectives and within agreed constraints such as time and budget.

British Codes of Advertising and Sales Promotion A new instrument introduced in January 1995 to combine the *BCAP* and the *BCSPP*.

Broadcasting Act 1990 The Act under which the *Radio Authority* and the Independent Television Commission (*ITC*) get their powers.

CAP (Committee of Advertising Practice) The organisation which draws up the codes for the control of non-broadcast advertising and sales promotion.

Card decks　Sets of postcard-sized advertisements with pre-printed Freepost backs so that enquirers or purchasers can return only those in which they are interested.

CAVIAR　The Cinema and Video Industry Audience Research organisation.

Channel dominance　A position of power and influence over a channel of distribution which may be held by either the manufacturer or the retailer.

Circulation manager　The person responsible for maintaining the sales of a newspaper or magazine.

Classified advertising　Advertising in the classified section of a publication organised under distinct headings such as 'Situations Vacant' and often lacking a strong design element.

Claymation　A form of animation that uses clay figures which are manipulated frame by frame.

Clutter　Matter such as programme credits on television which detracts from the impact of an advertisement.

CMT (crisis management team)　A team of key personnel set up in advance to manage a crisis situation should one arise.

Codes of practice　Sets of ethical guidelines for practitioners in various professions such as advertising and public relations. They sometimes lack the force of law and rely on moral conviction and commitment for their observance.

Cognitive dissonance　A state of mind where two strongly felt ideas or beliefs conflict.

Cognitivism　An approach to the study of behaviour and decision-making which takes account of the mental and intellectual processes at work as opposed to *behaviourism* which does not.

Commission　A method of payment made to a salesperson or agency etc. on an agreed scale for the performance of specific duties and tasks.

Communications audit　A form of market research often associated with public relations which aims to discover how well the company is communicating its identity and activities to its publics.

Communications gap　A situation that arises when an organisation fails to communicate its activities to its target publics so that misunderstandings arise.

Conditioning　The process of shaping behaviour patterns in both animals and humans by the constant association of certain behaviours with either rewards or punishments. Behaviour, once conditioned, can become de-conditioned if the associations are discontinued and, subsequently, re-conditioned if the associations are resumed.

Consumer panel   A group of individuals (or families) which supplies market research data on a regular rather than a one-off basis.

Contact list   Names of people to be contacted in particular circumstances. Crisis contact lists and media contact lists are examples.

Contingency procedure   A 'back-up' procedure to be brought in if things do not work out as expected or planned or if some unexpected event occurs.

Continuous Research   Research undertaken on a permanent or semi-permanent basis.

Contracting out   Giving work to an external agency to perform rather than doing it in-house.

Convenience goods   Those goods for which convenience of purchase rather than price is the key factor in making a purchase.

Copy fitting   Making the *body copy* and other written elements of the advertisement or printed page fit into the space available.

Copywriter   The member of the creative team who is responsible for the actual message – slogans, straplines, body copy, etc.

Corporate hospitality   Hospitality extended by a company to shareholders, suppliers, wholesalers, retailers, etc. which may be in the form of a 'day at the races' or a lavish banquet. It may be extended to include the partners of people on the guest list.

Cover   The number of times an advertisement is heard or seen. Four Plus Cover (4+ cover) is the number of people who have had at least four opportunities to see the advertisement.

Coverage   Sometimes called *reach*, it measures the number of people in the target audience who have at least one opportunity to see (*OTS*).

CPT (cost per thousand)   The media cost of reaching 1000 members of the target audience. This takes no account of production costs.

Creative   A person who works on the creation of an advertising campaign. In a print campaign there are usually two, the *copywriter* who writes the words and the *art director* who controls the visual aspects. They may work under a creative director.

Creative brief   The document which sets out what the *creatives* on an advertising campaign are required to do.

Credentials pitch   A presentation which sets out the background and expertise of an agency to a prospective client. This may be a separate presentation from the proposals pitch or may be made at the same time.

Crisis manual   A prepared document specifying what should be done, and by whom, in the event of a crisis.

DAGMAR   Defining Advertising Goals for Measured Advertising Results. A concept based on the idea that advertising campaigns should be designed to achieve measurable results.

Data fusion The merging of two sets of data taken from different surveys so that two separate people, matched for age, income, etc., are treated as one person.

Decision influencer Person who does not actually make the decision but who, nevertheless, influences the way in which it is made. Office workers may influence the choice of computers or copying machines.

Decoding The process by which the receiver of a spoken or written message interprets and understands it. May also be applied to other non-verbal messages such as body language and facial expressions.

Deemed consent An arrangement whereby posters can be put up without prior permission. Commonly restricted to retailers using their own walls and to temporary postings on building sites.

Direct fax A relatively new usage of the fax machine to distribute promotional material rather than using the mailing system. It is frequently resented by its recipients.

Direct response advertising Advertisements which contain a telephone number, address or both to enable the customer either to ask for more information or to buy directly.

Display advertising Advertising which is designed and positioned within a newspaper or magazine to have maximum impact and to grab the reader's attention. It is usually next to or opposite editorial matter.

DMU (decision making unit) Group (which may vary in its permanency and formality) which makes significant purchasing (or other) decisions in either an organisational or a personal context.

Drive-time The early morning and evening times when people are driving to and from work and can be targeted for 'drive-time' radio campaigns.

Dummy A mock-up of an intended advertisement or magazine, etc. to give clients or advertisers an idea of what the actual finished article will look like. Dummies may be very crude, or 'worked up' almost to the final finished standard.

Economic shopper A person who plans shopping activities to minimise cost, time or both.

Editorial campaign A press relations campaign to obtain editorial coverage, possibly running parallel with an advertising campaign.

Editorial copy deadline The final date by which a story must be submitted to a media vehicle if it is to have any chance of being mentioned in articles, programmes, etc. Failure to meet an editorial copy deadline means that the opportunity for beneficial media exposure will be lost.

Editorial matter Anything in a newspaper or magazine which is not an advertisement (articles, features, etc.). In TV, or radio, programming such as quiz-shows and documentaries plays the same role.

Editorial promotions Devices such as competitions and special offers used by newspaper and magazine proprietors to boost circulation.

Embargo A time or date controlling the earliest permitted publication of information sent out in a press release.

Encoding The process by which the sender of a message converts thoughts into spoken and written messages. Encoding can also include such things as the choice of type-faces.

EPOS (Electronic Point of Sale) A system used at retail checkout points to read electronically product specifications and prices from a bar code.

Facility visit An inspection visit made by an events organiser to a potential venue to assess its suitability.

Facing matter A position for an advertisement in a newspaper or magazine facing editorial content rather than another advertisement.

Fixed fee An arrangement whereby a client pays an agency an agreed sum of money regardless of the amount of work involved.

Free funder Person who would ordinarily have bought the product anyway but who nevertheless gets the benefit of a manufacturer's special offers.

Frequency The total number of times the target group has the opportunity to see an advertisement at least once.

Frequency distribution More detailed than just *frequency*, it states what proportion of the audience might have had one opportunity only, what proportion might have had two opportunities and so on.

Front of mind The situation where the consumer (or other public) is thinking about and aware of the product as opposed to forgetting or ignoring it. Producers like to keep their products at the front of the consumer's mind.

Full service agency An advertising or public relations agency which offers a full range of services including design, photography, graphic art, printing, etc.

Gestalt A psychological concept which holds that we always attempt to make sense of the world around us even when presented with incomplete or unreliable information.

Gone away Direct-mail letter returned to sender because the addressee has 'gone away'.

Hidden cost A cost which is not immediately obvious but which, nevertheless, cannot be overlooked. The administrative costs involved in setting up a sponsorship deal are an example.

IBC (inside back cover) One of the 'premium positions' for a magazine advertisement.

Impact   The exposure of one person in the target group to an advertisement.

Inbound call   Telephone call coming in to a telemarketing operation from an enquirer or customer.

In-charge   The contract period when a poster can be in place. When the period expires the poster becomes *out-of-charge*.

In-house   Work undertaken by an organisation on its own behalf in its own internal departments. Market research, advertising and public relations are all examples of work which can be done in-house.

Insertion   One single appearance of an advertisement in the print media.

Inter-media decision   The decision as to which media group or groups to use in an advertising campaign.

Internal client   An internal department for which an in-house operation works. An internal design department may do work for the marketing department as its internal client.

Intervening variable   A variable such as perception which is a mental factor operating on inputs such as price to affect outputs, e.g. purchasing decisions.

Intra-media decision   The decision as to which vehicles to use within a particular group.

Involvement device   A gimmick such as a scratch-card attached to a direct mailing to get the recipient involved.

IPC   Institute of Practitioners in Advertising.

IR (Independent Radio)   The commercial part of the radio industry which sells advertising time. May be broken up into ILR (Independent Local Radio), IRR (Independent Regional Radio) and INR (Independent National Radio).

ITC (Independent Television Commission)   The statutory body which derives its power from the 1990 Broadcasting Act to regulate all commercial television including cable and satellite.

Joint promotion   Promotional campaign where two companies (a manufacturer and a retailer for example) share the cost and benefits. Two manufacturers of complementary (non-competitive) products such as washing machines and soap powder can also co-operate in this way.

Land-line   A method of delivering advertisements (or other copy) to media organisations.

Layout   The overall design of an advertisement or printed page showing where headlines, body copy, etc., are to go.

Lead-time   The amount of time required to do something as in production lead-time (the time required to make a television commercial).

Lifestyle group Market segment based on the idea that people with similar lifestyles will have similar consumption habits.

Line by line A process of buying either cinema screens or poster sites on a one-by-one basis rather than as a package.

List broker A organisation which arranges the rental and use of a mailing list on behalf of the direct mailer.

List maintenance The process of keeping a mailing list (or a contact list) up to date and accurate.

Mandatory inclusion (i) Anything which the client stipulates as an inclusion in an advertisement such as stockists' names and addresses; or (ii) anything required by law such as health warnings on tobacco advertisements.

Mark-up The percentage added to a charge by an agency for work contracted out when passing the charge on to the client.

MCA Manufacturer to Consumer Advertising.

Media brief The document which guides the media planners when preparing an advertising campaign.

Media buyers The people who buy space or time in the media on behalf of advertising agencies and their clients. They may work in-house or out-house and may also be involved in *media planning*.

Media contact list Names of journalists to be contacted with a particular story.

Media group There are six such groups: newspapers, magazines, television, radio, cinema and posters.

Media independents Organisations which buy space and time in the commercial media and re-sell it to advertisers and their agencies.

Media owners The businesses and corporations which own the media. Two or more owners may have shares in the same *media vehicle* and one owner may have interests in more than one vehicle. There are regulations governing the extent of media ownership permitted in each country.

Media planning The process of drawing up a *media schedule*.

Media schedule A timetable showing when advertisements are expected to appear in the chosen *media vehicles*.

Media vehicle A single unit within a *media group*. The *Daily Mirror* is a media vehicle within the newspaper group.

Mention A term which refers to the appearance of a company's name or products in the editorial content of the media.

Merchandising A term which can be applied to some of the sales promotion activities of either manufacturers or retailers.

Message model A model which recognises three types of messages: those which simply inform, those which change the receiver's opinions, those which lead to action.

Mixed media campaign A campaign which uses more than one *media group*.

Network planning A method for putting all the constituent parts of a project into a logical order so that they are all done at the right time and unnecessary delay is avoided.

Noise Any distraction which interferes with either the encoding or decoding process in communications with the possible result that what the audience eventually understands is not actually what the sender intended. *Clutter* is a form of noise.

OBC (outside back cover) One of the 'premium positions' for a magazine advertisement.

Off-air promotions Promotions using the non-broadcast media which are paid for by radio and television companies to announce programmes and to boost audience size.

Omnibus mailing A direct mail operation in which several companies are represented in the same envelope.

On-air promotions Promotional activities undertaken by radio and television companies in which they use their own air-time facilities to announce future programmes.

One-step communication Where messages are transmitted directly from the sender to the receiver without going through an intermediary. A direct mail letter is one-step.

Opinion leader Person who because of his/her position or strength of personality is able to influence the opinions of others.

OSCAR (Outside Site Classification and Audience Research) A poster industry organisation which gives each site a rating based on type of neighbourhood, proximity to supermarkets, etc.

OTC (over the counter) Refers to goods (in the pharmaceuticals industry, for example) which can be legally sold in retail outlets.

OTS (opportunity to see) A single opportunity given to a member of the target group to see the advertisement.

Outbound calls Telephone calls made out from the company in a telemarketing operation.

Out-house (*or* out of house) Work which an organisation gives out to an agency to do on its behalf rather than doing it itself. Advertising, market research and public relations, etc., can all be done out of house.

Out-of-charge When the contract period for a poster campaign comes to an end.

PAB (Poster Audit Bureau)   Set up in 1976 to ensure that posters were correctly posted according to contract.

Panel   The surface for a single poster of any size.

Parental yielding   Giving in by parents to the persistent demands of their children.

Peer-group pressure   The pressure put on individuals by their contemporaries to conform in the matter of clothing, behaviour, etc.

Performance gap   A situation which arises when an organisation fails to live up to its own claims or its *publics'* expectations.

Personalisation   Individually addressing each copy of a direct mail letter to show the name of the intended recipient.

Pester power   The ability of children to pester their parents into making purchases which the parents might not otherwise make.

Piggy-back mailing   Where one organisation pays another organisation (such as the electricity company) to include a direct mail letter with its regular accounts mailings.

Pink market   The collective purchasing power of the gay and lesbian community.

Pitch   (i) A presentation made by an agency to a prospective client to persuade the prospective client to give its account to the agency. If only two agencies are in competition this can be called a two-way pitch. If four agencies are involved it is a four-way pitch. Solo pitches involving only one agency are also possible. (ii) Media representatives also pitch to sell space and time.

POS (point of sale)   The place where the purchase is concluded, e.g. the checkout in a supermarket. Point-of-sale materials include display stands, dispensers and posters.

Poster contractor   An owner of one or more poster sites.

Poster specialist   An organisation which deals with poster contractors to plan and buy poster campaigns on behalf of an agency or advertiser.

Post-purchase dissonance   Feelings of doubt or anxiety following a purchase.

Pre-empt system   Found in television air-time buying where a second buyer can offer a higher price to pre-empt the first buyer's claim to the time.

Press conference   A pre-planned meeting to which journalists are invited to announce some event such as the launch of a new product.

Press information pack   Serves a similar purpose to a press release but contains more information such as prospectuses, price lists and even product samples (sometimes just called information pack).

Press relations The process of developing positive relationships with the media for the purpose of generating positive media exposure. Sometimes called media relations.

Press release A written statement sent to journalists containing the facts relating to some story which the sender desires to publicise (sometimes called media release or news release).

Primary market Made up of people who make purchasing decisions on their own behalf.

Primary research The process of discovering market or other relevant facts for the first time as opposed to relying on *secondary research*.

Pro-active Used to describe decisions or actions taken with the deliberate intention of bringing about a particular state of affairs or event such as the launching of a new product.

Product placement The practice of getting a product or service prominently discussed or displayed in the context of, for example, television and radio drama so as to gain publicity for it.

Product recall Withdrawing from the market place goods which have already been sold because, for example, they have been found to be faulty.

Production company An independent organisation which produces film and television commercials for advertising agencies.

Professional buyer A person whose occupation is wholly or partly concerned with buying essential supplies and services on behalf of an organisation.

Programme sponsorship A situation in either radio or television where the cost of making a programme is undertaken by an organisation in return for the publicity which the sponsorship generates.

Promiscuous nomad Consumer who changes from brand to brand depending on whatever special offer is available.

Psychic rewards (psychic income) Non-monetary benefits to a salesperson, for example, such as esteem and recognition.

Psychoanalytical models Explanations of consumer and other behaviour which rely upon subconscious motivation.

Public A group of individuals or organisations which have some recognisable interest in an individual or organisation and/or in which the individual or organisation has a recognisable interest. The interest may be friendly or hostile, solicited or unsolicited.

Publicity surround All of the publicity surrounding an organisation or individual whether favourable or unfavourable, authorised or unauthorised, accurate or inaccurate.

Pull factors Those aspects of a promotional campaign which pull the product through the channel of distribution by stimulating demand.

Push Factors Those aspects of a promotional campaign which push the product through the distribution channel so that it becomes available to the consumer at the retail outlet.

Qualitative research Research characterised as asking a relatively few people some fairly complex questions the answers to which require psychological or motivational analysis.

Quantitative research Research characterised as asking a lot of people some fairly direct questions the answers to which are capable of statistical analysis.

QUARTZ A simulation model of a test market operated by Nielsen.

Radio Authority The statutory body for the control of the independent radio industry which derives its power from the Broadcasting Act 1990.

Rate card The published list of prices for space or time in the advertising media.

RAJAR The Radio Joint Audience Research Board.

Reactive Used to describe a decision or action taken with the intention of responding to changes or events in the environment such as an aggressive advertising campaign by a competitor.

Recreational shopper A person who treats a visit to a shopping centre as a leisure trip with no serious intention of making a purchase.

Redeemable coupons Sales promotions coupons which can be redeemed against the price of a product or in exchange for a gift.

Relationship marketing Marketing with a view to developing long-term stable relationships with suppliers and customers rather than just exploiting short-term opportunities.

Remailing The practice of sending direct mail letters through another country in order to take advantage of cheaper postage rates.

Response management Dealing with the enquiries or sales generated from a recruiting or direct-response advertising campaign.

Retail audit A systematic collection of sales data related to pre-selected goods from pre-selected retail outlets. A trade audit includes wholesalers as well as retailers.

Retainer A fee paid by a client to an agency in return for which the agency agrees to act as and when necessary on the client's behalf.

ROP (run of paper) A non-premium positioning of a newspaper or magazine advertisement placed anywhere at the editor's discretion.

ROW (run of week) Buying TV time on the basis that the advertisement will be broadcast any time within a specified week. ROM (run of month) and ROY (run of year) also occur.

Sales promotion war   Competition between manufacturers which uses sales promotions to gain display and other advantages within the retail environment.

Satellite household   One which receives satellite as well as terrestrial television.

Scenario   (i) A possible situation in business strategy development. (ii) The story-line for a film, cinema or radio commercial. (iii) A method of describing a television commercial in words without the use of visuals.

Secondary market   Those people who influence the purchasing decisions of others (members of the family, for example).

Secondary research   Research based on the examination and analysis of existing reports, surveys, etc.

Self-regulation   Voluntary as opposed to statutory control, often administered through a trade or professional association.

Semi-display advertisement   A term used to describe advertisements which fall somewhere between full display and ordinary classified announcements.

Semi-solus   A term used to describe a poster site with just two panels or a magazine page with just two advertisements.

SFX   (i) Special effects as in science-fiction films. (ii) Sound effects as in radio commercials.

Share of mind   The extent to which a consumer, for example, thinks about one brand or product rather than about other brands or products.

Sheet   A unit of measurement for poster sizes. A single sheet is 20×30 in and posters can be single sheet up to 48 or 96 sheet and over.

Shopping goods   Goods which represent a significant purchase such as television sets for which the consumer will shop around to compare quality, prices, etc.

Simulation   (i) A mock-up of a television or film commercial used for research purposes which, as an example, employs stand-ins rather than the intended celebrities. It can be made on hand-held video. Expensive effects such as car crashes can also be simulated using models. (ii) A computer model of a test-market or other business situation.

Site   The actual geographical location of a poster panel. There can be solus sites of one panel only but the majority of sites have more than one panel.

SMP (single minded proposition)   The one clear proposal around which the campaign is built. It may feature some consumer benefit, a design element in the product or, indeed, any single noteworthy factor.

Social shopper   A person, often lonely, who prefers to patronise local corner-shops rather than supermarkets because of the more personal social environment.

Solus   An advertisement which stands alone, for example a solus poster site or a full-page advertisement in a magazine.

Solus mailing   A direct-mail operation in which only one company or its product is represented.

Space-plus   An arrangement where the advertisement department of a newspaper or magazine gives something more than just space to a media buyer. Free copies or guaranteed editorial space may be given.

Sponsee   The beneficiary of the support given by a *sponsor*. The sponsee may be a person or an organisation.

Sponsor   The provider of financial or non-financial support to some otherwise independent person, activity or event.

Stop-action   An animation technique which relies on stopping the camera while model characters are moved into their next position. The characters may be articulated or made of clay (see *Claymation*).

Storyboard   A visual depiction like a comic strip for demonstrating how a television or film commercial will develop. Often used for research purposes or to get client approval.

Strategy   A plan set over the medium to long term to bring about a particular objective such as entering a foreign market or increasing market share.

Tactic   A move taken in the short term as a step towards achieving a strategic objective: for example, using special offers as a tactic to achieve the strategic objective of increasing market share.

TC (till countermanded) site   An arrangement whereby an advertiser can arrange continuous booking of a poster site over a long period of time without the need for constant renewal.

Teaser copy   (i) Wording placed on the envelope of a direct-mail shot to stimulate interest in the contents. (ii) Any copy which is designed to arouse curiosity.

Telemarketing   Marketing using a telephone sales force to originate outbound calls or to handle inbound calls.

Terrestrial household   A household which has only terrestrial television and not cable or satellite.

Terrestrial television   A term used to distinguish the traditional broadcast technologies of the BBC, ITV and C4 from the newer technologies of cable and satellite transmission. One can also talk of terrestrial radio.

Tertiary market   The future market made up of those people who are potential buyers who are not yet in a position to buy.

Test market   A region or neighbourhood chosen to represent the country as a whole in which new products or new marketing strategies can be tried out prior to a national launch.

Third-party endorsement   An independent recommendation of a product or service, as when a journalist writes positively about a new car.

Traffic control (traffic management)   The function of making sure that everything proceeds according to plan and that deadlines are met. Most often found in the creative and production areas of campaign development.

Trial   A usage of a new or unfamiliar product or service to try it out for the first time (first time trial) or a re-trial if one trial is insufficient or if time has elapsed and the first experience is no longer clearly remembered.

TVR (television rating point)   A way of measuring the potential value of a television audience to an advertiser. One TVR equals 1 per cent of the target audience.

Two-step communication   A situation where the message does not pass immediately from the originator to the target audience but goes through an intermediary first.

Unmovable   Consumer who is so brand loyal that he/she cannot be swayed by special offers from other brands.

Value chain   A concept which recognises that suppliers, manufacturers and customers in the same chain will have a more mutually beneficial relationship if they share similar business values.

Venue buyer   An individual or organisation who contracts for the temporary usage of an exhibition or conference venue for the purpose of holding an event.

Venue seller   The management of an exhibition or conference centre which sells temporary access to that venue to venue buyers.

VFD (Verified Free Distribution)   The monitoring of the claimed distribution figures of free newspapers.

Voice-over   An off-screen voice used in television and cinema commercials. Sometimes distinguished as MVO (male voice over) etc.

White space   Areas in an advertisement or printed page deliberately left blank for creative and visual effect.

WOM (word of mouth)   Where positive messages about a company are conveyed by one individual to another. Companies may encourage WOM by such means as rewarding existing customers for introducing new customers.

Sources of further information

Books

Black, S., *Exhibitions and Conferences from A to Z*. The Modino Press (London, 1989).

Broadbent, Simon, *The Advertising Budget*. IPA/McGraw Hill (Maidenhead, 1989).

Broadbent, Simon and Jacobs, B., *Spending Advertising Money*. Century Business Books (London, 4th edn, 1984).

Chisnall, P., *Consumer Behaviour*. McGraw Hill (Maidenhead, 1995).

Cummins, J., *Sales Promotion: How to Create and Implement Campaigns that Really Work*. Kogan Page (London, 1990).

Douglas, Torin, *The Complete Guide to Advertising*. Macmillan (London and Basingstoke, 1988).

Dudley, J. W., *Successful Exhibiting*. Kogan Page (London, 1990).

Fogle, J. and Forsell, M. E., *Visual Concepts in Advertising*. Columbus Books (London, 1989).

Foxall, G., *Consumer Psychology in Behavioural Perspective*. Routledge (London, 1993).

Giles, C., *Business Sponsorship*. Butterworth-Heinemann (Oxford, 1991).

Harding, John, *The Craft of TV Copywriting*. Allison & Busby/W. H. Allen (London, 1988).

Hart, A. and O'Connor, J., *The Practice of Advertising*. Heinemann (London, 1990).

Howard, Wilfred (Editor), *The Practice of Public Relations*. Heinemann (London, 1988).

Jefkins, Frank, *Public Relations Techniques*. Butterworth-Heinemann (Oxford, 1994).

Johnson, G. and Scholes, K., *Exploring Corporate Strategy*. Prentice-Hall (Hemel Hempstead, 1989).

McNeal, James U., *Kids as Customers*. Lexington Books (New York, 1992).

Maiden Outdoor, *Posters in Perspective 2*. (1994).

Rank Screen Advertising (RSA), *The Cinema Handbook*.

Royal Mail, *The Royal Mail Guide to Successful Direct Mail*. (1991).

Smith, P. R., *Marketing Communications*. Kogan Page (London, 1992).

Stefanou, Rosemarie, *Success in Marketing*. John Murray (London, 1993).

Stevens, M., *The Handbook of Telemarketing*. Kogan Page (London, 1992).

Wells, W., Burnett, J. and Moriarty, S., *Advertising Principles and Practice*. Prentice-Hall International (Englewood Cliffs N.J., 1989).

Wheen, Francis, *Television*. Century Publishing (London, 1985).

Wilmhurst, John, *The Fundamentals of Advertising*. CIM/Heinemann (Oxford, 1990).

Wilson, Neil, *The Sports Business*. Piatkus (London, 1988).

Magazines and directories

Advance (six times per year). Themetree Ltd, 2 Prebendal Court, Oxford Road, Aylesbury HP19 3EY. Tel. 01296 28585.

Conference and Exhibition Fact Finder (monthly). Batiste Publications Ltd, Pembroke House, Campsbourne Road, London N8 7PT. Tel. 0181 340 3291.

Direct Marketing International (monthly). Detailextra Ltd, 3 Bridgefoot, Market Deeping, Peterborough PE6 8AA. Tel. 01778 380065.

Direct Response Magazine (monthly). Brainstorm Publications Ltd, 4 Market Place, Hertford, Herts SG14 1EB. Tel. 01992 501177.

Event Organiser (six times per year). The Event Suppliers Association, 29 Market Place, Wantage, Oxfordshire OX12 8BG. Tel. 01235 772207.

Exhibition Bulletin (monthly). The London Bureau, 266–272 Kirkdale, Sydenham, London SE26 4RZ. Tel. 0181 659 8495.

Institute of Public Relations Journal (monthly). IPR, The Old Trading House, 15 Northburgh Street, London EC1V OPR. Tel. 0171 253 5151.

Marketing Week (weekly). Centaur Communications Ltd, St Giles House, 50 Poland Street, London W1V 4AX. Tel. 0171 439 4222.

Meetings & Incentive Travel (monthly). Conference & Travel Publications Ltd, Ashdown Court, Lewes Road, Forest Row, East Sussex RH18 5EZ. Tel. 0342 824 044.

PR Week (weekly). Haymarket Marketing Publications, 30 Lancaster Gate, London W2 3LP. Tel. 0171 413 4543.

Radio Communication (monthly). Victor Brand Associates Ltd, West Barn, Low Common, Bunwell, Norfolk NR16 15Y. Tel. 01953 788 473.

Sales Promotion Magazine (monthly). Market Link Publishing, Market Link House, High Green, Elsenham, Bishops Stortford, Hertfordshire CM22 6DY. Tel. 01279 647 555.

Sponsorship News (monthly). Charter House Business Publications, PO Box 66, Wokingham, Berkshire RG11 4RQ. Tel. 01734 772770.

TV World (monthly). Emap Business Publications Ltd, 33–39 Bowling Green Lane, London EC1R ODA. Tel. 0171 837 1212.

Professional and official bodies

Advertising Standards Authority (ASA). Brook House, Torrington Place, London WC1E 7HN. Tel. 0171 580 5555.

Association for Business Sponsorship of the Arts (ABSA). 2 Chester Street, London SW1X 7BB. Tel. 0171 378 8143.

Association of Exhibition Organisers. 207 Market Towers, Nine Elms Lane, London SW8 5NQ. Tel. 0171 932 0252.

British Exhibitor Venues Association. Mallards, Five Ashes, Mayfield, East Sussex TN20 6NN. Tel. 01435 872244.

Chartered Institute of Marketing (CIM). Moor Hall, Cookham, Maidenhead, Berkshire SL6 9QH. Tel. 01628 524922.

Direct Marketing Association (DMA). Haymarket House, 1 Oxenden Street, London SW1W 9PY. Tel. 0171 321 2525.

Incorporated Society of British Advertisers (ISBA). 44 Hertford Street, London W1Y 8AE. Tel. 0171 499 7502.

Independent Television Commission (ITC). 33 Foley Street, London W1P 7LB. Tel. 0171 255 3000.

Institute of Practitioners in Advertising (IPA). 44 Belgrave Square, London SW1X 8QS. Tel. 0171 235 7020.

Institute of Public Relations (IPA). The Old Trading House, 15 Northburgh Street, London EC1V OPR. Tel. 0171 253 5151.

Institute of Sales Promotion (ISP). Arena House, 66–68 Pentonville Road, London N1 9HS. Tel. 0171 837 5340.

Institute of Sports Sponsorship (ISS). Francis House, Francis Street, London SW1P 1DE. Tel. 0171 828 8771.

Market Research Society (MRS). 15 Northburgh Street, London EC1V OAH. Tel. 0171 490 4911.

Public Relations Consultants Association (PRCA). Willow House, Willow Place, London SW1P 1JH. Tel. 0171 233 6026.

Radio Authority. Holbrook House, 14 Great Queen Street, London WC2B 5DG. Tel. 0171 430 2724.

Specimen examination questions

In this appendix there are 39 questions covering the scope of this book. They are typical of the questions that might be asked on a variety of courses for which this book is intended. The questions are in no particular order (much as you might find them on an examination paper) but the following list will help you to find particular areas of interest.

There are no questions relating to chapter 1. Some questions cover more than one chapter.

Chapter	Questions	Chapter	Questions
2	2	13	20, 22, 26
3	5, 37	14	5, 10, 15, 31
4	1, 4, 7	15	13, 15, 31
5	14, 20	16	13, 15, 32
6	21, 26	17	13, 23, 34, 36
7	8, 20	18	13, 16, 25, 28, 29
8	10, 33	19	3, 13, 30
9	4, 11, 18, 31	20	6, 29, 38
10	4, 5, 10, 11, 12	21	9, 16, 29
11	2, 8, 12, 17, 24, 27, 32	22	7, 35, 39
12	2, 8, 12, 18, 19, 24, 27		

1. Your company is thinking of launching a new product. What do you think would be the major considerations in deciding whether or not to appoint an advertising agency? Explain your reasons.

    (Chapter 4)

2. Explain the terms time-based media and space-based media. Pick one medium of each type and contrast them.   (Chapters 11 and 12)

3. You are the sponsorship manager for a large business corporation. List the things you would have to consider in deciding which event to sponsor. What might be your reasons for deciding to spread your company's sponsorship support around several smaller, diverse events rather than putting it into one large event?   (Chapter 19)

4. Explain the following terms and discuss the relationships between them:

    (i)   Client
    (ii) Advertisement manager
    (iii) Advertising agent
    (iv) Media independent.   (Chapters 4, 9 and 10)

5. Explain the relationship between advertising and promotions strategies on the one hand and business policy and strategy on the other. Why is it important for an advertising or public relations campaign planner to study a client's business plans?
(Chapters 3, 10 and 14)

6. Discuss the importance of attending trade fairs as part of the total campaign to launch a new product. (Chapter 20)

7. Client–agency relationships are very important but they do, all too often, go wrong. Explain some of the factors which can lead to a breakdown of client–agency relationships. (Chapters 4 and 22)

8. Explain, in broad outline, the differences between behaviourist and cognitive schools of psychology. Discuss, with examples, how both schools of thought can provide the basis for developing an advertising campaign. (Chapters 7, 11 and 12)

9. What does it mean to say that professional buyers should always behave rationally and in the interests of their employers? Do you think that professional buyers do always behave in this way?
(Chapter 21)

10. Discuss with specific reference to either advertising or public relations campaigns the importance of carrying out primary research.
(Chapters 8, 10 and 14)

11. Explain the term media vehicle. As a media buyer, what factors would you take into consideration before buying either time or space in a particular media vehicle? (Chapters 9 and 10)

12. Outline the major steps to be taken in drawing up and developing an advertising campaign. (Chapters 10, 11 and 12)

13. Discuss briefly four of the following terms:

   (i) Sales promotion
   (ii) Direct mail
   (iii) Sponsorship
   (iv) Media relations
   (v) Crisis public relations.
   (Chapters 15, 16, 17, 18 and 19)

14. Discuss critically the view that voluntary self-regulation is always to be preferred over government legislation. Illustrate your answer with reference to the work of the ASA and the ITC. (Chapter 5)

15. Discuss the role that public and media relations can play in a crisis situation. (Chapters 14, 15 and 16)

16. Explain with reference to the sales force how a company can get the best out of its people. (Chapters 18 and 21)

17. Discuss the major factors to be considered in setting up a poster campaign. (Chapter 11)

18. Discuss some of the positive benefits of running a radio advertising campaign. What disadvantages might radio possess as an advertising medium?   (Chapters 9 and 12)

19. Explain, using current examples of television advertisements, some of the different ways in which a story-line can be developed.
(Chapter 12)

20. There has been much talk of late of the 'battle for the child consumer'. Discuss some of the commercial and ethical aspects of this so-called 'battle'.   (Chapters 5, 7 and 13)

21. Distinguish between one-step and two-step communications and between one-way and two-way communications. Apply these terms to different aspects of the promotional activity.   (Chapter 6)

22. Explain the terms 'pester power' and 'parental yielding' and discuss some of the product categories where these are likely to occur.
(Chapter 13)

23. Discuss briefly four of the following direct-mail terms:

  (i)   Personalisation
  (ii) Teaser copy
  (iii) Remailing
  (iv) Involvement devices
  (v)   Piggy-back mailings.   (Chapter 17)

24. Discuss some of the methods which could be used in researching the copy for either a print or a broadcast advertisement.
(Chapters 11 and 12)

25. Sales promotions are often thought to have only short-term tactical value. Do you agree with this assessment? Explain your answer.
(Chapter 18)

26. Distinguish between primary, secondary and tertiary markets and discuss some of the advertising and promotional implications of each.   (Chapters 6 and 13)

27. Explain the term creatives and discuss their role in developing either a print or a broadcast campaign.   (Chapters 11 and 12)

28. Distinguish between sales-force incentives, trade incentives (or promotions) and consumer incentives (or promotions). (Chapter 18)

29. Discuss the use to which conferences could be put in promoting products and services.   (Chapters 18, 20 and 21)

30. What criteria would you use after the event in attempting to assess the benefits of a sponsorship deal? How could you decide whether or not your company would have been better off if it had spent the money on advertising instead?   (Chapter 19)

31. Discuss the different ways in which public and media relations and advertising make use of the media. How would you go about developing a combined advertising and media relations campaign?   (Chapters 9, 14 and 15)

32. You work for a commercial haulage company which has recently been through some severe crises. Things are now back to normal. How would you use advertising to restore confidence in your product? Identify your target audiences and write a suitable print advertisement. (Chapters 11 and 16)

33. Outline some of the difficulties involved in accurately assessing the effectiveness of an advertising campaign. What steps can be taken to improve the accuracy of such an evaluation? (Chapter 8)

34. Discuss the importance of having accurate and up-to-date mailing lists for a direct-mail exercise. Outline some of the ways in which an accurate mailing list can be obtained and maintained. (Chapter 17)

35. Outline the main factors to be considered in drawing up a total promotional plan. (Chapter 22)

36. What do you understand by the term direct-response advertising? Explain how direct response can be used in both a print and a broadcast campaign. (Chapter 17)

37. Discuss the importance of a corporate mission statement both as an act of publicity and promotion in its own right and as a reference for subsequent promotional activities. (Chapter 3)

38. Outline the logistical considerations involved in successfully attending a trade fair as an exhibitor. What steps could you take to ensure that you got the maximum benefit out of your attendance? (Chapter 20)

39. Discuss the usefulness of techniques such as network planning in planning a promotional campaign. (Chapter 22)

Index